Culture, Deafness & Music

Critical Deaf Studies: Teaching the World

VOLUME 1

The titles published in this series are listed at *brill.com/defn*

Culture, Deafness & Music

Critical Pedagogy and a Path to Social Justice

Edited by

Ana L. Cruz

BRILL

LEIDEN | BOSTON

Originally published in hardback in 2025.

Cover illustration: *Like a River*. Artwork by Nancy Rourke

All chapters in this book have undergone peer review.

The Library of Congress Cataloging-in-Publication Data is available online at https://catalog.loc.gov

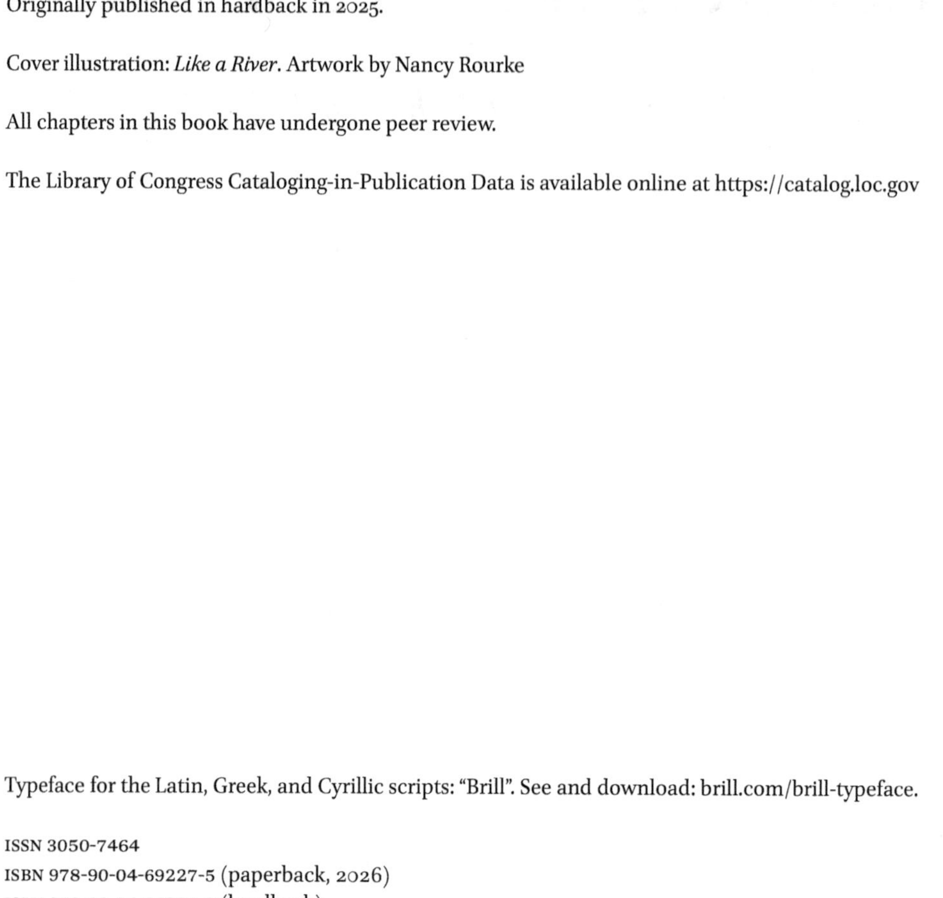

Typeface for the Latin, Greek, and Cyrillic scripts: "Brill". See and download: brill.com/brill-typeface.

ISSN 3050-7464
ISBN 978-90-04-69227-5 (paperback, 2026)
ISBN 978-90-04-69228-2 (hardback)
ISBN 978-90-04-69229-9 (e-book)
DOI 10.1163/9789004692299

This book is printed on acid-free paper and produced in a sustainable manner.

Advance Praise for
Culture, Deafness & Music: Critical Pedagogy and a Path to Social Justice

"*Culture, Deafness & Music: Critical Pedagogy and a Path to Social Justice* is an inexhaustibly fascinating and pathfinding collection; its overall message is direct, like a hammer blow on an iron girder, an indomitable force dedicated to dismantling grave injustices and nurturing the fertile ground of an inclusivity infused society. [...] This collection of works is brilliantly conceived, pleasurably unpredictable, filled with granular descriptions of the lived experiences and real-life struggles of Deaf people who are contributing to the Deaf community and to those outside the Deaf community in a myriad of ways, through theater, poetry, fiction writing, acting, music and serving as activists and advocates for Deaf people worldwide. The thematic weight of this volume is kept comfortably afloat by chapters that are beautifully written and filled with the roar of dissidence. This is not a book for the tranquil mind."
– Peter McLaren (Professor Emeritus, University of California Los Angeles, USA) from the Foreword

"This book and its authors have thus made a significant contribution towards the important task of assisting Deaf Studies and other Deaf domains to understand power relationships throughout history—including Deaf histories—in order to embrace these ongoing challenges and advance towards a more positive future."
– Paddy Ladd (former Reader, Centre for Deaf Studies, University of Bristol, UK) from the Afterword

"*Culture, Deafness & Music: Critical Pedagogy and a Path to Social Justice* addresses issues that are part of the core of contemporary views of being Deaf in today's society from a Deaf perspective. Audism has always been a central part of this perspective: it has been the gist in shaping the everyday life of a Deaf person. This book, through the contributors' powerful thoughts, is a vehicle to bring this reality to us while making the Deaf consciousness of life and culture present in our views in order to break the irony of oppressions fashioned from a hearing perspective."
– Ronice Müller De Quadros (Universidade Federal de Santa Catarina, Brazil)

"*Culture, Deafness & Music: Critical Pedagogy and a Path to Social Justice* is the first book of its kind to engage with the lives and liberation stories of Deaf people in education through the lenses of critical pedagogy and the arts. It is personable, powerful, and thought provoking, including chapters about music, poetry, and even humor as emancipatory forms of art and critical pedagogy in the Deaf community. It is a must read for practitioners and scholars of education."
– **Tricia Kress (Molloy University, USA)**

"That's really very informative! I believe this book will be of great help to readers in making connections between the events described in each chapter concerning the Deaf community. All contributions to the book are organized in a manner that facilitates understanding of how the Deaf community is constructed, perceived, maintained, and preserved for the sake of younger generations. It has been challenging for members of the Deaf community to hold their ground in mainstream society in affirming their linguistic and cultural identity through not just longtime advocacy, but also through poetry and music. It is also imperative not to ignore but to recognize the diversity and differences within the Deaf community."
– **Anthony Chong (Monash University Malaysia)**

"The frameworks presented in this edited volume provide fresh ways of critically viewing phenomena that have not been fully elucidated in Deaf Studies. The material does not just correct the lens through which the hearing view the Deaf person and, specifically, the Deaf artist; it also shows the Deaf person an insightful way to view the Deaf Self. This work calls the hearing to stand alongside the Deaf in their communities in naming their world and being radical. Together, they can end the marginalization of the Deaf and the lack of official recognition of their sign languages. This work is a valuable reader for the collection of any scholar in Deaf Studies and anyone who has an interest in the area."
– **Keren Cumberbatch (The University of the West Indies, Jamaica)**

To all "People of the Eye"—Deaf communities around the world—who for centuries have been marginalized and violated in their human rights

À todos os "Povos do Olho"—comunidades surdas ao redor do mundo—que por séculos tem sido marginalizadas e violadas em seus direitos humanos

To Roberta Sá Gomes, who was able to open my eyes to new multisensory possibilities through which music can be explored, experienced, and appreciated not only by Deaf people but by all peoples of the world

À Roberta Sá Gomes, que foi capaz de abrir meus olhos para as novas possibilidades multissensoriais pelas quais a música pode ser explorada, vivenciada e apreciada não apenas por pessoas surdas, mas por todos os povos do mundo

To my mother and first teacher, Maria da Conceição, who taught me my first words, first numbers, first symbols, and also taught me that to be literate was to continuously seek answers for (im)possibilities

À minha mãe e primeira professora, Maria da Conceição, que me ensinou as primeiras palavras, os primeiros números, os primeiros símbolos e também me ensinou que ser alfabetizada era buscar continuamente respostas para (im)possibilidades

In memory of my father, José Inácio, who was the first to introduce me to a bookcase full of books—books he collected with pride in the search for knowledge

Em memória do meu pai, José Inácio, que foi o primeiro a me apresentar uma estante repleta de livros—livros que ele colecionava com orgulho na busca do conhecimento

∵

The more radical the person is, the more fully he or she enters into reality so that, knowing it better, he or she can better transform it. This individual is not afraid to confront, to listen, to see the world unveiled. This person is not afraid to meet the people or to enter into dialogue with them. This person does not consider himself or herself the proprietor of history or of all people, or the liberator of the oppressed; but he or she does commit himself or herself, within history, to fight at their side.

PAULO FREIRE (1994, *Pedagogy of the Oppressed*, p. 21)

∵

Contents

Foreword

Peter McLaren

Today's Volksgeist, or national spirit of the times, is currently reverberating with fear and loathing: of the great replacement, where white 'legacy' Americans are allegedly being replaced by dark-skinned immigrants; of the great reset, where "global elites" are supposedly using the Coronavirus pandemic to push forward a globalist plot to destroy American sovereignty and prosperity and subdue all of humanity in a liberticidal health dictatorship; of teachers who dare say that systemic racism exists in America; and of an increasingly visible 2SLGBTQ+ community bent on 'grooming' our children. However, those fears that are actually grounded in reality, that have some sturdy basis in fact, such as eco-anxiety, a chronic fear of suffering an environmental cataclysm, and nuclear anxiety, fear of an imminent nuclear apocalypse, seem to rank last among wide swaths of the U.S. population, a growing number of whom are in the thrall of far-fetched conspiracy theories such as QAnon. It is as if we have been locked in a room at 221B Baker Street in London, and forced to listen to a Stradivarius churning out Beethoven's Violin Concerto in D Major in the trembling hands of its famous owner (the one in a deerstalker hat), who is sliding down his chair, feet on the desk, after a night filled with French wines and a bow arm pocked by recent injection marks.

Rarely in this age of murk and musty minds, have we felt as deeply isolated and persistently alienated as at this present historical moment. Having succumbed to the entangled nexus of rivalry and political tribalism, to the incitements of surplus desire—what modern scientists call the "hedonic treadmill"—we have fallen ever more inextricably under the thrall of the culture of consumption and neoliberal capitalism's swindle of prosperity. In so doing we have lost our ambition for discovering the essence and meaning of everyday life, preferring to scavenge in the rag-and-bone shop of lost memories of better times. Deaf people throughout time have been encapsulated within the limited notion of peoples with disabled bodies in need of fixing in order to gain visibility, respect, and full human rights. Deaf people have pushed against this notion of disability.

In this Foreword I want to acknowledge my positionality in relation to deafness and disability. As a university professor who is congenitally deaf in his right ear, who has lost approximately 50% of his hearing in his left ear, and who struggles with hearing loss, middle ear myoclonic tinnitus, Meniere's disease and chronic hyperacusis, and who was raised as part of the hearing world, I have experienced first-hand the calculated affront to human decency embodied in the limited extent to which both disingenuous and well-intentioned university administrators (including those who bloviate endlessly about their state-of-the-art disability programs) are willing to act in order to provide reasonable accommodation to professors with disabilities. I do not intend to impose the concept(s) of disability on Deaf persons but instead I want to point out that the battles and resistance of Deaf persons for the right of being Deaf have benefitted the struggles of all of those marginalized for being dismissed as persons with disabilities. The reductive notion that disability signifies a deficiency has been seamlessly integrated into the complex mosaic of identity politics and intricately interwoven into the very fabric of our educational system and broader societal structures. Consider the following remarks by Jay Timothy Dolmage:

> There is a phrase that many disability studies teachers have heard from colleagues over and over again, noted first by Amy Vidali who noticed how often other teachers said to her "but there are no disabled students in my class." This statement is a kind of apologia for not creating an inclusive classroom. The statement is something that Vidali and other disability scholars find sad and ironic and maybe a bit humorous: it is statistically and practically nearly impossible. The sad or scary part is that this statement sounds or feels like a wish or a desire. That wish or desire for higher education without disability is academic ableism in a nutshell, and it is rooted in eugenics [...]. But by more literally mapping disability as a reality and an important, contributing population in colleges and universities, there is a move to refuse this desire for academia and for an educational space without disability. (2017, p. 42)

The stigma of disability in U.S. culture, with its clinical aloofness, its multiple insinuations of inferiority, its instantiations of deficit ideology, its anatomizing of human identity, its viral social exclusions (what Dolmage calls "disability drift"), and its over signification as either an absence, a lack, or else a monstrous representation of all that is wrong with human nature depicted in proportions that rival the Furies, the Gorgons, and the Hydra of Greek mythology, has driven disability studies to an impasse, an historical-critical inflection point. To appreciate the advances made by Deaf scholars, artists and, yes, musicians, will require the hearing world to acquire new mechanisms of observation, new instruments of perception to appreciate fully the variety of aesthetic paths they have taken. While still regarded as an autonomous anthropological fact, disability is no longer spoken of in whispered tones. There have, indeed, been attempts to expand accessibility for persons with disabilities in the workplace and to increase their legal rights as productive citizens that go well beyond the urbanities of public relations performances. Yet there remains a self-veiling aspect to disability, a sense that while society-at-large increasingly recognizes the rights of persons with disabilities, engaging the full measure of persons with disabilities is not native to the temperament of most U.S. citizens who would prefer to celebrate their own despair in unrelenting isolation and doggedly thematize their own dread, rather than increase freedoms for persons with disabilities. Their ableist demons would, no doubt, unsparingly insist that their freedoms should be limited and circumspect rather than expanded in substance and scope, lest the 'disabled population' begin to permeate society more widely and mix with its 'able-bodied stock.' This, of course, is a symptomology of despair common to capitalist societies, largely responsible for spawning disablement. The crisis of capitalism and its effects on persons with disabilities was no more evident than during the COVID-19 pandemic which, as James Graham (2023) notes,

> has enabled the state-sanctioned purging of entire swaths of the disabled population, through mass death in privatized long-term care, preventable overdose deaths caused by a poisoned drug supply, and the destruction of homeless encampments (whose residents are more likely to be disabled than not), including during record-breaking low temperatures. Disability assistance programs, which have become more and more difficult to access, fail to provide recipients with the income needed to live with dignity in most cities. It is easier in many cases for disabled people to be approved for medically assisted death than to secure a place to live. The fact of the matter is that disabled people are viewed as disposable, as acceptable collateral damage, by society at large.

Students and teachers both with and without disabilities don't live in isolation—they live in the wider social universe of capitalism: of uncompromising social relations inundated by sectarian vitriol and political fraud, a lack of job security, unreasonable workloads and a lack of living wages. They live in a world of rampant homelessness and a lack of universal healthcare while CEOs sit on golden toilets filled with obscene concentrations of wealth. And they suffer multiple forms of abuse. For example, Dolmage (2017) draws our attention to the radically disproportionate number of sexual assaults against students with disabilities.

Dolmage's important work, *Academic Ableism: Disability and Higher Education*, reveals how education employs the logics of both *ableism* as well as *disablism,* recognizing the struggle for disability rights to be a contradictory practice that can reproduce the very social relations of inequality and asymmetrical relations of power and privilege that it ostensibly sets out to undermine. 'Disablism' focuses on the stigma of being disabled and desperately clings to a set of assumptions and suppositions that promote the contrastive pseudoscientific treatment of people because of real or presumed disabilities. In so doing, it negatively constructs disability under the presumption that being disabled is concomitant to being a criminal, or worse, a cypher. As a result, people with disabilities find themselves positioned inside a structure of domination, a carceral state overpopulated by capitalist social relations that have reordered the world into robust 'legacy' stock who have 'normal' tools of living, and defective stock (immigrants, the disabled), with non-disabled persons accorded a master status, able to privilege their experiences above that of others. The ableist judges others against a bifurcated backdrop of 'able-bodiedness and able-mindedness' that too often becomes the default identity for persons with disabilities.

Many people today consider deafness to be a medical disability, whose complex physiology is described in granular detail in a chapter by *Wafaa Kaf* on the auditory pathway and hearing loss. However, Kaf also addresses that when applying the medical model, Deaf people should have the voice to articulate whether they would like to use sound amplification (i.e., hearing aids, etc.) or use sign language to communicate, taking into consideration the heterogeneity of Deaf culture. It is important to realize that deafness can also be considered in a multitude of other ways. Deafness imposes its own reality as a culture, an ethnicity, an identity, a communication and performance genre, as a mode of being in, alongside and with the world, as a political movement, which makes research in Deaf Studies particularly challenging but also a cause for excitement and exhilaration. Deaf Studies researchers must pay considerable attention to numerous viewpoints and perspectives—epistemological, ethical, and ideological—when doing research in Deaf Studies. *Stephanie Cawthon* reminds us, first and foremost, that it is absolutely crucial that researchers become aware "that the majority of research is conducted from the point of view of a hearing person, living in a world that is designed to be maximally accessible for hearing individuals." Following from her observation, it becomes paramount to understand one's own positionality as a Deaf researcher or within a deaf community and how this impacts the content and context of one's work, including how decisions are made about research design, how to collect and analyze data, and how to present findings to specific audiences.

Douglas Baynton, who analyzes the history of Deaf peoples' relationship with the concept of disability, introduces us to the rich, deep and complex history of American Deaf culture that conceptualizes deafness in terms of social, cultural and disability models. We learn the many ways in which the values of Deaf people differ from those of hearing Americans, including the cultural distinction between being deaf and Deaf, as seen through the lens of recent linguistic research into language acquisition and development that suggests that Deaf people differ from hearing people in sensory ways that remain distinctly unaccounted for by cultural models alone. *Baynton's* perceptive insights underscore the failure of existing cultural models to explain Deaf identity, and we learn that it is common practice within Deaf communities to refer to the Deaf community as an ethnic group. To be clear, Baynton does not disparage the cultural model that "continues to be a powerful tool in Deaf Studies, as well as in the struggle for Deaf rights and community pride." Similarly, he finds merit in the ethnicity model which he regards as "a crucial concept because it provides a framework for exploring the ways in which Deaf Americans have maintained distinct community institutions and have passed down, over many generations, a common history, language, and culture." Yet at the same time Baynton expands the argument for understanding deafness as not only a cultural construction but also a bodily phenomenon as Deaf people clearly inhabit a different sensory world. But to model deafness as a defect or impairment—often within what is sometimes called a 'pathological model'—is wrenchingly problematic since it discredits Deaf people by viewing them as deficient and fails to account for the ways in which Deaf people experience disability in terms of their own engagement in complex social relations. Claiming disability as an identity for Deaf people can allow for an exploration of how sensory differences between hearing and deaf people shape their worlds, as well as how the concept of normality shapes both the attitudes of hearing people toward Deaf people and the sense of identity developed by Deaf children. It also provides an explanatory framework for rejecting the medicalization of deafness, and a theoretical framework for arguing that Deaf people are not disabled by hearing impairment, but rather by the oppression of difference. A key insight of Baynton is that in claiming disability as an identity, "disabled people name the oppression under which they live, declare solidarity with others similarly oppressed, and set themselves in opposition to it." Consequently, Baynton sees great value in the pan-disability rights movement.

According to Baynton, the cultural model alone cannot account for the ways in which Deaf people differ from hearing people in physical (sensory) ways. Yet sensory difference is not sufficient, either, to fully explain Deaf identity. *Baynton* argues that Deaf people are different from hearing people "in ways other than cultural"—deafness is more than a cultural construction, it is also a physical reality, it has to do with living in a very different sensory social universe. The more recent social model of disability locates disability in social structures and practices but does not include normal human variation. *Baynton* contends that while there is considerable resistance among Deaf people and Deaf Studies scholars to focusing on the physical aspects of deafness, an exploration of the body and the physical aspect of deafness, that moves well beyond any medical or pathological model of deafness, is essential to furthering the progress of Deaf Studies. What matters here, of course, is not simply a question of bodily differences but the ways in which human differences are interpreted. The cultural and social models thus offer much to our understanding of Deaf identity so long as the challenge of bodiliness is not forsaken.

Baynton makes the important observation that while contemporary legal, cultural and political histories shape, contain and variously imprison deafness, there nevertheless exists an alter-relationality that is not ruled by the rationality of the medical model and refutes the presumption of innate biological inferiority. In recent years, while some disability activists and scholars were busy developing an argument for the concept of disability as a culture and an ethnicity, Baynton was seeking to underscore that "there is no inherent contradiction in identifying a group as both disabled and as a cultural group." He argues that "the disability model should not pose a threat to Deaf people's sense of identity any more than does the ethnic model" since what is at stake is

> not a question about identity but rather about the need for a coherent category of analysis for scholars, for a unified, broad-based movement for effective activism, and for explanations that the general public, in particular the parents of deaf children, can find both plausible and persuasive.

He goes on to claim that

> a tenet of disability solidarity is that those less threatened should not abandon the more vulnerable. Disabled people differ significantly from one another, but they share common experiences resisting the medicalization of their identity, coping with inferior 'special' education, fighting for autonomy and self-determination—in short, they share a common experience of oppression and of struggle against it. Thus, sharing a common oppression, they have undertaken to forge a common liberation.

The concept of Deaf persons sharing a common culture of resistance has led the editor of this volume, *Ana L. Cruz*, to acknowledge a common link between their lived experiences of oppression, resistance and liberation and the work of Paulo Freire, the patron of Brazilian education, who was imprisoned for his literacy work and went into exile as a result of his success working with Brazilian peasants in the Northeastern state of Pernambuco. As a result of Freire's innovative efforts, poor peasants learned how to read and write in an extraordinarily short time, by sharing their lived experiences through dialogical encounters that they had in cultural circles organized by Freire and his assistants, and they began to think critically about their future and those of their families and neighbors in a country governed at the time by a brutal bureaucratic-military state dictatorship. Freire's approach to the development of critical consciousness (conscientização) and transformative praxis (the interpenetration of theory and practice), most clearly formulated in his pathfinding work, *Pedagogy of the Oppressed*, led his students to move beyond an anti-politics that simply repudiated the improprieties of the bourgeoisie in a non-threatening way; instead, Freire created the conditions of possibility for them to engage in acts of subversive intervention (via teachers unions, shop-floor organizations, landless peasants organizations, revolutionary movements) in order to identify and transform those oppressive structures and asymmetrical relations of power and privilege that treated them as objects to be acted upon, rather than as subjects worthy of being considered active agents of their own history. Ana L. Cruz has made significant contributions to critical pedagogy, an approach that has brought together a myriad of ideas from the labyrinthine expanse of critical social theory and whose tributaries have grown out of the vast reservoir of Freire's work and expanded into the rich transdisciplinary field of critical pedagogy.

Junhui Yang's chapter is a rich exploration of the roles of the media and education in improving the social status of Deaf people in China. While demonstrating a spirit of good will with respect to its Deaf citizens, China's government still regards Deaf people within an overall disability prism and this has led to an unintentional paternalism. However, China has also demonstrated effective care and employment policies. *Yang* stresses the importance of the government administration and disability organizations in their role of including the Deaf Chinese population in various aspects of Chinese society, emphasizing the crucial role of the family in the well-being of the deaf child. Recent advances in technology such as the Internet, as well as growing opportunities for Deaf people to travel internationally has led to "more open-minded thinking among deaf people, and within the general public, and has benefitted the Deaf community greatly."

Yang discusses the struggle of Chinese Sign Language (CSL) to achieve government recognition as a bona fide language and challenges faced by the older and younger generations of sign language users. Major gains for Deaf Chinese communities, such as the right to drive for deaf people, has led "to an increase in the socialization of Deaf people through better access to leisure activities, improved job prospects, and has enhanced the social status of Deaf people at large." This, in turn, has sparked a rise in deaf clubs, morning exercise groups for elderly deaf people, and evening street light gatherings for local deaf people in the heat of the summer. More formal organized activities include September Deaf Day Celebration events, Disability Awareness Day in May, "and special interest groups, such as stamp collecting workshops, fishing, painting, photography, and Chinese chess competitions, which are organized through a committee and demand a membership subscription." There are also formal, local, national and international associations for deaf people related to Deaf community capacity building. A major event is the government funded Deaflympics. Yang warns of a reduction in such activities in the U.S., because of inclusion and mainstreaming policies. In China there are in excess of 30 television programs that provide sign language on screen, and several hundred local TV news channels that offer sign language interpretation. President Xi Jinping and his wife Peng Liyuan were seen using some sign language phrases during their media appearances. The seed of Deaf culture has begun to grow in China. There now exist Deaf media companies and Internet sites that function with sign language. Yang reports concerns with the way that the media focus not on events within the larger Deaf community but on the achievements of single individuals. The under-reporting with respect to the larger Deaf community is coupled by "the tendency in the media to report crimes of theft, pocket-picking by groups of deaf people, which has led to an often negative view of deaf people and even a fear of deaf groups."

There would be less audism and its more traumatic version, surdophobia (an anxiety disorder coined by Gardy van Gils, who defines it as a hostility, intolerance, or fear against Deaf people, Deaf culture, and the Deaf community, and resistance toward the sign languages used (Thal, 2023), by recognizing the rich complexity of Deaf culture, including the unique approach of Deaf people to humor, an approach captured by *Rachel Sutton-Spence's* dynamic and compelling account of Deaf humor as a performance art and form of resistance, affirmation, and liberation. In her account she emphasizes the tension (sometimes unintentional) between the external imposition of the majority hearing community, which is uniformly regarded as disempowering and disenfranchising, and the Deaf community's embrace of linguistic self-affirmation, celebration and liberation (such as in the case of American Sign Language culture). Sutton-Spence shares an encounter with a community that creates written and spoken art, poetry and political humor that Sutton-Spence characterizes as a multi-vocal, multi-textual, and genre-resisting hybrid experience of Deaf folklore utilizing World Knowledge and Deaf World Experience.

We learn that Deaf people and hearing people alike appreciate similar types of humor that are visually accessible in both form and content and there are unique forms of humor that originate within the Deaf community, motivated by the specific knowledge and experience of Deaf people, what some consider a form of 'fusion humor,' blending the knowledge and experiences of Deaf people with the humor traditions in the wider society, although much of the community's humor is expressed in sign language. As Deaf humor relies entirely on sign language, it is the form that carries the humor and often it is lost in translation. Some Deaf humor relies upon a highly embodied and tactile production of entertaining images. Sutton-Spence draws upon several jokes considered classic within various Deaf communities that generate both cultural approval and resistance. While Deaf humor identifies areas of Deaf oppression, often the humor has affirmatory political interpretations ultimately supporting Deaf identities.

Karen Christie and Dorothy M. Wilkins celebrate the Deaf American women whose literary, artistic and powers of performance we can admire today such as Elizabeth Allen, Adele M. Jewel, and Laura Catherine Redden (who published under the name, Howard Glyndon), Agatha Tiegel, Ella Mae Lentz, Dorothy Miles, Kristi B. Merriweather and Nathie Marbury. In the main, however, it has been a long and brutal struggle for Deaf students and their teachers (especially Black Women and other women of color) to survive in college environments when oralism took over the Deaf schools (dominating eighty percent of them), and there existed a prevalence for Deaf students to being tracked into mainly vocational programs.

In her interview with Ana L. Cruz, *Patti Durr* offers a fascinating account of the works of art by De'VIA (Deaf View/Image Art) movement or genre that grew out of the Deaf Art Movement. According to Durr, the name originated in ASL and is signed "Deaf 'look-at-hand' art." The 'look-at' is meant to signify Deaf perspectives and points of view. The hand (open palm) points to the artwork. Durr notes that "[s]elf-assertion, cultural pride, creative expressions, the expansion of the field of ASL linguistics, interpreting and Deaf Studies in academia, all played a key role in the emergence of De'VIA." Prior to the birth of De'VIA, a small group of Deaf students at Gallaudet University had created the Deaf Art Movement DAM and a Deaf artists colony was formed in Austin, Texas, in the late 1970s. They convened in the Washburn Arts Center at Gallaudet University in 1989 and that is where their manifesto was given birth. De'VIA has grown into a movement that encompasses a large body of artists focused on expressing cultural or physical Deaf experiences. Recognizing that oralism "is a systematic way of teaching Deaf children speech which forbids the use of signing and often includes punishment to suppress a Deaf child's natural inclination to use their hands and eyes for language," De'VIA's early works promoted the use of American Sign Language (ASL), and now the movement has flourished and assumed an international reach. Durr notes that there are many issues facing Deaf people today that are addressed via ARTivism, that include

> access to information, job opportunities, equal education, cultural appropriation, Hearing actors taking Deaf roles, audism, oralism, genetic engineering, CRISPR, police brutality & murder, solitary confinement in prison, mental health access, human and linguistic rights, intersectionality, racism within the Deaf world, and more.

Clearly, the struggle is an ongoing one that is committed to a social justice agenda, with activists participating all over the world.

Before I had the opportunity to meet my life mentor, Paulo Freire, in person, my doctoral dissertation advisor, the great exponent of children's drama, Richard Courtney, introduced me to the work of Augusto Boal. Boal had developed what is called *Theater of the Oppressed*, that involved 'simultaneous dramaturgy' techniques in working with various populations in the Brazilian countryside and in the favelas. Eventually Boal created many different theatrical styles, such as forum theater, image theater and invisible theater, that motivated participants to make important changes in their lives and communities. One of my fondest memories is when I was invited to speak on a panel with Paulo and Augusto during a Pedagogy of the Oppressed conference held in Omaha, Nebraska. Boal's accomplishments in reinventing theater parallels similar moments of dramatic apprehension described by *Aaron W. Kelstone* in his fascinating discussion of Deaf Theatre from a Deaf-World point of view, especially as it developed in the United States. Deaf Theatre's important innovations were responsible for giving form and substance to more authentic representations of the Deaf community. Kelstone's recognition of the unique capability that ASL (American Sign Language) and English have in performing simultaneously on stage, in close proximity to each other (albeit masking inherent vulnerabilities in the process), underscores the singular power of Deaf Theatre to enable artists to share indigenous stories by means of new performance techniques. Such techniques are now formally identified and have led to a "critical social and language breakthrough for Deaf people." Deaf Theatre enabled the Deaf community to move closer to the center of public life, which attracted performers in the hearing world. Frustrated with the limitations of voice and text, these artists "found opportunities to actively participate with Deaf artists to support an alternative means of creative expression."

Multiple voices can be represented on stage, pirouetting through a complex web of heuristics and multimodal literacies, with some of the artists moving beyond the written and spoken word through the framework of sign language performances, using their bodies as expanded expressions with which to communicate with their audiences and find common ground for engaging in a "meaningful dialogue about what it means to be functional, creative, and human." To audience members outside the Deaf community, these performances may seem opaque but with certain members of the Deaf and hearing communities, there is a recognition that these performances are part of an ongoing attempt by the Deaf community to create "a new understanding of the lived experiences of Deaf people that can be acculturated across the boundaries of difference."

Deaf education and the larger struggle for people with disabilities means challenging the specter of ableism and disablism. The ableists have been around for centuries, hypostasizing the disabled and partitioning them into the bottom rung of a eugenicist ladder that measures their social wealth and social capital as worthless in comparison to the hearing community, or invisibilizes them completely. And, of course, the additive of color and race in relations between those who are considered able-bodied and those who are marked as disabled, illustrates that the former never acknowledges the latter since their ableist mindset deems them as less than human, or at least as having less social capital, in those material and social contexts where the disabled are meant to self-actualize inferiority, to participate in a contrastive extrapolation that ensepulchers them in a prison house of alienation, of placelessness, of ontological disablement, of unpurged images of violence and hate, that often leads to social death, the ultimate form of 'thingification' and reification.

Ableism is a process of instrumentalization and externalization, of becoming ontologically otherized, because your disability is negatively constructed against what is considered to be normal and designed to prevent a deep awareness of the ecology of one's self, of one's ontological vocation to become more fully human, as Paulo Freire might put it. Ableism (in which disablism is often comfortably nested) occurs when a person's (perceived) disability overrides all other individual characteristics. The negative effects of audism are brilliantly illustrated with considerable verve and power in *Christie and Wilkins' discussion* of the Deaf liberation movement. Here the authors explore, in their own words, the struggle

> for cultural identity, for self-determination, for the acceptance and recognition of our signed languages, and for access to literacy and quality education. It has been a struggle to unmask audism and the soft violence of benevolence perpetuated by the medical and educational systems. It is a struggle against the domination that silences Deaf bodies, particularly the bodies of Deaf Women and the literal and symbolic repression of their hands—a primary source of creative expression.

The authors warn that "the right to BE Deaf is still seriously challenged" and cites as an example "government-sponsored genetic counseling and genetic research [that] clearly promotes eliminating Deaf people." From these authors we learn about the perils of Deaf infants who are given a medicalized identity, government pressures faced by parents of Deaf children, the grievous inadequacy of educating Deaf children where Deaf students, tinctured by ableism and denied full inclusion, are forced into government "sites of colonization with the goals of forced assimilation into the spoken language community." Most shockingly, we learn that 80% of the world's Deaf population has no access to education at all. *Christie and Wilkins* prognosticate correctly that those with multiple identities are at the greatest risk of being denied their human rights (Deaf Women as well as Black Indigenous People of Color, Deaf Latinx, DeafBlind individuals, Deaf LGBTQIA, and disabled Deaf people), including Deaf people from lower socio-economic classes and oppressed minority religions and cultures. We shudder when we read their moving account of the banning of sign language from European schools of the deaf, in favor of oral-only instruction, including from the American School for the Deaf, where signing was relegated to bathrooms and dorm rooms. And yet there was an important push back from the National Association of the Deaf who challenged the discriminatory barriers to Deaf people applying for civil service jobs. There was the establishment of a Moving Pictures Committee as a counterpoint to the increasing encroachment of oralism. With racism so prevalent in the U.S., Deaf individuals of color had no access to education. The authors recount key events in the tumultuous history of Black Deaf education, with eighteen states in the South establishing segregated departments and/or segregated schools for Black Deaf students with a frequent focus on industrial/vocational training rather than academics. Gallaudet University did not accept Black Deaf students until the 1950s, while desegregation of these schools was a long and difficult battle and not complete until 1978. The impact of a pernicious entanglement among systematic racism, pervasive oralism and audism was devastating.

The historical absence of codetermination in the institutionalization of ASL and the lack of a functional precedence for outlawing mandates for oralism in educational settings, exemplified the difficulty in executing reasonable demands by the Deaf community and making it next to impossible for securing institutional governance except through insurrectionary direct action. These struggles are bound to happen when so-called 'mainstream culture,' against which Deaf culture is defined, is comorbid with what I have called 'predatory culture'—the detritus of settler colonialism, ethno-nationalism, white supremacism, panoptic surveillance, surplus enjoyment (finding pleasure in our own oppression), widespread homelessness, unaffordable health care, gun violence and government insurrection. It is a culture wrapped in neuroses and fixations and a miscellaneous clutter of indifferences, a culture defined by the excrescences of officialdom, neoliberal capitalism and the naked pursuit of power. It is a culture marked by the vagaries of fashionable apostasy and a proliferation of ideologically compromised public intellectuals scrubbed of any criticality, designated by the establishment to help us think through the glorious mess we constantly and consistently find ourselves in. Weave all of these symptoms together inside our digital universe (and there are many more) and the result is a toxic cyberculture marked by implacable frivolity, belligerent bigotry, hair-raising ineptitude and intellectual outlawry. As a form of cultural production, predatory culture functions as a vulgarizer of every aspect of our lives. Consider for a moment the case of capitalism. Dolmage notes that "[t]he ways in which disability is socially constructed in contemporary society can also be seen as, from top-to-bottom, economic." He asserts that over the past 150 years of disability history, especially during periods of economic collapse or downturn, "people with disabilities are the first to be constructed as drains or threats." He describes how disability became

> an object of charity rather than part of the social contract, the disabled body must be made productive or expendable, exhibited or warehoused for profit, the disability itself must be easily monetized—all of these things ensure that disability can be easily controlled in order to absorb or expel citizens from status positions. (2017, p. 109)

Against such a charred and desolate landscape, we can begin to understand why it is so difficult to challenge the psychodynamics of ableism and disablism, relative to established social, economic and political forms of domination marking 21st century America. This symptomology of predatory culture is not alien to Deaf culture. It affects everyone, in disproportionate ways, but singles out persons with disabilities with particular vehemence.

Lindsay M. Dunn and Kari F. Cooke's sweeping and inclusive chapter that examines the Deaf experience among Black communities throughout the U.S. highlights the "vibrant multiethnic, multilingual, and multicultural world of people whose cosmopolitanism connects the people of the world in intricate intersections of identities, one that crisscrosses the Deaf and Hearing worlds." Yet at the same time they sound a dire warning about the pressing need for greater scholarship with respect to the varied and complex experiences of Black Deaf communities. There is a danger that the stories created from their struggles against audism and racism will be lost to history, and with it the vast contributions of the Deaf Black world. They criticize the audio-dominant world for all but ignoring the Black Deaf and hard-of-hearing communities, and with it the history of their struggles, such as being "stabbed or shot at for signing on the streets in neighborhoods where gang members mistake ASL for gang signs;" or "being subjected to religious rituals or special prayer sessions designed to exorcise evil spirits that are assumed to cause deafness;" or being shunned in communities and towns by those who demand a life of implacable rectitude and "where people believe that deafness is a result of a familial curse." Dunn and Cooke also maintain, in a prefigurative sense, that by using the lens of Afrofuturism, we can emulate those communities and villages "where deafness is seen in more positive ways and a Deaf child is seen as a blessing." They share that "millions of Deaf children within Africa and some of its Diaspora who have never seen the inside of a school." And the situation in the U.S. is nothing to brag about. While Deaf scholarship has produced robust analyses showcasing the strengths and the challenges faced by Deaf ethnic communities in the U.S., there exists an egregious lack of research focusing on Black Deaf communities. The lack of culturally inclusive research on Black Deaf communities is compounded by the lack of Black instructors and administrators in schools for the deaf. It only adds insult to injury to learn that there have been only two Black Superintendents of a school for the deaf. Black communities have fought against cultural erasure since the days of Jim Crow and we can only hope that Dunn and Cooke's clarion call for more research on Black Deaf communities is taken up by the world of Deaf scholarship. Unless this occurs, the brilliance and cultural richness of the African Diaspora of Deaf people in the United States risks being rendered invisible.

To challenge the fetishistic mystifications of the capitalist system, which has medicalized, pathologized and dehumanized Deaf people struggling in the often conflictual social terrain of daily life, will take more than liberal compassion and a polyglot cosmopolitanism that smooths over the contradictions inherent in today's system of capitalist commodity production. The challenge becomes how to re-establish intersubjective connections with others and demand from society not only an affirmation of formal personhood but a transformation of the very structure of human relations. Many Deaf persons consider their identity within the context of a unique and vibrant culture. To use a phrase from critical pedagogy, they are "cultural workers" who are encapsulated by a larger culture of disability against which they have been fighting for generations, never having experienced their own bourgeois-democratic revolutions of the 17th and 18th centuries of England, the U.S. and France from which to build. The roots of this abject domination can be linked to the popularization of biological arguments, which were securely nested within the curriculum at North American colleges and universities since the 1920s, and which both fueled the rise of eugenics, and allowed eugenics to continue to be taught in more subtle or covert ways well after the Holocaust. In fact, one of the prime sites for the reproduction of eugenicist logic was, and is, the North American university, where today such institutions can be found to "work to suspend opportunities for disabled people, or use forms of disablement to suspend opportunities and privileges for marginalized groups" (Dolmage, 2017, p. 108). Dolmage writes:

> These eugenic practices, and in fact eugenics itself, can be seen as the invention of the North American university, which in turn was also built upon the exploitation of people with disabilities. Colleges and universities were colonial projects—places for settlers to continue the work of forcibly changing their landscapes and these landscapes' inhabitants, but also as sites of a sort of internalized imperialism, because universities were mainly where North Americans went to Europeanize. Eugenics was not just implicated in these moves, but was in many ways the perfect ideological vehicle for the settler colonialism of higher education. More simply, academia became the place where North Americans could most efficiently destroy what and who came before European settlement. Eugenics—the idea that certain bodies were biologically inferior—was rhetorical fuel for this very efficient destruction. (2017, p. 14)

Clearly, university politics related to people with disabilities has a long and sordid history. It is one reason to take seriously the old saying, "don't let school get in the way of your education." It's time to scrub ourselves clean of the ideological flotsam and jetsam and predilected rationality that has turned universities into dank warehouses of ableist thought, and ill-equipped for accommodating members of the Deaf community whose autonomy and independence is paramount. Trapped in a boneyard of forgetfulness, and too often content to display an obscene motivated amnesia regarding the origins and history of the treatment of people with disabilities, contemporary scholars, educators, and university administrators need to come face-to-face with their own culpability in failing to manifest themselves as subjects of praxis, by creating what Freire calls "a culture of silence" when it comes to addressing audism, ableism and disablism in their classes. When conditions of unfreedom are manifested in attacks on Deaf culture in particular and the politics of difference in general, Deaf activists, artists, poets, comics, and intellectuals have risen to the occasion and established a counter-public ground of being from which to fight the policies and practices that threaten being Deaf throughout the country. They have, in turn, displayed unconditional self-giving and civic courage and, by using the critical instruments of intelligibility found in their lived experiences, have been able to defend the rights of people of being Deaf. They fully understand that righteous rectitude, moral exertion, and pleas to the oppressor for assistance is not enough to redress this situation. Changing the world cannot be achieved by simply appealing to people's individual conscience. Because it avoids the social causes of capitalism's wretched symptomology. We need, instead, to change the structural determinations of the established social order, an order that produces and reproduces the destructive effects of capitalist social relations of exploitation and the law of value (the term value here is being used to refer to monetized wealth). In tandem with such work, we need to foster new reciprocal social relations premised on inclusion, equality and social justice, where ableism will not be papered over for the sake of a cosmetic harmony or used as a cover for class domination, and where the struggle to support people with disabilities will become inseparable from rediscovering what it means to be human in a dehumanizing and eugenicist society, whose foundations are deeply rooted in the structure of capitalist society.

Joseph C. Hill's chapter underscores the importance of resistance by Deaf activists. He reminds us that the

> medical model, often with governmental and corporation involvements, creates a conditional existence of signed languages of Deaf people, meaning that if deafness were to be completely cured, the necessity of signed languages would be severely undermined and Deaf cultures, which are intimately related with sign languages, would be drastically affected. This is an ongoing reality that determines how sign languages are recognized and accepted at local, national and international levels.

He concludes by arguing that "the deaf communities' resistance against oppression is what fuels the stubborn existence of sign languages as long as there is a basic human need for them."

The story of the Deaf community is very much a story about socio-historical captivity of people in the grip of the authoritarian pretentions of the hearing community, both of whom are the victims of predatory capitalism, a social universe co-constitutive of disablement. James Graham (2023) writes that

> Ableism is a distinct form of oppression that causes suffering and hardship regardless of the social class of those who experience it; disabled people, even those from bourgeois or petit-bourgeois economic backgrounds, are denied basic autonomy and made dependent on their families and partners, facilitating trauma and abuse.

Society at large needs to seriously engage the experiences of the Deaf community, for it is crucial for the health and maintenance of the struggle against that universal subjugator that is ignorance, an ignorance with its tentacular roots in ableism and disablism, an ignorance supreme in its pro-auditory audacity. But oppression cannot be adequately explained by experience alone. What is needed is an analysis of experience, a critical analysis of 'experience effects,' that is, an analysis that goes beyond experience to address intentionality, agency and material causality.

"You only learn from experiences that you learn from" is a phrase I heard from the great Appalachian educator, Myles Horton, during a panel we shared in Bozeman, Montana. He also said, "You can't teach anybody anything. You can only create the conditions for learning to take place, the conditions for people to learn." To me, this means that we are in dire need of languages of critique and possibility in order to help our students interpret their experiences, languages (systems of intelligibility) that can help us unpack the subjective and material conditions of experience and how they interlock catalytically in specific contexts. Critical pedagogy points to the social sciences and humanities as a means of developing new terminologies that can help us understand our experiences as resulting from both the structural determinations and contingencies of capitalism, which form part of capitalism's multi-layered and interrelated set of social relations, a chain of relationships that form a contingent totality. A pedagogy that locates experience in a world-historical frame, that leads to material change in society, and advances the conditions of possibility for a socialist alternative to a world geared towards the production of value (i.e., accumulated monetary wealth), is the type of pedagogy needed in our schools of education, if we want to build future disability activists that can envision a new society freed of economic necessity, where the idea of disability is firmly detached from its medical and social models, where people with disabilities are not denoted as unproductive workers, where structural ableism is smashed to pieces and the self-organization of people with disabilities occurs unmolested. It is a society where eugenics would be cast into the dung heap of history, where there would be accessible housing, universal healthcare and resources and accommodations necessary for a fully inclusive democratic society built on a socialist model in which there would be no dictatorship of a rich minority. All aspects of society would be managed by popular participation and people would set up methods of decision-making and conflict resolution. And there would be no need for legal protections such as the Americans with Disabilities Act to be enshrined. In such a social universe, those who cannot work would not be thrown to the wolves of marketized care. These values are worth fighting for.

Baynton records that

> one of the remarkable aspects of the pan-disability rights movement is its ability to bring together diverse groups of people into common action. It is a fractious coalition, riven by identity politics and conflicting agendas to be sure. Nevertheless, its very existence and dramatic growth is testament to a powerful idea—that the goal ought not to be for any one group to find liberation for itself, in effect merely reshuffling the deck, but rather to resist and disrupt the systematic translation of difference into structures of privilege and oppression.

Cruz's innovative application of critical pedagogy in Deaf Studies reveals the power and potentiality of an analytical and transformative theoretical framework and language that can functionally challenge the oppressive socio-cultural-political forces that create the conditions of unfreedom that affect subaltern groups most vulnerable in our society, including from the Deaf community. It is here that Cruz emphasizes the importance of intersectionality in terms of the myriad ways that race, class, gender and sexuality impact Deaf individuals. Such an understanding can develop a protagonistic agency "able to disrupt these oppressive forces, decolonize hegemonic meanings, and consequently result in social transformation and transcendence of all types of oppression." What I find fascinating is how Cruz was able to map ways in which deaf individuals construct meaning in music and based on auditory skills, how deaf individuals were able to translate their construction of meaning in such a way that they became aware of the oppressive forces arrayed against them in the larger society.

Contributors *Jody H. Cripps, Anita Small, Ely Lyonblum, Samuel J. Supalla, Aimee K. Whyte, and Joanne S. Cripps* share how Deaf performers use hands, movements and facial expressions to expand the definition of music. A particularly arresting result has been the way that signed music has helped to deepen the means of self-efficacy on the part of children, who can now be encouraged to become more educated and conscious of what constitutes signed music and to proactively develop signed language as an artistic performance. The authors reveal that music is not only a creative auditory phenomenon, not simply organized sound, but can be signed by Deaf people, using ASL—a fully-fledged human visual-gestural language possessing linguistic properties—drawing from Deaf culture, a culture that takes physicality and sensual blandishments with an ardent seriousness. One such example of a Deaf musician is *Marko Vuoriheimo* (artist name Signmark) a congenitally deaf rapper/hip-hop artist from Finland. Signmark performs worldwide with his band and is a recording artist for Warner Music Group. He uses his music to advocate for the rights of

Deaf people whom he considers as part of a dynamic linguistic minority with their own culture, history, and community. As a Deaf musician, Signmark placed a close second in the Finnish qualification at the 2009 Eurovision Song Contest. In an interview with Ana L. Cruz, Signmark expresses his interest in the music of various ethnic communities and the two audiences that he works with:

> I was always very interested in other music artists' work. I have gained much information from their lyrics and I know more about the world because I have been studying other music artists and their lyrics. For instance, Sami people or Maori and their own songs; when I am 'listening' to the music and reading those texts I get a feeling of a shared identity, that I have similar experiences with them, I kind of 'feel' them. At the same time, I am thinking about how I would write my own next song because I was inspired by their song, or how will this affect my songwriting because I am always writing for Deaf audiences. I start to think how could I make this for a Deaf audience, but at the same time, of course, I want the hearing people to be able to enjoy my music as well. I have these two audiences that I'm constantly thinking about. That is important for me in music.

It is important for Signmark to speak to the interests of the global Deaf community that is made up of individuals with multiple intersecting identities but who share common experiences and characteristics and whose rights deserve to be defended.

Signmark is correct. Shared Deaf identities performed locally and globally need to be defended. In addition, the importance of the pan-disability rights movement for the Deaf community cannot be emphasized enough, especially in light of recent history when, as President of the United States, Donald Trump mocked a reporter, Serge Kovaleski, who has arthrogryposis, a congenital condition affecting the joints.

Articles in the *The Atlantic* magazine written by Jeffrey Goldberg and in MSNBC News by Eric Garcia, shared a profile of General Mark Milley, the outgoing chairman of the Joint Chiefs of Staff. Milley revealed another shocking revelation about Trump and his loathsome view of disabled Americans, even the most patriotic whose features were disfigured and limbs lost in their service to their country. During Milley's welcoming ceremony as chairman, he invited a veteran, Luis Avila, to sing "God Bless America." Avila had served five combat tours, lost a leg, had two heart attacks, two strokes and suffered brain damage. At that rain-drenched ceremony, Avila's wheelchair almost toppled over. Invited guests at the ceremony did their best to keep him from falling. Milley reported that Trump said: "Why do you bring people like that here? No one wants to see that, the wounded" (Garcia, 2023). Trump ordered the general to never let Avila appear again in public. Apparently, Trump had previously wanted wounded veterans excluded from public events because, "Nobody wants to see that" (Garcia, 2023).

In a review of *Deaf People in Hitler's Europe* by Donnal L. Ryan and John S. Schuchman (Gallaudet University Press, 2002), Gilles Renaud (2003) points out that actions undertaken against people with disabilities were initially not viewed as central to the Holocaust. This is in stark contrast to a renewed understanding of Nazi eugenics that makes it clear that "people with physical and cognitive abilities were targeted for special measures, from forced sterilization to outright liquidation, but always under the umbrella of legislation." Wilhelm Ballier's 1932 film, *Verkannte Menschen* (Misjudged People), that championed the rights of deaf Germans, was the last time during the rise of Nazism that deaf people were portrayed in a positive light and able to escape the Nazi "euthanasia" effort (Renaud, 2003). The Deaf people who formed their own community through sign language, along with formal Deaf organizations, were forcefully taken over by the Nazi Association of Deaf People, the ReGeDe (The Reich Union of the Deaf of Germany), whose initial act was to forcefully sterilize many of its members (it is worth remembering that Adolf Hitler was an admirer of the American eugenics movement, Jim Crow segregation, and American citizenship and anti-miscegenation laws which influenced Nazi Germany's Citizenship Law and the Blood Law). As Renaud notes, the 1933 and 1935 racial hygiene laws declared Jews, Gypsies, and disabled people to be "unfit" and so they were eventually all targeted for "sterilization, marriage prohibitions, and death" (Renaud, 2003). The 1933 Hereditary Health Law mandated compulsory sterilization for hereditarily deaf individuals and it is unknown how many Deaf persons were among the 400,000 individuals forcibly sterilized by the Nazi regime between 1934 and 1945 (Hudson, 2019). To the German medical community, this was simply "applied biology" and some of their members even served in genetic counseling centers to screen for hereditary impairments (which makes me feel good that I denied an invitation to serve as an ethnographer for the Human Genome Project). Twelve million people with disabilities were eventually exterminated by the Nazis. While Deaf people might not be priority targets for an American fascist movement, it could be, in Donald Trump's words, "the Marxists, the communists, lunatic thugs, misfits, wackos, rapists, murderers, or the Japs."

This collection of works is brilliantly conceived, pleasurably unpredictable, filled with granular descriptions of the lived experiences and real-life struggles of Deaf people who are contributing to the Deaf community and to those outside the Deaf community in a myriad of ways, through theater, poetry, fiction writing, acting, music and serving as activists and advocates for Deaf people worldwide. The thematic weight of this volume is kept comfortably afloat by chapters that are beautifully written and filled with the roar of dissidence. This is not a book for the tranquil mind. It is clear that Deaf scholars, teachers, artists and performers are launching new, protracted experiments and struggles against the *fin de siècle* ableism and disablism of the twentieth century. The themes addressed by the writers of these chapters constitute a virtuoso repertoire of some of the most significant issues and debates surrounding Deaf culture, Deaf music, and overall Deaf Studies at the first quarter of the twenty-first century. Disability is being reconfigured in new ways, not in the physical bodies of individuals alone, but in socially produced boundaries linked to the fundamental social, cultural and economic relations of society (Marx thought poverty was a disability), including restrictive macroeconomic arrangements and ideational constructs (i.e., the materialist social model, Clear & Gleeson, 2002). There is an emphasis on boundary crossing rather than boundary maintenance, as well as creating new social formations and relations of production that enable new skills, capacities and potentialities. Deaf Studies is unveiling new epistemes which govern what constitutes a disability and disablement and offering bold new ways of interpreting human differences. This has sparked conversations on what it means to be human in the apocalyptic rubble of today's post-digital technoverse and the current crisis of the Capitalocene. Baynton is right when he argues that it is people "with particular physical differences from the majority [that] are disabled by the prejudicial beliefs and actions of the majority." He further notes that

> People with physical differences from the majority have increasingly moved away from the notion that they have a disability, or are persons with a disability, and instead refer to themselves as disabled people to indicate its centrality to their identity, and speak of "disablement" to refer to the social process of becoming disabled. Many people find it difficult to understand that anyone would willingly embrace the identity of "disabled person," since disability in our culture seems self-evidently a personally discrediting label. Just as most hearing people simplistically translate "deaf" into "cannot hear," so do most people equate disabled with unable.

There is a collective abhorrence that sets the writers of this volume squarely against those who remain ignorant of the value and accomplishments of Deaf people and who possess a studied refusal to acknowledge the creativity and vibrancy of Deaf culture. There is, too, a carefully cultivated sense of refusal of an America dominated by an image of itself as a place that welcomes all people equally, that battens on the kindness and generosity of its populace. *Culture,*

Deafness & Music: Critical Pedagogy and a Path to Social Justice is a tart warning to reconsider our prejudices and assumptions and to reject the obscene familiarities surrounding disability that throbs through our daily thoughts like a migraine. It is a book of tremendous verve and at times a pulverizing brute force without plunging into a strategic recklessness that is sometimes necessary in rescuing those who prefer complacency and stock responses over critical agency. For a true education warrior who has donned Freirean armor, Ana L. Cruz has accomplished a work of loving dedication to the cause of justice. By dint of persevering in what has become her lifelong struggle, and remaining undaunted by those forces designed to antagonize critical warriors at all turns and junctures, she has remained at the forefront of collaborative efforts to provide a new architecture for Radical Deaf Studies that can bring about ameliorative public acts without the salvationist alchemy pitched triumphantly by 'missionary' reformers. Freire, her mentor, has a long pedigree in critical studies, and Cruz has skillfully reinvented many of his key ideas in bold and innovative ways through her fusion of critical pedagogy with Deaf Studies by means of a skillfully crafted revolutionary praxis. In so doing she has redefined the boundaries between sound and silence, in that liminal space of 'betwixt and between' where Deaf people 'see music' externally and internally, and view musical instruments as extensions of the human body.

Culture, Deafness & Music: Critical Pedagogy and a Path to Social Justice is an inexhaustibly fascinating and pathfinding collection; its overall message is direct, like a hammer blow on an iron girder, an indomitable force dedicated to dismantling grave injustices and nurturing the fertile ground of an inclusivity-infused society. It is a powerful and urgent contribution to a Radical Deaf Studies that explicitly confronts, undermines and provides alternatives to ableist logics, audism and the self-destructive binary of disablement that separates the Deaf and hearing communities, that have for ages infected the state and academia. Helen Keller once remarked, "Blindness cuts us off from things, but deafness cuts us off from people." That need not be true any longer, so long as the hearing community recognizes that it is their own prejudices and biases that disable people who are deaf, that it is their own lack of understanding that has created ableism, audism and surdophobia. The community of Deaf persons has come out of the shadows imposed upon it, claiming the right to be Deaf. And it will resist any and all attempts to push it back towards oblivion.

References

Clear, M., & Gleeson, B. (2002, June). Disability and materialist embodiment. *Journal of Australian Political Economy, 49*, 34–55.

Dolmage, J. T. (2017). *Academic ableism: Disability and higher education*. University of Michigan Press.
Garcia, E. (2023, September 22). Disabled veterans seem to get respect from everyone except Donald Trump. *MSNBC News*. https://www.msnbc.com/opinion/msnbc-opinion/gen-mark-milleys-disturbing-reminder-trumps-disdain-wounded-vets-rcna111476
Goldberg, J. (2023, November). The patriot. How general Mark Milley protected the constitution from Donald Trump. *The Atlantic*. https://www.theatlantic.com/magazine/archive/2023/11/general-mark-milley-trump-coup/675375/
Graham, J. (2023). Socialism needs disability justice. *Midnight sun: A magazine of socialist strategy, analysis and culture*. https://www.midnightsunmag.ca/socialism-needs-disability-justice/
Hudson, M. (2019, May 27). Being deaf during the nazi era and the holocaust. *Disability history museum*. https://disabilitymuseum.org/dismuse/being-deaf-during-the-nazi-era-the-holocaust/
Renaud, G. (2003). Book review: Ryan, D. F. & Schuchman, J. S. (Eds.). (2002). Deaf people in Hitler's Europe. *Revue Générale de Droit, 33*(2), 346–349. https://www.erudit.org/en/journals/rgd/1900-v1-n1-rgd01602/1027462ar.pdf
Thal, M. (2023, July 28). Marginalization of the deaf: Marginalization and surdophobia. *Young Adult Books: The Blog*. http://michaelthal.com/marginalization-of-the-deaf-audism-and-surdophobia/

Preface

A Brief History

The seeds for this book—hence the theme of music & deafness and the social justice aspects—were laid in Brazil in the late 1980s. As a very young university professor with a commitment to serve the local community as a music instructor, I had the opportunity to work with a young congenitally deaf girl (profoundly deaf) who wanted to learn how to play the piano. She was eager to participate in the music activities of her family (all family members were hearing individuals who played music instruments). Upon her father's request to the academic department at the university at which I was an Assistant Professor at that time—linked to the university's Art/Music Center for Community Services—I agreed to provide piano instruction to this congenitally deaf girl by modifying the pedagogical approach that I used for teaching hearing students. The music instruction was successful and after about one year the young girl was able to read musical notation and play the piano with ease that many people to whom she played did not realize that she was congenitally deaf. She was enthusiastic and motivated; she followed the path that she chose, supported by her family, without negating her deaf identity. But even more important was my realization of the lack of viable possibilities for the deaf girl to follow her dream and to engage with music, for example the lack of schools and teachers prepared for providing deaf students with music opportunities/exposure to music instruments/instruction, a restricted education that did not allow for exploration and/or creativity, as well as the barriers erected by a hearing society used to prescribe to deaf people what they can and cannot do. This was the beginning of my commitment to social justice and equity for the Deaf community. Therefore, the term 'deafness' in the title of the book is not meant to reinforce a medical/pathological view, but 'deafness' is seen as a socio-cultural and ideological barrier to be overcome.

After working with the deaf girl for a few years in Brazil and learning what was made available for her to engage with music, I also recognized that knowledge about and work on music & deafness was scarce to nonexistent in Brazil. Consequently, I moved to the U.S. for graduate studies with an understanding that educational opportunities for d/Deaf people were more developed in the U.S. than they were in Brazil. However, I also quickly found out that linking deafness and music was a 'taboo' both in the hearing and also in the Deaf world in the U.S. The questions about the lack of opportunity, prejudice, oppression, and domination of Deaf people based on auditory skills first raised in Brazil continued, perhaps even more intensified, in the U.S.: once again, an issue of social justice, equity, and ethics.

Exploring and understanding the merger of music & deafness is complex and I soon realized that a space for this type of work did not exist in academia. Music therapy was the closest field of study linking music & deafness. My focus, however, was not on the therapeutic aspect but on the artistic aspect of music, on experiencing and enjoying music as an art form. As for academic fields, I experienced some marginal acceptance of my scholarly endeavors, based on the curiosity of some experts, in music education. I found myself as a broker between academic fields as knowledge seemed to be partitioned into separate cages. I also navigated through many professional conferences in music therapy, music education, education, and cultural studies, with the aim to find a space to share my scholarship and to advocate for the possibility of music & deafness. I found a professional home in the U.S. in the Teacher Education Program at a two-year academic institution that puts emphasis on teaching at the undergraduate level. This academic institution provided an opportunity for faculty to explore interdisciplinarity, where creativity was not only respected but also encouraged. One outcome due to this creative space was the design of a general education capstone course that was open to all students, not just to the teacher education students. This course, *Voices of Diversity: Culture, Deafness and Music*, was interdisciplinary in nature with subject areas that I have worked on as a graduate student and as a professor; it was an amalgam of Deaf Studies, cultural anthropology, history, pedagogy, sociology, audiology, research methodology, and cultural studies. The course aimed at a better understanding of Deaf people, Deaf culture, diversity in the Deaf community, music & deafness, and the concept of the social construction of deafness as a disability. With my interdisciplinary background and focus on critical pedagogy and social justice the design of this course was very exciting, it was a 're-beginning' of my engagement with the Deaf world. Not surprisingly, there was no textbook available to cover all the course topics envisioned for this course; Branson and Miller (2002) was chosen as a course text supplemented by a long list of additional reading materials and videos. Despite the focus on the Deaf world and being open to all college students, the course also proved particularly beneficial for teacher education students as it was relevant for Foundations of Education in addressing issues of diversity (including different abilities), social justice, multiculturalism, and the importance of interdisciplinary knowledge.

The aforementioned course became the basis for this book project which started eight years ago. The goal was to create a book that canvasses the Deaf world based on contributions from experts, Deaf and/or hearing, and to speak directly to readers interested in the Deaf world. There were many challenges in putting this book together, such as (1) the gap between the Deaf world and the hearing world; (2) engaging in editing a book about the Deaf world and Deaf culture as a hearing person (please see endnote for my own positionality[1] statement); (3) the various reactions of Deaf experts I contacted for contributions (some of whom naturally had to check me out by requesting a chat and/or an interview with me: some disregarded my inquiries, some dropped out of the project, and some fully embraced it); (4) personal life events of contributors (including my own) that delayed completion of the book. These challenges, however, were not seen as barriers but as learning opportunities; I believe that what I learned from those challenges enhanced the final outcome of the book. The book evolved, with some planned chapters that did not materialize and chapters that were added, but throughout those years the contributors stood together and kept their belief in the project; their patience and powerful contributions are a testament that this book is truly a labor of love. The book should be seen as a forum for *dialogue* about the Deaf world with an *emphasis on social justice*; it is intended for anyone interested in learning about the Deaf world and in bringing the voice of Deaf people to a wider audience. In addition, the book contains a substantial segment on Deaf art which closely connects with the theoretical framework of this book: critical pedagogy/social justice. As articulated by Ursula Le Guin in 2014[2] "[a]ny human power can be resisted and changed by human beings. Resistance and change often begin in art."

Outline of the Book

The book is divided into four parts: Encounters in Deaf Culture (Part 1), Deaf Art: Affirmation, Resistance, and Liberation (Part 2), 'Deaf Music:' Visions, Possibilities, and Social Justice (Part 3), and Understanding the Auditory System and Portraying the Diversity of Deaf Voices through Research (Part 4). Part 1 "Encounters in Deaf Culture" commences with *Douglas Baynton* (Chapter 1) addressing the concepts of culture, identity, ethnicity, and disability, including a discussion on how these concepts relate to Deaf people. The author details how the concept of Deaf culture in the field of Deaf Studies contributed fundamentally to an understanding of the Deaf experience. He argues that the cultural model to frame the study of Deaf communities and Deaf experience reached limits and should be expanded in order to address more adequately issues related to deaf people. Baynton invites us to consider the social model of disability that emphasizes 'difference' as opposed to the medical model of disability that emphasizes loss or impairment; the latter often leading to oppression. This social model of disability is firmly juxtaposed to the medical model of disability. The author argues that embracing the physical body and physical aspect of deafness (i.e., a different sensory relationship to the world) to augment the powerful cultural model will strengthen Deaf Studies and will be more encompassing in addressing issues related to Deaf communities and the Deaf experience.

Despite the diversity in the Deaf community, sign language is a cultural mark for Deaf people. The global scope of sign languages and their significance for Deaf people is the subject of the chapter by *Joseph Hill* (Chapter 2). Hill provides an overview of the history of sign languages and their validation as language based on linguistic research; the world-wide distribution of sign languages, including International Sign; and the impact of sign languages on the schooling of deaf people. He emphasizes that schools for the deaf were instrumental in the acquisition and maintenance of sign language and in the development of Deaf communities. World-wide, there are differences in sign languages based on geographical and social factors, an example being Black American Sign Language (BASL) developed due to racial discrimination and educational segregation in the U.S. Hill further argues that despite place-specific influences on the development of Deaf identity, Deaf culture, and sign language, the universality of the Deaf experience in navigating social and cultural spaces and sign language as its key component connects deaf people within the concept of Deafhood (Ladd, 2003). One shared experience by deaf communities around the world is the confrontation with audism, the systematic oppression, discrimination, and ignorance against Deaf people (Humphries, 1975, 1977; Bauman, 2004). With Deafhood as the metaphysical home, the author describes the scattered world-wide distribution of Deaf communities as diasporic.

Lindsay Dunn and *Kari Cooke* offer in their chapter a comprehensive description of the Deaf experience by Black Deaf people in the U.S. (Chapter 3). They provide a look at the Black Deaf American community characterized by varied historical and cultural roots, of multiethnic and multilingual makeup, with rich intersection of identities. Dunn and Cooke point out the strong Pan-African solidarity within the Black Diaspora (Deaf and hearing) in the U.S. and address issues of transnationalism and disidentification. They emphasize the twin barriers faced by Black Deaf Americans: racism within the Deaf community and racialized audism in the hearing world. Dunn and Cooke call for the integration of multiculturalism in the education of Deaf students and for an increase in the number of African-American teachers, counselors and school administrators at schools for the deaf. The chapter is also a clarion call for more scholarship to explore the intersectionalities of Black Deaf identities and experiences in the U.S., a field within Deaf Studies that is—up until now—mostly neglected.

In her chapter *Junhui Yang* shifts the geographical focus to China (Chapter 4). She describes the emergence of a Deaf culture in this second-most populous country on Earth sparked by exposure to the development of Deaf culture in North America and Europe. Deaf people, considered through the disability perspective, receive support from government administration and disability organizations but this support also reinforces the aspect of disability and leads to oppression. Emergence of a Deaf culture in China and especially the improvement of the social status of Deaf people were influenced by (1) exposure to deaf-related issues through traditional and social media, (2) increased educational opportunities for deaf children through mainstreaming—in a society that strongly values education—and also (3) through often strong family involvement in the education of deaf children. Junhui, furthermore, presents an example of deaf people engaged with music through a case study of a deaf dance troupe. Exposure of this deaf dance troupe through the media led to widespread awareness in China of Chinese Sign Language and the cultural rights of the Deaf community.

In Part 2 "Deaf Art: Affirmation, Resistance, and Liberation" the discussion revolves around the theme of artistic expression by d/Deaf people. A common thread is that artistic expressions are often political acts of affirmation—that is the celebration of Deaf culture—and/or resistance—that is the emphasis on injustice and oppression experienced by Deaf people (Durr, 1999). Artistic expressions, then, portray the d/Deaf lived experience, raise awareness regarding societal issues affecting the deaf community, and eventually offer the opportunity to work toward overcoming those oppressive and unjust circumstances. Christie and Wilkins (2007) refer to the path from resistance to affirmation as liberation.

In "Deaf Humor as a Political Tool" (Chapter 5), *Rachel Sutton-Spence* contrasts between Deaf humor and sign-language humor. She emphasizes that most Deaf humor is political as it navigates the space between the disenfranchised minority Deaf community and the dominating majority hearing society. Sutton-Spence provides examples of Deaf jokes, many of them recognized by Deaf communities worldwide, and inquires whether they can be considered acts of resistance or acts of affirmation.

Karen Christie and *Dorothy Wilkins* discuss (Chapter 6) English and American Sign Language (ASL) literature primarily by U.S. Deaf women. Christie and Wilkins provide a succinct history of Deaf education in the U.S. together with addressing the origin and development of ASL, and its recognition as a full-fledged language. Accompanying this historical trajectory is a discussion of the emergence and development of Deaf literature, involving works in English, works combining English and signing, and works fully composed in ASL. They highlight the Deaf liberation movement and literary contributions by Deaf women that originated within and supported this movement for Deaf rights and societal acceptance. The works of contemporary Deaf women poets—Kristi B. Merriweather, Nathie Marbury, and Ella Mae Lentz—are analyzed in light of their contribution to Deaf women's liberation. Christie and Wilkins make clear that sign language poetry is a contribution by Deaf people to humanity, part of the concept of Deaf Gain (Bauman & Murray, 2014), but also that the power of literary works by Deaf women for Deaf liberation has yet to be fully realized.

Chapter 7 by *Aaron Kelstone* offers a historical overview of the origin and evolution of U.S. Deaf Theatre, and of the individuals, institutions, singular events, and societal factors that influenced the course of this historical development. The chapter makes clear the importance of Deaf Theatre in contributing to the development of a Deaf cultural identity and viability, and to promoting the Deaf community as a linguistic minority based on American Sign Language. Kelstone emphasizes the transformative power of Deaf Theatre as it can challenge society's social, cultural, and political perceptions and misrepresentations of Deaf people. The chapter concludes with a look at the possibility of the modern Deaf Theatre to address issues of intersectionality of Deaf people and to provide opportunity for a better understanding of human diversity.

Patti Durr, in an interview with Ana L. Cruz (Chapter 8), provides a brief history of the De'VIA movement and references some of the major former and current artists of this movement. De'VIA stands for Deaf View/Image Art. This art movement is comprised of Deaf-themed visual art that provides a visual expression of the Deaf lived experience and it was significant in contributing to the development of a distinct Deaf culture and identity. De'VIA works celebrate Deaf culture (works of affirmation) or emphasize injustice and oppression toward Deaf people (works of resistance). As with surdism, a more recent Deaf-themed art movement which also incorporates art forms beyond the visual arts, De'VIA is an important means of contributing to consciousness raising for Deaf (and hearing) people leading to activism to change unjust and oppressive societal conditions for Deaf people.

Music, overall, has become a more prominent part of the Deaf experience. In Part 3 "'Deaf Music:' Visions, Possibilities, and Social Justice," *Jody Cripps, Anita Small, Ely Lyonblum, Samuel Supalla, Aimee Whyte,* and *Joanne Cripps* (Chapter 9) address the concept of signed music. Signed music by Deaf people is created through the use of hands, movement and facial expressions; it is music not related to the use of the auditory system and is not supported by auditory music. Cripps et al. argue that musical elements, such as rhythm, timbre, texture, and motif can be expressed in the signed modality. Signed music, as understood by them, is rooted in Deaf culture and the Deaf community, and its creation and performance should be carried out by fluent signers (e.g., American Sign Language—proficiency). Cripps et al. conclude by emphasizing that Deaf children should be exposed to signed music in school as this will contribute to self-efficacy and identity development.

Marko Vuoriheimo, a Finnish hip-hop artist, composer, performer, and recording musician known as Signmark, explains in an interview with Ana L. Cruz (Chapter 10) his path of becoming a Deaf professional musician who now performs to large audiences in concerts worldwide. He recounts the support and the opposition he experienced on this journey to fulfill his dream of becoming a Deaf artist, and also the reasons and artistic influences that let him to the genre of hip hop. In the interview he also reveals how he, as a Deaf person, experiences music; how he "learned" to become a musician; and why music is important to him. He also believes that there are great benefits to be gained by exposing Deaf children to music. Marko also emphasizes the social impact of music, especially through the lyrics, and he uses his music to inspire Deaf people and to raise awareness throughout the world about socio-economic and political issues affecting Deaf people.

The contribution by *Ana L. Cruz* (Chapter 11), emanating from her experiences with music & deafness, addresses issues of domination and oppression faced by Deaf individuals because of audism and ableism, and, in addition, she also proposes a 'new pedagogical approach' for educating d/Deaf people in music. Cruz, furthermore, highlights opposition faced by Deaf individuals who engage in musical activities not only from the hearing world but also from within the Deaf world. She argues for a transdisciplinary fusion of critical pedagogy (especially concepts such as conscientização and emancipatory literacy) with Deaf Studies to contribute to the theoretical foundation of Deaf Studies and, as a Radical Deaf Studies, to create an opportunity for another theoretical lens to further analyze oppressive forces affecting Deaf people while supporting the development of Deaf agency for transformation.

One of the initial ideas in the design of this book was for its readers to develop an understanding of how Deaf people are (re)presented in research studies, and to learn about the research process and research methodologies. In Part 4 "Understanding the Auditory System and Portraying the Diversity of Deaf Voices through Research" *Stephanie Cawthon* (Chapter 13) introduces the reader to the nature of conducting research with a special emphasis on research involving d/Deaf and hard-of-hearing individuals. The chapter provides a succinct guide through the research process from design to data interpretation (both qualitative and quantitative research designs); the special ethical concerns when d/Deaf and hard-of-hearing individuals are involved; and the factors that affect how deaf experiences are represented. This contribution by Cawthon is significant since research involving d/Deaf and hard-of-hearing individuals requires special considerations to avoid issues of domination, oppression, and cultural appropriation. While teaching the course *Voices of Diversity: Culture, Deafness and Music,* there were many questions not only from hearing but also from a set of Deaf students about the auditory system and the various types and causes of hearing loss. Therefore, the chapter by *Wafaa Kaf* (Chapter 12) provides a detailed overview of the anatomy and physiology of the auditory system and the circumstances that can lead to different types of hearing loss. She also provides an introduction to audiological testing and amplification measures. Kaf, while considering the use of amplification measures, also emphasizes the importance of a discussion about Deaf culture, shared decision-making with Deaf individuals, and expert counseling. The focus of the book, however, is aimed at an understanding of the Deaf experience through the socio-cultural framework and not viewing it from the/a medical perspective.

The appendices include the *De'VIA Manifesto* (Appendix A) and the *Surdism Manifesto* (Appendix B). Appendix C, in contrast, is a qualitative case study of a teacher at a school for the deaf who integrates music in the education of d/Deaf children. The study shows the use of music as an instructional technique in a middle school for d/Deaf students and students with multiple disabilities. The study reveals the acquaintance of d/Deaf children to music by extensive exposure through media in its multiple forms; specific approaches and techniques used by the teacher in using music for instruction of d/Deaf children; the benefits derived from using music with d/Deaf children; and problems encountered through the teaching practice. The study emphasizes the applicability of music for teaching d/Deaf children and supports the argument against the ideological concept that music & deafness are mutually exclusive. This appendix is a reproduction of a conference (1996) proceedings paper that was formerly available as a digital publication on the Internet. It generated some interest from scholars and is made accessible again through this appendix.

Notes

1 I am a hearing educational researcher with scholarly interests in critical pedagogy and music & deafness. I am a multiethnic-racial (black, indigenous, white) female from Brazil teaching at a Higher Education Institution in the U.S. in a teacher education program. I have a strong connection to the arts as a former music education professor and as a classical pianist.

My (limited) dexterity in American Sign Language diminished because of a lack of practice, especially since moving to St. Louis where oral communication in schools for the deaf is more prevalent.

2 The quote is from Ursula Le Guin's acceptance speech for the *Medal for Distinguished Contribution to American Literature* from the National Book Foundation in 2014. The source for the quote is the *The Guardian* (November 20, 2014) https://www.theguardian.com/books/2014/nov/20/ursula-k-le-guin-national-book-awards-speech

References

Bauman, H.-D. L. (2004). Audism: Exploring the metaphysics of oppression. *Journal of Deaf Studies and Deaf Education, 9*(2), 239–246.

Bauman, H-D. L., & Murray, J. J. (Eds.). (2014). *Deaf gain: Raising the stakes for human diversity*. Minneapolis, MN: University of Minnesota Press.

Branson, J., & Miller, D. (2002). *Damned for their difference: The cultural construction of deaf people as disabled.* Washington, D.C.: Gallaudet University Press.

Christie, K., & Wilkins, M. (2007). Themes and symbols in ASL poetry: Resistance, affirmation and liberation. *Deaf Worlds, 22*(3), 1–49.

Durr, P. (1999). Deconstructing the forced assimilation of deaf people via De'VIA resistance and affirmation art. *Visual Anthropology Review, 15*(2), 47–68.

Humphries, T. (1975). *Audism: The making of a word* [Unpublished essay].

Humphries, T. (1977). *Communication across cultures (deaf-hearing) and language learning* [Unpublished Doctoral Dissertation]. Union Institute and University.

Ladd, P. (2003). *Understanding deaf culture: In search of deafhood.* Clevedon, UK: Multilingual Matters.

Acknowledgements

I want to first acknowledge the support I received for this book project from Peter De Liefde and Evelien Witte-van der Veer. Further thanks go to Athina Dimitriou, Christine Hededam, and the whole team at Brill for seeing the book project come to fruition. The book benefitted from comments by anonymous reviewers, and I also thank the colleagues who wrote endorsements for the book. Special thanks must be extended to Peter McLaren and Paddy Ladd for accepting the invitation to write the Foreword and Afterword, respectively, and to Nancy Rourke for permission to use her painting 'Like A River' for the book cover. I am grateful to the University of Minnesota Press for allowing to reprint 'Beyond Deaf Culture' by Douglas Baynton as Chapter 1 of the book and to the QUIG Conference Proceedings editors for permission to reproduce a Proceedings article as Appendix C. I need to express my deepest gratitude to all contributors to the book, for their patience during a long gestation process and the trust they put in me—especially the trust extended to me by the Deaf contributors.

I also want to acknowledge the support I received when I was a graduate student at my alma mater, The University of Tennessee-Knoxville: from the Office of the Graduate School that embraced me as part of their 'family,' from Dean Clarence W. Minkel, and from Olga Welch, Marvelene Moore, and Faye Harrison, who also sharpened my understanding of culture(s) and diversity.

My access to the Deaf world and the subject of music & deafness would not have been possible without that young deaf student in Manaus, Brazil, Roberta Sá Gomes (and her family). Roberta's curiosity, tenacity, and unwavering positive attitude opened my eyes to the constant oppression faced by Deaf persons and that, nevertheless, the 'impossible is possible.' At the University of Tennessee, Donald Ashmore further guided me into the Deaf world and took me on a journey about the manifold possibilities for a Deaf person and music.

I am indebted to the late Joe Kincheloe, critical pedagogue extraordinaire, for supporting my work—he saw in my work on music & deafness and Freirean critical pedagogy something others could not. Sincere thanks also go to Marcus Barros, former Rector of the Universidade Federal do Amazonas, for his unwavering support. I also want to thank Antônio Paulo Graça, Professor of Literature at the Universidade Federal do Amazonas, for his support, friendship, wisdom, sage advice, being an older academic compadre, and inexhaustible fountain of knowledge—my great regret is that he cannot see this book and my work—he left this Earth much too early!

I want to extend my special thanks to my family, particularly my mother Maria da Conceição, my sister Teresa Cristina, my brother Carlos Eduardo, and my cousin Maria do Carmo, for their constant support and love. Lastly, the most heartfelt gratitude to my husband Joachim; this book would not have been possible without his patience, support, guidance, love, and companionship in the struggle for a better world!

It is not possible to thank by name, in this limited space, all those who supported and encouraged me throughout the years—therefore, many thanks to all of you.

About the Cover Art

The painting on the cover of this book is entitled *Like a River*. The artwork depicts how a deaf girl was raised wearing her cochlear implant since the age of 21 months. She was taught to listen and talk, and not to use sign language. Her parents worked many hours training her to listen to music. While the girl was growing up, her parents would tell friends and relatives that their daughter was 'hearing.' The painting shows two worlds: one is Culturally Deaf, where there is sign language; and the other one is the hearing world, where there are ears, mouths and musical notes. The Culturally Deaf side of the painting shows more vivid colors than the hearing world side. The colors are bold on the Culturally Deaf side because Deaf people are visually-wise, while on the hearing world side, the colors are limited which means not deaf-friendly and lack of any accessibilities. When the deaf girl enters the hearing world, she feels limited and uncertain. She becomes the river—she flows between the two worlds. She is in-between two worlds and struggles to find her own identity. The river shows a hidden image of that deaf girl and there is a hidden message that says 'AUDISM.' Because the word audism is shown there, it means turning a content baby deaf girl into a 'hearing' baby girl after the cochlear implant surgery, she had no control. She has to learn how to listen and talk and to be raised in a hearing world. This has become a violation of human rights. With this painting I hope to inspire and to educate new parents of a deaf child about the Culturally Deaf, its history, and the values of life; to encourage them to learn sign language and to develop language acquisition for a deaf child age zero to five before entering kindergarten. The color scheme used in my oil paintings is often referred to as *Rourkeism* and is based on primary colors and some uses of monochrome. The meaning behind the color scheme: red represents empowerment; yellow represent hope and light—Culturally Deaf people use to sign to each other; blue represents oppression; black and white do not have a meaning behind it, but they help make the vivid colors to pop out more. Motifs I use often are Mouth, Ear and Eye and they represent Culturally Deaf and Oral Deaf (and predominantly audist environments). My paintings are strongly influenced by De'VIA, as in *Deaf View/Image Art*, and the colors I use are influenced by the Fauvism movement.

Nancy Rourke

Figures and Tables

Figures

Tables

Abbreviations

AAE	African-American English
ASHA	American Speech-Language-Hearing Association
ANSD	Auditory Neuropathy Spectrum Disorder
APD	Auditory Processing Disorder
ASL	American Sign Language
ASD	American School for the Deaf
Auslan	Australian Sign Language
BASL	Black American Sign Language
BDA	British Deaf Association
BIPOC	Black, Indigenous, and People of Color
BSL	British Sign Language
BTE	Behind the ear receiver
CDS	Centre for Deaf Studies (University of Bristol)
CHL	Conductive Hearing Loss
CIC	Completely in the canal receiver
cm	Centimeter
CODA	Child of a Deaf Adult
COED	Commission on the Education of the Deaf
CRISPR	Clustered Regularly Interspaced Short Palindromic Repeats
CSD	California School for the Deaf
CSL	Chinese Sign Language
CT	Computerized Tomography
DAM	Deaf Art Movement
DASL	A Dictionary of American Sign Language on Linguistic Principles
DCAL	Deafness Cognition and Language Research Center (University College London)
De'VIA	Deaf View/Image Art
dB	Decibels
dBA	A-weighted decibels
DIF	Differential Item Functioning
DPN	Deaf President Now
EAC	External Auditory Canal
EDHI	Early Hearing Detection and Intervention
EU	European Union
FDA	Food and Drug Administration
FDP	Federation of Deaf People
GU	Gallaudet University

HBCUs	Historically Black Colleges and Universities
HIV	Human Immunodeficiency Virus
HL	Hearing Loss
Hz	Hertz
ICED	International Congress on the Education of the Deaf
ICSD	International Committee of Sports for the Deaf
INES	Instituto Nacional Educação de Surdos (National Institute of Education for the Deaf)
IRB	Institutional Review Board
ITC	In the Canal Receiver
ITE	In the Ear Receiver
LDVP	London Deaf Video Project
Libras	Lingua Brasileira de Sinais (Brazilian Sign Language)
LGBTQ	Lesbian, Gay, Bisexual, Transgender, Queer
LGBTQIA	Lesbian, Gay, Bisexual, Transgender, Queer, Intersex, Asexual
LSF	Langue des Signes Française (French Sign Language)
mm	Millimeter
MRI	Magnetic Resonance Imaging
NAD	National Association of the Deaf
NAACP	National Association for the Advancement of Colored People
NBDA	National Black Deaf Advocates
NCHAM	National Center for Hearing Assessment and Management
NMM	Nonmanual Markers
NTD	National Theatre of the Deaf
NTID	National Technical Institute for the Deaf
NUD	National Union of the Deaf
NYTF	National Yiddish Theatre Folksbiene
OSHA	Occupational Safety and Health Organization
OFSL	Old French Sign Language
PHU	Partially hearing units
RIT	Rochester Institute of Technology
RITE	Receiver in the ear
ROI	Return on investment
SNHL	Sensorineural Hearing Loss
SOC	Superior Olivary Complex
STD	Speech Detection Threshold
TC	Total Communication
TM	Tympanic Membrane
UN	United Nations

UNICEF	United Nations International Children's Emergency Fund / United Nations Children's Fund
VL2	Visual Language and Visual Learning
VV	Visual Vernacular
WFD	World Federation of the Deaf
WHO	World Health Organization
WPSD	Western Pennsylvania School for the Deaf
WRT	Word Recognition Testing
YES	Youth Empowerment Summit

Notes on Contributors

Douglas C. Baynton

is Professor Emeritus of history at the University of Iowa, where he also taught courses in Deaf Studies for the ASL program. He is the author of *Forbidden Signs: American Culture and the Campaign against Sign Language* (University of Chicago Press, 1996); co-author with Jack Gannon and Jean Bergey of *Through Deaf Eyes: A Photographic History of an American Community* (Gallaudet University Press, 2007); and author of *Defectives in the Land: Disability and Immigration in the Age of Eugenics* (University of Chicago Press, 2016), a history of the concept of "defective persons" in the making of American immigration policy.

Stephanie Cawthon

is a professor in the College of Education at the University of Texas at Austin and Executive Director of the National Disability Center for Student Success, a $5 million, 5-year research initiative funded by the U.S. Department of Education. Dr. Cawthon is an internationally-renowned deaf scholar who investigates issues of access and equity for disabled people. Her books include in-depth discussion of education reform, research design, and pathways to postsecondary success. For a full slate of Dr. Cawthon's work see her website at stephaniecawthon.com.

Karen Christie (she/her) (name sign "KC")

is a Deaf white sighted cis woman who found the Deaf community in adolescence. At the National Technical Institute for the Deaf/Rochester Institute of Technology, she taught Deaf cultural studies and English courses. Christie curates the website https://deafwomeninhistory.wordpress.com and along with Patti Durr has edited and produced *The HeART of Deaf Culture: Literary and Visual Expressions of Deafhood* (https://heartdeaf.com). Through Suridists United, she has written children's books as well as an independent reader, *WHO THAT? George W. Veditz*. She currently works as the educational coordinator for Deaf Refugee Advocacy.

Kari F. Cooke

is a political appointee serving as Cabinet Member and Inaugural Director of the D.C. Mayor's Office of Deaf, DeafBlind, & Hard of Hearing. She is dedicated to using a liberation ethic to address societal transformation. In recognition of her accomplishments, she is an alum of the New Leaders Council and a Fellow of the Stagen Leadership Academy. Previously, she was appointed to the New York State Independent Living Council and to the Obama Administration's FCC Disability Advisory Council. Her commitment to public service includes terms as a U.S. Delegate with the United Nations-IYLA and board member of International Deaf Education Advocacy and Leadership.

Joanne S. Cripps
is founder of JC Consulting, is a consultant in Deaf Arts, renowned Deaf leader, author, and an active mentor. She was Executive Director and Co-Founder of the DEAF CULTURE CENTRE promoting Deaf arts and heritage. Joanne also recruits artists in developing and producing work, as well as reaching the public, for example with the world premiere The Black Drum, signed musical Deaf-led performance. She implemented expansion of the national certification process for Sign Language instructors, coaches and consultants and was instrumental for the expanded development of the Sign Language Institute Canada (SLIC) and CEFR (Common European Framework of Reference for Languages) as the main training for sign language instructors.

Jody H. Cripps
(Ph.D.) is an American Sign Language faculty in the Department of Languages at Clemson University, Clemson, South Carolina. Cripps' latest grant allows for conducting ground-breaking ethnomusicological research on the creative process and production of a signed music showcase titled, The Black Drum. This first of its kind musical incorporates Cripps' signed music theories and was recently selected as one of ten acts to be featured in a showcase at Clin d'Oeil in France. He conducted qualitative research on the pre-production of The Black Drum and observed and interviewed one-to-one with the production team members and actors as well as the audience members.

Ana L. Cruz
a native of Brazil, Dr. Cruz is Professor of Education at STLCC-Meramec. Her research interests are in critical pedagogy, social justice, the work of Paulo Freire, and music as an art form for d/Deaf people. She previously was Assistant Professor of Music/Art Education at the Federal University of Amazonas (Brazil), and held visiting positions at the University of Barcelona (Spain), the University of British Columbia (Canada), the Federal University of São Carlos (Brazil), and Hunan Normal University (China). She chaired the 3rd International Conference Paulo Freire: The Global Legacy (2021) and received the Paulo Freire Democratic Project Award of Social Justice (2022).

Lindsay M. Dunn
taught in the Deaf Studies Department at Gallaudet University for 15 years after serving as Special Assistant to the President for Diversity and Community Relations and as Special Assistant to the President for Advocacy at Gallaudet University. He was co-director of the Center for Black Deaf Studies which was founded in 2020. Mr. Dunn is the author and co-author of numerous papers and book chapters with an emphasis on Black Deaf history and culture. Mr. Dunn is a native of South Africa and resides in Prince Georges County, MD.

Patti Durr
born partially Deaf, Patti Durr grew up without sign language and did not learn ASL until she was 20. She has received RIT's Eisenhart Award for Outstanding Teaching, RIT's Vagina Warrior Award, NTID Student Congress Staff Humanitarian Awards and Outstanding Staff Awards. Durr has made several award-winning short films and educational videos and had her artworks accepted and exhibited in juried shows. She has been arrested for peaceful civil disobedience during the Occupy Movement and Black Lives Matters protests in Rochester, NY, where she lives with her family. Her latest role is caregiver to her mom who has Alzheimer's.

Joseph C. Hill
is Professor of Deaf Studies and Linguistics and Director of the Center for Black Deaf Studies at Gallaudet University. His research interests include socio-historical and -linguistic aspects of African-American variety of American Sign Language and attitudes and ideologies about signing varieties in the American Deaf community. His contributions include *The Hidden Treasure of Black ASL: Its History and Structure* (Gallaudet University Press, 2011), which he co-authored with Carolyn McCaskill, Ceil Lucas, and Robert Bayley, and *Language Attitudes in the American Deaf Community* (Gallaudet University Press, 2012).

Wafaa Kaf
is an audiology professor at Missouri State University, Dr. Kaf, M.B.B.Ch, M.Sc., Ph.D., FAAA, has over 120 research publications and conference presentations for objective hearing threshold estimation, neural adaptation, cochlear synaptopathy, and sound hypersensitivity in ASD. Dr. Kaf has received several awards, including the Margo Skinner Award for Outstanding Audiologist in Missouri (2009), and MSU Foundation Awards for Excellence in Teaching (2009) and Research (2017), Accomplished Professor (2019), Outstanding Bear-Bridge Mentoring Award (2021). She has been featured in several national and

international magazines. Dr. Kaf currently serves as a member-at-large on the American Academy of Audiology Board of Directors.

Aaron W. Kelstone
formerly a Principal Lecturer at the National Technical Institute for the Deaf (NTID) in the Department of Performing Arts. His Doctorate is in Education from Northeastern University. He taught for 22 years at NTID in the areas of the Humanities, Deaf Studies and Performing Arts. Prior to NTID Dr. Kelstone was actively involved as an actor, director, playwright and artistic director with Cleveland Signstage Theatre and the National Theatre of the Deaf.

Paddy Ladd
is a Deaf scholar, activist, film-maker, artist, and former Reader and M.Sc. coordinator at the Centre for Deaf Studies, University of Bristol. In 2009 he received the E.M. Gallaudet Award for 'International Leadership in Promoting the Well-Being of Deaf People of the World' from Gallaudet University. Best known for the groundbreaking book *Understanding Deaf Culture: In Search of Deafhood* (Multilingual Matters, 2003), he has also published *Signs of Freedom* (Dot Sign Language, 2019) and *Songs of Deafhood* (Dot Sign Language, 2019). His most recent book, *Seeing through New Eyes, Deaf Culture and Deaf Pedagogies: The Unrecognized Curriculum* (DawnSignPress, 2022) examines the work and philosophies of Deaf educators.

Ely Lyonblum
is a facilitator of research and creative practice. His work, largely focusing on cultural equity, ranges from the history of sound recording, American Sign Language performance art, and storytelling through music. Ely trained as a documentary filmmaker at the Centre for Visual Anthropology at Goldsmiths, University of London, and completed a Ph.D. in Music at the University of Cambridge. He regularly co-produces events with academic and not-for-profit collaborators, as well as contributes to the development of training programs for artists. Ely's work has been presented and exhibited by the MIT Media Lab, CBC Radio 1, the Smithsonian Institution, the British Library, and cultural institutions across six continents.

Peter McLaren
is Professor Emeritus at the School of Education and Information Studies, University of California Los Angeles, where he taught for twenty years. Most recently he served as Distinguished Professor in Critical Studies, Co-Director of The Paulo Freire Democratic Project, and International Ambassador for Global Ethics and Social Justice at Chapman University. An award-winning

scholar and author, he has published hundreds of articles and 50 books including recently *Pedagogy of Insurrection* (Peter Lang, 2015) and *Critical Theory: Rituals, Pedagogies and Resistance* (Brill, 2022). His writings have been translated into over 25 languages.

Nancy Rourke

is a Deaf artist whose paintings call attention to social justice, artivism, human rights, and solidarity. The paintings make a clear political statement and can be categorized as resistance art, affirmation art, and liberation art. As an artist she is influenced by painters such as Jean-Michel Basquiat, Jacob Lawrence, and overall, by the Fauvism and Neo-Expressionist movements. Nancy Rourke is a prominent member of the De'VIA movement. Some of her paintings can be accessed at https://www.nancyrourke.com/oilpaintingsyears.htm

Anita Small

(M.Sc., Ed.D.) is a sociolinguist, educator, arts programmer, cultural mediator and researcher. Co-Founder/past Co-Director, DEAF CULTURE CENTRE, Canada; Founder/Owner, *small* LANGUAGE CONNECTIONS, Dr. Small works with artists, theatres, broadcast companies, museums, educational/arts institutions to co-create empowering, award-winning productions/resources and organizations. She has researched sign language performing arts in the Netherlands and collaborated to research signed music for the past decade. She has provided cultural-interaction training/consultation in Canada, U.S., Japan, Italy, Netherlands, and France for 30 years, is recipient of numerous international arts awards, including the singular national award from the Canadian Deaf community given to a hearing individual. anitasmall.com

Samuel J. Supalla

is Associate Professor Emeritus in the Department of Disability and Psychoeducational Studies at the University of Arizona. Dr. Supalla's research focuses on investigating deaf children's capacities in the language and literacy domains. Dr. Supalla also serves as President for the Society for American Sign Language (ASL). This organization promotes the concept of linguistic accessibility and addresses the need to recognize deaf people as signers and identify and tap into their abilities. Dr. Supalla is proud to be an accomplished ASL storyteller who has made pioneering contributions to ASL literature.

Rachel Sutton-Spence

has been a teacher and researcher in the Department of Brazilian Sign Language (Libras) at the Federal University of Santa Catarina, Brazil since 2013. She has been engaged in sign language research since 1989 (in the Centre for

Deaf Studies at the University of Bristol) and has published on linguistic and sociolinguistic aspects of British Sign Language, co-authoring *The Linguistics of British Sign Language* (Cambridge University Press, 1999) with Bencie Woll. Her current research interests are in signed folklore and creative signing, including signed humour, poetry and narratives. In 2016 she published *Introducing Sign Language Literature* (Bloomsbury, 2016), co-authored with Michiko Kaneko.

Marko Vuoriheimo
is a Deaf musician and recording artist from Finland who performs under the artist name Signmark to audiences across the globe. He is the first Deaf performer to sign a recording deal with a major music label. Marko's hip-hop concerts are bilingual and attract both Deaf and hearing audiences with Marko rapping in sign language and a partner using spoken English. Marko is a strong advocate for Deaf rights and through his art/music aims at increasing society's awareness of the Deaf community as a linguistic minority. His latest full album is *Silent Shout* and latest EP is *Viva La Parola.*

Aimee K. Whyte
a Deaf, white, cis lesbian, is Senior Lecturer at the Rochester Institute of Technology/National Technical Institute for the Deaf (RIT/NTID) and a Ph.D. candidate at the University of Rochester Warner School. She holds a B.S. in professional and technical communication from RIT/NTID and an M.A. in mental health counseling from Gallaudet University. Her dissertation (in progress) is a phenomenological study of music/musicking, intersectionality, and meaning-making among students at a Predominantly Deaf Institution.

Dorothy M. Wilkins (she/her)
is a white Deaf woman who graduated from the Rochester School for the Deaf. She is a Professor Emerita at Keuka College where she taught ASL, ASL-English Interpretation and Deaf Studies in addition to directing the ASL Program. Her master's degree was from the Teaching ASL Program (TAP) at McDaniel College. Wilkins has presented on various topics related to ASL teaching and learning. Previously, Wilkins and Karen Christie have collaborated on research related to ASL poetry and perspectives of Deaf womxn. Wilkins is a certified Hatha Yoga Instructor. As a certified Life Coach, she has developed a Deaf-centered Life Coach Training Program with Deborah S. Meyer.

Junhui Yang
is Senior Lecturer in Deaf Studies at the University of Central Lancashire, UK. She obtained a Ph.D. in Deaf Education from Gallaudet University, Washington, DC, in 2006. She was born in Beijing and attended schools for the

deaf. She has been involved in many international projects, including a British Council's UK-China Partnership project that developed online English learning resources for sign language users; and Erasmus+ projects: *Deaf Museum Project, SignTeach, Signs2Cross* that created an online course for learning International Sign, and *Language Skills for EU Mobility* focusing on English literacy for Deaf students.

INTRODUCTION

The Tapestry of the Deaf Soul

Ana L. Cruz

> Human existence cannot be silent, nor can it be nourished by false words, but only by true words, with which men and women transform the world. To exist, humanly, is to *name* the world, to change it. Once named, the world in its turn reappears to the namers as a problem and requires of them a new *naming*.
>
> FREIRE (1994a, p. 69; 'name' and 'naming' emphasized in the original)

•••

> However, if you B U I L D a political discourse, through A-R-T and creative expression, you will be building an insurmountable mountaintop which the waves of oppression will not be able to dismantle. We will survive.
>
> LADD (2009 interview, in Christie & Durr, n.d.)

•••

> Colour is the keyboard, the eyes are the hammers, the soul is the piano with many strings. The artist is the hand which plays, touching one key or another, to cause vibrations in the soul.
>
> KANDINSKY (2020, p. 25)

∵

Critical pedagogy, as espoused by Paulo Freire (e.g., 1994a, b; see also discussion by Kincheloe, 2008; McLaren, 2015), constitutes the theoretical framework for this book. Approaching a definition of critical pedagogy, Leistyna and Woodrum (1999) posit that critical pedagogy:

> challenges us to recognize, engage, and critique (so as to transform) any existing undemocratic social practices and institutional structures that

 | DOI:10.1163/9789004692299_001

> produce and sustain inequalities and oppressive social identities and relations. (p. 2)

There is much beauty in silence, but not in being silenced, in being dismissed, in being oppressed and dehumanized! Paulo Freire, in the quote above, refers to true words, meaning to encompass action and reflection leading to transformation; false words, on the other hand, are deprived of either reflection or action leading to either activism ("action for action's sake—negates the true praxis and makes dialogue impossible." Freire, 1994a, p. 69) or verbalism without the ability then to transform reality (Freire, 1994a). Freire calls us not to be 'silent,' to name the world to identify problems and then to work on transforming and overcoming those problems. Through their various forms of expression, particularly the Arts (including music) Deaf people can name the problems afflicting the Deaf world, while using true words and with it creating agency for transformation. Therefore, critical pedagogy can be a path to social justice that can *educate* the hearing and Deaf worlds and in addition informing and making *accountable* policy makers. This book attempts to look with much respect at the Deaf world and to learn from Deaf people's experiences. It is guided by the questions 'How can the Deaf experience be portrayed?' and 'How do Deaf people as a marginalized group deal with oppression?' I hope that this book can generate a dialogue between the contributors and the readers, and that readers may become advocates for equal opportunities for (and respectful interactions with) Deaf people to transform experiences of Deaf people in schools, public spaces, and society, and consequently transforming society into a better place for all.

Culture, identity, ethnicity, and sign language are central themes in Deaf studies (e.g., Baynton, Chapter 1; Yang, Chapter 4; Hill, Chapter 2) but one has to recognize the wide diversity within the Deaf world. This is exemplified by the number of diverse major sign languages (such as ASL—American Sign language, CSL—Chinese Sign Language, Libras—Brazilian Sign Language, etc.) and also by varieties within major sign languages and more local sign languages (such as native/indigenous) due to geography, culture, history, economics (Hill, Chapter 2; Dunn & Cooke, Chapter 3). For example, oppressive forces, such as racism and racial segregation, were responsible for the development of Black American Sign Language (BASL) in the U.S. (Hill, Chapter 2). Diversity within the Deaf world is further illustrated by the concept of intersectionality as Deaf individuals can have multiple intersecting identities (Dunn & Cooke, Chapter 3; Kelstone, Chapter 7), with levels of oppression engendered from both outside and within the Deaf world experienced, for instance, by Black Deaf Americans (Dunn & Cooke, Chapter 3).

Deaf art, I believe, has become the fulcrum for radical possibilities for the Deaf community. The wide variety of deaf artistic expressions are often political as either affirmation, celebrating Deaf culture, or as resistance, highlighting the hegemonic relationship and oppression brought about by the hearing world (Durr, 1999), and can lead to liberation (Christie & Wilkins, 2007). Emelife (2022, p. 21) emphasizes that "[e]vents, the subjectivity of history, and narratives that have been taken for granted without question find vivid interrogation through art." The political aspect of Deaf art is illustrated by Deaf humor (Sutton-Spence, Chapter 5), Deaf literature—especially poetry—(Christie & Wilkins, Chapter 6), Deaf Theatre (Kelstone, Chapter 7), the visual arts (Durr, Chapter 8; Rourke, book cover and *About the Cover Art* section of this book), and music (music as a means of raising awareness, transformation, education, and identity formation; Vuoriheimo, Chapter 10; Cruz, Chapter 11; Cripps et al., Chapter 9). As highlighted in the book chapters, the arts are a critical medium for analyzing hegemonic attitudes, practices, and policies, and for challenging a dominant hearing authority. Through the arts, therefore, one can promote awareness which can lead to agency and transformation, all themes intimately associated with critical pedagogy. Furthermore, through their art Deaf people communicate with each other and beyond, become part of a "culture of resistance" (Lampert, 2013, p. XI)—through their art they show the soul of Deaf people.

Artistic expression with music, engagement with music, or enjoyment of music by Deaf people, in a majority and hegemonic hearing world, is fraught with obstacles: lack of (music) education, lack of opportunities, and also socio-cultural barriers exclude Deaf people from music activities, or yet make engagement with music activities very difficult. In addition, opposition within the Deaf world, that equates engaging in music with the hearing world or associates it with oralism (Ladd, 1994), further hinders Deaf people in pursuing their interest in music. Many Deaf people seemed to have internalized ideologies perpetuated by a myopic hearing world. A hearing world encaged by the knowledge of its contextual times that has learned to experience music only through the auditory pathway (more on the auditory system by Kaf, Chapter 12). Deaf people's holistic way of experiencing music by not focusing on one sense (hearing) only should not be considered as a limitation, but a groundbreaking opportunity for all of us to radically think beyond our cages of knowledge. How more holistic the teaching and learning of music could become if we expand our knowledge of what music encompasses, how it is experienced, and how individuals (Deaf and hearing) attach meaning to their lived musical experiences (Cruz, 1997). The important (but not exclusive) component of experiencing music by Deaf people through the eyes can also be emphasized through musical notation that transcends 'western' rules; here the example of Anthony Braxton and the Association for the Advancement of Creative Musicians (AACM) is instructive as they attempt to "blurring the boundaries between the aural and the visual: music for the eyes and painting for the ears" (Beckwith & Roelstraete, 2015, p. 73).

It is important to note that what can be perceived as disability in certain contexts and historical times, based on who has the narrative voice (see also Cawthon, Chapter 13), can become new opportunities for discovery and new ways of experiencing the world. Therefore, deafness in itself, as many (Deaf) scholars argue, is not a disability but another way of experiencing the world. The initial working title for this book had the word '(dis)ability' in it because the idea was to contest the perception of Deaf people as disabled. However, as the book evolved, it became clear that the fight against oppression and dehumanization is not limited to the particular concept of disability but requires the uprooting of an entire ideology that has been trying to impart on Deaf people a sense of inferiority for their difference while marginalizing them. Consequently, if the goal is not just to inform and to address fundamental inequities, but to resist and to transform the world, we need to be anchored in critical pedagogy; we need to establish collaborative agency and political solidarity between the hearing and Deaf worlds to understand the difference between "marginality that is imposed by oppressive structures and that marginality one chooses as site of resistance—as location for radical openness and possibility" (hooks, 1990, p. 153) in order to overcome our cages of knowledge, we need to explore 'culture, deafness & music, and critical pedagogy as a path to social justice.'

I am a hearing researcher,[1] editor of and contributor to this book. I am on the border (Sutton-Spence & West, 2011), an 'outsider' and cannot claim a Deaf lived experience, being part of the Deaf world, or immersed in Deaf culture. I am honored, therefore, that so many Deaf contributors trusted me with this book project. On a path to social justice, I cannot speak alone, it always will need many, and I cannot speak for Deaf people, as this can lead to domination and myself to become an 'oppressor.' To quote Paulo Freire (1994a) "[c]onsequently, no one can say a true word alone—nor can she say it *for* another, in a prescriptive act which robs others of their words" (p. 69; original emphasis).

My interest in this book project was driven by curiosity, respect and love;[2] love as a commitment to humanity and a commitment to engage in social justice issues, and—most importantly—to work on creating awareness of and lay the groundwork for possibilities for Deaf individuals to engage in music if they choose to do so. With respect to the latter, I experienced numerous instances when my 'sanity' was questioned. It is much easier to dismiss or call an idea or a person 'insane' if there is no vision or understanding of possibilities. My commitment to music & deafness, to educate about possibilities, and to try to overcome barriers also can be described as armed love which Freire (1998) describes as "the fighting love of those convinced of the right and the duty to fight, to denounce, and to announce" (p. 41).

This book can serve as a true foundation for our education about people that society casts to the margins. It can be a foundation of education in which we can renew our commitment to the diversity of ways of being (ontologies) and ways of knowing (epistemologies) and to ways in which we communicate these 'knowledges;' it can be the foundation from which we re-envision a world of more equity and respect for the beauty of the diversity and differences in humankind (Cruz, 2017). This book may make (hearing) people understand that there is no need to 'acquire hearing capabilities' to be 'fixed' in order to be seen as (fully) human, as 'normal.' Instead it is important to expand the knowledge about and understanding of humankind realizing that there is beauty and also 'privileges' in being different, in engaging with the world through different sensorial experience(s)—there is, according to the contributors to this book, much beauty in being Deaf! Understanding the one who is Deaf is discovering humanity in oneself: it is a mirror.

As a final and personal note, I want to remark that as a Brazilian living away from Brazil[3] for more than half of my life now, I clearly can see, from afar, how special, how rich, how creative, how persistent, and how diverse the soul of my people—the Brazilian Soul—is. It was in Brazil that a deaf girl, by touching the keys of a piano, caused vibrations in my soul[4] and opened my eyes to the Deaf world. And, with this book, I also hope that the readers can see and understand how special, beautiful, robust, and diverse the tapestry of the Deaf Soul is!

Notes

1 My positionality is provided in the Preface.
2 Paulo Freire discusses the concept of love, the profound love for the world and people, love as an act of courage, and love as commitment in *Pedagogy of the Oppressed* (1994a, chapter 3).
3 A Brazilian deaf girl changed my life and opened my eyes to the possibilities of music & deafness in the late 1980s which made me travel abroad seeking for answers—answers I could not find in my native Brazil during that time—on how music & deafness could have a happy marriage and, consequently, seeking more equal opportunities for d/Deaf people.
4 Alluding to the Kandinsky (2020) quote at the beginning of this chapter.

References

Beckwith, N., & Roelstraete, D. (Eds.). (2015). *The freedom principle: Experiments in art and music 1965 to now*. Chicago, IL: Museum of Contemporary Art Chicago in association with The University of Chicago Press.

Christie, K., & Durr, P. (Eds.). (n.d.). The HeART of Deaf culture: Overview – interviews – Paddy Ladd. Rochester Institute of Technology. https://heartdeaf.com/overview/#tab-b89232fce48deb46f8b

Christie, K., & Wilkins, M. (2007). Themes and symbols in ASL poetry: Resistance, affirmation and liberation. *Deaf Worlds, 22*(3), 1–49.

Cruz, A. L. (1997). *An examination of how one deaf person constructs meaning in music: A phenomenological perspective* [Unpublished Doctoral Dissertation]. University of Tennessee: Knoxville, TN.

Cruz, A. L. (2017). A world in special need(s): Diversity and social justice. *Tijdschrift Voor Orthopedagogiek, 56*(7/8), 358–365.

Durr, P. (1999). Deconstructing the forced assimilation of deaf people via De'VIA resistance and affirmation art. *Visual Anthropology Review, 15*(2), 47–68.

Emelife, A. (2022). *A brief history of protest art*. London, UK: Tate Publishing.

Freire, P. (1994a). *Pedagogy of the oppressed*. New York, NY: Continuum. (Original work published 1970)

Freire, P. (1994b). *Pedagogy of hope: Reliving pedagogy of the oppressed*. New York, NY: Continuum. (Original work published in Portuguese 1992)

Freire, P. (1998). *Teachers as cultural workers: Letters to those who dare teach*. Boulder, CO: Westview Press. (Original work published in Portuguese 1993)

hooks, b. (2015). *Yearning: Race, gender, and cultural politics*. New York, NY: Routledge. (Original work published 1990)

Kandinsky, W. (2020). *Concerning the spiritual in art* (Enhanced Edition). Brattleboro, VT: Echo Point Books & Media.

Kincheloe, J. L. (2008). *Critical pedagogy primer* (2nd ed.). New York, NY: Peter Lang.

Ladd, P. (1994). Deaf culture: Finding it and nurturing it. In C. J. Erting, R. C. Johnson, D. L. Smith, & B. D. Snider (Eds.), *The deaf way: Perspectives from the international conference on deaf culture* (pp. 5–15). Washington, D.C.: Gallaudet University Press.

Ladd, P. (2009). Interview. In K. Christie & P. Durr (Eds.). The HeART of Deaf culture: Overview – interviews – Paddy Ladd. Rochester Institute of Technology. https://heartdeaf.com/overview/#tab-b89232fce48deb46f8b

Leistyna, P., & Woodrum, A. (1999). Context and culture: What is critical pedagogy? In P. Leistyna, A. Woodrum, & S. A. Sherblom (Eds.), *Breaking free: The transformative power of critical pedagogy* (pp. 1–7). Cambridge, MA: Harvard Educational Review No. 27.

Lampert, N. (2013). *A people's art history of the United States: 250 years of activist art and artists working in social justice movements*. New York, NY: The New Press.

McLaren, P. (2015). *Life in schools: An introduction to critical pedagogy in the foundations of education* (6th ed.). Boulder, CO: Paradigm Publishers. (Original work published 1989)

Sutton-Spence, R., & West, D. (2011). Negotiating the legacy of hearingness. *Qualitative Inquiry, 17*(5), 422–432.

PART 1

Encounters in Deaf Culture

∵

How is it possible for us to work in a community without feeling the spirit of the culture that has been there for many years, without trying to understand the soul of the culture?

PAULO FREIRE (1990, in We Make the Road by Walking: Conversations on Education and Social Change, by Myles Horton & Paulo Freire, p. 131)

CHAPTER 1

Beyond Culture

Deaf Studies and the Deaf Body

Douglas C. Baynton

Abstract

In recent decades the cultural attributes of the American Deaf community have been documented and described in depth. The concept of Deaf culture, however important it has been, increasingly appears inadequate by itself as an explanation of Deaf communities and the experiences of Deaf people. For example, research has shown that Deaf people process visual information differently than hearing people. This has complemented a growing emphasis on the centrality of vision to Deaf experience, with some suggesting that Deaf people also be referred to as 'seeing' or 'visual' people. The term 'deaf eyes' has been used to describe a characteristic and recognizable way Deaf people have of using the eyes. Since the nineteenth century many have argued that it is the nature of deaf people to use signed languages, a view that is supported by research on language acquisition among Deaf children. All of these suggest that Deaf people differ from hearing people in physical (more precisely, sensory) ways that are not explained by the concept of Deaf culture. Deaf Studies should move beyond the culture model to talk also about the body and the significance of living in a particular kind of sensory world.

Keywords

ASL – Deaf culture – Deaf Studies – disability – ethnicity – medical model – normality – social model

1 Introduction

The concept of Deaf culture is fundamental to the field of Deaf Studies. In recent decades, the distinctive cultural attributes of the American Deaf community have been documented and described at length, among them a shared history, a rich literary culture, rules of etiquette and naming practices that differ from those of the larger hearing society, a strong tendency to marry within

 | DOI:10.1163/9789004692299_002

the group, a unique means of transmitting cultural knowledge between generations, and of course a complex visual language. In addition, like other cultural minority groups, Deaf people have established a variety of social, political, and economic organizations, as well as a periodical press, dating from the mid-19th century. Perhaps most importantly, Deaf people share fundamental values that differ from those of the hearing Americans around them, in particular having the value of American Sign Language (ASL) and the Deaf world. The existence of a deep, rich, and longstanding culture of American Deaf people is now beyond reasonable dispute (Padden & Humphries, 1988; Van Cleve & Crouch, 1989; Lane, Hoffmeister & Bahan, 1996; Buchanan, 2002; Burch, 2002).

As important and useful as it has been, however, the concept of Deaf culture increasingly appears inadequate by itself as an explanation of the Deaf community and the experiences of Deaf people. For example, recent research has shown that Deaf people process visual information differently than hearing people, and in some ways more efficiently. This has complemented a growing emphasis in recent years on the centrality of vision to Deaf experience, with some Deaf people suggesting that they instead be referred to as "Seeing people" or "Visual people" (Lane, Hoffmeister, & Bahan, 1996, pp. 111–116; Alden, 2002, p. 8; Bahan, 1989, pp. 30–31). The statement by George Veditz that Deaf people "are facing not a theory but a condition, for they are first, last, and all the time *the* people of the eye," has become a popular aphorism among Deaf activists (Veditz, 1912, p. 30). Deaf people now often speak of "deaf eyes," a characteristic and recognizable way Deaf people have of using the eyes. Under an exclusively cultural model, how do we discuss such phenomena? What, moreover, is the implication of arguing, as Deaf people long have argued, that it is in the *nature* of deaf people to use signed languages, a view that has been given support by linguistic research into language acquisition and development among Deaf children? All of these suggest that Deaf people differ from hearing people in physical (or, more precisely, sensory) ways that are not explained by culture.

This is not to say that sensory difference by itself is sufficient to explain Deaf identity. For example, many people identify themselves as hearing impaired, hearing disabled, deaf, or hard-of-hearing who are not culturally Deaf: they do not share the values of Deaf people, they are not (or only partially) fluent in the language of the community, and they do not identify as Deaf and are not seen as Deaf. The cultural distinction between deaf and Deaf, while sometimes ambiguous, is nevertheless a crucial one.

Consider, however, another kind of outsider to Deaf identity: hearing people who grow up within a Deaf family, marry into the Deaf community, or for whatever reason immerse themselves in the Deaf world. They may be as fluent in ASL, cognizant of Deaf cultural beliefs and etiquette, familiar with Deaf folklore, and involved in the social life of the Deaf community as any Deaf person. They may be accepted, respected, well liked, included in the community "as if" they were Deaf, and they may even be referred to as "Deaf" in certain circumstances. Yet they are recognized as not *really* Deaf. As Padden and Humphries note in *Deaf in America*,

> Hearing children of Deaf parents represent an ongoing contradiction in the culture: they display the knowledge of their parents—skill in the language and social conduct—but the culture finds subtle ways to give them an unusual and separate status.

Cultural explanations by themselves are insufficient to explain Deaf identity (Padden & Humphries, 1988, p. 3).[1]

The cultural model also fails to adequately account for the stories Deaf people commonly tell of their first weeks at the residential school, of feeling that they had found their true home. Culture cannot explain that experience, for they are not yet "Deaf" when they arrive. Similarly, many young deaf people grow up in oral schools or in mainstream programs who do not encounter ASL or Deaf culture until adulthood, yet as young adults (often as students at Gallaudet University) choose to learn ASL as best they can, to principally associate with Deaf people, and to identify themselves as culturally Deaf. This includes many people who were considered to be "oral successes" by their teachers and parents. Under a simple cultural model, this ought not to happen with such frequency. Children raised in the hearing world are culturally hearing, not Deaf, yet in large numbers choose to join the Deaf world. An explanation of why they make this choice must point beyond culture.

Moreover, how do we explain the strong connections that Deaf people often feel to other Deaf people from outside their own country, to people from very different and distant cultures? Deaf cultures, like hearing cultures, vary a great deal from country to country.[2] Carol Padden is currently studying the Bedouin deaf, who are fully integrated in a hearing community where everyone signs, and who consequently have not created a distinct Deaf culture. Yet Padden sees her research as part of Deaf Studies and of interest to American Deaf people. Why should that be, if culture alone is what defines Deaf people and binds them together? Indeed, in spite of major cultural differences, Padden tells me that upon meeting the Bedouin deaf, she felt the same sense of commonality and connection that Deaf people typically feel upon meeting.[3] The cultural model needs a great deal of stretching to cover such phenomena. A more plausible and straightforward alternative is to posit that Deaf people are different from hearing people in ways other than cultural.

It has become standard practice in Deaf Studies to speak of the Deaf community as an ethnic group. While that term fits in many ways, in other ways it can be misleading. As Jeffrey Nash pointed out in 1987, "in conventional ethnic groups, members of the first generation have the ethnic mother tongue as native, and ... second and third generations shift from the ethnic to the dominant language" (Nash, 1987, p. 11).[4] In other words, ethnic groups in America typically assimilate during the second and third generations. Deaf people do not. Nor do Deaf people tend to marry outside the group, as do second- and third-generation children of ethnic groups. Furthermore, ethnicity is typically an identity shared within families, while deafness is typically not. Recent research estimates that only about 3 percent of Deaf people have two Deaf parents. Ethnicity, then, offers a misleading model for the childhood experiences of 97 percent of Deaf people (and of that 3 percent, a majority have hearing siblings, again an experience unlike that of most ethnic groups) (Mitchell & Karchmer, 2004).

When I wrote my book, *Forbidden Signs: American Culture and the Campaign against Sign Language*, I worked within the cultural model. One of the criticisms I encountered from historians who read my early drafts, however, was that I argued that deafness was a cultural construction while simultaneously contending that oralism was *necessarily* harmful to deaf people. They pointed out to me that if deafness was truly just a cultural construction, there were no grounds for taking the position that deaf people everywhere in all times *needed* signed language. In making that claim I was necessarily making a claim about the *nature* of deafness. In response to that criticism, I wrote the following in my introduction to the book:

> Deafness is ... very much a cultural construction that changes over time. But it is also a physical reality. The hearing people who have traditionally made most of the decisions concerning the education of deaf children can spend entire careers contented within these constructions of deafness, unconstrained by physical reality, but deaf people cannot. When the cultural climate of the nineteenth century changed to make sign language objectionable, hearing people could simply say, "Away with sign language," and imagine that this could be accomplished. Deaf people could not, for they are both members of a species that by nature seeks optimal communication, and inhabitants of a sensory universe in which that end cannot be achieved by oral means alone. (Baynton, 1996, p. 10)

In the book's conclusion I added that being deaf

> is more than a cultural construction. It means most fundamentally that one occupies a different sensory world from those who hear, and this has

> certain consequences that cannot be *constructed* away. This physical reality (upon which culture works, certainly, and with which culture intertwines and interacts) transcends culture. (Baynton, 1996, p. 160)

I did not pursue the matter any further, however. Constrained by the cultural model, I simply did not know what to do with these ideas. Increasingly, I have become convinced that if the field of Deaf Studies is to progress, it must move beyond the culture model to talk about the body, about the significance of living in a different sensory world.

There is an understandable resistance among Deaf people and Deaf Studies scholars to focusing on the physical aspect of deafness. In the past, such a focus has meant defining deafness in terms of defect and deficiency. It has meant talking about what Deaf people have in common with other disabled people, which has seemed a dangerous path to start down, given that most people think of disability in terms of inability, absence, and loss. Many Deaf people have tried to distance themselves from this image by distancing themselves from any notion of disability and insisting that their identity is based on cultural rather than physical difference from the hearing majority. They explain that being Deaf is not a defect, that being Deaf offers no less rich and rewarding a life than being hearing, and that being Deaf is neither a pathology nor a medical matter. Most of us in Deaf Studies have correspondingly defined our work as a branch of ethnic studies, separate and distinct from Disability Studies.

However, what most people have in mind when they think of disability is a medical model (a.k.a. the functional limitations or pathological model). According to this model, disability is simply a physical, mental, or sensory impairment. It resides solely or largely in the individual with the impairment. Prevention, cure, and rehabilitation are of primary importance. When Deaf people say that "disabled" does not describe them, it is generally this model that they reject.[5] It is precisely this model, however, that Disability Studies scholars (and disability rights activists) also reject. In recent decades they have advanced a social model that locates disability not in individual bodies but rather in social structures and practices that do not take account of normal human variation. Just as gender and race are not merely matters of bodily difference, so is disability not simply inherent in bodies but rather a way of interpreting human differences. People with particular physical differences from the majority are *disabled* by the prejudicial beliefs and actions of the majority. When buildings, technology, and media are designed for certain types of people but not others, when communication is carried out in ways accessible to certain types of people but not others, or when school curricula are designed for certain types of learning but not others, disability results. Disability, in short, is a product of oppression (e.g.,

Oliver, 1990; Swain, French, Barnes & Thomas, 1993; Hahn, 1996; Shakespeare & Watson, 1997; Barton & Oliver, 1997; Priestley, 1998; Barnes, Oliver & Barton, 2002; for the social model of disability; Longmore, 2003; Garland Thomson, 1997; Mitchell & Snyder, 1997; Davis, 1995; Longmore & Umansky, 2000; for recent[6] examples of disability studies in the humanities; see also overviews by Baynton, 2000; Kudlick, 2003).

In this, disabled people have followed a trajectory similar to other oppressed groups. It was once also generally accepted that the bodies of women and members of "inferior races" limited their capacity to participate in social and economic life. As Harlan Hahn has noted, "unlike other disadvantaged groups, citizens with disabilities have not yet fully succeeded in refuting the presumption that their subordinate status can be ascribed to an innate biological inferiority." They have made considerable progress in recent years, however. People with physical differences from the majority have increasingly moved away from the notion that they *have* a disability, or are persons *with* a disability, and instead refer to themselves as *disabled people* to indicate its centrality to their identity, and speak of "disablement" to refer to the social process of becoming disabled. Many people find it difficult to understand that anyone would willingly embrace the identity of "disabled person," since disability in our culture seems self-evidently a personally discrediting label. Just as most hearing people simplistically translate "deaf" into "cannot hear," so do most people equate *dis*abled with *un*able. By claiming disability as an identity, however, disabled people name the oppression under which they live, declare solidarity with others similarly oppressed, and set themselves in opposition to it (Hahn, 1996, p. 43).[7]

Our bodies matter because they shape how we experience, understand, and interact with the world, and because they affect how others view us. On both counts, the body is intensely relevant to Deaf people. The appropriate vocabulary is that of difference, however, not loss. Just as deafness brings into being new ways of using the other senses, so does any physical difference result in a new configuration of abilities. Merely equating disability with impairment reduces a way of life, a complex relation to the environment, and a web of social relationships and cultural meanings to a simple and concrete absence. It fails utterly to account for the human experience of disability. Like Deaf people, disabled people experience disability in terms of social relations rather than as personal deficiency, and it becomes just one aspect of the world in which they live, in all its complexity.

This does not mean that disabled people experience no limitations, but rather that the experience of limitation is a universal one, not characteristic merely of a subset of humanity. Relative to most of the animal kingdom, after all, humans live in a flat and unvariegated scent world. Their vision is severely impaired by the standards of, say, a hawk, and their night vision is abysmal compared to an owl or a cat. They are deaf to frequencies heard well by dogs, bats, whales, and elephants. They are poor swimmers, slow runners, and incapable of flight absent assistive technology. The list of abilities that other creatures enjoy and that humans lack is long indeed, yet somehow the human species manages to limp along without nursing feelings of grief or loss. The reason we do not consider ourselves disabled is that the term is relative to notions of normality around which we structure our societies. Radio programs do not employ frequencies beyond normal human hearing, jobs do not demand the eyesight of an eagle, and schools do not require students to stand all day like horses without sitting. We establish expectations based on what is normal for the majority and design our built environment to serve that norm—and to exclude, often, any who fall outside it. Deaf people are disabled in the sense that they fall outside most cultures' notions of normality and are on that basis denied equal access to social and economic life.

2 Culture

The common argument that Deaf people are a cultural and linguistic group and *therefore* are not disabled wrongly characterizes culture and disability as mutually exclusive. Saying that Deaf people share a culture says nothing about the usefulness or validity of speaking of Deaf people as disabled. The social model of disability is entirely compatible with an understanding of Deaf people as a cultural minority group and, as a complement to the cultural model, accounts for much about Deaf experience that the cultural model cannot. Not only is it entirely possible for Deaf people to be both a distinct cultural group *and* disabled, it is necessary if Deaf and Disability Studies scholars are to provide a coherent account of the Deaf community.

What do we mean when we say that people "have" a culture? If there are any words with fixed, definite, and unchanging meanings, this one is certainly not among them. Until fairly recently, "culture" referred to a quality acquired through education, an elevated and learned ability to discern the finer from the baser aspects of the world. It was acquired through *cultivation*. Only in the 20th century did its current anthropological meaning become prevalent, and that meaning is still by no means standardized. Speaking of *a culture* is a shorthand way of saying that a defined group of people share certain distinctive beliefs, practices, and ways of interpreting the world that persist across generations. It refers, in essence, to what a group of people typically think (as expressed in language) and what they typically do.

Some have resisted the term Deaf culture, arguing that Deaf Americans partake in the larger American culture and therefore constitute a *sub*culture within it. The flaw in this reasoning is that it assumes the nation-state to be the natural level on which culture operates, and cultures on a smaller scale to be necessarily subordinate. The concept of culture, however, has no necessary affiliation with the nation-state. It would make equal sense to speak of "Western culture," to assume "the West" to be the level on which culture resides and national cultures as subcultures. Alternatively, one might situate "culture" on the level of region or ethnicity, and argue that modern nations are too diverse to claim a unitary and cohesive culture. The distinction between culture and subculture is an arbitrary one. We make the distinction as a matter of practical utility not of logical or natural necessity. "Culture" is variously used to describe national linguistic groups (even when these share languages with other, distinct national cultures), stateless linguistic groups, supranational and subnational groups with or without shared languages (including *movement cultures* when these involve significant, shared structures of thought). It has been used in these diverse ways because in each case *it has proved useful* in understanding the attributes of a given group. Describing the distinctive beliefs and practices of the American Deaf community in terms of culture has been tremendously productive in a variety of ways, both for Deaf people themselves and for the academic study of their community. It is a powerful idea and therefore has, in the pragmatic sense, truth value. While there is still resistance to the idea of Deaf culture in some quarters, it now seems to be an idea that is here to stay.[8]

It may also turn out to be useful to speak of a disability culture. A number of disability activists and scholars think so and have been busy developing an argument for it in recent years. If it helps us to understand the experience of disability and the lives of disabled people—if it turns out, that is, to have truth value—then the idea will have staying power. If it does not, if it distorts or obscures more than it clarifies, then it will not. The evidence for such usefulness is not very strong yet, in my opinion, but it is still a relatively new idea and its proponents have not yet elaborated it to any great extent, so it is too early to judge. The idea of Deaf culture, after all, took a couple of decades to work out and to begin to make sense to both scholars and Deaf people. And unlike Deaf culture, which is understood to date in the United States from the 19th century, disability culture is usually understood as something that has emerged only in recent decades, in part as a movement culture (Longmore, 2003; Barnartt, 1996; Charlton, 1998; Crutchfield & Epstein, 2000; Fries, 1997).

Whether or not the concept of disability culture turns out to have merit, the point here is that there is no inherent contradiction in identifying a group as both disabled and as a cultural group. The terms do not describe mutually exclusive states of being. "Disability" describes a particular kind of relationship between a majority and a minority, between socially constructed notions of normality and deviance. "Culture" describes a set of values and beliefs within a group. Saying that Deaf people share a culture says nothing about the usefulness or validity of speaking of Deaf people as disabled. It is not necessary to say that Deaf people are *either* a cultural group *or* disabled. It is entirely possible to be both.

3 Pragmatic Considerations

Considered as a purely practical matter, what good and what harm come from Deaf people aligning themselves with disabled people and the concept of disability? This is by no means a simple question. In the past, the emphasis of the disability rights movement on educational inclusion or mainstreaming has been a point of serious contention. Disability rights activists have increasingly come to understand and respect the Deaf position on this question, in addition to increasingly questioning the often ideologically rigid, one-size-fits-all approach of the early years of the movement. *Disability Watch*, the periodic assessment of the status of disabled people in the United States published by Disability Rights Advocates, pointed out that while inclusion has been good for most disabled people, it "is proving disastrous for deaf children." It went on to describe how "the Deaf community has vigorously opposed these ill-considered practices, but its cogent dissent has gone largely unheeded" by school authorities.[9] Of course, as with any coalition made up of groups with diverse interests and experiences, disagreements are unavoidable. Still, cooperation between Deaf and disability rights groups has accomplished much good, most notably the Americans with Disabilities Act. The constant refrain heard from the Deaf community that "we are not disabled," however, threatens to undermine the basis for that cooperation. Disabled and nondisabled people alike increasingly respond that if Deaf people really do not want to be considered disabled, then they ought not to claim the protections of that designation.

In any case, alignment with disabled people clearly holds more promise than one with ethnic groups. If there are differences among disabled groups, they pale in comparison with the distance between Deaf and other ethnic communities. Can we imagine the Chinese-American community agitating in favor of Deaf teachers? What reason would hearing Spanish speakers have for supporting residential schools for Deaf children? (After all, in California a majority of Hispanic-American voters recently joined other citizens in voting to end bilingual education). In battling the resurgence of eugenics, are disabled people or

Cuban-Americans going to be more steadfast allies? Who have been powerful allies of Deaf people in the past, ethnic Americans or disabled Americans?

If the disability model tends to have a bias toward assimilation, contrary to the interests of the Deaf community, the ethnic model in the United States does as well, but without accommodations for physical differences from the majority. The rights and services that Deaf people demand are of the kind demanded by disabled people not ethnic groups. Interpreters, for example, are provided to linguistic minorities in the United States only in a limited number of unusual situations, such as court appearances and medical emergencies. Those who wish to attend college or take up a profession are expected to master and use the national language. College instructors and graduate students whose first language is not English must pass an exam demonstrating their ability to make themselves clearly understood in spoken English before they are permitted to teach. Deaf people, on the other hand, rightly demand subsidized interpreting services that allow them to participate in cultural, social, and economic life on an equal basis with hearing people. The demand for captioning and relay services is even less compatible with the ethnic group model. To the extent that these services are provided, it is in the name of disability rights, not ethnic group rights, since no other minority requests, let alone asserts a right to, such services. The principle at work in the provision of these services is that it is wrong to construct, for example, a phone system that serves some people and excludes other, or to offer a college education that is accessible to some but not others, merely on the basis of physical, sensory, or mental differences. As far as I am aware, every useful law in the United States protecting Deaf rights has been based on this principle, rooted in the demand for disability rights rather than in protections for ethnic minorities. Furthermore, aside from the pragmatic considerations of political efficacy, the ethnic model fails conceptually even to explain the kinds of rights that Deaf people assert.

In the struggle to provide a decent education for deaf children, the cultural model also falls short, and in fact is counterproductive. Hearing parents of deaf children are rarely persuaded of the value of ASL by being told about Deaf culture, and often resist the notion that their children ought to be part of a culture other than their own. In fact, they frequently express fears of "losing their children to the Deaf culture." More persuasive arguments stress the importance of ensuring linguistic input via the eyes while children are still very young, to achieve their fullest social and intellectual development. That is, it focuses on the ways in which their children's sensory needs differ from those of hearing children.

The Deaf culture model by itself has always posed a troublesome incongruity when used to discuss deaf children. When we speak of deaf adults who are not culturally Deaf, no one objects to referring to them as disabled. However, when we speak of mainstreamed deaf children in hearing families, we often speak of them as Deaf even when they have had no contact with Deaf culture, in part because we think that they *ought* to be Deaf, and in part because they are likely to become Deaf at some point in the future. Some of them, however, will never be culturally Deaf, and it is clearly contradictory to speak of deaf children as Deaf, only to reclassify some of them as disabled when grown, when nothing substantive has changed other than their age. We are stuck with making this incoherent argument because, under the cultural minority model, there is no other logical way to assert their linguistic rights as children. To claim, however, that children who have no connection to or even knowledge of the Deaf community are culturally Deaf is unpersuasive to say the least. It is utterly unpersuasive to their hearing parents, who often view it as presumptuous as well as absurd, and it is intellectually implausible to scholars to suggest that Deaf people, unlike any others in the world, might somehow be born with a culture inherent within them.

An alternative that resolves the incongruity, as well as offering a more plausible line of argument in favor of early ASL for all deaf children, is to take seriously the truism that (in Padden and Humphries words), "Deaf people are both Deaf and deaf" (Padden & Humphries, 1988, p. 3). That is, Deaf people are both a cultural minority *and* disabled. This allows us to say that a deaf child is physically different from hearing children, therefore has fundamentally different needs from hearing children, and therefore if denied access to effective bilingual education *is disabled by that denial*. It allows us to say, further, that both Deaf and hard-of-hearing persons are disabled by social practices designed to accommodate only hearing people, and to demand arrangements that accommodate them as well as hearing people.

Indeed, those writing within the Deaf culture model often do say that deaf children who are denied access to ASL and to the Deaf community by parents and schools are disabled by that denial (e.g., Lane, 1992; Branson & Miller, 2002). This is precisely in line with the social model of disability. The Disability Studies model would go further, however, to argue that even Deaf children who attend bicultural/bilingual educational programs and are fully acculturated in the Deaf community *continue* to be disabled by discriminatory practices that extend beyond secondary school. It is disabling to be denied equal access to television, movies, theater, civic and public events. It is disabling to be denied reasonable accommodations, in higher education or on the job, such as competent interpreting services. According to the social model of disability, both deaf and Deaf people are disabled not because they do not hear, but because society is structured and everyday business is conducted in ways that exclude them: mass media and public services are often inaccessible; education is generally inferior; information in public places comes over aural but not visual channels; prejudice, demeaning stereotypes, and discrimination are widespread; and in general the hearing majority assumes a hearing norm and does not accommodate those who deviate from it.

Thus when disability activists claim that Deaf people are in the same boat with them, they do *not* mean to suggest that Deaf people are afflicted with a defect which ought to be fixed or eliminated, or that they are not whole, or that something is wrong with them, as Deaf people often seem to assume. Rather, they mean that Deaf people have a sensory difference from the majority that requires a different way of life; that the majority hearing population often tries to obstruct or thwart that way of life, or at the least does not make reasonable accommodations for it; and that the hearing majority thereby disables Deaf people. It is understood that if Deaf people were to live entirely in a Deaf world they would not be disabled, just as it is understood that the same is true of many other disabled people. This way of understanding disability does not seem to contradict in any fundamental way how Deaf people already view themselves.

The cultural model also has had little practical relevance to the debate over cochlear implants. Even if all hearing people were to become convinced that Deaf people are "not disabled" and constituted a cultural minority, would that affect the implanting of deaf children? After all, minority cultures in the United States come and go without much fanfare. There used to be strong Italian-American communities in many cities, for example, that have mostly disappeared. There were once thriving Scandinavian cultures across the rural upper Midwest and Polish-American communities in the cities. Asian-Americans and Jewish-Americans are increasingly assimilating today. A marked and distinct ethnic identity usually persists only to the extent that majority prejudice prevails over the tendency toward assimilation, as has been the case for most African-Americans. The charge of "ethnocide" sometimes raised in the case against cochlear implants is not a persuasive one in the United States, for the disappearance of minority cultures—whatever opinion one may hold about this—is not only commonplace but has often been held up as an ideal. Not only are Americans generally unwilling to offer bilingual education for the purpose of preserving ethnic cultures, opposition to the persistence of minority cultures is one of the main arguments deployed against bilingual education, which is on the defensive and in decline across the country. If it is true that implants threaten Deaf culture (which is a subject of debate within the Deaf community), hearing Americans seem unlikely to support the idea of preserving deafness in order to preserve Deaf culture when they have shown no widespread concern for preserving other minority cultures.

Medicalization of difference is as much an issue for disabled people generally as it is for Deaf people. Disabled people are equally concerned about the attitudes that lead to excessive, risky, and often ineffective surgeries performed on children in valiant attempts to restore "normal function"—for example, to enable someone to walk about with difficulty, rather than modifying public spaces in ways to enable them to roll about with ease. The problem Deaf people face is not that they are not recognized as an ethnic group, but rather, as Alice Dreger has written, that in the modern west "the most prevalent myth is that an unusual anatomy must be considered a medical pathology." It is equally a problem for deaf and all disabled people that "most children with unusual anatomies are born to parents who do not share the unusual trait, and so the parents' reaction often involves fear, confusion, shame, guilt, and distress ... The parents often can't imagine living 'that' way" (Dreger, 2004, pp. 55, 77).

Like Deaf people, many disabled people see disability as central to their identity and have no desire whatsoever to join the nondisabled "other" (Shapiro, 1994, p. 14). This is particularly true of those born disabled or disabled from an early age. Disabled people are in fact very similar to Deaf people in this way, and use similar language when they speak of disability as their norm, as something in which they have pride, as essential to their identity. The question is not so much whether one is Deaf, blind, or a wheelchair user, but rather whether that is an integral part of one's identity, which is in large part a question of time and life stage. People who grew up with an atypical body or set of senses tend to see themselves as "normal" and experience little or no desire to change. Those who experience a dramatic change in bodily or sensory configuration go through a period, some longer than others, of wishing they could return to their earlier norm, but in most cases this sense of inhabiting an abnormal body passes with time. As Susan Triano told a reporter at the 2004 International Disability Pride Parade in Chicago,

> We're trying to unite all people with all different kinds of disabilities to send a message that disability is a natural and beautiful part of human diversity. We don't need to be cured. We don't need to be fixed. We are whole human beings just the way we are. (Ritter, 2004)

Although I have long known that disabled people routinely express satisfaction with their identity and way of life, I was nevertheless surprised to learn recently that only once in history have conjoined twins expressed a desire to be separated. Of course, parents and surgeons routinely decide to surgically separate them in infancy, but when conjoined twins reach an age at which they can speak for themselves, they nearly always express satisfaction with their lives.

Why was I surprised? Because I had imagined what it would be like to live such a life and concluded that it would be intolerable. That is the problem. Hearing people imagine what it must be like to be deaf, and envision a gray and lonely existence. Walking people imagine life as a wheelchair user, and see only limitation and constraint. Deaf people know that deafness is not deprivation, but imagine other disabilities much as hearing people do. Blindness looms especially large in the Deaf imagination as the negation of their identity as visual people, and has been a felt presence in the Deaf community in the form of Usher Syndrome. John Lee Clark, however, writes that while Deaf people fear blindness and blind people fear deafness, they need not, for

> we all share the same capacity for human experience. And that capacity can be filled in infinite ways, from a bank of small spigots to a fewer but larger ones. However the reliance on senses are distributed, we all hold equal access to living full lives. (Clark, 2004)

Resistance to technological normalization flies in the face of powerful social forces and is an uphill battle no matter what arguments are deployed. Nevertheless, the disability critique of the modern tendency to homogenize human experience, to regulate human appearance and behavior, and to lessen human variation is a broad and powerful argument. Claiming that implanting deaf children constitutes ethnocide is not, for the children who are implanted are neither culturally Deaf nor members of an ethnic group. As individuals, they possess no elements of a minority culture. What they do possess is a different sensory relationship to the world around them. It is the value of *that* difference that is at issue. If an effective counterargument is to be constructed, it is more likely to be based upon the good that comes from preserving sensory and physical diversity rather than upon ethnic identity.

4 Ethnicity

The desire among Deaf people to be defined only by cultural and not physical difference has striking parallels with the mid-20th-century campaign by European immigrants to be redefined as ethnic groups. In the 19th and early-20th centuries, what we now term "ethnic groups" were typically referred to as "races." It was common to speak of a multi-racial Europe populated by the Irish race, the Italian race, the Jewish race, the Slavic race, and so on. The concept of race denoted *both* body and culture, inherited *and* environmentally influenced characteristics, nature *and* nurture, which were all seen as inextricably linked. A study of immigration in 1926, for example, identified fifty-six races of people employed in American industry. Among those described as distinct races were Poles, Slovaks, South Italians, North Italians, Magyars, Lithuanians, Croatians, French-Canadians, Hebrews, Spanish, and "native-born White Americans." The study described how the "bodily form" and "shape of the skull," as well as the temperament and personality, varied from race to race (Sipress, 1997, p. 179).

Proponents of immigration restriction, such as Edward Ross, sociology professor at the University of Wisconsin, maintained that recent immigrants to the United States tended to be physically inferior: "South Europeans run to low stature," he wrote.

> A gang of Italian[s] ... filing along the street present, by their dwarfishness, a curious contrast to other people. The Portuguese, the Greeks, and the Syrians are, from our point of view, undersized. The Hebrew immigrants are very poor in physique ... the polar opposite of our pioneer breed ... The physiognomy of certain groups unmistakably proclaims inferiority of type. (Ross, 1914, pp. 258–290)

This is why restricting the immigration of these "inferior types" was so important to eugenicists at the time, because their "defects" were seen as inherent racial traits. Eugenicists stigmatized both disabled people and "inferior races" as prisoners of defective bodies, and sought to exclude immigrants who were "degenerate," whether due to racial characteristics or individual disabilities. In effect, both racial and disabled minorities came under the purview of a medical model. From this medical model came increasing attacks on the liberties of disabled people and racial minorities, including widespread institutionalization, sterilization, and exclusion from American economic and social life.

A similar kind of medicalization of difference was prominent in the justification of slavery and, after slavery's demise, of other forms of racial oppression. For example, an article on the "diseases and physical peculiarities of the negro race" in the *New Orleans Medical and Surgical Journal* explained,

> It is this defective hematosis, or atmospherization of the blood, conjoined with a deficiency of cerebral matter in the cranium, and an excess of nervous matter distributed to the organs of sensation and assimilation, that is the true cause of that debasement of mind, which has rendered the people of Africa unable to take care of themselves. (Cartwright, 1851, p. 693)

African-Americans were assumed to become ill or disabled more easily than whites, especially under the stressful conditions of freedom. Diseases of blacks were generally attributed to "inferior organisms and constitutional weaknesses," which were claimed to be among "the most pronounced race characteristics of the American negro." Women's physical differences, as well, have been endlessly medicalized (to a lesser degree still are today). One of the important strategies of the opponents of women's suffrage was to attribute various disabilities to women, among them irrationality, uncontrolled emotionality with a tendency to hysteria, and constitutional weakness. The supposed tendency among "inferior races" to feeblemindedness, mental illness, deafness, blindness, and other disabilities have been repeatedly invoked in arguments for racial inequality and discriminatory immigration laws. Time and again, when categories of citizenship are in question, a medicalized notion of disability has been called upon to discredit and to stigmatize (Fredrickson, 1971, pp. 250–255).[10]

European-American minorities began arguing that they should be considered ethnic groups rather than races in the 1930s to escape the imputation of physical and biological inferiority. Ethnicity suggested that all European-Americans were members of the "white race," and therefore culturally but not biologically different. The ethnicity model excluded African, Asian, and Native-American minorities, who continued to be stigmatized by a medical model that associated them with disabled people: prisoners of defective bodies, degenerate by nature, and likely to pass on their defective characteristics to future generations. European-American minorities, on the other hand, were so successful at shedding the notion of race and becoming "white ethnics" that most people soon forgot that they had ever been considered members of different races at all (e.g., Jacobson, 1998; Brodkin, 1999; Ignatiev, 1996; Sipress, 1997—on the social construction of ethnicity and of "whiteness").

The claim today that disabled people differ from the nondisabled by dint of physical difference, while Deaf people differ from the hearing only by culture, mirrors the division of ethnicity from race. Just as the decision of European-Americans early in the 20th century to identify themselves as ethnic groups rather than racial groups was in part a political decision, and just as the identity of "white person" is in part a political choice, "Deaf" and "disabled" are also, at least in part, political choices. These are constructions of history—always contested, never settled, and always open to question. There is nothing timeless or "natural" about them.

This is not to argue that the idea of ethnicity is disreputable, but rather that it is a construct that arose under particular historical conditions and was used for particular purposes. Whatever the particular origins of the concept and its problematic relationship with the notion of race, ethnicity is a useful model because it provides a framework for exploring the ways in which Deaf Americans have maintained distinct community institutions and have passed down, over many generations, a common history, language, and culture. Nor is this to say that Deaf people should not be conceptualized as an ethnic group, or that Deaf Studies scholars cannot learn much from Ethnic Studies (not to mention Women's Studies, Race Studies, and Queer Studies). It is undeniable that the cultural/ethnic group model has been extraordinarily useful and beneficial in many ways to both Deaf Studies and the Deaf community. It is nevertheless useful to reconsider in light of its history what purposes the model is serving today, and whether an exclusive reliance on the cultural model serves ends that scholars and Deaf people wish to pursue.

5 Historically Created Identities

The statement that "Deaf people are not disabled" suggests that current definitions of Deaf and disabled are natural, timeless, and universal categories. These are not fixed definitions, however, but rather historically created and impermanent identities. Padden and Humphries put the matter more accurately when they wrote in *Deaf in America* that, "'disabled' is a label that historically has not belonged to Deaf people," but still they left open the question of which historical period they meant (Padden & Humphries, 1988, p. 44). My preliminary research suggests the possibility that the "Deaf people are not disabled" claim *may* be of fairly recent origin.

In the 19th century it seems to have been common to talk of Deaf people as disabled. Laurent Clerc, one of the founders of the American School for the Deaf, in an 1818 address, spoke of "the infirmities of the bodily organization, such as deafness, blindness, lameness, palsy, crookedness, ugliness." In 1835, John Burnet wrote of his deafness as one of the "long catalogue of infirmities which flesh is heir to." He went on to explain that,

> [Our] misfortune is not that [we] are deaf and dumb, but that *others* hear and speak. Were the established mode of communication … by a language addressed not to the ear, but to the eye, the present inferiority of the deaf would entirely vanish; but at the same time the mental and social conditions of the blind would be far more deplorable, and their education far more impracticable, than that of the deaf is now.[11]

This seems a perfect expression of the social model of disability, applied to deafness and blindness.

In 1855, John Jacob Flournoy argued that Deaf people should abandon the hearing world that oppressed them and establish their own state, and at the same time saw no contradiction in describing Deaf people as disabled. Responding to William Turner's statement that a Deaf man was as unsuited to serve in a legislature as a blind man was to lead an army, Flournoy wrote (in his wonderful phrasing): "The old cry about the incapacity of men's minds from physical disabilities, I think it were time, now in this intelligent age, to *explode*!" He made his case by referring to great disabled military heroes and blind philosophers: "Have you ever heard how Muley Moloch had himself borne in a litter, when lamed by wounds, to the head of his legions …? So much for a *lame* man. Then, as for a *blind* one" Flournoy described Deaf people as a distinct and oppressed community *and* as sharing a common oppression with other disabled people.[12]

Nor does it seem to have been very common for Deaf people to reject the association with disability (at least in print) through most of the 20th century. In *Illusions of Equality*, Bob Buchanan describes two significant instances, during the 1908 battle over the hiring of deaf people for the Civil Service, when Deaf community leaders objected to an association with disability: George Dougherty wrote that being classed in Civil Service regulations with "the insane, the crippled, and criminals" might prejudice employers against them, and George Veditz warned, "once let the government brand deafness as a disability that renders us ineligible for its service, and it will not be long before the prejudice will spread among the employers at large." Both of these instances, however, had to do specifically with concerns over employment discrimination rather than a general aversion to being thought of as disabled. The Veditz quotation is ambiguous in that he does not reject the idea that deafness is a disability, but specifically that deafness is *a disability that renders us ineligible* for employment. The term "disability" at the time was often used in this more specific sense to refer to a trait that disqualified a person for certain rights and privileges. Buchanan also documents occasions on which Deaf leaders decided against collaboration with disability groups, but while this *may* suggest a rejection of the concept of disability, it does not do so necessarily. The ethnic group model, after all, is not weakened by the fact that Deaf people do not typically collaborate with other ethnic groups (Buchanan, 2002, p. 42).

Susan Burch, in *Signs of Resistance*, suggests that Deaf people began to reject the association with disability in the early 20th century. It is a plausible suggestion, but Burch provides only one significant source for the claim. An editorial in the *Empire State News*, supporting a proposal for a labor bureau for deaf people and responding to an argument that it ought to serve all disabled people, asserted that "the average deaf worker belongs in the classification of foreign-language groups rather than that of the physically handicapped." This would appear at first glance to be an endorsement of the cultural model and rejection of the disability model. However, the editorial then went on to explain that a worker's

> deafness is sure to raise difficulties of communication which may hinder his effectiveness until he becomes accustomed to the routine of work in that particular place. Hence, some follow-up work would be necessary in a placement service for the deaf. This is an additional detail which the regular service cannot handle.

That is, the editorial is focused entirely on the issue of *what deaf people need from a labor bureau,* not their identity. Deaf people have employment needs that are distinct from those of "other handicapped groups," the editorial continued, because

> one has to have effective communication between the placement officer and the deaf applicant. No such difficulty exists in the case of the blind, the crippled, and other groups, for all of these possess in common with the director and his assistants the great blessing of combined hearing and speech, which facilitate the interview.

The point is the specific employment needs of deaf people, nothing broader. Moreover, the editorial twice refers to "*other* groups of handicapped people," which suggests no aversion to being thought of as one of those groups (Burch, 2002, p. 121).[13]

In my (admittedly not exhaustive) research so far, I have found no unambiguous and explicit examples of Deaf people rejecting association with disability before the 1970s in the United States.[14] While it would not be surprising to find such examples, it does seem suggestive that I have come across no published examples so far, while I have found numerous examples of Deaf people who referred to themselves as disabled or handicapped. For example, in 1930, Albert Ballin, in *The Deaf Mute Howls,* referred to deafness as a "handicap," as did Thomas Ulmer, a Deaf contributor to the *American Annals of the Deaf,* in 1945. In 1941, Tom Anderson, then president of the National Association of the Deaf (NAD), urged President Roosevelt to "give handicapped persons a break in working for the defense program," by which he clearly meant to include Deaf people. He was quoted in a *New York Times* opinion column by a disabled man writing in favor of greater employment opportunities for disabled people, and in 1942 the *Empire State News* approvingly reprinted that piece. The president of the California Association of the Deaf, Toivo Lindholm, in 1953 referred to Deaf people as handicapped. In 1970, NAD president Frederick Schreiber wrote of deaf people having a "disability." In 1974, in his book *A Deaf Adult Speaks Out,* Leo Jacobs described Deaf people as a minority group and simultaneously as people who have a "handicap."[15]

Clearly more careful research than what I have done here is needed. The history of Deaf peoples' relationship with the concept of disability is no doubt far more complex than I am able to describe in this essay. However, if these preliminary findings are borne out, it is possible that the argument that Deaf people are not disabled came to prominence alongside the Deaf rights movement and the rise of the culture model in the 1970s and 1980s. If so, the claim that Deaf people have long rejected identification as disabled might be an example of an "invented tradition," a common phenomenon in all cultures but particularly those reacting to rapid change. Historians have become increasingly interested in recent years in the ways that societies seek to reinforce the legitimacy of their values by projecting their origins back in time and defending them as long-standing cultural traditions (e.g., Hobsbawm & Ranger, 1983).

The rejection of disability since the 1970s seems mainly intended as a refutation of the demeaning focus on deafness as defect. In their desire to avoid the focus on the ear to the exclusion of all other aspects of Deaf experience, and to emphasize the legitimacy of their culture, Deaf people increasingly denied that physical difference had any significance in the formation of Deaf identity. Just as early ASL studies downplayed the importance of fingerspelling, iconicity, and any other element that seemed to make signed languages less like "true languages" (that is, conforming to definitions and standards derived from the study of spoken language), so also did early Deaf Studies deny the importance of sensory difference in order to emphasize the cultural aspect of Deaf identity. Just as it was thought that a "true language" would not rely on iconicity or the spelling of borrowed words, a "true culture" could have nothing to do with physical difference. However, just as ASL scholars now have enough confidence to explore the significant place of iconicity and fingerspelling in the language, so too has Deaf Studies begun pointing toward the significance of physical difference in defining the Deaf community.

6 Conclusions

Nothing I have written here should be construed as an argument against the cultural model. It has been and continues to be a powerful tool in Deaf Studies, as well as in the struggle for Deaf rights and community pride. Ethnicity is a crucial concept because it provides a framework for exploring the ways in which Deaf Americans have maintained distinct community institutions and have passed down, over many generations, a common history, language, and culture. As Ella Mae Lentz recently pointed out to me, it may also more closely reflect the way in which Deaf people experience their relationships with hearing people. When encountering a nonsigner, she maintained, a Deaf person does not think, "I cannot hear and therefore cannot communicate with this person," but rather, "Our languages are different and therefore we cannot communicate with each other." In this way, the Deaf individual's experience is that of a linguistic minority.

However, the social model of disability can account for much that the cultural model cannot. The disability model allows us to explore how sensory differences between hearing and deaf people shape their worlds, as well as how the concept of normality shapes both hearing people's attitudes toward Deaf people and the development of Deaf children's sense of identity. It provides an explanatory context for the medicalization of deafness, and a theoretical framework for the argument that Deaf people are not disabled by hearing impairment, but rather by the oppression of difference. It provides powerful arguments for ASL in Deaf education. It shows us that the response of hearing people to deafness is not unique but rather part of a larger response to disability. It makes sense of the fact that Veditz wrote *not* that Deaf people were people of sign language, but that they were people of the eye.

Moreover, the disability model should not pose a threat to Deaf people's sense of identity any more than does the ethnic model. After all, until fairly recently most Deaf people would have strongly objected to being identified with ethnicity. Once Deaf people in the 1970s and 1980s began to identify themselves as an ethnic group, they felt no less Deaf than they had before, and they felt no compulsion to merge their identities with Vietnamese-Americans, Italian-Americans, or other ethnic groups. Deaf Americans (or for that matter Chinese-Americans) are not expected to feel a close affinity for Cuban-Americans just because, for purposes of explaining their experiences as minorities, we describe both as ethnic groups. The same holds true for disability. Deaf people will doubtless always feel far more affinity for other Deaf people than for other disabled people (or for other ethnic groups). It is not a question about identity but rather about the need for a coherent category of analysis for scholars, for a unified, broad-based movement for effective activism, and for explanations that the general public, in particular the parents of deaf children, can find both plausible and persuasive.

Most groups who now identify themselves as disabled have done so only recently. Blind people in particular long resisted both the label and association with the larger universe of disabled people. People with mental disabilities and those with physical disabilities have long had an uneasy relationship. Those with acquired disabilities, such as disabled war veterans, often have resisted association with people who have lifelong disabilities. The tendency of those with less stigmatized disabilities to distance themselves from those with more highly stigmatized disabilities is a common phenomenon. Throughout American history, disabled people have been more likely to identify themselves in terms of a specific group than as disabled.

Only recently has the identity of "disabled person" been widely embraced. This is in part a conscious political decision, in part the product of a new consciousness of shared experience, and in good part is due to increasing awareness of the social model of disability. It was once common to hear wheelchair users say, "Just because I use a wheelchair doesn't mean you should treat me like I'm retarded." Today it is more common to hear something like, "Nobody, regardless of their disability, should be treated that way." Some disabled people are far more vulnerable to discrimination, institutionalization, and eugenic assault than others, but a tenet of disability solidarity is that those less threatened should not abandon the more vulnerable. Disabled people differ significantly from one another, but they share common experiences resisting the medicalization of their identity, coping with inferior "special" education, fighting for autonomy and self-determination—in short, they share a common experience of oppression and of struggle against it. Thus, sharing a common oppression, they have undertaken to forge a common liberation.

Indeed, one of the remarkable aspects of the pan-disability rights movement is its ability to bring together diverse groups of people into common action. It is a fractious coalition, riven by identity politics and conflicting agendas to be sure. Nevertheless, its very existence and dramatic growth is testament to a powerful idea—that the goal ought not to be for any one group to find liberation for itself, in effect merely reshuffling the deck, but rather to resist and disrupt the systematic translation of *difference* into structures of privilege and oppression.

Acknowledgements

The author wishes to thank Robert Buchanan, Bryan Eldredge, William Ennis, Christopher Krentz, Anna Mollow, and Joseph Murray, as well as the participants in the 2002 Deaf Studies Think Tank at Gallaudet University, for their helpful comments on earlier drafts. This chapter is a revised version of H.-D. L. Bauman. (Ed.). 2008. *Open your eyes: Deaf Studies talking* and is published with permission from the University of Minnesota Press.

Notes

1 Bryan Eldredge has a wonderful discussion of the complicated place hearing people occupy in the Deaf community; see chapter 1 in *The Role of Discourse in the Formation and Maintenance of Deaf Identity and the Deaf-World*, (PhD dissertation, Department of Anthropology, University of Iowa, 2004). Some Deaf people, most notably World Federation of the Deaf president Markku Jokinen and the editors of *The Tactile Mind*, have argued recently for thinking in terms of "sign language users" rather than "Deaf persons," as this would emphasize culture and language rather than lack of hearing. Markuu Jokinen, "The 'Sign Language Person'—A Term to Describe Us and Our Future More Clearly?" in *Looking Forward: EUD in the Third Millennium—The Deaf Citizen in the 21st Century*, ed. Lorraine Leeson (Coleford, UK: Douglas McLean Publishing, 2001), pp. 50–63. Paddy Ladd, in his recent and important book, *Understanding Deaf Culture: In Search of Deafhood* (Clevedon, UK: Multilingual Matters, 2003), suggests that in the absence of oppressive relations Deaf people would welcome culturally Deaf hearing people as full members of the community. I would maintain that sensory differences matter, regardless of the cultural setting. Ladd, in another section of his book, suggests this point by arguing that "blindness, being a sensory impairment, might well involve certain psychological patterning which, when reinforced by time spent together, might add up to a phenomenon with some notable cultural features" (p. 194). Human beings are cultural beings, and they are also physical beings. To deny one or the other, to say that our fates are entirely decided by our bodies, or conversely that we are all culture and that our bodies do not shape who we are, is equally wrong.

2 Arkady Belozovsky, for example, spoke at the 2004 Deaf Studies Today conference about cultural differences between Russian and American Deaf people, such as attitudes toward physical contact and ways of introducing people. Arkady Belozovsky, "Learning Foreign, Linguistically Related Sign Languages: What are the Benefits to ASL/Deaf Studies Instructors," (paper presented at the Deaf Studies Today conference held at Utah Valley State College, April 12–14, 2004).

3 Carol Padden, "A New Language" (paper presented at the Deaf Studies Today conference held at Utah Valley State College, April 12–14, 2004). Joseph Murray suggested to me that Padden's experience of a sense of connection might also be explained by her *expectation* that Deaf people should feel such a connection with one another. This indeed suggests an alternative explanation in general for Deaf experiences of kinship across national lines; biological kin often feel a similar sense of connectedness and mutual responsibility in spite of cultural divides. Still, I would argue that the shared experience of sensory difference from the majority, and the knowledge that another's experiences of the world are in this fundamental way like one's own, would be likely in itself to produce a sense of commonality.

4 Nash also points to important similarities between Deaf and other ethnic groups.

5 Ladd, in *Understanding Deaf Culture*, acknowledges the significance of the disability model, writing that Deaf people should be "seen as intrinsic 'dual-category members'—that is, that some of their issues might relate to issues of non-hearing whilst others relate to language and culture" (16). He notes that the concept of "access" has provided a rationale for important services to Deaf people such as interpreting services, text telephones, captioning and the like (while it has also created problems, as in the debate over separate versus mainstreamed education). On the whole, however, he downplays deafness and focuses almost entirely on what he aptly terms "Deafhood." The emphasis is understandable, given that he is trying to reach a public ignorant of Deaf culture and that views Deaf

people simply as people burdened with nonfunctioning ears. Nevertheless, it leads him to understate the importance of sensory difference in constructing the Deaf community and determining its membership (pp. 41–42, 74 n. 8) And while he gives a serviceable description of the social model of disability, he then goes on to equate recognition of "physical deafness" with "the medical concept," which is precisely the equation that the social model rejects (pp. 16, 166–169).

6 Please note: this chapter is a reprint and was originally published in 2004 (please also see Acknowledgements).

7 Simi Linton defines disability as "a marker of identity" that has brought together a coalition of people stigmatized by physical, sensory, and mental differences from the majority, in *Claiming Disability: Knowledge and Identity* (New York: New York University Press, 1998). Anna Mollow suggested to me that the social model assumes a false opposition between the medical and the social, and excludes disabling conditions that originate in progressive, chronic, or terminal illnesses such as AIDS, cancer, and diabetes. She argues that some disabilities are best understood as both social and medical. While I think that a conceptual distinction can be made between illness and disabilities associated with illness, Mollow's point may well indeed indicate a need for a more nuanced model of disability. However, since it does not directly affect the argument I present here, I have to plead the standard excuse that it is a question beyond the scope of this essay.

8 Lawrence Goodwyn's *Democratic Promise: The Populist Moment in America* (Oxford: Oxford University Press, 1976) is a prominent example of this use of "movement culture." Paddy Ladd, *Understanding Deaf Culture,* has a useful discussion of culture and subculture in which he posits language as a crucial element in distinguishing the two.

9 Reprinted in Longmore, *Why I Burned My Book*, p. 26.

10 On the ways in which the concept of disability has been used to justify discriminatory practices against women and minority groups, see my essay, "Disability and the Justification of Inequality in American History," in Longmore and Umansky, *New Disability History*, pp. 33–57.

11 Laurent Clerc, "Address to the Connecticut Legislature," and John Burnet, "What the Deaf and Dumb are before Instruction." In C. Krentz (Ed.), *A mighty change: Deaf American writing, 1817–1864* (pp. 17, 40). Washington, DC: Gallaudet University Press, 2000.

12 John Jacob Flournoy, "Mr. Flournoy's Plan for a Deaf-Mute Commonwealth," *American Annals of the Deaf* (1858), reprinted in Krentz, *A Mighty Change*, p. 166.

13 Burch cites two other issues of the *Empire State News*, but I could find nothing in them related to this question. The first briefly alludes to dissatisfaction with the work of the New York State Employment Service and endorses the idea of a deaf labor bureau. The other discusses concerns that the New York State Employment Service "claims to have 19 specially trained interviewers for the handicapped, but that none of these specially trained interviewers are equipped by experience or training to deal intelligently with the problems of the deaf." Again, the point is to address the particular needs of deaf people, not to make any conceptual distinctions between them and other "handicapped" persons.

14 A Deaf Frenchman, Henri Gaillard, did write in 1893 that, "Infirm we are not. In order to be infirm in the true sense of the word, it is necessary to be deprived of a limb, be bandy-legged, one-armed, crippled, blind or blind in one eye." *Proceedings of the World Congress of the Deaf and the Report of the Fourth Convention of the National Association of the Deaf* (Chicago, 1893), p. 176. This is the kind of unambiguous statement that has not yet been produced from research on the American Deaf community. The extent to which American Deaf people (or French Deaf, for that matter) agreed remains to be established. Thanks to Joe Murray for bringing Gaillard's statement to my attention.

15 Albert Ballin, *The Deaf Mute Howls* (1930; reprinted., Washington, D.C.: Gallaudet University Press, 1998), p. 57. Thomas A. Ulmer, "A Review of the Little Paper Family for

1944–45," in *Deaf World: A Historical Reader and Primary Sourcebook*, ed. Lois Bragg, (New York: New York University Press, 2001), p. 260. Anderson was quoted in Jay McMahon, "Rehabilitation Urged," *New York Times* (April 28, 1941): E6; reprinted in a regular column by Charles Joselow, "For Your Record," *Empire State News*, (January-February, 1942), p. 3; both cited in Buchanan, *Illusions of Equality*, p. 175 n. 10. Toivo Lindholm, "Place of the Adult Deaf in Society," in Bragg, *Deaf World*, p. 272. Frederick Schreiber, "What a Deaf Jewish Leader Expects," in ibid., p. 34. Leo M. Jacobs, *A Deaf Adult Speaks Out* (1974; reprinted., Washington, D.C.: Gallaudet University Press, 1989), pp. 13, 23. For a more recent example, see Tom Willard's 1998 essay in which he wrote of his frustration with "the misconception that people with disabilities are not happy or whole until they have overcome their disability." Tom Willard, "What Exactly Am I Supposed to Overcome," in Bragg, *Deaf World*, p. 273.

References

Alden, B. (2002). Visualist theory 101. *Tactile Mind*.

Bahan, B. (1989). Notes from a 'seeing person.' In S. Wilcox (Ed.), *American deaf culture: An anthology* (pp. 17–20). Silver Springs, MD: Linstock Press.

Ballin, A. (1930). *The deaf mute howls* (Reprinted 1998). Washington, D.C.: Gallaudet University Press.

Barnartt, S. (1996). Disability culture or disability consciousness? *Journal of Disability Policy Studies, 7*(2), 1–20.

Barton, L., & Oliver, M. (Eds.). (1997). *Disability studies: Past, present and future*. Leeds, UK: Disability Press.

Barnes, C., Oliver, M., & Barton, L. (Eds.). (2002). *Disability studies today*. Cambridge, UK: Polity Press.

Baynton, D. C. (1996). *Forbidden signs: American culture and the campaign against sign language*. Chicago, IL: University of Chicago Press.

Baynton, D. C. (2000). Bodies and environments: The cultural construction of disability. In. P. Blanck, (Ed.), *Employment, disability and the Americans with Disabilities Act: Issues in law, public policy and research* (pp. 387–411). Evanston, IL: Northwestern University Press.

Baynton, D. C. (2001). Disability and the justification of inequality in American history. In P. K. Longmore & L. Umansky (Eds.), *The new disability history: American perspectives* (pp. 33–57). New York, NY: New York University Press.

Blanck, P. (Ed.). (2000). *Employment, disability and the Americans with Disabilities Act: Issues in law, public policy and research*. Evanston, IL: Northwestern University Press.

Bragg, L. (Ed.). (2001). *Deaf world: A historical reader and primary sourcebook*. New York, NY: New York University Press.

Branson, J., & Miller, D. (2002). *Damned for their difference: The cultural construction of deaf people as disabled*. Washington, D.C.: Gallaudet University Press.

Brodkin, K. (1999). *How the Jews became white folks and what that says about gender and white supremacy*. New Brunswick, NJ: Rutgers University Press.

Buchanan, R. (2002). *Illusions of equality: Deaf Americans in school and factory, 1850–1950*. Washington, D.C.: Gallaudet University Press.

Burch, S. (2002). *Signs of resistance: American deaf cultural history, 1900 to 1942*. New York, NY: New York University Press.

Cartwright, S. A. (1851). Report on the diseases and physical peculiarities of the negro race. *New Orleans Medical and Surgical Journal, 7*, 693.

Charlton, J. I. (1998). *Nothing about us is without us: Disability oppression and empowerment*. Berkeley and Los Angeles, CA: University of California Press.

Clark, J. L. (2004). *On sensory unloss*. https://web.archive.org/web/20040416181107/http://www.johnleeclark.com/mainthing2.html#osu

Crutchfield, S., & Epstein, M. (Eds.). (2000). *Points of contact: Disability, art, and culture*. Ann Arbor, MI: University of Michigan Press.

Davis, L. J. (1995). *Enforcing normalcy: Disability, deafness and the body*. London, UK: Verso Press.

Dreger, A. (2004). *One of us: Conjoined twins and the future of normal*. Cambridge, MA: Harvard University Press.

Eldredge, B. (2004). *The role of discourse in the formation and maintenance of Deaf identity and the Deaf-world* [Unpublished doctoral dissertation]. University of Iowa, Iowa City, IA.

Fredrickson, G. M. (1971). *The black image in the white mind*. New York, NY: Harper Row.

Fries, K. (1997). *Staring back: The disability experience from the inside out*. New York, NY: Plume.

Garland Thomson, R. (1997). *Extraordinary bodies: Figuring physical disability in American culture and literature*. New York, NY: Columbia University Press.

Goodwyn, L. (1976). *Democratic promise: The populist moment in America*. Oxford, UK: Oxford University Press.

Hahn, H. (1996). Antidiscrimination laws and social research on disability: The minority group perspective. *Behavioral Sciences and the Law, 14*, 41–59.

Hobsbawm, E., & Ranger, T. (Eds.). (1983). *The invention of tradition*. Cambridge, UK: Cambridge University Press.

Ignatiev, N. (1996). *How the Irish became white*. New York, NY: Routledge.

Jacobs, L. M. (1974). *A deaf adult speaks out* (Reprinted 1989). Washington, D.C.: Gallaudet University Press.

Jacobson, M. F. (1998). *Whiteness of a different color: European immigrants and the alchemy of race*. Cambridge, MA: Harvard University Press.

Jokinen, M. (2001). The sign language person' - A term to describe us and our future more clearly? In L. Leeson (Ed.), *Looking forward: EUD in the third millennium - The Deaf citizen in the 21st century. Proceedings of a conference to celebrate 15 years of the European Union of the Deaf* (pp. 50–63). Coleford, UK: Douglas McLean Publishing.

Krentz, C. (2000). *A mighty change: Deaf American writing*. Washington, DC: Gallaudet University Press.

Kudlick, C. J. (2003). Disability history: Why we need another 'other.' *American Historical Review, 108*, 763–793.

Ladd, P. (2003). *Understanding Deaf culture: In search of deafhood*. Clevedon, UK: Multilingual Matters.

Lane, H. (1992). *The mask of benevolence: Disabling the Deaf community*. New York, NY: Alfred Knopf.

Lane, H., Hoffmeister, R., & Bahan, B. (1996). *A journey into the Deaf-world*. San Diego, CA: DawnSign Press.

Linton, S. (1998). *Claiming disability: Knowledge and identity*. New York, NY: New York University Press.

Longmore, P. K. (2003). *Why I burned my book and other essays on disability*. Philadelphia, PA: Temple University Press.

Longmore, P. K., & Umansky, L. (Eds.). (2001). *The new disability history: American perspectives*. New York, NY: New York University Press.

Mitchell, D. T., & Snyder, S. L. (Eds.). (1997). *The body and physical difference: Discourses in disability*. Ann Arbor, MI: University of Michigan Press.

Mitchell, R. E., & Karchmer, M. A. (2004). Chasing the mythical ten percent: Parental hearing status of deaf and hard of hearing students in the United States. *Sign Language Studies, 4*, 138–136.

Nash, J. E. (1987). Policy and practice in the American sign language community. *International Journal of the Sociology of Languages, 68*, 7–22.

Oliver, M. (1990). *The politics of disablement*. New York, NY: Palgrave McMillan.

Padden, C., & Humphries, T. (1988). *Deaf in America: Voices from a culture*. Cambridge, MA: Harvard University Press.

Priestley, M. (1998). Constructions and creations: Idealism, materialism and disability theory. *Disability and Society, 13*(1), 75–94.

Ritter, J. (2004, July 19). 650 walk, roll and bike in city's first Disability Pride Parade. *Chicago Sun-Times*.

Ross, E. A. (1914). *The old and the new: The significance of past and present immigration to the American people*. New York, NY: Century.

Shakespeare, T., & Watson, N. (1997). Defending the social model. *Disability and Society, 12*, 293–300.

Shapiro, J. (1994). *No pity: People with disabilities forging a new civil rights movement*. New York, NY: Random House.

Sipress, J. M. (1997). Relearning race: Teaching race as a cultural construction. *History Teacher, 30*(2), 175–185.

Swain, J., French, S., Barnes, C., & Thomas, C. (Eds.). (1993). *Disabling barriers - Enabling environments*. London, UK: Sage Publications.

Van Cleve, J. V., & Crouch, B. A. (1989). *A place of their own: Creating the deaf community in America*. Washington, DC: Gallaudet University Press.

Veditz, G. (1912). President's message. *Proceedings of the Ninth Convention of the National Association of the Deaf and the Third World's Congress of the Deaf, 1910* (pp. 6–13). Philadelphia, PA: Philocophus Press.

CHAPTER 2

Diasporic Deaf Places and Spaces

A Comparative Overview of Sign Languages

Joseph C. Hill

Abstract

Sign language communities are scattered around the world and the communities differ by nationality, culture, history, and language and yet there is one thing that binds them all in a visceral sense: the experience of being the 'other' and the ability to navigate social and cultural spaces as deaf people. Universally, they are experientially connected in their daily battle against audism, which is a systematic oppression, discrimination, and ignorance against Deaf people. With the universality of the Deaf experience and sign language as their treasured resource, it is appropriate to use the term *diaspora* to describe the dispersion of the Deaf communities around the world. With the traditional meaning of *diaspora*, it typically focuses on racially, ethnically, or religious homogenous groups that have the ancestral ties to their homeland from where they were dispersed either by force or by will. Even though there is no physical home for the Deaf communities and where they live defines their experiences and lives differently, their metaphysical home is Deafhood where sign languages and their experience as Deaf people runs deep.

Keywords

Deafhood – audism – Sign Language – international sign – diaspora – variation

1 Introduction

Deafness is an auditory disorder that involves damaged or disrupted sensory organs or bones in the ear that negatively affect the ability to perceive sound. Deafness can be congenital, which may be hereditary- or fetal development-related, or it can be acquired, for example, through trauma, accident, aging, medical complications, or prolonged exposure to excessive noise. The effects of hearing loss include communication problems, difficulty in maintaining

 | DOI:10.1163/9789004692299_003

relationships, difficulty in gaining or maintaining employment, and reduced pleasure in sound-based activities. This is a typical reality based on the medical model of disability that, in a pathological sense, describes people with hearing loss as individuals suffering from affliction that limits their major life activities. However, this is just one reality. Counter to the disabling reality is the reality of biodiversity, a world that happens to include people from the Deaf communities who view themselves as part of marginalized minorities with human and language rights. To them, deafness is just part of human biodiversity (Bauman & Murray, 2014). Some members may go as far as claiming that they are not disabled and use sign language and Deaf culture to justify their distance from the disability community and movement (see Lane, 2002 and Mauldin, 2015 for further discussion on the intersection and separation of deafness and disability). However, deafness is often viewed as a condition that requires medical and technological interventions to reduce the effects of hearing loss as described above so the hearing and speaking abilities of the affected individuals can be normalized (Lane, 2002). Medicine is generally accepted as a necessary part of life, and it is critical to everyone's survival so this makes the medical model of deafness much more prevalent than the cultural model. The medical model, often with governmental and corporation involvements, creates a conditional existence of signed languages of Deaf people, meaning that if deafness were to be completely cured, the necessity of signed languages would be severely undermined and Deaf cultures, which are intimately related with sign languages, would be drastically affected. This is an ongoing reality that determines how sign languages are recognized and accepted at local, national and international levels (see Reagan, 2010; Monaghan, 2003).

Sign language, like with any spoken language, is a natural language that possesses the universal linguistic properties that are recognized and interpreted by the brain despite the difference in the communication modality (Petitto, 2014). In the early childhood, children using sign language reach each milestone of the typical language development at the similar rate as children using spoken language (Petitto, 2000, 2014). Through centuries, sign languages can be transmitted from generation to generation through families and peer cohorts at residential schools (Lane, Hoffmeister, & Bahan, 1996). Sign languages are typically acquired at residential schools because the majority of deaf people who was born and reared in families where deafness is not typical and communication is normally spoken. Like spoken languages, the origin of sign languages can be traced to modern and ancestral sign languages based on the similarity in phonology, lexicon, and syntax based on lexicostatistical studies.

Sign language communities are scattered around the world and the communities differ by nationality, culture, history, and language (see Fenlon &

Wilkinson, 2015 on multilingualism within the world's deaf communities) and yet there is one thing that binds them all in a visceral sense: the experience of being the 'other' and the ability to navigate social and cultural spaces as deaf people. Their experiences and their abilities are unified in the framework of deafhood. Deafhood, coined by Paddy Ladd (2003), is a decolonizing process that reframes the meanings and experiences associated with deafness free from limitations which are set by the medical model of disability and allow people to individually and collectively define what it means to be Deaf. The operative words are 'individually and collectively' because all deaf people live and experience life differently in their own surroundings and their social networks. Universally, they are experientially connected in their daily battle against audism, coined by Tom Humphries (1975) and popularized by H-Dirksen L. Bauman (2004), which is a systematic oppression, discrimination, and ignorance against Deaf people. With the universality of the Deaf experience and sign language as their treasured resource, it is appropriate to use the term *diaspora* to describe the dispersion of the Deaf communities around the world. With the traditional meaning of *diaspora*, it typically focuses on racially, ethnically, or religious homogenous groups that have the ancestral ties to their homeland from where they were dispersed either by force or by will. Even though there is no physical home for the Deaf communities and where they live defines their experiences and lives differently, their metaphysical home is deafhood where sign languages and their experience as Deaf people runs deep.

2 Sign Language on the Global Scale

The U.S. Census Bureau (2017) reports that the world's population count is over 7 billion people. Out of this number, the estimate—although it is questionable considering the disability count is not always available in the countries' census data—is that there are 70 million Deaf people (World Federation of the Deaf, 2017). That is around 1 percent of the world's population who has hearing loss. It should be noted that the population estimates of deaf and hard-of-hearing people can vary so one should take caution by investigating the methods of population estimate (see Mitchell, Young, Bachleda, & Karchmer, 2006). With no direct data available, researchers often resort to use their own sources to make an estimate of deaf and hard-of-hearing population. With deafness as a low-incidence disability and the number of Deaf people who are proficient in sign language, it can be safely determined that the proportion of deaf and hard-of-hearing people to hearing people is extremely low in the context of the general population in a respective nation. For example, in the

United States, we have nearly 313 million people and the unconfirmed estimate of Deaf people runs between 100,000 and 2,000,000 (Mitchell et al., 2006). That is less than 0.6%. In New Zealand, out of 4 million New Zealand citizens, the estimate of the Deaf population is between 4,500 and 7,700, which is less than 0.17% (McKee, McKee, & Major, 2011). In Australia, the number of Deaf population is estimated to be 7,000 people out of 22,685,018 (Johnston, 2004, p. 367). That's less than 0.03%. An estimate of 6,500 Deaf people living in Ireland accounts for 0.14% of 4.6 million residents. An unconfirmed estimate of 1 million users of Ethiopian Sign Language accounts for 1% of the Ethiopian population (Tamene, 2016).

Even though sign languages are generally used in the world's communities of deaf and hard-of-hearing people, it is important to know that not all deaf and hard-of-hearing people use sign language. It depends on how they were raised and how they identify themselves: Deaf as a person with an entrenched cultural identity and a carrier of sign language; hard-of-hearing as a person with residual hearing and speech capacity and a range of signing proficiency; oral deaf as a person with little or no hearing but has a strong preference in oral communication over signing; and late-deafened as a person who possessed normal hearing and speech abilities before losing them due to medical conditions, e.g. illness, genetic predisposition, or accident. And that is not all of the identities that appear to be relevant in the world's deaf communities. Leigh (2009) presents a nice and detailed account on the complexity of identities related to deafness. Also, hearing people, meaning people who have normal hearing and speech abilities, who have personal or professional ties to members of the Deaf communities (e.g., family, friend, teacher, interpreter, or researcher) and can converse comfortably in sign language can be considered members or allies, but even so, it is unlikely that there is a sizable segment of the hearing population who are skilled in sign language and maintain connection with Deaf communities on a regular basis, except in some rural or village communities where everyone depends on each other for their livelihood as long as they are able to contribute.

As reported in the *Ethnologue*, there are 7,097 living languages in the world. The number includes institutional languages, developing languages, and endangered languages; out of all living languages, 138 sign languages have been documented (Lewis, Simons, & Fennig, 2016). However, there are questions about how they are counted: how are those sign languages counted as actual sign languages?; do mutually intelligible sign languages count as dialects of a same language or as different languages?; how are sign languages named in their respective communities and how are they known to the outsiders of the communities?; and how many sign languages are erroneously counted as a single sign language that is considered a standard sign language in a respective community? (Woll, Sutton-Spence, & Elton, 2001; Padden, 2011). These questions are important to consider when it comes to the socio-political nature that defines the signing communities and the sign languages they are using.

According to Schembri (2010), sign languages can be divided into two general categories: sign language macro-communities and micro-communities. Sign language macro-communities include large stable communities with sign languages that are used widely in nation states and urban city centers, for example, Auslan (Australian Sign Language), Libras (Língua Brasileira de Sinais, Brazilian Sign Language), BSL (British Sign Language), LSF (Langue des Signes Française, French Sign Language), ASL (American Sign Language), and Hong Kong Sign Language (Fenlon & Wilkinson, 2015). Sign language micro-communities include indigenous, rural, or village sign languages used by minority communities whose livelihood is dependent on the local economy of businesses, occupations, and resources (Fenlon & Wilkinson, 2015). The general observation is that these communities have a higher incidence of deafness than observed in the signing macro-communities due to a high number of intermarriage and familial relationships between deaf and hearing members in the micro-communities (ibid). The signing micro-communities have been uncovered by sign language research in different parts of the world, for example, Alipur, India; Chican, Mexico; Bedouin Arab communities in Israel; Adamorobe, Ghana; and so forth (see Fenlon & Wilkinson, 2015 on the list of micro-communities). Like spoken languages that fall into vulnerable and endangered categories, sign languages of the micro-communities are vulnerable due to economic and socio-political pressures that affect their local economic and political powers, and they are especially vulnerable to the pressures relating to educational, medical, and technological advances in the treatment of deafness.

In the areas where multilingualism is common, people employ different strategies to communicate with each other in a language contact encounter: speaking each other's language, using a form of foreign talk, speaking a language of the majority in a respective nation, using a form of code-mixing, or using an international auxiliary language like Esperanto which is constructed for social spaces with people of multiple nationalities. The strategies are similar in many contact situations between signers of different nationalities where they use each other's sign language or a form of code-mixing, foreign talk, or co-construction of iconic gestures which is different from conventionalized lexical signs. One form of co-constructed translingual practice is called "International Sign" and it often used in various places where deaf people of different nationalities gather and participate in sport activities, conferences, tourism, or on social media where deaf people share their videos of signed messages.

To a non-signer's eye, International Sign appears to be a sign language, but it is not a language by definition. Sign language is considered a language if it meets the language characteristics which are as follows: symbols such as words or signs that are conventionalized by a particular community; particular organization of symbols and their relationships; discreteness of symbols which can be divided into parts; recursive property of the system where a string of symbols can be nested in another string of symbols; conveying information using displacement to refer to things that are not immediately present in a physical or temporal sense; productivity, complexity, and creativity in using symbols and expressing information; cultural transmission between generations; and social contexts related to semantics and pragmatics that heavily influences the meaning of symbols. Sign language is also tightly bound with culture in a particular community or region. Sign language is unique in the way how information is encoded in a particular modality, which is gestural and spatial modality. A visual perception does play a part in the modality, but for deaf people who are also blind, they can perceive sign language through haptic perception by touching another person (see Collins & Petronio, 1998). In that sense, the gestural and spatiality modality is fitting for sign languages that can be perceived by sight and through touch.

International Sign is also of the gestural and spatial modality, but it is a distributed translingual practice that is greatly dependent on a shared context that international signers use to accommodate each other (Rosenstock, 2008; Mesch, 2010; Kusters, 2024). It is used for particular activities or encounters at conferences and sport competitions, through personal or group travels, or on social media where the intended audience is international deaf signers. International conferences, for example the World Federation of the Deaf organization and the World Association of Sign Language Interpreters, hold their conferences in different countries every few years and deaf signers as well as hearing signers from different countries are welcome to attend as participants or as presenters. Often, International Sign is a preferred communication of choice for the conference attendees who use different sign languages. The same is true for international sports competitions for deaf athletes which are managed by, for example, the International Committee of Sports for the Deaf (ICSD) that hosts Deaflympics that occurs every two years with the alternating sport events which are winter and summer games. The origin of ICSD is dated back to 1924 when a governing body was established by two notable deaf leaders as a response to the need to create and maintain the standard rules and regulations to run the international sport events in a fair and honest manner (ibid). It must be noted that the founders were from France and Belgium that were involved in the international soccer matches that were first started by deaf athletes from England and Scotland (Ammons, 2009).

International Sign, however, is different from sign languages in many respects. It is a form of distributed communication practice with a limited set of conventionalized signs, and it is typically combined with iconic signs from the signers' primary sign languages which offer more lexical and semantic choices (Rosenstock, 2008; Kusters, 2024). Unlike natural sign languages, conventionalized signs of International Sign tend to remain at the superordinate level where their meanings can be easily inferred based on the iconic and metaphorical forms of signs, for example, the gesture of a round breast in reference to a woman or the depiction of a vertical space from top to bottom to indicate a power differential between an employer and an employee. The syntactical and semantic contexts of the conventionalized signs can vary between the signers depending on their knowledge of International Sign and their sign languages so the signers may have to frequently negotiate meanings and check for comprehension with each other. If in the case of a monologic discourse where a signer has less of a communication exchange with an audience, for instance in a lecture or in a video, the signer needs to be mindful of the sign and gesture choices that clearly communicate the intended meanings to the multilingual audience of different nationalities and cultures.

Even though International Sign is used by signers from different countries, not all deaf signers in different countries are familiar with International Sign, just as not all hearing people use Esperanto for various reasons. International Sign is used widely in European countries where the multilingualism of sign languages suggests a relatively high number of contacts between deaf signers, which makes sense considering the international deaf organizations' home offices, for example the World Federation of the Deaf and the International Committee of Sports for the Deaf headquarters, are often located in Europe (Rosen, 2009; Ammons, 2009). International Sign is not as widespread outside of Europe and deaf people in the developing countries may not have resources and credentials that privilege their access to international conferences and sport events in order to be exposed to International Sign. Even though, International Sign has been used for decades, the studies on the linguistic features and structural analysis of International Sign are still very much in the early stage (Fenlon & Wilkinson, 2015).

Prior to the mid-1900s, there have been sporadic instances of sign language analysis, but the most influential is the 1965 seminal analysis of American Sign Language done by William Stokoe and his deaf colleagues, Dorothy Casterline and Carl Croneberg. This inspired a host of studies on sign languages in the world, but it is still a young field. The origin of sign languages and other gestural forms of communication is difficult to trace since the historical forms of natural signing between deaf signers were rarely documented except for signs used at certain monasteries in place of speaking to honor the vow of silence (Bragg, 1997; Padden & Gunsauls, 2003) and manual alphabets that were designed as an educational tool (Sutton-Spence, 2003). The records of signs are usually found in the scholarly texts produced by monks and by educators who were typically the religious types that documented their attempts in educating deaf students. Religion is a common factor in the establishment of educational institutions that changed the lives of deaf students in many ways, including their ability to communicate with sign language and their sense of belonging in a community, particularly a deaf community.

3 A Brief Historical Overview of Sign Languages

With deafness as a form of disability which can be congenital or acquired that can affect any person, deaf people have always been in existence as long as there have been human beings. Earliest mentions about deaf people can be found in the ancient texts, for example the dialogue of Greek philosopher Aristotle in 355 B.C., but in this particular historical context the popular view was that deaf people were "dumb" as to mean, "unable to speak" (Jankowski, 1997). This signifies the metaphysical nature of what it means to be human, that to be human is to speak (Bauman, 2004). Somehow, the inability to speak was defined as lacking in intelligence and that translated into a conventional view that deaf people were not educable. Deaf people would be severely marginalized within a community where a community membership was based on social interaction and communication exchange in a spoken language, unless deaf people had valuable skills that redeemed them as full members of a community with rights and responsibilities or they were in a community that accepted alternative forms of communication, especially of the visual and gestural communication mode. In spite of the difficulty, deaf people could carry on in a form of visual and gestural communication with people around them. If there was a group of two or more deaf people, they might share a more developed and specialized gestural communication system based on the frequency of interaction and usage.

The history of the instructional methods for deaf children would be incomplete if the intersection of religion, science, nationalism, and internationalism is not mentioned. There are historical records of people who went against the conventional ideology about language and communication and attempted to educate deaf children through various means, which are often based on the religious motivation to proselyte deaf children by teaching them religious subjects (Leeson & Saeed, 2012; Lane et al., 1996). The earliest records of educating deaf children are dated from about 1550 when monks tutored deaf children of noble families (Plann, 1997). It was then that education was exclusive to people of privileged class. A group of deaf children needed to be brought together to reach a critical mass that would lead to a stable deaf community. That happened in France.

One of the most successful education models of teaching deaf children is the French National Institute of Deaf-Mutes, the first public school for the deaf in Paris, France founded in 1760 by l'Abbé Charles-Michel de l'Épée, a hearing Frenchman who studied to be a Catholic priest. The model includes methodical signing which is a system of signing with signs borrowed from signing deaf students and modified in a way that follows French grammar and vocabulary. This is known as the French Method and this was primarily for instructional purpose. A sign language is typically different from a spoken language within a respective community because of the difference in modality and the number of articulators (meaning the use of body parts) to express meanings. If the sign language is modified to follow the grammar of a spoken language, some natural features of the sign language are likely to be reduced or omitted, for example, spatial references, non-manual signals, and prosody. During the same time period, there existed another method in Germany that was used to educate deaf children: the German Method, an oral method that was designed to teach deaf children to speak. The French and German methods came about during the time when the relationship between France and Germany became politically tense, particularly when Germany sought to replace France as the European center (Monaghan, 2003). As German power grew, Germany garnered the international admiration for its advances in education, science, and technology and that slowly set the stage for the international spread of oralism since oralism happened to be connected with the innovative advances coming out of Germany.

During the 1860s, a small movement for making deaf schools exclusively oral started gaining momentum and this continued through the years until the fateful days in Milan, Italy. During September 1880 a conference, hereby called the Milan Congress, was attended by delegates of deaf schools from France, Italy, and the U.S.A. and the delegates held a passionate debate about the effective mode of communication in deaf education. American delegates had reservations about the effectiveness of instructing deaf students through the means of oral communication, but for most European delegates, the goal was to normalize deaf children so they could conform to the mainstream society. At the closing of the conference, the majority had made a final decision to ban sign languages from school properties and to train deaf students to use their remaining hearing and speaking facilities. This created an enormous consequence for the future of deaf people in education and employment and the stability of deaf communities with the prompt dismissal of deaf school staff and faculty (Baynton, 1996).

Whereas spoken languages are practiced in different units of the hearing communities from individuals to families to institutions and they are widely available for children to acquire, sign languages are not as widely practiced in the hearing communities in which deaf and hard-of-hearing are members. In that sense, the population factor functions as a constraint on the transmission of sign language for deaf and hard-of-hearing people. And yet what contributes to the success of a sign language transmission among deaf and hard-of-hearing people is the educational factor, despite the long-held ban on sign languages at the educational institutions simply because sign languages are perceived more effectively through visual and haptic senses.

4 The Impact of Sign Languages for the Schooling of Deaf People

In a world without the educational institutions for the deaf people, deaf communities would not be easily formed and signed languages would not be used as widely as they are today (Monaghan, 2003). Schools for the deaf have long been considered to be the crucibles for the acquisition and maintenance of sign language (Lucas, Bayley, & Valli, 2001); they are also the seeds in the formation of deaf communities (Monaghan, 2003). This is not to say that all of the world's deaf communities were formed because of the schools; not all deaf people were fortunate enough to go to school. There are a number of deaf communities that were also formed due to the social isolation of a community with a high incidence of deafness and the employment availability and potential for deaf people in specific locations where they could work for their livelihoods. Those deaf people who were fortunate enough to go to school would eventually have to find work after they completed their schooling, so employment was another factor in the formation of deaf communities as well. Despite the long period of suppression of sign languages after the Milan Congress, the schools continued to be a place for deaf and hard-of-hearing students to be immersed in a sign language-rich environment, although they had to be very discreet lest they received a corporeal punishment for transgressing the oral schools' ban on sign language (Baynton, 1996; Lane et al., 1996).

Long before the decisive vote on the ban of the signing method at the Milan Congress, the educators who supported the signing method and its variants were more concerned about deaf students' reading and writing ability than they were with deaf students' oral communication skills (Baynton, 1996; Lane et al., 1996). For the educators, deaf students' ability to learn a variety of subjects was much more important than how well their oral and aural communication skills should be. Since the majority of deaf students were born to families who did not use sign language, it was typical for deaf students to arrive at the schools with little or no knowledge of sign language. In those days, the schools were usually hard to reach for many families who lived farther away, and transportation was not easily available so many schools had dormitories for deaf children to stay through the end of the school year except for scheduled breaks and holidays. With so much time away from their families, their peers were their family and the school staff their custodians. With the exception of the minority of deaf students who acquired sign language at home with their signing deaf families, many deaf students learned sign language in the company of older deaf peers. This is known as "horizontal transmission" which is normal for the cohorts of deaf and hard-of-hearing children to learn from each other at the schools as opposed to "vertical transmission" which is typical for hearing children to acquire their native language from their families passing down through generations. With the familial-like bond between the deaf peers that developed at the schools for the deaf, it created the cultural attributes that became typical of Deaf culture in a respective deaf community and the schools were where the community members acquired and used signed language, formed lifelong friendships, and developed their community identities as deaf people.

Teaching of deaf students could occur anywhere in the world and at any time in history, but with the lack or loss of historical documents, it is difficult to go farther back and beyond the border of the European continent where the records of deaf education have been found. For many schools for the deaf before the 20th century, religion was the main influence in the establishment of the schools. Many educators had a religious background and for them, deaf people's lack of access to and knowledge about religious subjects was a major concern. A variety of communication methods were tried and one of the most successful was the signing method. The educational and sign language influences of the schools for the deaf that were founded throughout Europe, North America, South America, and some parts of Africa can be traced back to the National Institute in France and the schools used their signing methods that included signs from French Sign Language and students' pre-existing signs.

Before the establishment of the National Institute for the Deaf in France, there were instances of tutoring and academies, for example Thomas Braidwood's Academy in Great Britain, but they were only for families who could afford to pay for the education of deaf children. In 1760, the French National Institute of Deaf-Mutes in Paris was the first state-supported school in the world that made it possible for deaf children to receive education regardless of their family's ability to pay. Its renowned status and success inspired many religious educators to teach deaf children in sign language. Sign language used at St. Mary's School for Deaf Girls founded in 1846 in Cabra, currently a suburb of Dublin, Ireland, can be traced back to Old French Sign Language (OFSL) at the National Institute (Leeson & Saeed, 2012). A decade later in the same suburb, St. Joseph's School for Deaf Boys was founded in 1857, but their sign language was heavily influenced by American Sign Language (ASL) that was developed at the American School for the Deaf in Hartford, Connecticut (Leeson & Saeed, 2012). Despite the difference in the influence, ASL is related to OLSF. OLSF's influence can also be found in Brazilian Sign Language (Língua Brasileira de Sinais, Libras). Libras was developed at the institution known as the Instituto Nacional Educação de Surdos (INES, National Institute of Education for the Deaf) in 1857 (Guarinello, Santana, Berberian, & Massi, 2009). The founder was a deaf Frenchman named Ernest Huet who was educated at the National Institute in France. This is the same founder of the first Mexican school for the deaf in 1865 (Monaghan, 2003).

In a similar fashion, OFSL was exported to the United States with a deaf Frenchman, but it occurred much earlier. The deaf Frenchman was Laurent Clerc who was an educator at the National Institute. Clerc met with Thomas Gallaudet who had been searching for a school that was successful at teaching deaf children so he could learn the method and establish a similar school in Connecticut. It must be noted that Gallaudet had a religious inclination since he studied to be a priest. After Gallaudet persuaded Clerc to move with him to the United States, they founded the first American public institution for the deaf, the American School for the Deaf (ASD), in Hartford, Connecticut in 1817. OFSL was used at the school but like with any language that is transported to another community, the language is mixed with other forms of language or communication that is particular to the community. Before ASD was established, there existed the indigenous sign language that was used at Martha's Vineyard, an island just south of mainland Massachusetts. Martha's Vineyard Sign Language was a shared language used by deaf and hearing people in the community where the rate of incidence of deafness was higher than the rest of the United States (Groce, 1985). OFSL was also mixed with the indigenous sign language of Henniker, New Hampshire and deaf children's home signs which is homemade gestures co-created by deaf children and their hearing families (Lane et al., 1996, p. 56). The mixture of sign languages led to the formation of what is now called American Sign Language (ASL). ASL continued to flourish through generations of deaf children at ASD and other institutions for the deaf. Some of those deaf children became teachers and served as the signed language models for deaf children at the institutions. The founding of other institutions for the deaf spread southward and westward from the first institution in Hartford and deaf communities formed around the institutions to maintain community ties (Lane et al., 1996; Padden & Humphries, 1988).

In 1957, an African-American deaf missionary named Andrew Foster travelled to Ghana and founded the first school for the deaf in that country. Before his unfortunate death in 1987, he had remarkably founded 32 schools for the deaf in 13 West and Central African countries during his 30-year career as an educator (Ilabor, 2009). Still to this day, his advocacy, his courage, and his drive are celebrated by many deaf Africans who are grateful for language and education which offer far more opportunities than if they had not gone to the schools. The language they acquired at the school was not a language but a signed communication system in the form of methodological signing that combined ASL and English forms. It was called Total Communication which was a compromise made by the educators in the United States to reintroduce the signing method, albeit modified, in classrooms after the ban on sign language. Foster's version of Total Communication was based on signs he learned in the Michigan School for the Deaf and Gallaudet University. It is also possible that he used Black ASL since he attended a segregated school for black deaf children in Alabama before he moved to Michigan, but there is no evidence of Black ASL used in the African schools for the deaf.

Schools for the deaf in other countries began in a similar manner, but with the technological advances that changed how people travelled and communicated, educational institutions and laws changed as well. Following the advent of mainstreaming with deaf and hard-of-hearing students attending regular schools with or without accommodation, the role of the schools for the deaf has become increasingly smaller as a source of sign language input for deaf and hard-of-hearing children. For example, before the 1960s, almost 80 percent of the deaf children in the US attended residential schools for the deaf (Lane et al., 1996); by 2010, the percentage had declined to 24.3% (Gallaudet Research Institute, 2011). The educational and age factors are clearly related based on the passage of mainstreaming laws that encourage the placement of deaf and hard-of-hearing students in regular educational settings. In a large-scale sociolinguistic study of ASL, Lucas and her colleagues (2001) observed the age factor as an external constraint based on the division of three generational age groups (15–25, 26–54, and 55+). The age division has been motivated by developments in language policy in deaf education in the early 1970s with the passage of Public Law 94–142 (the Education of All Handicapped Children Act of 1975) and in the change of communication methods from oral to signed which may not have included ASL (Lucas, Bayley, & Valli, 2001). In Italy, a similar trend emerged in the late 1970s with the passage of the legislation on the mainstreaming of children with disabilities, including deaf and hard-of-hearing children (Geraci, Battaglia, Cardinaletti, Cecchetto, Donati, Giudice, & Mereghetti, 2011). It is also true for New Zealand when the mainstream placement of deaf and hard-of-hearing children has become increasingly favored starting in 1980s (McKee & McKee, 2011). The legal, educational, and communication developments in deaf education have produced a clear effect on the communication background of generations of deaf and hard-of-hearing people.

5 Sign Languages Contextualized in Place and Space

Throughout the world, deaf communities are a microcosm of the larger communities, reflecting the social diversity as it exists in the societies (Pray & Jordan, 2010). Deaf identities and a notion of Deaf culture may not be the same in all deaf communities because "the nature of deaf and Deaf identity in a given community depends on the forms of community and language" and with respect to forms, "the form any sign language takes is intertwined with the nature of the community that uses it" (Monaghan, 2003, p. 20). As it has been mentioned above, the majority of deaf people were born to hearing families; through their families, deaf people are usually socialized into the social institutions at the macro and micro levels. In addition, deaf people who have attended educational institutions, be it mainstreamed or specialized, are also socialized by the teaching staff into the social institutions as well.

The percentage of deaf and hard-of-hearing people born to families of deaf and hard-of-hearing adults using sign language as primary communication is much smaller than the percentage of deaf and hard-of-hearing people who were born to non-signing families with normal hearing. For instance, in the United States, approximately 8 percent of deaf children have at least one parent who is deaf or hard-of-hearing (Mitchell & Karchmer, 2005). To break it down even further, about 4.8 percent of the deaf children have one hearing parent and one deaf or hard-of-hearing parent and approximately 3.5 percent have two deaf or hard-of-hearing parents. Unfortunately, the account of how many homes use American Sign Language (ASL) as the home language is not available (Mitchell & Karchmer, 2004), and the same can be said for many sign languages in the world. In contrast, 92 percent of deaf children were born to hearing parents and it is very likely that these deaf children are not initially and/or perpetually exposed to sign language at home with their families (Mitchell & Karchmer, 2004). Although, there are exceptions that hearing families are aware of the existence and benefits of sign language and choose to use it with their deaf children. With deafness as a low-incidence disability and the genetic mutation that appears as a factor for the minority of Deaf population in a nation state, it is likely that the percentages of deaf and hard-of-hearing people born to hearing people are similar in different countries and territories. This is not to say that deaf people who were born to signing families with deaf members are not likely socialized in the social institutions of the larger communities. They are in many ways, but with the low percentage of deaf people from signing deaf families, they are in a rare status in the families whose sign language transmission is truly vertical from parent to child as opposed to the horizontal transmission of sign language which is common for the majority of deaf people born to hearing families. The vertical transmission is just as important in the maintenance of sign language as the educational institutions that still have sign language as a medium of instruction. But in these days, mainstream education has become very much a norm for the majority of deaf students and the difference in communication methods in the classroom instructions convey implicit beliefs and values about languages.

In deaf education, language of instruction is intricately linked with language acquisition and exposure for deaf and hard-of-hearing students because schools are usually the primary places for the students to acquire a language in a variety of communication modes: sign, speech or sign-supported speech modes. Behind every language of instruction, there is an educational philosophy that explains the choice of the language and the values that teachers and administrators want to instill in their students. If the language of instruction is sign language, the teachers and administrators may have the same respect for sign language as they do for spoken language and convey the positive values of sign language by using it with their deaf and hard-of-hearing students. The positive values can be, for example, the status of sign language as a true language, the awareness of linguistic and cultural values of sign language, the pride of being bilingual with spoken/written and sign languages, and the sense of being normal with the use of sign language. If the medium of instruction is strictly in an oral or sign-supported speech mode, the teachers and administrators may not have as much respect for sign language as they have for spoken language and they convey the negative values toward natural sign language by using only a speech-based communication method with their students. The negative values can be the unacknowledged status of sign language as a true language, the perpetuation of the misconceptions of sign language, and the indignity of using sign language. If the language of instruction contains both speech and sign components, it depends on how the teachers and administrators convey the message to the students with their actions and use of language.

Besides the educational factor that affects the use of language, there are two other factors that influence the formation and maintenance of sign languages and they are related to the particular regions where signers live and the social groups which their identities are based on.

Geographical and social factors, which explain the natural or man-made boundaries between existing communities, often play a role in the formation of language varieties (see Wolfram & Schilling-Estes, 2006). The geographical and social factors can also be compounded by other factors that are particular to the communities, for example legal, political, educational, and economic. In the geographical sense, communities can be separated by natural or man-made boundaries, e.g., natural geographic barriers (e.g., rivers, mountains, or swamps), settlement patterns, political borders, social stratification, and economic ecology, which is geographic concentrations of occupations (Wolfram & Schilling-Estes, 2006). With communities in relative isolation from one another, language varieties naturally form in the respective communities and the varieties are defined by the communities' culturally bound communication practices passed down through generations.

As it has been mentioned in the earlier section, Ireland had two schools for the deaf that were geographically segregated by gender in Cabra: St. Mary's School for Deaf Girls and St. Joseph's School for Deaf Boys (Leeson & Saeed, 2012). Single sex education is not unusual since it is a traditional practice in many parts of the world, but what is unusual about this case is that the gender segregation is a factor in the difference of sign languages between two genders. Deaf female students were instructed in a sign language that was very different from the sign language used by deaf male students at their school. When the students graduated from their schools and began their courtship that eventually led to marriage, the spouses had to understand each other's signing variants. Oralism became increasingly enforced in the 20th century following the decision made at the Milan Congress to ban sign language in schools, to the point where the students' literacy skills became a problem because of their ineffective communication with their other peers and their families (Leeson & Saeed, 2012). Signing had returned to education in the late 20th century when the deaf community became politically active and called for Irish Sign Language as a language of instruction.

In the U.S., racial segregation in its modern form began in the late 1800s on a much larger scale. Despite the Supreme Court's landmark decision in the case of *Brown v. Board of Education* in 1954, segregation was still in practice within the later decades in some parts of the South. Not surprisingly, black deaf people were affected by the same discrimination of the segregation era that affected black hearing people and the same social isolation and marginalization due to race that contributed to the development and maintenance of African-American English (AAE). Racial segregation is the influential geographic and social factor in the formation of Black ASL which is an African-American variety of ASL. Schools for Black deaf children certainly met these conditions of the geographic and social factors that include the isolation of one community from another; physical and political boundaries; and separation based on social identities. Separate schools, as well as so-called 'Colored Departments' of White schools, were established in southern and border states. Sometimes, the 'Colored Department' was on the same campus as the White school (e.g. Kansas, Missouri), but in other states, these departments were physically separated (e.g. Georgia, Mississippi) (Baynton, 1996).

Following the founding of the American School for the Deaf in Hartford, Connecticut in 1817 that occurred before the U.S. Civil War, more schools were established in northern states such as New York, Pennsylvania, and Ohio and these schools had small Black populations. After the Civil War, the 'separate but equal' residential schools for Black Deaf students slowly began to emerge in a large number of states in the South (Gannon, 1981). In the north, no separate schools for Blacks were established, but Baynton (1996) reported that the Clarke School in Northampton, Massachusetts, which favored oral instruction, in 1908 affirmed a policy of excluding Black students. However, some states did allow Black Deaf students to attend classes with their White Deaf counterparts. In seventeen Southern and border states, Deaf schools followed the patterns of segregation that characterized the public schools (McCaskill, Lucas, Bayley, & Hill, 2020). These schools were designed to house both Black Deaf and Black Blind students. The average number of years it took to establish the school for black deaf children after the establishment of the school for white deaf children is 33. In some states, however, the time was considerably longer: 61 years in Kentucky, 56 years in West Virginia, 70 years in Virginia, and 86 years in Louisiana. The average number of years of the existence of the Black schools before desegregation is 72.8. The striking exceptions are 101 years for Washington, DC and 98 years for North Carolina, but these schools were established much earlier than most schools for black deaf children.

Racial discrimination was present in local, state, and regional organizations in the deaf community as well. The National Association of the Deaf (NAD) was founded in 1887. At first the Association welcomed Black Deaf Americans. However, in 1925 at the Cleveland Conference they revoked the membership of the Black members, changing the bylaws to prohibit Black Deaf membership (Burch, 2002; Tabak, 2006). Black people had to wait until 1964 to gain the right to vote in the Association (Burch, 2002). Studies of Black people in the Chicago and Washington, DC Deaf communities in the 1980s reported that clubs and congregations were still segregated, and the races rarely intermingled (Aramburo, 1989; Higgins, 1987).

Desegregation occurred around the same period when the educational laws allowed deaf students to be educated in the mainstreamed setting. The apparent differences on the phonological, lexical, and discourse levels between the signing of black deaf people and of white deaf people had become less apparent over time since black deaf students began to be educated in the racially integrated settings and the horizontal transmission of Black ASL that was active at the racially segregated schools was forever interrupted. In the stories shared by the participants over the age of 55 in the Black ASL project, those who had integrated with white deaf children after some years at a segregated school often mentioned that they discontinued to use their signs with their white peers and perceived the signing of white deaf people positively than they did with their own signing (McCaskill et al., 2020). Even though segregation is no longer legally sanctioned, the U.S. communities are still socially segregated and this remains a reason for the degree of difference in the signing of black and white deaf people.

6 Sign Language as a Form of Empowerment for Deaf People

Sign languages had existed long before the Milan Congress where the majority of the educators who were the proponents of the oral method voted to ban sign languages from school premises. The deaf school staff was eventually dismissed from the schools and their positions were replaced by hearing teachers who taught speech (Baynton, 1996). In schools, the majority of education of the deaf students was dedicated to speaking as normal as possible. If the students failed with the oral method approach, they were deemed 'oral failures' and they would be sent to schools that used signs, but they were already past their prime in acquiring a language at the optimal level. This resulted in a possibly critical and long-lasting consequence for their language, social, and cognitive development. In spite of this, oralism continued to be pervasive and the validity and benefits of sign language as a language of instruction continued to be undermined.

Until the early 1960s, the sign language that was used in America since 1817 was simply called 'the sign language' (Padden & Humphries, 2005). It finally received a name in 1965 when William C. Stokoe, Carl Croneberg, and Dorothy Casterline published the seminal linguistic analysis of what they called American Sign Language (ASL) (Liddell, 2003). Linguistic work on ASL and the new official name of the language should have been a moment of celebration for the American Deaf community because it validated the linguistic status of ASL, but instead it was a moment of anxiety and anger (Liddell, 2003; Padden & Humphries, 2005). Anxiety emerged because it was a struggle for the community to understand ASL as more than just a way to communicate with hands and eyes and equate its linguistic status with that of English that had been long held as standard. Anger arose because the belief about ASL as an imperfect system was challenged and Stokoe was attacked by people inside and outside of the American Deaf community out of anxiety about the proclamation of ASL as a valid linguistic system and its role as a medium of instruction in the education systems for deaf children (Padden & Humphries, 2005).

But somehow, the seminal analysis of ASL has grown into the respectable field of linguistics and its branches, interpreting, Deaf Studies, and more, with dedicated and reputable professionals studying sign languages and its respective cultures. There are active research projects at universities and centers throughout the world: Visual Language and Visual Learning (VL2), a National Science Foundation supported science center of learning at Gallaudet University in Washington DC; the Brain and Language Laboratory for Neuroimaging at Gallaudet University; the Laboratory for Language & Cognitive Neuroscience at the San Diego State University in California; the Deafness Cognition and Language (DCAL) Research Centre at the University College London in the United Kingdom; the National Research Council (Consiglio Nazionale delle Ricerche) in Rome, Italy; the Institute of German Sign Language and Communication of the Deaf at the University of Hamburg in Germany; the Auslan (Australian Sign Language) Corpus Project at La Trobe University in Melbourne, Australia; and there are more to add to the list. With the expanding research literature on sign languages, the body of evidence of linguistic and cognitive advantages continues to grow and the validity of sign language as a language has become less questionable. Yet, audism is a global issue that continues to be a major problem for deaf people in education, employment, medicine, politics, and even family. Speech and hearing continue to be the rule.

Recently as of 2016, a deaf male in the U.S. has gained fame as a winner of the 22nd cycle of the America's Next Top Model and the 22nd season of Dancing with the Stars. His name is Nyle DiMarco. He is not the first deaf contestant to appear on a reality TV competition. There have been other deaf reality TV contestants before him and there is a long history of deaf actors and entertainers who have used sign language on TV in the U.S. and abroad, but what is special about DiMarco is his activism and the movement he espouses. He is a 4th generation in a deaf family who uses sign language. He graduated from Gallaudet University with a degree in math education. He uses his fame and his camera time as a platform to send messages about language deprivation that deaf children are experiencing with the omission of sign language. He promotes his own foundation, Nyle DiMarco Foundation, as a philanthropic resource for individuals, organizations, and institutions to empower the Deaf communities and to facilitate access to research-based information about early language acquisition and bilingual approach for deaf children. He also lends his fame and support to the national campaign, LEAD-K, with the goal to end the epidemic of language deprivation by promoting the use of ASL as well as English as a basic human right for deaf children before kindergarten. DiMarco has defied the general pre-conception of deaf people as the Deaf winner of the model and dance competitions in which he has no prior training or professional experience. He mentioned in the interview published as a news article that he, as a young child, stopped attending speech therapy because he felt it was taking his time away from education. DiMarco has done all of these in the public eye. The sign language movement had been steadily building before he entered as a contestant in America's Next Top Model, but his sudden fame draws the national spotlight to the issues of deaf education and language deprivation rarely noticed by the public, to the disappointment of critics who are supportive of oral-only approach with hearing assistive devices and auditory verbal therapy. Through it all, the deaf communities' resistance against oppression is what fuels the stubborn existence of sign languages as long as there is a basic human need for them.

References

Ammons, D. K. (2009). International committee of sports for the Deaf and deaflympics. In D. F. Moores & M. S. Miller (Eds.), *Deaf people around the world: Educational and social perspectives* (pp. 368–373). Washington, D.C.: Gallaudet University Press.

Aramburo, A. (1989). Sociolinguistic aspects of the Black Deaf community. In C. Lucas (Ed.), *The sociolinguistics of the Deaf community* (pp. 103–22). New York, NY: Academic Press.

Bauman, H.-D. L. (2004). Audism: Exploring the metaphysics of oppression. *Journal of Deaf Studies and Deaf Education, 9*(2), 239–246.

Bauman, H.-D. L., & Murray, J. J. (2014). Deaf gain: An introduction. In H.-D. L. Bauman & J. J. Murray (Eds.), *Deaf gain: Raising the stakes for human diversity* (pp. XV–XLII). Minneapolis, MN: University of Minnesota Press.

Baynton, D. C. (1996). *Forbidden signs: American culture and the campaign against sign language*. Chicago, IL: University of Chicago Press.

Bragg, L. (1997). Visual-kinetic communication in Europe before 1600: A survey of sign lexicons and finger alphabets prior to the rise of deaf education. *Journal of Deaf Studies and Deaf Education, 2*(1), 1–25.

Burch, S. (2002). *Signs of resistance: American Deaf cultural history 1900–1942*. New York, NY: New York University Press.

Collins, S., & Petronio, K. (1998). What happens in tactile ASL? In C. Lucas (Ed.), *Sociolinguistics in Deaf communities, vol. 4: Pinky extension and eye gaze: Language use in Deaf communities* (pp. 18–37). Washington, D.C.: Gallaudet University. Press

Fenlon, J., & Wilkinson, E. (2015). Sign languages in the world. In A. C. Schembri & C. Lucas (Eds.), *Sociolinguistics and Deaf communities* (pp. 5–28). Cambridge, UK: Cambridge University Press.

Gallaudet Research Institute. (2011). *Regional and national summary report of data from the 2009–2010 Annual Survey of Deaf and Hard of Hearing Children and Youth.* Washington, D.C.: GRI.

Geraci, C., Battaglia, K., Cardinaletti, A., Cecchetto, C., Donati, C., Giudice, S., & Mereghetti, E. (2011). The LIS corpus project: A discussion of sociolinguistic variation in the lexicon. *Sign Language Studies, 11*(4), 528–574.

Groce, S. (1985). *Everyone here spoke sign language: Hereditary deafness on Martha's Vineyard.* Cambridge, MA: Harvard University Press.

Guarinello, A. C., Santana, A. P., Berberian, A. P., & Massi, G. A. (2009). Deafness: Educational-historical aspects in the Brazilian context. In D. F. Moores & M. S. Miller (Eds.), *Deaf people around the world: Educational and social perspectives* (pp. 271–283). Washington, D.C.: Gallaudet University Press.

Higgins, P. (1987). *Outsiders in a hearing world: A sociology of deafness*. Beverly Hills, CA: Sage.

Humphries, T. (1975). *Audism: The making of a word* [Unpublished essay].

Ilabor, E. (2010). *Dr. Andrew Jackson Foster: The most courageous educator and the most visionary missionary to deaf Africans*. Ibadan, Nigeria: Christian Mission for the Deaf.

Jankowski, K. (1997). *Deaf empowerment: Emergence, struggle, and rhetoric*. Washington, D.C.: Gallaudet University Press.

Johnston, T. A. (2004). W(h)ither the Deaf community? Population, genetics, and the future of Australian Sign Language. *American Annals of the Deaf, 148*(5), 358–375.

Kiyaga, N. B., & Moores, D. F. (2009). Deafness in Sub-Saharan Africa. In D. F. Moores and M. S. Miller (Eds.), *Deaf people around the world: Educational and social perspectives* (pp. 145–154). Washington, D.C.: Gallaudet University Press.

Kusters, A. (2024). More than signs: International Sign as distributed practice. *Signs and Society, 12*(1), 37–57. https://doi.org/10.1086/728113

Ladd, P. (2003). *Understanding Deaf culture: In search of Deafhood.* Clevedon, UK: Multilingual Matters Ltd.

Lane, H. L. (2002). Do deaf people have a disability? *Sign Language Studies, 2*(4), 356–379.

Lane, H. L., Hoffmeister, R., & B. Bahan. (1996). *A Journey into the Deaf World.* San Diego, CA: DawnSignPress.

Leeson, L., & Saeed, J. I. (2012). *Irish Sign Language*. Edinburgh, UK: Edinburgh University Press.

Leigh, I. (2009). *A lens on Deaf identities*. Oxford, UK: Oxford University Press.

Lewis, M. P., Simons, G. F., & Fennig, Ch. D. (Eds.). (2016). *Ethnologue: Languages of the world (19th ed.)*. Dallas, TX: SIL International. http://www.ethnologue.com

Liddell, S. (2003). *Grammar, gesture, and meaning in American Sign Language*. Cambridge, UK: Cambridge University Press.

Lucas, C., Bayley, R., & Valli, C. (2001). *Sociolinguistic variation in American Sign Language*. Washington, D.C.: Gallaudet University Press.

Mauldin, L. (2015). *Made to hear: Cochlear implants and raising deaf children*. Minneapolis, MN: University of Minnesota Press.

McCaskill, C., Lucas, C., Bayley, R., & Hill, J. (2020). *The hidden treasure of Black ASL: Its history and structure*. Washington, D.C.: Gallaudet University Press.

McKee, D., McKee, R., & Major, G. (2011). Numeral variation in New Zealand Sign Language. *Sign Language Studies, 12*(1), 72–160.

McKee, R., & McKee, D. (2011). Old signs, new signs, whose signs? Sociolinguistic variation in the NZSL lexicon. *Sign Language Studies, 11*(4), 485–528.

Mesch, J. (2010). Perspectives on the concept and definition of international sign. *Digitala Vetenskapliga Arkivet*. http://www.diva-portal.org/smash/get/diva2:683050/FULLTEXT01.pdf

Mitchell, R. E., & Karchmer, M. A. (2004). When parents are deaf versus hard of hearing: Patterns of sign use and school placement of deaf and hard-of-hearing children. *Journal of Deaf Studies and Deaf Education, 9*(2), 133–152.

Mitchell, R. E., & Karchmer, M. A. (2005). Parent hearing status and signing among deaf and hard of hearing students. *Sign Language Studies, 5*(2), 231–244.

Mitchell, R. E., Young, T. A., Bachleda, B., & Karchmer, M. A. (2006). How many people use ASL in the United States?: Why estimates need updating. *Sign Language Studies, 6*(3), 306–335.

Monaghan, L. (2003). A world's eye view: Deaf cultures in global perspective. In L. Monaghan, C. Schmaling, K. Nakamura & G. H. Turner (Eds.), *Many ways to be Deaf: International variation in Deaf communities* (pp. 1–24). Washington, MN: Gallaudet University Press.

Padden, C. (2011). Sign language geography. In G. Mathur & D. J. Napoli (Eds.), *Deaf around the world: The impact of language* (pp. 19–37). Oxford, UK: Oxford University Press.

Padden, C., & Gunsauls, D. C. (2003). How the alphabet came to be used in a sign language. *Sign Language Studies, 4*(1), 10–33.

Padden, C., & Humphries, T. (2005). *Inside Deaf culture*. Cambridge, MA: Harvard University Press.

Petitto, L. A. (2000). The acquisition of natural signed languages: Lessons in the nature of human language and its biological foundations. In C. Chamberlain, J. P. Morford & R. I. Mayberry (Eds.), *Language acquisition by eye* (pp. 41–50). Mahwah, NJ: Lawrence Erlbaum Associates.

Petitto, L. A. (2014). Three revolutions: Language, culture, and biology. In H.-D. L. Bauman & J. J. Murray (Eds.), *Deaf gain: Raising the stakes for human diversity* (pp. 65–76). Minneapolis, MN: University of Minnesota Press.

Plann, S. (1997). *A silent minority: Deaf education in Spain, 1550–1835*. Berkeley, CA: University of California Press.

Pray, J. L., & Jordan, I. K. (2010). The deaf community and culture at a crossroads: Issues and challenges. *Journal of Social Work and Disability Rehabilitation, 9*(2), 168–193.

Reagan, T. G. (2010). *Language policy and planning for sign languages*. Washington, D.C.: Gallaudet University Press.

Rosen, R. (2009). The World Federation of the Deaf. In D. F. Moores and M. S. Miller (Eds.), *Deaf people around the world: Educational and social perspectives* (pp. 374–391). Washington, D.C.: Gallaudet University Press.

Rosenstock, R. (2008). The role of iconicity in international sign. *Sign Language Studies, 8*(2), 131–159.

Schembri, A. (2010). Documenting sign languages. In P. Austin (Ed.), *Language documentation and description* (pp. 105–143). London, UK: School of African and Oriental Studies.

Stokoe, W., Casterline, D. C., & Croneberg, C. G. (1965). *A dictionary of American SignLanguage on linguistic principles.* Silver Spring, MD: Gallaudet College Press.

Sutton-Spence, R. (2003). British manual alphabets in the education of Deaf people since the 17th Century. In L. Monaghan, C. Schmaling, K. Nakamura & G. H. Turner (Eds.), *Many ways to be Deaf: International variation in Deaf communities* (pp. 25–48). Washington, D.C.: Gallaudet University Press.

Tabak, J. (2006). *Significant gestures: A history of American Sign Language*. Westport, CT: Praeger.

Tamene, E. H. (2016). Language use in Ethiopian Sign Language. *Sign Language Studies, 16*(3), 307–329.

U.S. Census Bureau. (2017). U.S. & world population clocks. http://www.census.gov/main/www/popclock.html

Woll, B., Sutton-Spence, R., & Elton, F. (2001). Multilingualism: The global approach to sign languages. In C. Lucas (Ed.), *The sociolinguistics of sign languages* (pp. 8–32). Cambridge, UK: Cambridge University Press.

World Federation of the Deaf. (2017). *Who we are.* https://wfdeaf.org/who-we-are/

Wolfram, W., & Schilling-Estes, N. (2006). *American English* (2nd ed.). Oxford, UK: Blackwell Publishing.

CHAPTER 3

Black and Deaf in the United States

Call for Research Exploring Intersecting Identities

Lindsay M. Dunn and Kari F. Cooke

Abstract

This chapter evaluates the growing genre of Black Deaf identities. It is argued that Black Deaf people, far from being monolithic, are replete with multiple intersections of identities that are seldom explored in consideration with one another. Additionally, examples of experiences of racialized audism and racism in deaf communities highlight the need to expand on the literature regarding Black Deaf people in the United States. Finally, it is argued that studies of deafness, American cultures, and Black culture are more likely to tell a true story if they are grounded in an inclusive lens, which utilizes multiple standpoints that take into account the intersections of race, ethnicity, class, gender, sexuality, and other systems of domination and subordination.

Keywords

Black Deaf identities – intersectionality – audism – racism – ethnicity – Pan-Africanism – disidentification – Black Diaspora – race – Black American Sign Language (BASL)

1 Forgotten Legacies

Although neglected by scholars and academics, Black Deaf Americans have filled in the gaps in their own ways to memorialize their experiences growing up Black and Deaf. Mary Herring Wright's memoirs, *Sounds Like Home* and *Far from Home* offer perhaps the first ever widely published account of growing up Black and Deaf during and after World War II. It also offers one of the very first in-depth accounts of life at a school for Black deaf in the south that has ever been published. Wright, an alumnus of the North Carolina School for Coloured Deaf and Blind in Raleigh, North Carolina, is one of several alumni of this school who went on to live fulfilling and successful lives before desegregation shut down the schools for Black Deaf and Blind children. Another one of the most famous

 | DOI:10.1163/9789004692299_004

alumni of the North Carolina school was a Black Deaf man, Roger Demosthenes O'Kelly who completed the entire law school curriculum in one year at the oldest HBCU, Shaw University. He was admitted into Yale University School of Law, graduating in 1912 and going on to have a highly successful law practice. It is worth noting that O'Kelly used the manual method of communication, Black American Sign Language (BASL) also known as the Raleigh Method (McCaskill, Lucas, Hill, & Bayley, 2011). These stories are but two examples of the ways Black Deaf people in the U.S. have endeavoured to not only continue their stories, but to showcase Black Deaf people as a crucial community worthy of scholarship. This essay will explore the Black Deaf world in the U.S., with several of its complexities to offer a more inclusive description of the varied Deaf experience in America, highlighting needed areas of scholarship.

2 Who Are Black Deaf People in the United States?

Pan-Africanism thrives within the Black Deaf communities just as it does within the global Black world. Among Black Deaf Americans are the African-Americans with roots from the slaves who were forced into building this country's economy, along with descendants of African-Americans born of free people in the U.S. Some Black Deaf people in America are first generation that come from colonized nations, bringing with them the added layer of remnants of neo-colonialism in their identities. Others are now several generations in this country with their own legacies of slavery, such as those from South America and the Caribbean. These first-/second- generation immigrants bring the sign language of their home nations and integrate it with American Sign Language (ASL) to create a sign language unique in its use among those with permission to inhabit the spaces within their particular ethnic enclaves. ASL is a living language and hence is flexible enough to accommodate the various cultures that use the language. In so doing, Black Deaf Americans enrich both U.S. Deaf culture along with the greater hearing world in the U.S.

While 'race' is a social construct that refers to a person's physical appearance, such as skin color, hair color, etc., 'ethnicity' refers to cultural factors such as nationality, ancestry, language, and beliefs (Nagel, 2003). Being deaf neither excludes us nor denies Black Deaf people from participating in cultural traditions and rituals such as marriage, birth of a child, and death in the family or community. In the United States Blackness renders ethnicity invisible to the mainstream culture (Nagel, 2003), but does not fully describe the ethnic self-identification that informs the individual's experience. Within the greater (hearing) socio-cultural enclaves are 'elders' who perform the common traditions that are typical of the ethnic enclaves of origin. These elders are also keepers of histories that connect the ethnic culture to the mainstream one and in some cases also serve as community leaders. Black Deaf elders perform the same responsibilities within the deaf tribal/ethnic communities in the United States. The Black Deaf existence and persistence within these two worlds should pique the interest of social scientists and encourage further research.

Those who migrated to the United States connect with hearing ethnic peers who are family, or by blood or fictive kinship with roots in the countries, villages and towns of origin. Like others within the Deaf Community in the United States, they live with varying degrees of hearing loss and varying proficiency in native spoken/written languages or sign language. However, these Black Deaf immigrants may not necessarily have as strong a need to perceive their hearing brethren as the binary opposite of their deaf selves. In the Black Diaspora the cultural marker of forming kinship despite forced separation of family members during slavery, or lack of blood relations among modern immigrants, is a powerful bond that binds them to a greater Pan-African solidarity (Dill, 1998). A strong example of this kinship is the effect of slavery in America, wherein the slave-owners forced families to separate and be sold off as property; slaves developed new families with those in their new homes (Dill, 1998). Some escaped slaves and free slaves intermarried with Indigenous men and women, along with widespread rape by slave masters and overseers (Jennings, 1990), and the mutual intimacies across racial lines (Jennings, 1990) this added to the ethnic histories of the innately multiethnic community that is Black, and whose experience criss-crosses the breadth and width of humanity. In most major cities within the United States today, Black neighbourhoods reflect this rich intersection of identities (Lee & Bean, 2004). Most Black Deaf people in the U.S. are comfortable in these neighbourhoods that offer them the connectedness, sense of belonging and freedom to feel safe in exploring the deaf and hearing world outside their ethno-cultural milieu. It also provides a 'home base' to seek refuge in when the Euro-dominant Deaf and Hearing worlds conspire to threaten and diminish their humanity.

Black Deaf people do not deny the existence of audism within their hearing ethnic communities. However, they are less inclined to reject these communities in favour of total immersion in the White Deaf world where racism is a far more painful experience for most than audism. This act of selecting/prioritizing certain identity markers from the mainstream white deaf community, while redefining what it means to be deaf in America is an example of disidentification (Muñoz, 1999). The most commonly-experienced barriers faced by members of the Black Deaf community are racism and audism. This can be exemplified by the experience of Dr. Glenn Anderson, Ph.D. who from humble beginnings in the South Side of Chicago went on to become the first Deaf African-American to earn a doctorate degree and later to become Chair of the Gallaudet University Board of Trustees (Anderson & Watson, 1993). In 2006 Dr. Anderson was a candidate for the Presidency of Gallaudet University; incredibly and to the stunned dismay of the Black Deaf community, he was not selected among the finalists. This stunned reaction was from the fact that among the three white finalists, one of them did not even possess an earned doctorate degree at the time of candidacy and did not have the higher education administration experience needed for such a position. This rejection and simultaneous elevation of comparative mediocrity sent a clear message to the Black Deaf community: despite the many gains in race relations in America, a Black Deaf candidate—even with the privilege of male gender—is not qualified enough to be a candidate for the presidency of Gallaudet University, whether or not he may have superior credentials than the competition. The Black Deaf community rallied in objection to the Gallaudet decision and made a strong case that the flaw in the selection process was due to blatant racism. This was repeatedly denied by the White deaf community, which persisted in their assessment that the selection process was fair and that it should be allowed to take its course without acknowledging or addressing the role of white privilege/supremacy in the process.

This remains among one of the most powerful symbols of blatant racism within the Deaf community in the United States. Black Deaf people continue to maintain connections as a community with links that reach into various intercultural spaces. Inter-ethnic and interracial marriage takes place within Black Deaf communities, making it a microcosm of the interconnections resulting from globalization and transnational movements of people. 'Transnationalism' refers to the socio-cultural concept wherein the importance of social remittances which provide a distinct form of social capital between migrants living abroad and those who remain at home are elevated (Levitt, 2001). With these inter-relationships comes the integration of cultures, spoken languages, and signed languages. A significant number of people within the Black Deaf community are thus bilingual/multilingual, given that they reside in the United States while still sharing a connection to their cultures of origin. Black deaf people make frequent trips to their native countries to maintain family connections and connections to the deaf communities of their nations of origin. This in turn maintains a continued proficiency in both the native signed languages and their adopted American Sign Language. The role of language and cultural transitioning enriches the diversity within the Black Deaf community of the United States.

Andrew Foster, a deaf African-American from Alabama who attended the Alabama School for Coloured Deaf and Blind, was the first Black deaf person to graduate from Gallaudet University in 1954 (going on to receive an honorary doctorate from Gallaudet University in 1970). Foster went on to found over 30 schools for the deaf in 13 West and Central African countries (Gannon, 1981). His work in West and Central Africa was so far reaching in its impact on African deaf lives that he is considered the "Father of African Deaf Education" (Gannon, 1981). While he indeed brought American Sign Language (ASL) to his schools, it is evident by the sign language used by alumni of his various schools in Africa that this ASL was subsequently 'localized' and adapted to reflect cultural realities in each country or region where a school was founded (Monaghan, Schmaling, & Nakamura, 2003). Many alums of these schools for the deaf founded by Andrew Foster have themselves gone on to graduate from Gallaudet, making the legacy of Dr. Foster come full circle.

Transnationalism and cross-cultural experiences will have strong repercussions in the educational settings for students of color. Lack of understanding of different cultural beliefs/perspectives may have potentially negative implications for Black Deaf youth in the K-12 grades given that schools for the deaf are made up of primarily White teachers (Nicolarakis, 2020). This in turn fails to acknowledge the fact that the students themselves reflect the 'browning of America' (Rodriguez, 2003). It becomes even more imperative that scholarship and research reflect this demographic reality within the Deaf community in the United States.

3 Navigating the Landmines of Racism and Audism in Creating Next Steps

Racism in Deaf communities and racialized audism in the hearing world at large are twin barriers confronting Black Deaf Americans on a regular basis. Dunn (2008) offers a glimpse into this experience of living with audism and racism in his chapter (Burden of Racism and Audism) in the book *Open Your Eyes, Deaf Studies Talking* (Bauman, 2008). While it is necessary that every deaf person of color will navigate these twin landmines individually and in their own unique way, it is difficult to imagine that the process is natural and without psychological implications, especially for Deaf people of color who must frequently navigate these –isms in unsafe spaces. There is scant literature describing the psychological implications of carrying multiple burdens on a daily basis. There is an abundance of literature that describes the burden of being Black in America, coined by DuBois as 'double consciousness' (DuBois, 1903). Additionally, there is an abundance of literature that describes the psychological condition of being Deaf in America. Literature from these lenses offers readers with insights into various spaces, but not revelations of the intersections. There remains much opportunity to study deaf people of color who carry these multiple experiences. Future scholarship can showcase the ways it informs Black Deaf people's views of women/gender-variant folks, as LGBTQ people, as members of religious communities, within Deaf Disabled/ DeafBlind experiences and identities, and more. The research can show how socio-economic status in society mitigates or exacerbates societal barriers, and determines positionality in both deaf and hearing worlds. We need to understand the irrational justification that accepts that a white deaf person with a Master's degree is considered better qualified for a leadership position at the university level than a Black deaf person with a doctorate degree.

So, what are some next steps, some concrete ways in which the deaf community in the United States can begin to explore retooling the system that impacts students of color the most: the educational system? Scholars such as Sass-Lehrer, Gerner de Garcia and Rovins (1995), Moores (1998), Christensen (2000), and others have long championed the urgency for educational curriculum transformation by including multiculturalism in both the education and counselling disciplines that will provide intensive training to professionals that frequently interact with students of color. However, the fact that the National Education Agenda, led by the Conference of Education Administrators Serving the Deaf (which serves administrators of schools for the deaf across the country), has brought together individuals and organizations and none of them are Black, is cause for concern. That was the same mistake made by the Commission on the Education of the Deaf (COED), which did not have a single Black person among the commissioners. Johnson (2003), Andrews, Leigh, and Weiner (2004), Fernandes and Myers (2010), and Pray and Jordan (2010) have joined many others over the years in making a more recent case for a multicultural lens in training, research, and discourses on the deaf culture in America. These researchers have repeatedly argued that discourses on the deaf experience in America are incomplete without a multicultural lens.

The Black church has long been a major source for recruiting Black interpreters adept at both ASL and BASL given the proliferation of 'deaf ministries' in many Black churches. Historically, HBCUs supplied the teachers, administrators and other professionals who provided education and social services to Black deaf people prior to integration of schools for the deaf. These resources need to be renewed and tapped sufficiently to increase the number of Black students in interpreter, teacher, and social services training/education programs around the nation. Actively increasing the ranks of Black hearing, deaf and hard-of-hearing professionals in the educational and service fields will enhance the availability of role models and provide unique perspectives to problem-solving and policy-forming processes. It has the potential to offer valuable solutions to efforts needed to remove the burden of racism and audism on Black deaf people. Black deaf and hard-of-hearing professionals are familiar with the painful experiences of audism within hearing families, ethnic enclaves, and in the general audio-dominant world (Valentine, 1996). Experiences can be replete with the taunting from peers and relatives who make fun of being deaf by mimicking sign language as gang signs. In some cases Black Deaf people have real experience of being stabbed or shot at for signing on the streets in people neighbourhoods where gang members mistake ASL for gang signs. There have been numerous stories of Black Deaf people being subjected to religious rituals or special prayer sessions designed to exorcise evil spirits that are assumed to cause deafness. In some cases, Deaf people of color come from communities and towns where people believe that deafness is a result of a familial curse. Yet, using the lens of Afrofuturism, communities can evolve, as there is also the converse knowledge that in other cultures, there are communities and villages where deafness is seen in more positive ways and a Deaf child is seen as a blessing. There are spaces where Deaf and hearing people are conversant in sign language and Deaf people are not excluded from the routine activities within their communities. While more and more Black Deaf people are obtaining education, there remain millions of Deaf children within Africa and some of its diaspora who have never seen the inside of a school. There is experiential knowledge that Black Deaf and hard-of-hearing professionals can bring with them in the school settings, and it is important to consider this when recruiting and hiring professional staff in institutions and agencies. As the deaf community in the United States moves forward, we must consider the scholarship on the intersectionalities of Black deaf identities and experiences of paramount urgency and importance.

4 Conclusion: There Is Work to Do

In conclusion, Black deaf communities in the United States remain aware of the history and existence of audism within ethnic communities and are similarly not naïve to imagine a space of safety from racism among mainstream deaf communities; and this manifests itself at various intersections, which makes the lack of research even more appalling. Literature on Deaf people has cited the strong desire among Deaf people to marry Deaf and hopefully have Deaf offspring (McCaskill, Lucas, Hill, & Bayley, 2011). There is no specific study that explores if the same sentiment exists among Black Deaf people. There is no research that investigates whether or not large percentages of Black parents of Deaf children have a willingness to relocate to a state school for the deaf that might offer their child a better education. In fact, there has been little research that evaluates whether a Black Deaf child would receive an education equal to a White Deaf child at a school for the deaf. The lack of culturally inclusive research is staggering, and in the field of education, it is needed now more than ever.

African-Americans represent only 7% of the teaching faculty[1] and there have been only two Black deaf persons (the late Dr. Reginald Redding and Ernest Garrett III) who served as Superintendents of a school for the deaf. Albert Couthen and Dr. Angela McCaskill are the only deaf African-Americans who have served as Principals of schools for the deaf (Mississippi School for the Deaf and the Model Senior Secondary School for the Deaf, respectively). At the 2015 National Black Deaf Advocates, Inc. conference in Louisville, Kentucky, a community forum, featuring superintendents of schools for the deaf, was held to discuss concerns that lack of representation in administration and in the classrooms hinders the success of Black deaf children. An annual meeting of superintendents and communities of color within the Deaf world should be held to discuss and address these glaring disparities in the academic achievement of Deaf children.

Navigating this world is brutally difficult for anyone, more so for Black Deaf people. However, Black Deaf communities are communities of perseverance, and if their stories are not told in research projects, they nevertheless thrive and are passed on through productions in fine arts, performance and poetry. There are spaces to congregate on the local, regional and national levels through personal friendships and organization affiliations. The African Diaspora of Deaf people in the United States is a community that has brought together the vibrant worlds of Africa, the Caribbean and Latin America and fused it into the culture of those whose ancestors were forced into slavery in this country. Deaf Studies, Black Studies, American Studies and more cannot be complete until the added knowledge of Black Deaf peoples' history and future is explored and researched. Until then, Black Deaf people will always be other-ized, always be strangers. The experience of Black and Deaf is a vibrant multiethnic, multilingual, and multicultural world of people whose cosmopolitanism connects the people of the world in intricate intersections of identities, one that criss-crosses the Deaf and Hearing worlds.

Note

1 http://www.deafed.net/diversity/why_diversity.htm

References

Ahmad, W., Darr, A., Jones, L., & Gohan, N. (1998). *Deafness and ethnicity: Services, policy and politics.* Bristol, UK: The Policy Press.

Anderson, G. B., & Grace, C. A. (1991). The black deaf adolescent: An underserved minority. *The Volta Review*, 73–86.

Anderson, G., & Watson, D. (1993). The Black deaf experience: Excellence and equity. *Selected proceedings of the National Black Deaf Experience: Excellence and equity conference.* Little Rock, AR: Rehabilitation Research and Training Center for Persons who are Deaf or Hard of Hearing. University of Arkansas.

Andrews, J. F., Leigh, I. W., & Weiner, M. T. (2004). *Deaf people: Evolving perspectives from psychology, education and sociology.* Boston, MA: Pearson Education.

Appiah, K. A. (2006). *Cosmopolitanism: Ethics in a world of strangers (Issues of our time).* New York, NY: Norton & Co.

Aramburo, A. (1989). Sociolinguistic aspects of the Black Deaf community. In C. Lucas (Ed.), *The sociolinguistics of the Deaf community* (pp. 103–119). San Diego, CA: Academic Press.

Askar, Y. (2013, November 12). Addressing the growing demand for sign language interpreters. *University of Arizona News.*

Bauman, H.-D. L. (Ed.). (2008). *Open your eyes. Deaf studies talking.* Minneapolis, MN: University of Minnesota Press.

Bauman, H.-D. L. (2009). Postscript: Gallaudet protests of 2006 and the myths of in/exclusion. *Sign Language Studies, 10*(1), 90–104.

Brooks, D. K. (1996). In search of self: Experiences of a postlingually deaf African-American. In I. Parasnis (Ed.), *Cultural and language diversity and the Deaf experience* (pp. 246–257). New York, NY: Cambridge University Press.

Brown, M. C. (2013). *On the beat of truth: A hearing daughter's stories of her Black Deaf parents.* Washington, D.C.: Gallaudet University Press.

Chibbaro, L. J. (2012, October 11). Md. marriage equality group opposes suspension of Gallaudet administrator. *Washington Blade.*

Christensen, K. M. (Ed.). (2000). *Deaf plus: A multicultural perspective.* San Diego, CA: DawnSign Press.

Christensen, K. M., & Delgado, G. L. (Eds.). (1993). *Multicultural issues in deafness.* New York, NY: Longman Publishing Company.

Clancy, M. (2013, April 5). *Women's role in DPN explored.* Gallaudet University News. https://www.gallaudet.edu/news/dpn_women_role_explored.html

Coalition of Students of Color (CoSC). (2006, November 17). *CoSC members respond to FSSA open letter.* Gallaudet University Faculty, Students, Staff and Alumni Association (GUFSSA). http://bit.ly/1021OXN

Cohen, O. P. (1997). Giving all children a chance: Advantages of an antiracist approach to the education of deaf children. *American Annals of the Deaf, 142*(2), 80–82.

Dill, B. T. (1998). Fictive kin, paper sons, compadrazgo: Women of color and the struggle for family survival. In K. V. Hansen & A. I. Garey (Eds.), *Families in the U.S.: Kinship and domestic politics* (pp. 431–445). Philadelphia, PA: Temple University Press.

DuBois, W. E. (1903). *The souls of black folk.* Chicago, IL: A.C. McClurg & Co.

Dunn, L. (2008). Burden of racism and audism. In H.-D. L. Bauman (Ed.), *Open your eyes. Deaf studies talking* (pp. 235–250). Minneapolis, MN: University of Minnesota Press.

Dunn, L. (1994). Education, culture and community: The Black Deaf experience. In M. D. Garretson (Ed.), *Deafness: Life & culture: A deaf American monograph* (pp. 37–41). Silver Spring, MD: National Association of the Deaf.

Erting, C., Johnson, R., & Smith, D. (Eds.). (1994). *The Deaf way; Perspectives from an international conference on Deaf culture.* Washington, D.C.: Gallaudet University Press.

Fernandes, J., & Myers, S. (2010). Inclusive deaf studies: Barriers and pathways. *Journal of Deaf Studies & Deaf Education, 15*(1), 3–16.

Figueroa-Ruiz, E. (2014, March 15). *Role of intersectionality in privilege* [Interview]. (K. Cooke, Interviewer).

Figueroa-Ruiz, E., & Holcomb, T. (2013, Fall). Why intersectionality matters. *National Association of the Deaf Magazine*, 15–19.

Gannon, J. (1981). *Deaf heritage: A narrative history of Deaf America.* Silver Spring, MD: National Association of the Deaf.

Harrington, T. (2006, October). *Library guides: Deaf African and African-American slaves.* Gallaudet University Library: http://libguides.gallaudet.edu/content.php?pid=352126&sid=2880871

Jennings, T. (1990). "Us colored women had to go through a plenty": Sexual exploitation of African-American slave women. *Journal of Women's History, 1*(3), 45–74.

Johnson, H. A. (2003). *U.S. deaf education teacher preparation programs: A look at the present and a vision for the future* (COPSSE *Document No.* IB-*9*). Gainesville, FL: University of Florida, Center on Personnel Studies in Special Education.

Johnson, J. H. (1971). Ebony pictorial history of Black America. Chicago, IL: Johnson Publishing Co.

Kendell, K. (2005). Race, same-sex marriage, and white privilege: The problem with civil rights analogies. *Yale Journal of Law and Feminism, 17*, 133.

Khanna, N. (2010). "If you're half black, you're just black": Reflected appraisals and the persistence of the one-drop rule. *The Sociological Quarterly, 51*(1), 96–121.

Kiyaga, N., & Moores, D. (2003). Deafness in Sub-Saharan Africa. *American Annals of the Deaf, 148*(1), 18–24.

Kusters, A. (2012). Adamarobe: A demographic, sociolinguistic and sociocultural profile. In U. Zeshan (Ed.), *Village Sign Languages: Anthropological and linguistic insights* (pp. 347–351). Berlin: De Gruyter.

Lamelle, S., & Kelley, R. D. (1994). *Imagining home: Class, culture and nationalism in the African diaspora.* London, UK: Verso Books.

Lee, J., & Bean, F. D. (2004). America's changing color lines: Immigration, race/ethnicity, and multiracial identification. *Annual Review of Sociology, 30*, 221–242.

Levitt, P. (2001). *The transnational villagers.* Berkeley, CA: University of California Press.

Lomicky, C. S., & Hogg, N. M. (2010). Computer-mediated communication and protest: An examination of social movement activities at Gallaudet, a university for the Deaf. *Information, Communication & Society, 13*(5), 674–695.

Maxwell, M., & Smith-Todd, S. (1986). Black sign language and school integration in Texas. *Language in Society, 15*(1), 81–94.

McCaskill, C., Lucas, C., Hill, J., & Bayley, R. (2011). *The hidden treasure of Black ASL: Its history and structure.* Washington, D.C.: Gallaudet University Press.

McConnell, L. (1993, Spring). Embracing Diversity. *Gallaudet Today*, 18–20.

Miles, M. (2005). *Deaf people living and communicating in African histories, c. 960s – 1960s.* Independent Living Institute (ILI). https://www.independentliving.org/docs7/miles2005a.html

Monaghan, L., Schmaling, C., & Nakamura, K. (Eds.). (2003). *Many ways to be Deaf: International variation in Deaf communities.* Washington, D.C.: Gallaudet University Press.

Moores, D. F. (1998). Race, ethnicity, and minority status. *American Annals of the Deaf, 143*(4), 291–292.

Muñoz, J. E. (1999). *Disidentifications: Queers of color and the performance of politics (Cultural Studies of the Americas).* Minneapolis, MN: University of Minnesota Press.

Nagel, J. (2003). *Race, ethnicity, and sexuality. Intimate intersections, forbidden frontiers.* New York, NY: Oxford University Press.

Ndurumo, M. (2003). Where eagles dare: The legacy of Dr. Andrew Foster. *African Annals of the Deaf, 1*(1), 1–2.

Nicolarakis, O. D. (2020). *An examination of the writing strategies used by deaf and hearing adults: Similarities and differences in cognitive, linguistic and conventional components* [Unpublished doctoral dissertation]. Teachers College, Columbia University. New York, NY.

Nuckols, B. (2012, October 19). Gallaudet University roiled by Angela McCaskill gay marriage petition controversy. *Huffington Post.*

Nussbaum, M. C. (1994, October 1). Patriotism and cosmopolitanism. *Boston Review.* http://bostonreview.net/martha-nussbaum-patriotism-and-cosmopolitanism

Padden, C., & Humphreys, T. (2005). *Inside Deaf culture.* Cambridge, MA: Harvard University Press.

Pray, J. L., & Jordan, I. K. (2010). The deaf community and culture at a crossroads: Issues and challenges. *Journal of Social Work in Disability & Rehabilitation, 9*(2-3), 168–193.

Rodriguez, R. (2003). *Brown: The last discovery of America.* East Rutherford, NJ: Penguin Group USA.

Sass-Lehrer, M., Gerner de Garcia, B., & Rovins, M. (1995). Creating a multicultural school climate for deaf children and their families. *Perspectives in Education and Deafness, 14*(1), 1–6.

Smith, J. C. (1999). *Emancipation: The making of the Black lawyer, 1844–1944.* Philadelphia, PA: University of Pennsylvania Press.

Solomon, A. (2012). *Far from the tree: Parents, children and the search for identity.* New York, NY: Charles Scribner's Sons.

Valentine, V. (1996, January). Listening to deaf blacks: They want community access and acceptance. *Emerge*, 56–61.

Van Cleve, J. (1993). *Deaf history unveiled.* Washington, D.C.: Gallaudet University Press.

Warren, C. (2013). The utility of empathy for white female teachers' culturally responsive interactions with Black male students. *Interdisciplinary Journal of Teaching and Learning, 3*(3), 175–200.

Wright, M. H. (1999). *Sounds like home: Growing up black and deaf in the south.* Washington, D.C.: Gallaudet University Press.

Yep, G. A. (2003). The violence of heteronormativity in communication studies. *Journal of Homosexuality, 45*(2-4), 11–59.

CHAPTER 4

The Notion of Deaf People as Disabled and the Emergence of Deaf Culture in China

Junhui Yang

Abstract

This chapter explores the emergence of Deaf culture in China and the roles of the media and education in improving the social status of Deaf people. The longstanding association of Deaf people with disability is considered in relation to the struggle for the rights of the Chinese Deaf community, and attention is paid to the importance of government administration and disability organisations' support in all aspects of social inclusion. In addition, the relationship between the education of deaf children and societal attitudes towards deaf people are discussed and the vital role of the family in the well-being of the deaf child is highlighted. Through a case study of musical performance by deaf dancers, the chapter considers the role of the media in raising awareness of the language and cultural rights of Deaf people, and, finally, the gains and struggles for the rights of the Deaf community are explored in depth.

Keywords

Deaf culture – Chinese Sign Language – disability – China – deaf dance troupe – Deaf education – attitudes

1 Introduction

This chapter explores the emergence of Deaf culture in China and the roles of the media and education in improving the social status of deaf people. Traditionally, deaf people have been regarded as bearing a physical disability and this has led to paternalistic views of deaf people in accordance with the pathological perspective. China's commitment to protecting its vulnerable citizens is commendable and comes from a position of caring and goodwill, but this has unintentionally led to assumptions that all deaf people require care and support in order to function in daily life. Social care and employment policies

 | DOI:10.1163/9789004692299_005

are effective in many contexts but can lead to forms of oppression by reinforcing notions of disability. The longstanding association of deaf people with disability is considered in this chapter in relation to the struggle for the rights of the Chinese Deaf community, and attention is paid to the importance of government administration and disability organizations' support in all aspects of social inclusion. In addition, the relationship between the education of deaf children and societal attitudes towards deaf people is discussed and the vital role of the family in the well-being of the deaf child is highlighted. Misconceptions of Deaf culture in China have led to a belief that all deaf people are skilled in art and drawing. Deaf children are often regarded as best expressing themselves through the medium of art, and colleges and universities readily offer art courses to deaf applicants, assuming some form of innate skill and pleasure in this field. However, there is no basis for assuming that deaf people are any more or less likely to excel in art than their hearing counterparts.

There is, though, some veracity to the notion that a lot of deaf people enjoy the expression of Deaf culture through dance, and the success of the China Disabled People's Arts Troupe's international tours of the Dance of a Thousand Hands is testament to this belief. Engagement with such forms of dance have attracted the attention of many people, who are taking a keen interest in how deaf people, who are usually considered as having relatively low social status, can achieve such precision and creativity in performance. The inclusion of sign language in deaf people's performances has recently led to more interest and deaf people are beginning to be seen in the light of positive achievement through sign language, rather than in terms of an inability to achieve that the disability perspective has perpetuated. Along with the increase in teaching sign language to hearing people, and demonstrations of signed songs that has become widespread through social media, the dance troupe is now showcasing the Deaf community as a group of highly functioning, independent people. During performances, deaf people rely on vibration and eye gaze precision in order to precisely synchronize dance routines, rather than relying on hearing people who have acted as puppeteers at stage sidelines, attempting to help deaf people to access the rhythm and tempo of music and dance.

There is increasingly, in China, a sense of Deaf Gain that a perception of deaf people as sign language users, rather than as disabled people, brings about. The advances in video technologies have enabled sign language communication to take place readily across social media platforms and this is enabling hearing people to see the achievements and positive elements of Deaf culture and of functioning as a sign language user in society. This is emancipatory for deaf people, and rising levels of confidence in deaf communities is the result of this perspective shift. Deaf people are becoming more visible and included and afforded a higher status in society than they received during earlier days when deaf people were hidden away and patronized. Through a case study of musical performance by deaf dancers, the chapter considers the role of the media in raising awareness of the language and cultural rights of deaf people, and, finally, the gains and struggles for the rights of the Deaf community are explored in depth.

2 Culture

The term 'culture' has historical and political connotations in China and is not often applied in the context of deafness. There is some awareness among the population that Deaf people communicate and behave differently in some ways, using sign language for social interaction, and attending special educational institutions that are different to the mainstream society, but this is rarely referred to as 'Deaf culture' in Chinese language. This is a term that has recently migrated into the language and is accepted only by a small minority of people (Zhang, 2010). The larger population across China does not consider the lives of its Deaf citizens to hearing people as culturally different, and this is due to the complex sociolinguistic implications of being deaf (Callaway, 2000; Lytle, Johnson & Yang, 2005/2006). There have developed, in fact, multiple meanings attached to the term 'culture,' and particularly negative associations to such historical events as the 'cultural revolution' (1966–1976), which had a lasting impact in society. This is seen in two areas that directly affect Deaf people. Firstly, the China Deaf Association, which had been established in 1956, was closed down during the cultural revolution and many years of sign language work, which aimed to unify and promote sign language use and welfare work in support of all deaf people, was disbanded for ten years (from 1968 to 1978, Wen, 1992). This resulted in many archived resources being lost. Secondly, the general education system became fraught with lack of development. While schools for deaf children remained open, there was very little development in Chinese literacy and vocational education for deaf students until a visit to Beijing No. 3 School for the Deaf by Prime Minister Zhou in 1971 along with several foreign diplomats, after which some attention was paid to education and employment of young deaf people.

In another sense, culture is also seen as a reference to the high levels of literacy through education that some people achieve, rather than a particular way of life or worldview. This is so engrained that the concepts of culture and of literacy are referred to by the same word 文化 (*Wenhua*) in Chinese, and the sign for 'culture' in Chinese Sign Language is a compound of the signs for 'writing' and 'bloom.' Where the term is applied to a way of life other than that of the majority Chinese culture (the Han ethnic group), it is primarily used in relation to the ethnic minorities from the 57 indigenous groups of Chinese citizens, who have a collective cultural difference in relation to their own languages, traditions, values, foods, clothing, arts, dance, lifestyle, and so on. Such minority groups have assimilated as much as possible to majority Chinese ways and values, through school education and social policies, due to the Chinese philosophy of integration of all people; hence, Deaf people are also not viewed as a group of people that are distinct and separate from the majority Chinese culture (Zhang, 2003). Moreover, Deaf children from ethnic minorities often have limited access to information about their minority culture and language at home, and they also have been educated in schools where only the majority Chinese culture and language (Mandarin) are taught. This is with the exception of children born to the Tibetan culture, which is taught explicitly, alongside the majority culture, in a school that was established only in the year 2000. Tibet Sign Language has since come to be recognized as a minority sign language in China (Handicap International, 2002; Yang & Wu, 2014).

3 Associations of Deafness and Disabilities

Deaf and hard-of-hearing people are undoubtedly categorized as people with 'hearing disabilities' according to China's Law on Protection of Persons with Disabilities of 1990 and revised in 2008,[1] and have benefitted from the support services and financial welfare that this categorization has brought. Along with this, however, all deaf people have traditionally been seen as a socioeconomically disadvantaged group, who are vulnerable and in need of care and compassion from the semi-government disability organizations; in addition, medical companies have sought financial gain from the production of hearing aid and cochlear implant technologies that rely on deaf people needing to be cured. Debates around the labelling of Deaf people as disabled have continued for many years but remain less substantial to the development of the social status of deaf people than the debates about the usefulness of deaf people in a society. It is more important, therefore, that Deaf people are seen as useful and contributory, rather than the focus being laid intensely on the status of Deaf people as disabled or non-disabled (Dai & Song, 1999; Yang, 2011). The acceptance of the label of 'hearing disability' among Deaf people lies largely in the pragmatics of the welfare and benefit systems that require this status in order for Deaf people to receive appropriate funding and support. The increasing success of the disability movement in China also offers a form of strong campaigning that the Deaf community can only benefit from. The campaign for deaf people to be permitted to hold a driving license (which was not successful until both Deaf and disabled groups joined together in the same campaign) is an example of how joining with other groups of disabled people can boost the number of protesters and improve campaign outcomes. Other initiatives, such as free bus travel and discounted SIM cards for mobile telephones, have also been successful due to joint campaign strategies (Xu Jianping, personal communication, December 2015). Deaf people have adopted technologies available for use with mobile phones, such as video recorded information and communication apps, which means that they are now more readily able to access information in the mainstream society, and this is proving effective in improving the quality of life for many deaf people. Accepting deaf people as a disability group but with their own (sign) language, communication and social approaches, values and educational provisions is an important element towards improving the social status and cultural life of Deaf people in China.

Initially, then, many Chinese people viewed all deaf people from the firmly established medical or disability perspective and resisted the notion that some deaf people may constitute a distinct cultural group with their own language, culture, values and traditions. In addition, the long-standing desire of hearing parents for their deaf children to acquire speech was at the forefront of retaining this group under a medical guise (Callaway, 2000). This is seen also in regular Chinese media broadcasting of any success in the ability of deaf children to speak, and broadcasting related to the cultural aspects of being Deaf is only very slowly increasing. Through Deaf awareness workshops and sign language conference gatherings, and the media, it was often Deaf sign language users themselves who embraced the Deaf culture and began to exhibit pride in their Deaf identity and became more assertive but continued to struggle for their rights as a cultural minority group (Wu, 2009; Zhang, 2014). Furthermore, there was little socioeconomic benefit to be made from deaf people as a cultural group, especially given that the teaching of sign language has been done voluntarily by Deaf people for the last 15 years (Liu Chundan, personal communication, April 2016), as has most sign language film production or media-based sign language provision.[2] It is only very recently that a few Deaf people have begun providing their services, such as online media companies and art galleries, under a business model which promotes Deaf culture and Deaf role models.

4 The Notion of Deaf Culture

Understanding of deafness as a culture began to emerge across China primarily during the latter part of the 20th century, after academics returned from trips to Europe, the U.S. and Canada where they were exposed to notions of Deaf culture (Yang, 2008). During this period of international travel opportunities, Chinese Deaf people also began to travel abroad, and knowledge of the cultural issues related to being Deaf were often disseminated through the community on their return. Amid its massive population, the voice of Deaf and hard-of-hearing people began to be heard and the concept of Deaf culture began emerging. This saw a continuing development in the early 21st century with several sign bilingual- bicultural education initiatives, such as those sponsored by UNICEF (in Tianjin, Biggs, 2004), Save the Children (in Hefei), the Amity Foundation (in Nanjing, Callaway, 2000), and the Signo (Norway) Foundation's SigAm Deaf Bilingual Education Experimental projects (Yang, 2008; Kruse & Yang 2011). Through increased international exposure and partnerships with North America and Europe in teacher training and post-secondary education for deaf students (Callaway, 2000; Mudgett-DeCaro & DeCaro, 2009), Deaf culture is becoming increasingly recognized in society and more visible in the Chinese context, positively reflecting the country's socioeconomic growth.

During these early years of emergence, specialist schools and special educational colleges brought deaf people together naturally and provided a forum for community development. Some Deaf people would travel regularly in groups to meet and socialize with other Deaf groups and this led to awareness of the need for deaf people to come together locally, nationally, and even internationally. The continued socialization of Deaf communities led to the formation of many local and regional deaf organizations. After attending the World Federation of the Deaf (WFD) congress of 1955,[3] government officials began to discuss and understand the importance of opportunities for Deaf people to socialize, leading to the establishment of the China Deaf Association and its regional branches in Beijing, Shanghai and Tianjin in 1956. This association was later rechristened (in 1979) and evolved to include blind people and eventually disabled people in general, the result being that the element of being Deaf was diluted within the organization, disability becoming its most noticeable aspect. This change is evident in many ways. For example, in 1980 the China Deaf Association produced a bi-monthly magazine, titled *China Deaf People* and edited by Wen Damin, the vice-chief editor and sole Deaf member of the editorial team. The inclusion of blind people, and people with other disabilities, into the organization led to the magazine being renamed *The Voice of the Deaf and Blind* in 1986 and subsequently *The Chinese People with Disabilities (monthly)* in 1988, and content about Deaf people began to be reduced. On Wen Damin's retirement, no other Deaf person was appointed to the editorial team in his place, though he continued to influence Deaf correspondents to contribute by bringing Deaf people with good literacy skills together to write for the magazine (Zou Dezhen, personal communication, January 2014). The magazine has, in any case, remained an important avenue for people with disabilities to voice their rights and experiences in order to influence the government towards a philosophy of improved support and to learn about new government working plans on disability issues; it is also an important format for government officials in disability organizations to report on relevant visits and investigations, and to provide up-to-date political information and theories on the rights of people with disabilities, as well as for keeping up to date with current community issues themselves, hence its mutual benefit.

5 The Social Status of Deaf People and Education

Through indirect means, the social status of deaf people in China can be improved with the compulsory and post-secondary education of its deaf people. The New China government clearly announced in 1951 that deaf and blind children must be educated in special schools. The government immediately adopted all private schools for deaf children and opened new schools and, in addition, took full responsibility for funds, administration, teacher hiring and training, and school curricula (Piao, 1992). At this time, attitudes towards deaf children in society were still predominantly negative and ordinary schools did not enroll children with disabilities. The benefits that being educated bring to the individual's ability to function socially are significant to the social development path. Increased levels of education among the nation's deaf people, for example, has often resulted in successful employment in the arts and in the manual trade industries. This has also led to Government officials visiting schools for deaf children to witness the educational potential of the children.

The longstanding infrastructure of extreme government influence over people has a significant impact on the social status of deaf people. This was seen most explicitly after visits to schools for deaf children by President Jiang Zemin in 1992 and President Hu Jintao on 10 September, 2008 resulted in a sudden increase in school funding awarded to pay for building refurbishment or development, equipment for teaching, and aural-speech and vocational training, media attention, and employment opportunities. The government announcement that the education of deaf children was a progressive success, and the encouragement of businesses to employ deaf people by government officials, resulted in employers from many sectors considering applications from deaf applicants. The government also contributed in this area of employment by funding the establishment of a welfare industry and enterprise in the form of production factories predominantly for deaf workers, which also led to an immediate increase in deaf employment. The government control of these factories eventually diminished due to changes to the market and moves towards integrating people with disabilities into mainstream employment (see Regulations on the Employment of Persons with Disabilities of 2007[4]), and many, under private ownership, have since closed but some remain in successful operation. At the governmental level, the influence that policy makers have on the social status of deaf people also extends to the level of access that is provided. Decisions to award funds and support for access to information for deaf people is an area that has also developed and improved through the years and is of paramount importance in order for deaf people to be able to contribute as useful members of society.

The benefits of a move towards integration in mainstream education include an increase in the enrolment rate of children with disabilities attending all levels of education. This change in the education system, while removing the socialization that specialist schools naturally provided, enables deaf students to access higher levels of education and a natural progression into further and higher education opportunities. The inclusion of deaf children into mainstream schools also leads to a greater awareness in society of the educational potential of deaf children and this, as we have seen, is an important element in improving the social status of deaf people. When the only educational provision for deaf children was based in specialist schools, deaf children were segregated and there was little integration between deaf and hearing children in Chinese society; the mainstream education of deaf children, therefore, has a direct impact on attitudes towards deaf people. This inclusion can only be achieved with the support of allies, hence the importance of deaf people being integrated into the wider society where allies are found.

6 Family Involvement

The role that the family plays in the deaf child's educational and social development cannot be overstated. A family with limited knowledge of how to raise a deaf child, and the cultural and linguistic implications involved, will need to seek information and advice. This may come from the school, if the child attends one of the special schools for the deaf; or it may come from a specialist speech rehabilitation center for deaf children. The ability to develop an understanding and awareness of the whole family's needs is paramount and can result in the family providing a positive and inclusive environment for the deaf child. Where this is achieved, the child will develop the social and emotional skills required to achieve independence and positive socialization as an adult. Furthermore, a deaf child will thrive in a typical family environment where the parents are driven by their love for the child and strive to educate the child through any means. There have been many parents of deaf children who have shown this unconditional love and provided an educational home environment that has led to the child becoming a successful and well-rounded adult. Such parents have often shared their experiences and knowledge with other parents of deaf children in order to continue to support deaf children, and many advice and information centers have been established by parents over the years (Callaway, 2000). Shared advice has led to an increase in the entry rate of deaf children in local mainstream schools, as parents have fought to secure places and to have the required support put in place for the child that would not have previously existed. This has even led some parents to change their career paths to the field of early education for deaf children, and some parents have published books that have a direct impact on people in society and have contributed to increase the number of documentaries and films about raising and educating deaf children.

It is relevant here to bear in mind the fact that the educational opportunities available to a child in China are often dependent on the socioeconomic situation of the family. Children from wealthy backgrounds, where the family income is high, often have access to a good level of family support in relation to their education, with parents supplementing learning with home teaching and motivation. Children from such backgrounds have a higher chance of attending post-compulsory education. In cases where the socioeconomic status of the family is much lower, and the family is managing a low income, the level of support for learning from the family may also be much lower, impacting both on the child's level of learning and on their motivation to progress. In this case, attrition rates may be higher and, in cases where the parents are both out of the home working long days, the child may grow up and lose contact with the family as they move into the adult world more independently. This socioeconomic division naturally impacts on the educational opportunities and achievements of deaf children.

With regards to further and higher education, it is relevant to consider the events following the Chinese Revolution (1966–1976) and the closure of higher education institutions across the nation. When universities re-opened in 1977, deaf people were not immediately accepted into courses and were denied higher educational opportunities. In 1987, Changchun University in Northeast China was the first to establish Art and Design programs for deaf students. The need to travel many miles to attend school, and the limited choices for further and higher education led to a group of over 200 parents of deaf children to campaign for the rights of deaf children to enter colleges and universities. The level of educational success of the first few deaf students to enter higher education was paramount, as it would be the catalyst to show that deaf students, regardless of the limited employment opportunities thereafter, could achieve this high level of education. The continued campaigning by parents to the government and to educational establishments, and the continued success of deaf students at this level, eventually led to colleges and universities across China opening their doors to deaf students. This has also impacted on employment opportunities, which have increased over the years and highly educated deaf people are now able to attain levels of employment that were previously unattainable, aiding the social status of deaf people and raising some awareness of the differences between Deaf and disabled people.

7 Case Study: A Deaf Dance Troupe Since Deaf Way II

The turn of this century saw the beginnings of a new awakening for the visual culture of Deaf people in China. In July 2002, Deaf Way II, a prestigious conference on Deaf culture held in Washington D.C. in the U.S., attracted high profile members of many Deaf communities from across the globe. A large delegation from China was invited by Gallaudet University to attend (Johnson, Lytle & Yang, 2009). Prior to the conference, Zhou Fang, a Chinese Deaf artist working at Gallaudet University, won an award for creating the conference logo and designing the Deaf Way II poster. This inspired many Chinese individuals to attend and to pursue the possibility of studying abroad. The number of Chinese delegates at the event had a twofold effect: firstly, both Deaf and hearing people from many countries were awakened to the fact that prominent Deaf community members from China were eager to be involved in the growing academic awareness of the social and cultural rights of Deaf sign language users; secondly, on return from the conference, many of the Chinese delegates were able to disseminate their learning and awaken interest across the Deaf community nationwide as to the benefits that such recognition can bring. The seed of Deaf culture was truly planted.

At the Deaf Way II Opening Celebrations, a prominent team of 21 deaf dancers, the *China Disabled People's Performing Art Troupe*, was invited to perform their 'My Dream' (Thousand-Hand Bodhisattva) dance. This unique and spectacular performance mesmerized the international audience with its visual display of color and precise rhythmic movements. The troupe also received Chinese government officials' praise, bringing further attention to the abilities and talents of Deaf people. This dance team performed 'Thousand-Hand Bodhisattva' and demonstrated the verse 'love is our common language' in Chinese Sign Language during the Chinese New Year's Eve celebrations on 8

February 2005 which was televised on Central China TV Channel (Yang, 2011). This event was watched by millions of viewers and had a dramatic impact across the nation. The positive image of Deaf people as being capable of achievement began to be promoted in many parts of the country. As a direct result of this media attention, the following years saw an explosion of awareness of Chinese Sign Language (CSL) and of the Deaf community, leading to cultural growth and resulting in the establishment of many CSL courses. This developing period also saw Deaf people using sign language with pride, and the overwhelming presence of deaf dancers' performance at the Paralympic Games in Beijing in 2008 was a major milestone for the emergence of Deaf culture. The *China Disabled People's Performing Art Troupe* was also invited to perform at the Deaflympics a year later in Taipei, and the success and popularity of the performance led to increased intercultural communication between Taiwan and mainland China.[5]

Dance performances by Chinese Deaf troupes such as this often incorporate music, which attracts a hearing audience and aids the integration of Deaf people into mainstream society. Many Deaf dancers from the disabled performing art troupes have achieved high levels of success in musical performance often to the bewilderment of the hearing audience. Hearing people clearly find performances by Deaf troupes remarkable and very poignant. It is understandable that it is difficult for hearing people to imagine enjoying music and partaking in musical performances without being able to hear, as hearing people make use of sound for timing and rhythm. Many Deaf dancers, however, have become skilled in the rigorous practice of sequences in order to marry the time and the vibration of the rhythm together, and their performance is often successful due to the level of rehearsal and hard work that they have to commit to each performance. "I was thrilled with joy when the rhythmic vibration passed over my body from under my feet," Dancer Tai Lihua informed a Beijing Week reporter on March 5, 2005. While some deaf people have a small amount of residual hearing and are able to hear some musical beats, many profoundly deaf people rely solely on the vibrations and on rehearsal and memory skills in order to take part in musical activities. Successful dance troupes tour the country and perform with the assistance of sign language interpreters, making the event accessible for hearing people. The use of music in Deaf dance performance has often brought hearing and Deaf people together and this common interest has helped to bridge the two communities and aid the continued emergence of Deaf culture.

This case study of musical performance and its relation to the development of Deaf culture also demonstrates the gains that such exposure can bring to the advancement of Deaf people in society. There are now funding streams available, especially from charities with an interest in disability, that enable disabled troupes to run and offer training courses and professional job opportunities for disabled performers. Media reporters often take pleasure in interviewing performers to find out more about their individual backgrounds and have reported that many successful Deaf dancers graduated from specialist schools for deaf children, where they expressed interest in the performing arts. A Taiwan television series named *Listening Eye* in July 2015 recorded interviews and documented the activities and backgrounds of the Deaf dancers from the *China Disabled People's Performing Art Troupe,* and found that many of the dancers had attended specialist schools before becoming full time, professionally employed dancers with the troupe. Lead dancer, Tai Lihua, noted during one interview[6] that the dance troupe was often perceived with sympathy as an amateur group due to the continuing paternalistic attitudes towards disabled people, and its professionalization has led many people to enjoying the performance with respect rather than with sympathy. This clearly indicates a change in attitude towards performing troupes once they become professionally paid artists. Tai Lihua also serves as a vice-chair of China Deaf Association and is a political advisor, representing the Deaf community at the National People's Political Consultative Conference with a sign language interpreter, and advocates for improved access for people with disabilities. She was reported to be in the first group of Chinese Deaf driving license recipients in 2010.

The Deaf dance team also continues to seek new recruits to keep the troupe running, as there is a high turnover of dancers due to the brief nature of this particular career. Schools for deaf children continue to nurture a natural interest in dance and music, with many aspects being incorporated into the curriculum. Young deaf children continue to be encouraged to partake in a variety of performance activities and talent is consciously nurtured. Tai Lihua's hometown, Yichang City in Hubei Province, has established a specialist performing arts school for deaf children, where performance potential is identified and children demonstrating a high level of skill in this area are prepared for future participation in the disability performing arts troupe. Since 2013, the troupe, now of 23 Deaf dancers, has combined their performance training with university courses to obtain a degree for the purpose of future employment. This expands the opportunities available to them. Media reports have found that successful Deaf social workers, teachers, beauticians, and business people have often been educated with a similar performing arts background.

In sum, it is evident that notions of Deaf people as disabled have begun to develop from paternalistic and sympathetic towards respectful and understanding of the capabilities of Deaf people. Media attention and awareness is seen as the key to improved social status for Deaf people and this cannot be achieved without the aforementioned linguistic and cultural rights for sign language users. The important cultural value that is placed on education in Chinese society, and subsequently on deaf education, is also paramount in aiding Deaf people growing up to become independent and successful adults who are useful to society and can contribute to its development, as the case study has shown.

8 The Gains and Struggles for the Rights of the Deaf Community in China

The history of Deaf people in China has seen many gains, alongside its many struggles. Firstly, the benefit that sign language has brought to Deaf people must be stated. While sign language has provided a gain of many aspects within the Deaf community, Chinese Sign Language (CSL) has struggled to achieve government recognition as a bona fide language, affecting the emergence of Deaf culture (Gong, 2009). A survey conducted by National Centre for Sign Language and Braille in 2011, as Liu, Gu, Cheng and Wei (2014) note, found that the language has also struggled to demonstrate its natural and organic nature, largely because of the tendency at government level towards standardization. The publication of books with pictures of signs, amongst other things, has led to people viewing the vocabulary as static and standard, and the younger generation of sign language users is influenced by the demand to learn Mandarin and to develop oral skills, both of which impact on the use of CSL (Lin, Garcia & Pichler, 2009). Fisher and Gong (2010) reported that the natural, heritage language, with its many sociolinguistic variations, is now used mostly by the older generation of Deaf people.

One of the most significant gains in relation to the rights of the Deaf community in China is of course the right to drive. Awareness of the right to drive for deaf people in other countries, largely due to increasing travel to and from other countries by deaf people during the last few decades, generated this urge to campaign for the equal right to drive (Feng Gang, personal communication, April 2013). Historically, people with disabilities were not permitted to drive due to the association of a license to drive a vehicle with a professional job. This was during times when cars were driven only for business purposes, until economic growth across the country led to the use of cars for personal and leisure use. There was in fact a period of time when many deaf people were benefitting from the economic growth in terms of personal finances and a car was certainly affordable, but the prohibition meant that they were unable to drive until Deaf people joined the campaigns run by people with other disabilities and the impact of the larger group led to the decision to overturn the ruling. The 'Drive across China' campaign, led by Zhang Haidi, famous writer and later Chair of the Chinese Disabled Persons' Foundation, resulted in a ruling that people with single leg amputations could drive, and the campaign continued until the right to drive was given to more people with disabilities in 2003. This intensive campaign took many forms, including internet forums and wide consultation and, once successful, deaf people were able to begin contacting driving schools in order to express interest to learn. During the first years of the new ruling, many deaf people relied on gestural communication with instructors in order to learn if they were unable to find an instructor fluent in CSL. Many driving schools were reluctant to take deaf people on board and this time saw some deaf people having to fly to parts of China where learning to drive was accepted for deaf people (Liu Ping, personal communication, April 2013). Though many deaf people now drive cars, they are careful in the event of breakdown or accident, as they need to rely on mobile telephones and writing messages in order to communicate with the relevant vehicle services (Yu Qianghua, personal communication, April 2013). This right to drive has led to an increase in the socialization of Deaf people through better access to leisure activities, improved job prospects, and has enhanced the social status of Deaf people at large.

A further gain for deaf people is seen in the rise of deaf clubs over the years, which has led to increased socialization for many grassroots deaf people who were isolated from other CSL users. Organized gatherings for deaf people have led to many social activities through the years, such as a morning exercise group in a park for elderly deaf people, and evening gatherings under a street light during very hot summer months for local deaf people to come together and communicate with each other. There have also been more formally organized activities in the form of the Deaf Day Celebration events in September, Disability Awareness Day in May, and special interest groups, such as stamp collecting workshops, fishing, painting, photography, and Chinese chess competitions, which are organized through a committee and demand a membership subscription. Also, on a formal level, local, national and international associations for deaf people have been established through the years, often holding annual workshops and conferences on issues related to Deaf community capacity building and its social and political agendas. Membership in the larger organizations at times provides an opportunity for Deaf people to represent the organization at international sporting events, such as the Deaflympics, with government funding for support. This support includes funding for travel and for the essential training prior to the sporting event. This increased socialization of Deaf communities has occurred on a global level, but Padden (2008) warns of the reduction in such activities in the U.S. due to inclusion and mainstreaming policies that are driving Deaf people into mainstream events (also Atherton, 2012, for the UK). The large numbers of Deaf people, and the thriving internet as a source of communication, may have helped to maintain the socialization of sign language users in China.

Media reporting, however, focuses often on individual deaf people's achievements, rather than on the contribution that the larger Deaf community makes to the social status of deaf people. Larger Deaf community events are reported in the media occasionally and the on-going support and awareness that the community works hard to achieve is under-reported. This is also undermined by the tendency in the media to report crimes of theft, pocket-picking by groups of deaf people, which has led to an often negative view of deaf people and even a fear of deaf groups. Up until 2014, however, there are now 30 television programs that provide sign language on screen, and as many as 201 local TV news channels that offer sign language interpretation.[7] Interpreted programs include the news and access to Congress announcements and reports, and the improved acceptance of sign language in society was epitomized by the televised showing of President Xi Jinping and his wife Peng Liyuan using some sign language phrases. This area has seen further advances in the form of television programs for Deaf people, and there are now several Deaf media companies and internet sites that function with sign language. It is interesting to note, however, that many CSL users struggle to fully understand the language produced by the sign language interpreters on television and this service is in need of further development (Xiao & Li, 2012; Liu et al., 2014). The increased level of access and inclusion has undoubtedly contributed to higher levels of acceptance of deaf people among the general public and has helped to improve the social status of deaf people.

9 Conclusions

Notions of Deaf people as people with disabilities remain across China, despite the eventual emergence and increasing awareness of Deaf culture. The socialization of Deaf people in its large communities has benefitted from the advances in technology of recent years, especially Internet communication, and from the increased opportunities for international travel. Learning from other cultures and experiencing other languages has led to more open-minded thinking among deaf people, and within the general public, and has benefitted the Deaf community greatly. Attitudes towards deaf people, as we have seen, have been improving rapidly since the turn of the century and the seed of Deaf culture has begun to grow. The dynamic relation between education, family values, and the language and cultural rights of deaf people has been noted as a vital aspect of the increasing social status of deaf people.

Notes

1 See http://english.cdpf.org.cn/2017-07/30/c_914832.htm
2 For example, Shouyuzhe Prosigner https://www.facebook.com/DeafProsigner/, New Deaf TV site by Wang Jiangbin https://www.facebook.com/newdeaftv/ and Shouyu Hutong Vlog by Feng Gang https://m.weibo.cn/u/2774856385
3 The New China government accepted an invitation from the WFD and sent an official delegation to attend the second congress in Yugoslavia in 1955 and later became a member of the organization.
4 See http://english.cdpf.org.cn/2016-03/03/c_914834.htm
5 See the Listening Eye TV program Vol. 652, 2 July 2015. Retrieved from https://www.youtube.com/watch?v=GZLiHVgO-50
6 See the *Listening Eye* TV program Vol. 652, 2 July 2015. Retrieved from https://www.youtube.com/watch?v=GZLiHVgO-50
7 Statistical Communiqué on the Development of the Work on Persons with Disabilities in 2014. Retrieved from http://english.cdpf.org.cn/2016-03/23/c_914839.htm

References

Atherton, M. (2012). *Deafness, community, and culture in Britain: Leisure and cohesion, 1945–1995*. Manchester, UK: Manchester University Press.

Biggs, C. (2004). *Bilingual and bicultural approach to teaching Deaf children in China.* United Nations International Children's Emergency Fund (UNICEF).

Callaway, A. (2000). *Deaf Children in China.* Washington, D.C.: Gallaudet University Press.

Dai, M., & Song P. (1999). *Meng yuan yi dangnian* [When dreams come true, We will remember]. Shanghai: Education Publisher.

Fischer, S. D., & Gong Q. (2010). Variation in East Asian sign language structures. In D. Brentari (Ed.), *Sign Languages* (Cambridge Language Survey series) (pp. 502–521). Cambridge, UK: Cambridge University Press.

Gong, Q. (2009). A linguistic discussion on issues of Chinese Sign Language and Chinese in deaf education. *Chinese Journal of Special Education, 3*, 63–67.

Handicap International-Belgium. (2002). *Tibetan Sign Language dictionary*, Vol. I & II. Lhasa, Tibet: Tibet People Press.

Johnson, K., Lytle, R., & Yang, J. H. (2009). Deaf education and the deaf community in China: Past, present, and future. In D. E. Moores & M. S. Miller, (Eds.) *Deaf people around the world: Educational and social perspectives* (pp. 17–32). Washington, D.C.: Gallaudet University Press.

Kruse, S. E., & Yang, J. H. (2009). *An evaluation of SigAm bilingual education project for deaf children in China 2004–2009*. Oslo, Norway: The Signo Foundation.

Lin, C., de García, B. G., & Pichler, D. C. (2009). Standardizing Chinese Sign Language for use in postsecondary education. *Current issues in Language Planning, 10*, 327–337.

Liu, Y., Gu, D., Cheng, L., & Wei, D. (2014). *The use of sign language and Braille in China*. Beijing: The Commercial Press.

Lytle R., Johnson, K., & Yang, J. H. (2006). Deaf education in China: History, current issues, and emerging deaf voices. *American Annals of the Deaf, 150*(5), 457–470. (Original work published 2005)

Mudgett-DeCaro, P. A., & DeCaro, J. J. (2009). Postsecondary education for deaf people in China. In. D. E. Moores & M. S. Miller (Eds.), *Deaf people around the world: Educational and social perspectives* (pp. 33–45). Washington, D.C.: Gallaudet University Press.

Padden, C. (2008). The decline of Deaf clubs in the US: A treatise on the problem of place. In H.-D. L. Bauman (Ed.), *Open your eyes: Deaf studies talking* (pp. 169–176). Minneapolis, MN: University of Minnesota Press.

Piao, Y. (1992). *Teshu jiaoyu gailun* [Special education: An introduction]. Beijing: Huaxia Press.

Wen, D. (1992). *Xulun* [Preface]. In Y. Piao (Ed.), *Zhongguo Shouyu Jiaoxu Fudao* [A teacher's book of Chinese Sign Language] (pp. 1–24). Beijing: Huaxia Press.

Wu. A. (2009). SigAm deaf bilingual education programmes in China. *Chinese Journal of Special Education, 3*(Supp.).

Xiao, X., & Li, F. (2012). Sign language interpreting on Chinese TV: A survey on user perspective. *Perspectives: Studies in Translatology*, 1–17.

Yang, J. H. (2008). Sign language and oral/written language in deaf education in China. In C. P. Pust & E. Morales-Lopez (Eds.), *Sign bilingualism: Language development, interaction, and maintenance in sign language contact situations* (pp. 297–331). Amsterdam, The Netherlands: John Benjamins.

Yang, J. H. (2011). Social situations and the education of Deaf children in China. In: G. Mathur & D. J. Napoli (Eds.), *Deaf around the world: The impact of language* (pp. 467–486). Cambridge, UK: Cambridge University Press.

Yang, J. H. & Wu, A. (2014) *An introduction to Chinese Sign Language and Deaf culture* [Chinese]. Zhengzhou, Zhengzhou University Press.

Zhang, J. (2003). Silent river: Culture elements in Chinese and foreign deaf films. *Culture Studies, 4*(1), 150–162.

Zhang, N. (2010). *Deaf culture: An introduction* (1st ed.). Zhengzhou: Zhengzhou University Press.

Zhang, N. (2014). *Deaf culture: An introduction* (2nd ed.). Zhengzhou: Zhengzhou University Press.

PART 2

Deaf Art: Affirmation, Resistance, and Liberation

∵

Art constitutes one of the rare locations where acts of transcendence can take place and have a wide-ranging transformative impact.

BELL HOOKS (1995, *Art on My Mind: Visual Politics*, p. 8)

CHAPTER 5

Deaf Humor as a Political Tool

Rachel Sutton-Spence

Abstract

Much of deaf humor can be seen as political in the light of the relationship between deaf communities and the majority, powerful hearing society. In this chapter, I distinguish between deaf humor and sign language humor. The former is defined by the (deaf) people who create it, its content (relating to deaf people) and its intended (deaf) audience, while the latter is defined by the languages in which the humor is produced—the visual-spatial sign languages of deaf communities. Both these cultural and linguistic aspects are shown to have political elements, although these politics change through time and not all deaf humor is political. By asking what makes deaf people laugh, we see striking similarities in the humor of different national deaf communities, and that deaf humor can often be seen in terms of Resistance and Affirmation. Deaf humor has a wider scope than deaf jokes, encompassing different elements of language play and culturally approved carnivalesque inversions of common deaf experiences. In the deaf jokes presented and analyzed here, drawn from a range of sign languages, we see that deaf humor supports and challenges members of the in-group, and serves to demarcate the out-group of 'non-deaf.'

Keywords

deaf humor – sign language humor – deaf jokes – deaf resistance – deaf affirmation – world deaf communities

1 Introduction

Although most hearing society views deafness as a disability or a medical problem in need of a cure, many Deaf[1] people challenge this perception, identifying instead as members of a minority language community with its own culture (see, among many, Ladd, 2003, and Lane, Hoffmeister & Bahan 1996). The tensions between the two labels—one of disability, that is disempowering and oppressive, imposed externally, and the other of linguistic and cultural identity,

 | DOI:10.1163/9789004692299_006

that is empowering and self-affirming, chosen from within the group—often emerge in Deaf humor.

Much of the form and content of Deaf humor can be seen as highly political in the light of the relationship between the minority, disenfranchised Deaf community and the majority, powerful hearing society that dominates the everyday experience of Deaf people. The political importance of Deaf humor has already been noted, for example in Bouchauveau (1994), Jacobowitz (1996), and Pol (2014). We should note, however, that plenty of Deaf humor is not overtly political and even where it can be interpreted as such, the Deaf person creating the humor may not explicitly intend this at the time.

2 Deaf Humor as Resistance and Affirmation

Deaf people's expressions of their experience have already been analysed within a framework of political acts of resistance and affirmation (Miller, 1994; Durr, 1999, chapter 8; Christie & Wilkins, 2007, chapter 6) and I will apply this framework to consider the politics of Deaf humor. Durr (1999), in consideration of fine art created by Deaf people, notes that disenfranchised people's art can serve as an act of resistance when it shows "how disenfranchised group members experience domination by the majority culture" (Durr, 1999, p. 4). Affirmation art "involves members of a disenfranchised group celebrating and highlighting the positive aspects of their culture" (Durr, 1999, p. 4), where that celebration may be of "identity, collective history, cultural values and cultural survival" (Christie & Wilkins, 2007, p. 4). Drawing on Durr's work, Christie and Wilkins (2007, chapter 6) used ideas of resistance and affirmation to identify themes in American Sign Language poetry, adding the concept of liberation, as the journey from resistance to affirmation. As the poetry and humor of Deaf people form part of the multi-vocal, multi-textual, genre-resisting hybrid experience of Deaf folklore (Peters, 2000; Kincheloe, 2015), we may expect these same forces of resistance, affirmation and liberation to occur in Deaf humor.

Political humorous acts serve to create positive Deaf identities. The defining characteristic of Deaf culture and Deaf identity relates to Deaf people's linguistic identity, which results from the experience of sign language and written and spoken language (Carty, 1994). A Deaf social identity derives partly from a Deaf person's sense of belonging (or not) to the Deaf community, and Deaf cultural identity, which Bahan (1994) defines as possessing Deaf World Knowledge and Deaf World Experience, stems from, and interrelates closely with, these two. Any political analysis of Deaf humor needs to take these characteristics into account.

3 What Makes Deaf People Laugh?

Within the Deaf community, Deaf people laugh at many types of humor that are visual in form and, preferably, in content (Sanders, 1986). In many instances, Deaf people and hearing people find the same things amusing. Members of Deaf communities enjoy plenty of hearing society's humor when it is visually accessible, and laugh at jokes told in sign language translation, although those that rely on language play in the spoken language may be less entertaining. Some Deaf humor is similar to (and influenced by) the humor of the surrounding hearing society, in terms of its structure, content and function (Raskin, 1985), but there are other forms that originate within the Deaf community, motivated by the specific knowledge and experience of Deaf people (Rutherford, 1989). In many cases, Deaf humor can be seen as a form of 'fusion humor', blending the knowledge and experiences of Deaf people with the humor traditions in wider society (Sutton-Spence & Napoli, 2009).

Deaf communities are bilingual in their signed language and the language of the surrounding hearing society, so some Deaf humor is written by Deaf people for Deaf readers (Holcomb, 1985; Holcomb, Holcomb, & Holcomb, 1994), for example in books and journals as well as in texts and posts on social network sites. However, as sign language is integral to Deaf culture, much of the community's humor is expressed in sign language. Content-based, conceptual humor that is delivered through sign language can be translated reasonably easily into other languages, although readers of the translation may lack the knowledge or experience to appreciate what community members find funny about it. Where Deaf humor relies entirely on sign language, however, the form carries the humor and is lost in translation (Raphaelson-West, 1989). It is important to note, too, that some visual Deaf humor goes beyond what is normally seen as linguistic and its performance relies upon a highly embodied production of entertaining images. This last type of humor is easily understood by Deaf signers in other countries who use other sign languages, and partly accounts for the popularity of international Deaf humor, which spreads through meetings at international events and via the Internet.

Popular forms of humor such as Deaf practical jokes, entertaining games and slapstick are non-linguistic and many of these involve tactile humor as well as visual elements, reflecting culturally Deaf norms of behavior. In one party game, the Master of Ceremonies asked the participants standing in a circle (a Deaf cultural norm so everyone can be seen) to imagine they had found an ant, which they should place somewhere on the body of the person to their left. As the ant was passed round the circle, it was placed on shoulders, arms, ears, necks, knees, noses and other parts of the anatomy, each one possibly violating norms of personal space in other contexts but licenced by the game. At the end of the round, the MC informed the group that they must now kiss the ant where they had left it. For a culture that is usually more tactile than its hearing host society this was very entertaining and liberating because it gave members of the Deaf community licence to behave in a way that would be frowned upon in hearing society.

Cartoons, either written or in film (created by hearing society or within the Deaf community) may be non-linguistic, or use only the minimum of language, and are also popular among Deaf people, because of their visual appeal (Luckner & Yarger, 1997). Video clips showing slapstick events or practical jokes are another form of visual, non-linguistic humor. Within the Deaf community, however, language-based humor is most noticeable, seen in Deaf jokes, language games, theatre, storytelling, humorous conversation and witty asides. Indeed, many non-linguistic forms of humor often have linguistic forms as, for example, signers use sign language to retell a slapstick event or describe a cartoon. Jokes—whether translated from wider hearing society, original from within a Deaf community, or drawn from international Deaf humor—constantly vary and mutate, as tellers add new twists to known jokes, tell them in new ways, or tell them in new situations. As jokes are content based, their content often reflects political challenges for society, highlighting inequalities or presenting remedies. This chapter will draw on several jokes that are considered classics within various Deaf communities (Hessel Silveira, 2015). The fact that they are classics shows how communities present acts of culturally approved affirmation and resistance through humor.

4 The Functions of Deaf Humor

Humor pervades cultural life, whether of Deaf or hearing people. The various functions of humor are well documented, as it is widely accepted that humor is physically, socially, psychologically and educationally important, for Deaf and hearing people (Luckner & Yarger, 1997). Theoretical attempts to understand humor and laughter may relate to its incongruity, its means of creating release of tension or its portrayal of superiority of a social group, through inclusion and exclusion. All of these may be seen within Deaf humor (Pol, 2014) but this final aspect will be the focus here.

Clearly, a primary function of humor is to entertain and provide enjoyment in life, and it has long been associated with physical wellbeing as well as mental. Release of tension, ability to cope better with problems and reduction of frustration are known results of humor, which can all be useful for Deaf people faced with the daily frustrations living within hearing society. Hal Draper, a well-known and widely respected British Deaf comedian, noted (reported in Sutton-Spence & Napoli, 2012):

> [All-Deaf] audiences ... identified with the experiences and so they laughed. They could sit and watch and laugh and think, "Yes, I remember the same thing happening to me before." Also, for some Deaf people who were new to the Deaf community it brought out a lot of things from deep inside about themselves. They watched things being performed that they felt embarrassed about and realized, "I am not the only one who's had this problem—all Deaf have this problem." So, in some ways the show was about humor and laughter but in other ways it was a little bit of therapy for some Deaf people who found their identity. (p. 312)

As we can see from the quotation above, humor also serves to educate and enculturate members of the community, particularly those who are new to it. Many people only join their Deaf community as adults, having been brought up in hearing society, so humor can help them learn about the values and experiences of other members. It also allows them to explore and develop sign language as they play with it, pushing its boundaries. This simple ludic act is political in itself for a community whose language has traditionally been proscribed and belittled by the dominant hearing society. Humor and joke telling give the tellers an opportunity to show their humor skills and position themselves within the hierarchy of their social group (Robinson & Smith-Lovin, 2001).

A powerful political aspect of humor focuses on the question of inclusion and exclusion (Twark, 2014). Socially, humor serves to maintain the identity of the group by creating bonding among its members, building rapport and negotiating relationships within a particular community, as it provides positive reinforcement of current behavior of the group, establishes consensus and reduces social distance. Bienvenu (1994) has noted that this occurs with Deaf humor. It has long been observed that a primary political function of humor is to strengthen the in-group, which may be achieved by valorising the in-group (showing pride in its characteristic behavior and norms, and particularly for Deaf people, pride in sign language), attacking the out-group, or even by attacking the in-group (Martineau, 1972).

Humor valorizing the Deaf in-group is an act of affirmation that occurs whenever a signer produces a joke or witticism in sign language, because it promotes the status of the sign language. Humor occurs regularly within signed discourses other than jokes, such as sign language narratives and in daily conversation. Mimicking another individual through the process of 'embodiment' by showing the person's characteristics and behavior is highly valued as a form of wit and is frequently funny, especially if shown in an exaggerated way. Where it tips over into caricature it may become more negative, but the general concept is well established as a positive form of humor. Skilled and witty signers can provide unfamiliar representations of familiar objects, and anthropomorphic devices in signing to show the behavior, perspective, intensions or reactions of inanimate objects, often produced swiftly and spontaneously, are a source of sign language humor that shows the beauty and potential of the community language. In this sense, as Miller (1994) notes, it is highly affirming.

5 Sign Language Humor—Acts of Affirmation

Christie and Wilkins (2007) cite Byrne's (2005) suggestion that sign language poetry that does not show influence of the dominant culture and language is an act of cultural resistance. Similarly, we can suggest that using sign language in any humor is an act of affirmation at some level—whether intentional or not—simply because it is free of the dominant culture of hearing society. However, humor that relies explicitly on sign language for its effect, because the language is the humor, is perhaps the strongest form of this affirmation.

Language play in sign languages was first described through linguistic analysis by Klima and Bellugi in 1975. Every sign is made from a selected hand configuration, location and movement, which may be seen as analogous to spoken language phonemes, and their research described the ways that signers can alter a single parameter of a sign to create a new meaning for humorous affect. Some of this language play is simply part of wit, as it explores creative possibility in the language and the signer is valorised for their production. For example, a sign in Brazilian Sign Language (Libras) meaning PROUD normally made at the chest can be moved to the head (with the same handshape and movement) to mean 'proud of intellectual achievement'. A Libras sign INTERESTING that is normally made with a single finger on one hand, can be made with all fingers on both hands (with the same location and movement) to mean 'very interesting indeed'. This humor can also be made to belittle or insult, and is especially political when used to insult out-group members. The sign used in many sign languages APPLAUD-IN-SIGN-LANGUAGE is normally made with all the fingers on both hands open and spread, but can be made with just the little finger extended, to mean the applause is ironically intended. A widespread sign in British Sign Language (BSL) to mean A-HEARING-PERSON uses the index finger, but when this is replaced with the little finger, it belittles hearing people, reversing the usual power difference between the two communities. In BSL, there is extra meaning in this handshape change because the extended little finger has widespread formational connotations of negativity (used, for example, in the signs WRONG, BITTER, ILL, SWEAR, POISON and FAIL), so substituting this handshape in BSL is an even stronger act of resistance.

Taking a different perspective from Byrne's view that signing without any influence from spoken or written language is an act of cultural resistance, Peters (2000) claims with justification that mixing forms of the majority group's language with sign language can be an act of cultural liberation, because it appropriates the language for its own ends. Humor can play with the out-group's language, as Peters notes for American Sign Language (ASL), in a Bakhtinian 'carnival' burlesque, where it is distorted and loses its power. For example, the manual alphabet is a way of spelling out written words within sign language, and this is normally something that must be done carefully, creating written spelling accurately to avoid risking censure and ridicule from the powerful hearing out-group. In Deaf humor, however, fingerspelling can be recruited for puns and language games, such as ABC stories, which are popular in ASL and not part of hearing society. In an ABC story, each sign is made with the hand configuration of successive letters of the manual alphabet and the skill and wit lies in telling a coherent signed story within the constraints of the letter sequence. Many of these stories deal with traditionally taboo subjects (Rutherford, 1993) and one extremely funny one in BSL runs from A to Z to show a couple engaged in passionate love-making in the most explicit way. Using this form of language, originally imposed on Deaf children by hearing educators, to tell a racy story in sign language is a fine act of resistance against the powerful hearing out-group, and can be seen primarily as affirmation, as the language is used with such creative wit.

Another form of bilingual humor occurs in riddles relating to signed puns that are macaronic loan translations. Following Peters (2000), these can also be an affirmation of the power of sign language to play with the normally threatening dominant language. This is true, even when the translations are innocuous, such as signing RULE with the thumb rather than the conventional index finger to mean 'rule of thumb' or signing WHO at the nose instead of at the chin to mean 'who knows?'. However, when they are used with taboo meanings, the symbolic political statement is stronger (such as moving the sign FUCK as though it is flying, while shrugging, to mean 'couldn't give a flying fuck' or placing it at the nose to mean 'fuck knows').

Signed humor that relies upon using devices in the language to produce powerful visual images celebrates the pride that signers have in their visual meaning-making of the world. It can also mark the in-group from the out-group simply by its intelligibility. Although I am a hearing person and a non-native signer, and thus part of the 'out-group' I was once invited to observe an all-Deaf sign language humor workshop, at which the coordinating instructor worked with participants to produce a story based on a single photograph of a car. By the time one participant had finished his story, the group members were crying with laughter (showing the powerful affirming effect of the language play) but I was baffled. The coordinator asked him to 'sign it so the hearing can understand'. He obliged immediately and I found it very funny, but it was noticeably different and less potent than the first telling, and clearly marked the in-group and out-group status of those present.

6 Deaf Jokes—Resistance and Affirmation

When Deaf jokes refer to problems caused by Deaf life, it is a liberating act that leads to affirmation of Deaf survival, such as seen in jokes about cochlear implants and the disadvantages of sign language. Jokes about cochlear implants (often focussing on bizarre accidents caused by the magnet in the Deaf person's head) can reflect negative views towards an invasive technology imposed upon Deaf people by a hearing majority intent on 'normalization' and as such may be seen as forms of resistance. However, as most Deaf communities now accept that cochlear implants are part of their social reality, an ability to laugh at them on their own terms is a liberating act on the way to affirmation.

Jokes that present sign language in any sort of negative way may seem contrary to the idea that they affirm and celebrate the core of Deaf culture. However, the very act of highlighting its disadvantages shows how much signers value it. Chirico (2015), reviewing the work of Krefting, notes the use of 'minstrelsy' among stand-up comedians from minority groups who reproduce the stereotypical traits of their society, knowing that their audiences will recognise and enjoy the exaggerated impersonations. Laughing at these stereotypes allows group members to acknowledge them and 'confirm cultural belonging' but also 'releases anxiety' (Chirico, 2015, p. 755) caused by knowing that outsiders hold these stereotypes.

One Deaf joke of many about the perils of sign language involves a Deaf couple who fall into a passionate embrace. As the man tells the woman in sign language that he adores her, he uses a two-handed sign, and drops her so she hits the floor, then she slaps him and storms out. In another Deaf classic joke 'King Kong', a Deaf King Kong accidentally kills a human girl he holds in the palm of his hand because he uses that hand to sign that he wants to marry her.

In some sign languages (including ASL and Libras), the sign MARRY involves the clasping of hands, so he squashes her. In others (including BSL), the sign is motivated by the act of placing a wedding ring on the finger, which involves turning the hand so that palm faces down, and she falls off his hand.

Humorous Deaf stories and jokes that support Deaf culture by showing pride in characteristic Deaf behavior and norms are widespread. Many humorous stories are affirming as they show Deaf ingenuity in solving problems (often caused by being Deaf in a predominantly hearing society). An example of such an affirming joke concerns a Deaf hunter who always returns with more game than his hearing friends. He finally explains to them that he watches his horse's ears twitch towards the sounds of an approaching animal. Other examples are less obviously affirming to a non-Deaf viewer, such as the classic joke about the barber who gives free haircuts (taken here from Sutton-Spence & Kaneko, 2016 but also given in Hessel Silveira, 2015 and generally well-known in many countries).

A blind man goes to a barber for a haircut. The barber cuts his hair and refuses payment, saying he's doing community service for the handicapped this week. The next morning the barber finds a thank you card and a dozen roses at his shop. Later a man in wheelchair comes in for a haircut. The barber cuts his hair and refuses payment, saying he's doing community service for the handicapped this week. The next morning the barber finds a thank you card and a box of a dozen muffins waiting at his shop. Later a Deaf man comes for a haircut. The barber cuts his hair and refuses payment, saying he's doing community service for the handicapped this week. The next morning he finds a dozen Deaf people waiting at his door.

Hearing people might see this as an act of ingratitude (and part of the humor for Deaf audiences lies in knowing that the behavior violates hearing norms) but this joke is affirmatory because telling others about a good opportunity shows social responsibility in Deaf society. The fact that the hearing barber has to suffer a little despite his kind intent (perhaps as punishment for his misguided view of Deaf people as 'handicapped people') is part of the Deaf resistance in humor.

Deaf humor attacking the out-group usually involves showing hearing society (its members, or its norms of behavior) in a negative light. This is perhaps the clearest form of Deaf resistance. In the words of Hal Draper, (in an interview with Jenny Smith, in March 2005), "I think most humor that Deaf people like is based on hearing people making idiots of themselves". Some Deaf people might deny this, especially any younger Deaf people who have had the good fortune to grow up in a slightly more enlightened society than older members of the community. However, there are many Deaf jokes, skits and funny stories in which the humor lies in the discomfort of a hearing person, especially medical or educational professionals who wield considerable power.

One classic Deaf joke refers to a Deaf man who gets to his motel late at night and cannot remember which room his Deaf wife is in. He sounds his car horn until the lights come on in every room where a hearing guest has been awakened, so that he knows his wife is in the one remaining darkened room. Bienvenu (1994) notes that this joke is clearly told against hearing people who are sensitive to noise, although it also valorises Deaf ingenuity at problem-solving. In another classic joke, a Deaf army recruit counts to ten in sign language while holding a grenade before throwing it to explode with perfect timing. He is able to do this because his sign language uses one hand for all numerals. A hearing recruit tries to do the same and counts on his fingers, but he needs the other hand when he gets to six so he holds the grenade between his legs until he reaches ten—with predictably explosive results (both jokes widely known in many Deaf communities and described in Hessel Silveira, 2015 and Sutton-Spence & Napoli, 2009).

The role of sign language interpreters in the Deaf community is another area of political tension that is a source of jokes. Although Deaf people communicate freely when everyone uses sign language, it is acknowledged that sign language interpreters are needed to communicate with hearing non-signers. The trust required by Deaf people to operate with interpreters is costly to the Deaf community, especially when that trust, and the power necessarily invested in the interpreter, might be abused. There are many jokes about sign language interpreters that place the Deaf person in control, to the detriment of the interpreter. One such example follows the classic 'Three Men' structure in a specific Deaf format:

> A Blind man dies and his friends at the funeral throw his white cane into the grave with him saying, "Take this with you on your final journey." A man who used a wheelchair dies and his friends at the funeral throw his wheelchair into the grave with him saying, "Take this with you on your final journey." A Deaf man dies and his friends at the funeral throw the interpreter into the grave with him saying, "Take this with you on your final journey."

In keeping with the process of liberation, moving towards affirmation, many jokes place the Deaf person in control of the hearing person in an explicit reversal of everyday Deaf experience. The humor is surprisingly violent, and jokes see the hearing person thrown from the tops of buildings, tossed out of moving trains, gored by a bull or eaten by a lion, while the Deaf person escapes any penalty. Even though it is based on the full understanding that 'it is only a joke,' placing the powerful out-group members as victims of the normally disenfranchised in-group members is significant. In the jokes that put out-group members in a negative light, it is not necessary or expected that they should laugh along with the jokes. Indeed, I have often observed when discussing Deaf humor with students that some hearing students find Deaf humor that lampoons hearing people hurtful, childish or simply unfunny. This 'unlaughter' (Smith, 2009) is a characteristic response of the out-group when it is attacked by humor. Smith concludes that

> When jokes are aimed at outsiders or marginal group members, shared laughter is not always expected; instead, the unlaughter of these salient individuals, contrasted with the shared laughter of the rest of the group, heightens group boundaries by mocking and ostracizing the outsiders. (2009, p. 166)

Chirico (2015) notes that the 'charged humor' that comedians use to attack social inequality expects audiences to be players in the social scenarios under attack, either showing their complicity or suggesting ways to redress the balance. This is seen in Deaf humor, where the behavior of hearing people in relation to Deaf people, and Deaf people's own behavior are both held up for scrutiny.

Deaf jokes focus on political tensions within the Deaf community as well as between Deaf and hearing society, and humor in sign language can insult the in-group, as self-disparaging humor in which group members admit their own faults, in order to control in-group behavior. Jokes that highlight violation of social norms ensure that those norms are followed, for example, tensions between seeing oneself as a proud member of a linguistic minority culture or taking support from hearing society offered to disabled people provide a rich seam of jokes and riddles. Deaf people know that life lived interacting with hearing society is easier with financial benefits provided for disabled assistance, while at the same time taking pride in not being dependent. Jokes such as the following (originally told by Clark Denmark in BSL and cited in Sutton-Spence & Napoli, 2012) can highlight and release some of the tensions this political situation creates.

> A Deaf man, a blind man and a man in a wheelchair are all in the pub one evening, complaining that the beer is weak and the pub is too crowded. Just then, God walks in and sees them looking miserable and dissatisfied. He comes over to their table and says to the man in the wheelchair, "Be

> healed!" The man in the wheelchair stands up and runs from the pub shouting, "Praise the Lord!" God says to the blind man, "Be healed!" and the man looks around him at everything he can now see. He runs from the pub shouting, "Praise the Lord!" God turns to the Deaf man but before He can say anything, the Deaf man says in panic, "No, please don't heal me! I don't want to lose my disability benefits!"

The "Deaf Swingers" riddle runs,

Q: At a Hearing "swingers" party, people throw their car keys onto the table to decide who they go home with. How do Deaf swingers decide?
A: They throw their disabled person's bus pass onto the table.

The complicated issue of deafness and disability is highlighted in the specific 'three men' joke genre of Deaf humor, of which we have already seen two examples. Three contrasting scenarios are always presented, during which the Blind man and the man in the wheelchair behave according to mainstream (and Deaf) preconceptions,[2] so that the behavior of the Deaf man, while recognised by the audience as 'typically' or recognisably Deaf, breaks expectations, frequently of the Deaf norms of social acceptability.

Gently used, humor critical of a Deaf individual can promote good behavior, especially among newcomers to the community, to allow communication to continue without the transgressor losing face. For example, a young Deaf person new to the Deaf community signed too fast for the older Deaf people to understand. A respected community member signed an entertaining image of the air blast created by the young woman's flying hands that made his hair fly in the wind and had blown his glasses clean off, and suggested she might like to slow down. This she did, among supportive smiles.

7 Conclusion

While Deaf humor occurs daily in sign language discourse for many reasons, we may see political aspects in much of it. Some, particularly in jokes, is overtly resistant, identifying areas of Deaf oppression by hearing society. However, other Deaf humor has a more affirmatory political interpretation, as it implicitly or explicitly valorises and celebrates Deaf culture and sign language on community members' terms, where hearing society is simply irrelevant. While much of Deaf humor is spontaneous and privately told within small group interaction, the classic canonical Deaf jokes of many Deaf communities show that the form, content, aims and reception of the jokes can contribute to powerful messages supporting Deaf identities, while also having a good laugh.

Notes

1 It is conventional to use upper case 'D' for the word 'Deaf' when referring to Deaf people as members of a cultural linguistic group.
2 Preconceptions helpfully critiqued by Greg Judge, a hearing wheelchair user in one of my undergraduate classes at the University of Bristol.

References

Bahan, B. (1994). Comment on Turner. *Sign Language Studies, 83*, 241–249.

Bienvenu, M. J. (1994). Reflections of Deaf culture in Deaf humor. In C. Erting, R. Johnson, D. Smith, & B. Snider (Eds.), *The Deaf way: Perspectives from the International Conference on Deaf culture* (pp. 16–23). Washington, D.C.: Gallaudet University Press.

Bouchauveau, G. (1994). Deaf humor and culture. In C. Erting, R. Johnson, D. Smith & B. Snider (Eds.), *The Deaf way: Perspectives from the International Conference on Deaf culture* (pp. 24–30). Washington, D.C.: Gallaudet University Press.

Carty, B. (1994). The development of Deaf identity. In C. Erting, R. Johnson, D. Smith, & B. Snider (Eds.), *The Deaf way: Perspectives from the International Conference on Deaf culture* (pp. 40–43). Washington, D.C.: Gallaudet University Press.

Chirico, M. (2015). All joking aside: American humor and its discontents by Rebecca Krefting (Review). *Theatre Journal, 67*(4), 754–755.

Christie, K., & Wilkins, C. (2007). Themes and symbols in ASL poetry: Resistance, affirmation and liberation. *Deaf Worlds, 22*(3), 1–49.

Durr, P. (1999). Deconstructing the forced assimilation of deaf people via De'VIA resistance and affirmation art. *Visual Anthropology Review, 15*(2), 47–68.

Hessel Silveira, C. (2015). *Literatura Surda: analise da circulação de piadas clássicas em Língua de Sinais* [Unpublished doctoral dissertation]. Universidade Federal do Rio Grande do Sul, Porto Alegre, Brasil.

Holcomb, R. (1985). *Silence is golden, sometimes*. San Diego, CA: Dawn Sign Press.

Holcomb, R., Holcomb, S., & Holcomb, T. (1994). *Deaf culture our way: Anecdotes from the Deaf community*. San Diego, CA: Dawn Sign Press.

Kincheloe, P. (2015). Bridges to understanding: What happens when a Bakhtinian critical lens is applied to an American Sign Language poem. *Sign Language Studies, 16*(1), 117–138.

Jacobowitz, E. (1996). Deaf humor and positive political skills in communication. *Deaf studies* IV: *Visions of the past, visions of the future* (pp. 97–110). Washington, D.C.: Gallaudet University.

Klima, E., & Bellugi, U. (1975). Wit and poetry in American Sign Language. *Sign Language Studies, 8*, 203–224.

Ladd, P. (2003). *Understanding deaf culture: In search of Deafhood.* Clevedon, UK: Multilingual Matters.

Lane, H, Hoffmeister, R., & Bahan, B. (1996). *A journey into the Deaf-world.* San Diego, CA: DawnSignPress.

Luckner, J., & Yarger, C. (1997). What's so funny? A comparison of students who are Deaf or hard of hearing and hearing students' appreciation of cartoons. *American Annals of the Deaf, 142*(5), 373–378.

Martineau, W. H. (1972). A model of the social functions of humor. In J. Goldstein & P. McGhee (Eds.), *The psychology of humor: Theoretical perspectives and empirical issues* (pp. 101–125). New York, NY: Academic Press.

Miller, B. (1994). De'VIA (Deaf View/Image Art). In C. Erting, R. Johnson, D. Smith, & B. Snider (Eds.), *The Deaf way: Perspectives from the International Conference on Deaf culture* (pp. 770–773). Washington, D.C.: Gallaudet University Press.

Peters, C. (2000). *Deaf American literature: From carnival to the canon.* Washington, D.C.: Gallaudet University Press.

Pol, C. (2014). *Deaf humor. A theater performance in Italian Sign Language* [Unpublished master's thesis]. Università Ca' Foscari Venezia, Venice. http://hdl.handle.net/10579/5425

Raskin, V. (1985). *Semantic mechanisms of humor.* Dordrecht: Kluwer Academic.

Raphaelson-West, D. (1989). On the feasibility and strategies of translating Humour. *Meta: journal des traducteurs / Meta: Translators' Journal, 34*(1), 128–141.

Robinson, D. T., & Smith-Lovin, L. (2001). Getting a laugh: Gender, status, and humor in task discussions. *Social Forces, 80*(1), 123-–158.

Rutherford, S. (1989). Funny in Deaf: Not in hearing. In S. Wilcox (Ed.), *American Deaf culture: An anthology* (pp. 65–82). Silver Spring, MD: Linstok Press.

Rutherford, S. (1993). *A study of American Deaf folklore.* Burtonsville, MD: Linstok Press.

Sanders, D. (1986). Sign language in the production and appreciation of humor by Deaf children. *Sign Language Studies, 50*, 59–72.

Smith, M. (2009). Humor, unlaughter, and boundary maintenance. *Journal of American Folklore, 122*(484), 148–171.

Sutton-Spence, R., & Kaneko, M. (2016). *Introducing sign language literature: Creativity and folklore.* Basingstoke, UK: Palgrave Press.

Sutton-Spence, R., & Napoli D. J. (2009). *Humour in signed languages: The linguistic underpinnings.* CDS Monograph, Trinity College Dublin Press.

Sutton-Spence, R., & Napoli D. J. (2012). Deaf jokes and sign language humour'. *International Journal of Humor Research, 25*(3), 311–338.

Twark, J. (2014). The politics of humour: Laughter, inclusion, and exclusion in the Twentieth Century. *Monatshefte, 106*(2), 323–326 (Review).

CHAPTER 6

'Here Are My Wings'

Deaf Women's Liberation through the Poetry of American Sign Language and Written English

Karen Christie and Dorothy M. Wilkins

Abstract

Literature created by disenfranchised people is an act of both resistance and liberation. In this chapter, the works of Deaf Women poets in the United States is contextualized in a review of the history of Deaf education and the Deaf liberation movement. The literary traditions of Deaf Women poets creating in English and American Sign Language with a particular focus on the evolution of ASL poetry is described. A close analysis of select works of three contemporary Deaf Women poets demonstrate how these literary artists address racism, sexism and audism, providing a robust foundation for future generations of Deaf Women poets.

Keywords

Deaf Women poets – ASL poetry – English poetry

1 Introduction

> ...Is she to be
> Abandoned
> Stifled
> Knowing the foul darkness
> Of sure extinction?
> ...Ella Mae Lentz, "The Rosebush"[1]

The Deaf liberation movement has been a long struggle for assertion of the rights of personhood. It has been a struggle for cultural identity, for self-determination, for the acceptance and recognition of our signed languages, and

 | DOI:10.1163/9789004692299_007

for access to literacy and quality education. It has been a struggle to unmask audism[2] and the soft violence of benevolence perpetuated by the medical and educational systems. It is a struggle against the domination that silences Deaf bodies, particularly the bodies of Deaf Women and the literal and symbolic repression of their hands—a primary source of creative expression.

While the historical reality of infanticide and child genocide is behind us, the right to BE Deaf is still seriously challenged. Government-sponsored genetic counseling and genetic research clearly promotes eliminating Deaf people.[3] Because the majority of Deaf people are born into families and communities that do not use sign language, shortly after birth, Deaf infants are often saddled with a medicalized identity—one which medical practitioners strive to *heal* via surgical cures or early interventionists *treat* via spoken language clinical conditioning. Ironically, while signing has become more accepted and popular with many Hearing parents signing with Hearing babies, parents of Deaf babies are pressured to withhold signing.

Human rights for Deaf people are bound up with our rights to sign language and cultural identity. The UN Convention of the Rights of Persons with Disabilities states that people are entitled "to recognition and support of their specific cultural and linguistic identity, including sign languages and deaf culture."[4]

Human rights also include the right to a full quality education. The World Federation of the Deaf has asserted that Deaf children are often in educational programs that "do not meet their needs educationally, socially or emotionally." Full inclusion in education is delineated as a totally supportive, signing and student-centered environment in which students are able "to acquire full mastery of their sign language as their 'mother tongue,' as well as to learn the language(s) used by their family and community." While Deaf people in the United States (as well as other capitalist industrialized countries) have more opportunities than most, 80% of the world's Deaf population does not have ANY access to education.[5]

Deaf people who experience the greatest risk in being denied their human rights and in being safe in our culture are Deaf people of intersectional identities including: Deaf Women as well as Black Indigenous People of Color, Deaf Latinx, DeafBlind individuals, Deaf LGBTQIA, and disabled Deaf people. Deaf people from lower socio-economic classes, oppressed minority religions and cultures who are also part of the Deaf community are often less visible.

In general, literary creation requires one to become literate in ASL and/or English and to assert one's right to self-expression. When asked about the importance of artistic and literary creation of a people for cultural survival,

Paddy Ladd, a Deaf scholar, turned to a quote someone had shared with him in which she said: "The first thing oppression kills is creativity" (as cited in Christie & Durr, 2012). Clearly, the creation of ANY poem in ASL or written English, particularly by a Deaf Women of intersectional identities, is an act of true liberation.

In this chapter, we will explore the history of the education of Deaf people and the creation of literary works in both ASL and English. In addition, we closely examine the poetry of three Deaf women to show how ASL poetry, in particular, is a vehicle for Deaf Women's liberation.

2 The Language and Literature of Deaf Americans: Educational Evolution

In this section, we provide a brief historical overview of literary creation by Deaf people including an outline of the evolution of Deaf American education, ASL, ASL literature and ASL poetry. This will include literary works in written English by Deaf people. It will serve to contextualize our discussion of contemporary poetry created by Deaf Women in ASL and English.

> Wherever the deaf have received an education the method by which it is imparted is the burning question of the day with them, for the deaf are what their schooling makes them more than any other class of humans. They are facing not a theory but a condition, for they are first, last, and all the time the people of the eye. (Veditz, 1910)

> We possess and jealously guard a language different and apart from any other in common use—a language which nevertheless is precisely what all-wise Mother Nature designed for the people of the eye, a language with no fixed form or literature in the past, but which we are now striving to fix and give a distinct literature of its own by means of the moving picture film. (Veditz, 1910)

In the quotes above by George Veditz, who was the President of the National Association of the Deaf (NAD) in the early part of the 20th century, it is notable that he twice refers to Deaf people as "people of the eye." It was an assertion by Deaf people at that time that they identified themselves NOT by their ability/inability to hear, but by their human condition as visual beings—people whose language and literature were visually based. Today, we acknowledge this assertion as distanism which excludes and oppresses DeafBlind members of our community. Today, we all claim an agency in which we subvert being defined as subtractive individuals.

In the first quote, Veditz states that the accomplishments of Deaf people have been intimately connected with our educational experience. He also identifies one of the most prevalent and controversial issues in education related to Deaf people—the *method* of education. Educational methods for Deaf students have often been practiced as a binary opposition of either using a natural sign language for teaching academic subjects or using some form of the national spoken language for training Deaf students for 'the Hearing world.' Thus, while our schools have often been sites of colonization with the goals of forced assimilation into the spoken language community, having access to ANY education has long been a struggle for Deaf people throughout history. Certainly, the education of Deaf people has impacted our literary accomplishments. The second quote relates to the development of ASL literature, its 'oral' (face to face) literary tradition, and how technology for recording and preserving it has influenced its development. These are all areas we wish to address leading to an understanding of the foundations of poetry created by contemporary Deaf Women.

2.1 *Beginnings of Deaf Education and American Sign Language*

The majority of Deaf people have been born into families and communities that do not use sign language. Shortly after birth, a healthy Deaf infant's hearing is tested and multiple medical professionals descend on the family for intervention decisions. Deaf infants are then medically tracked and may undergo multiple audiological assessments, some under sedation; cochlear implant surgeries; and 'treatment' which focus almost exclusively on aggressive training of audition and speech.[6] While many Deaf children are exposed only to inaccessible or fragmented spoken language during their early years, Deaf children are clearly humans in search of language in their environments. Traditionally, accessible language and cultural experiences do not begin until they are enrolled in a Deaf school or program with Deaf peers who sign. There they meet signing Deaf children from Deaf and Hearing families who have easily achieved the normal milestones for language development. These children have served as language/cultural models, particularly in formal educational settings which do not use ASL.

Without an accessible language during early years, many Deaf individuals grow up with language deprivation which has severe cognitive, educational, economic, social and emotional consequences (Humphries et al., 2012). As Veditz attested, we are what our schooling makes us.

But how did education for Deaf children come to be in the United States? It is because of our educational heritage that Deaf Americans and Deaf people in a number of other nations have a historical kinship to France. There, in 1760, the first signing public school for Deaf children in the world was established by a monk, the Abbé de l'Épée. Deaf people in France and the United States have a folktale, told in their respective sign languages and handed down through the generations, of how l'Épée came to recognize the need for a school after meeting two Deaf sisters—who were never given names in the narration.

Two specific historical events occurring in France had a lasting impact on the legacy of Deaf literary artists and Deaf education in America. One event was the first known book published by a Deaf writer and the other was the emigration of one of the pupils of l'Épée's Paris school to America.

In 1779, Pierre Desloges, a Parisian bookbinder, published *Observations of a Deaf-mute on an elementary course of Education for Deaf Mutes* (Lane & Philip, 2006). While primarily a text defending l'Épée's educational methods, this publication provides us with some of the earliest themes and topics related to the 'Deaf Experience' that appear in later writings by Deaf Americans in English as well as other Deaf people world-wide. Desloges' writing served to confirm that a community of Deaf signers existed in Paris prior to the school's establishment. Furthermore, Desloges developed and discussed a number of issues which remain important today, 300 years later, such as

- the value of the lived experiences of Deaf people;
- the right of an oppressed person to defend one's own language;
- the assertion that the French Sign Language was a full language equal to others linguistically;
- the use of particular signs for identifying an individual;
- the difficulties of using a written language to write about a sign language; and
- recognition of the methods controversy (oral-only vs. signing) in the education of Deaf students.

Thus, even in the first-known published writings of a Deaf person we find assertions of Deaf humanity and responses to oppression toward Deaf people and our language.

The second Deaf individual we wish to highlight who made a lasting impact on the education of Deaf people in America was Laurent Clerc, a graduate of the Paris school, who is recognized as the first Deaf teacher in America. A Hearing American pastor, Thomas Hopkins Gallaudet enlisted the help of 30-year-old Laurent Clerc to help establish the first permanent Deaf school following the Paris school model. Founded in 1817, the Connecticut Asylum for the Education and Instruction of Deaf and Dumb Persons (later, the American

School for the Deaf—ASD) became the 'mother school' which produced a network of state schools spreading across the United States.

At ASD, Clerc and Gallaudet taught using modified French signing with a one-handed alphabet.[7] There were no formal signing classes for the students as they were expected to adapt their home-signs and become fluent through exposure and interaction. In 1818, just a year after the school opened, Clerc noted that a large number of students were coming from Martha's Vineyard, a small island off the coast of Massachusetts, with a fully developed sign language (Groce, 1985; Rée, 1999). Thus, certain students coming from Martha's Vineyard and others from Deaf families brought American signing traditions, which in turn, influenced the signing initially used by Clerc and Gallaudet in the classroom. Such was the beginning of American Sign Language and the system of education for the Deaf in America. For Black Deaf Americans, however, the beginning of formal education was much later.

2.2 *The Early Written Literary Tradition of Deaf American Women (1830–1910)*

The dearth of writings by Deaf American Women prior to the turn of the century was due to limited educational opportunities and sexist publishing practices. The works of four white Deaf Women who were published authors contain hints of how they navigated historical social attitudes toward being Deaf and being Women.

One of the earliest volumes of poetry published by a Deaf individual in the United States was *The Silent Harp: or Fugitive Poems* by Elizabeth Allen (1794–1849). Published in 1831/1832, most of her poems which focused on being Deaf reflected the dominant culture's attitudes of sympathy and misfortune (she became Deaf as a teenager). However, one notable poem, *Lines [Addressed to Mrs. E. C. of the Hartford Asylum, who is both deaf and dumb]* shows a shift in her perception (Allen, 1832, pp. 90–91). The third and last two stanzas are shown below:

O, come Eliza—haste with me,
  And to the meadow's stream repair,
Where nature's wonders we may see,
  Above—below—in earth or air.

•••

Alas! dear friend—we list in vain,
  Nor note, nor sound affects our ear,

And oh, their sweet enchanting strains,
We never—*never* more shall hear.

But hush, our sighs—we'll murmer not,
Since we unnumbered charms can view;
And though to hear be not our lot,
We'll see and praise our maker too.

Allen shows mastery of the poetic form that was common during her time. Her poem is constructed of quatrains with ending cross-rhymes and each line consisting of 8 iamb syllables. In this poem, she walked with another Deaf Woman (it is likely that the poet is referring to Eliza Boardman Clerc, the Deaf wife of Laurent Clerc) in an Eden-like countryside. Their shared experience of appreciating the visual beauty of nature led her to proclaim and affirm that Deaf people, and Deaf Women as well, were a natural part of God's creation.

A Brief Narrative of the life of Mrs. Adele M. Jewel, (being Deaf and Dumb) was one of the first autobiographical writings we have of an American Deaf individual. Published in various forms between 1859 and 1873, this work is instructive in that we learn about her impressions of life as a Deaf child before learning language and her first contact with another Deaf person after believing she was the only Deaf person who existed in the world. Below she writes of this first meeting with another Deaf person, which appears in many literary works by Deaf people in both English and ASL:

> Here I formed the acquaintance of a young lady also deaf and dumb, who had been educated at an Asylum in Ohio. She was the first mute I ever saw and the *mysterious ties of sympathy* immediately established a *friendly feeling* between us. I was surprised and delighted at her superior attainments. She could write a beautiful hand on her slate to those who knew not the use of signs, and in a little while taught me the sign language by which we conversed very easily together. (Jewel, p. 124, in Krentz, 2000, original emphasis)

Not only is the meeting of another Deaf person for the first time an important event in many life stories of Deaf people, Adele Jewel also met another Deaf Woman who served as a role model. After this meeting, Adele M. George (Jewel) (Kerr) (1834–1921) was educated briefly in the early years of the Michigan School for the Deaf. While struggling with poverty most of her life, she raised a Deaf son, and earned money to help support herself from her publications. Writing of her poverty and evoking religious pity, her sentimental style is in accord with the cultural expectations of the time while also defying the expectations by writing as a Woman who was both Deaf and extraordinarily literate.

One of the most prolific and well-known Deaf Women writers published works under the name of Howard Glyndon. Laura Catherine Redden (Searing) (1839–1923) was a graduate of the Missouri School for the Deaf and published in a wide variety of newspapers, such as *The Silent Worker* and *The New York Times*. In 1861, she wrote about the injustices of unequal pay for men and Women in the St. Louis public schools. As a Civil War correspondent for the *St. Louis Republican*, she traveled to Washington, DC and interviewed both President Lincoln and General Grant via pen and pencil. In 1862, she published a book, *Notable Men in the House of Representatives* followed by an 1864 volume of poetry, *Idylls of Battle and Poems of the Rebellion*. While much of her work addressed patriotism and the Civil War experience, she wrote poetry honoring figures from Deaf history such as Thomas Hopkins Gallaudet and celebrating the work of Deaf sculptor Douglas Tilden.

By the time it became known that Howard Glyndon was a Deaf Woman, it did not deter those who went on to publish her works. However, Deaf poet and scholar John Lee Clark (2005) states: "When critics did learn of the fact (that she was Deaf), … many of them lowered their earlier opinion of Redden's poetry" (p. 165). Redden used this experience in creating her short story, *The Realm of Singing*. The story presents an allegory in which a bird's singing is criticized only after it was noticed that the bird had a 'defective' wing. She is regulated to the lower branches ('down low') with the high branches symbolizing status and recognition in the world of poetry. These voices say:

> What have we here? A crippled bird that tries to sing? Such a thing was never heard of before. It is impossible for her to sing correctly under such circumstances and we were certainly mistaken in thinking that there was anything in such songs. Our ears have deceived us. They then withdrew adding, "We will forgive you poor thing, for trying to sing. And all the circumstances being considered, you do *quite nicely*. But then you know this isn't singing. The birds who do the real singing are not crippled as you are. Don't you know that birds in your unfortunate situation never succeed in singing? … and you cannot hope to be an exception to the general rule." (Jones & Vallier, 2003, pp. 208–209)

The story is successful in revealing the patronizing social attitudes toward disability and being Deaf. In addition, the trope as a bird representing a Deaf person appeared in many Deaf literary works hereafter.

Many of Redden's poems explored love and intimate relationships. Concerning her poem *Corinna Confesses*, the editors of a book on Redden's poetry note

"The first verse of this poem contains the only literal description of the female orgasm in nineteenth-century women's poetry" (Jones & Vallier, 2003, p. 187). The poem contains fifteen stanzas, we reproduce the first, third and final stanzas here:

To think that my eyes once could draw your eyes down for a moment,
  From their lifting and straining up toward the opulent heights—
To think that my face was the face you liked best once to look on
  When fairer ones softened to pleading 'neath shimmering lights!

•••

Too dark was the shadow that fell from your face bending over me—
  Too hot was the pant of your breath on the spring of my cheek!
I but dimly divined, yet I shrank from the warring of passions
  So strong that they circled and shook me while leaving you weak

•••

And yet, if I went to you now in the stress of your toiling—
  If we stood but one moment alone while I looked in your eyes—
What a melting of ice there would be! What a quickening of currents!
  What thrills of despairing delight betwixt claspings and cries!

In addition to expressing sexual excitement and pleasure, Redden also wrote about the social pressures upon young Women in the 19th century. The epic poem *Sweet Bells Jangled* is over 275 stanzas long and structured into over 70 sections. It describes a girl maturing into womanhood experiencing conflicts of love and work. Early on, the verses challenge the marriage expectations placed on young Women, pressures to keep up appearances, and the denial of her right to intellectual pursuits.

'Wilt thou be an ancient maiden?'
  Say the matrons unto me;
'Wilt thou have no chubby children,
  Clinging fondly to thy knee?'
'Ruddy matrons! happy mothers!
  What are children unto me?'

'Will thou live alone forever?'
  Say the matrons unto me.
Light I answer: 'Who is single

Should be ever blithe and free.
Sober matrons! thoughtful mothers!
Liberty is sweet to me!'

And later ... in a stanza describing her nineteenth year:

I pore above my books
So late of nights; and Mother does not like
To have me different from other girls,
Except that I should show the freshest face,
The prettiest dresses, and the readiest smile.
And ah! How shocked she would be, if she knew
That I write poems sometimes,--nay not poems,
But wretched verses...
My rhymes—my very own—(Jones & Vallier, 2003, pp. 82–83)

The poem contains hints of autobiography, as Redden did not marry until later in life, and then, only briefly. She was one of few Women poets who made writing a career, taking on audism, sexism and the right of Women to celebrate sexual experience.

The higher education of Deaf Women beyond Deaf residential schools became a real barrier for Deaf Women's achievement and literary creations. When the National Deaf-Mute College (which later became Gallaudet University) was inaugurated in 1864, it did not specifically deny Deaf Women entry to the college. However, by the late 1870s the president of the college was turning away female applicants. Under pressure, he admitted female students in 1887 on an experimental basis.

Agatha Tiegel (Hanson) (1873–1959) was one of the Women who entered Gallaudet during the experimental phase. A graduate of the Western Pennsylvania School for the Deaf, Tiegel later wrote

> I resented being on trial, both at Gallaudet and the world at large ... I resented that there might be any question of the right, the God given right, of my sisters and myself to make our places in the sun. (Hanson, 1937 pp. 6, 8)

As valedictorian of her 1893 graduating class, she helped put an end to the experimental nature of the education of Women at Gallaudet. Her graduation address, *The Intellect of Woman,* was a powerful anthem proclaiming the right of Women to an education. Her presentation, to an audience of predominantly men, confronts sexist child rearing practices, the primary goal of marriage

FIGURE 6.1 Agatha Tiegel Hanson (1873–1959)
ARTWORK: ELLEN MANSFIELD

for women, and the perceived inequality of women's intellectual capacities (Jankowski, 2001). At the conclusion of her presentation she states:

> There yet remains a large fund of prejudice to overcome, of false sentiment to combat, of narrow-minded opposition to triumph over. But … she herself is too strongly impelled by a noble hunger for something better than she has known, too highly inspired by the vista of the glorious future, not to rise with determination and might and move on till all barriers crumble and fall. (Tiegel in Jankowski, 2001, p. 293)

Her poem, *What's an Education For?*, published four years after graduation, echoes some of the same themes as her graduation presentation:

> To behold our limits widen
> Glories open to our view…
>
> To attain our soul's full stature
> Larger, loftier than our dream…

To feel that our proudest learning
Is entwined with something higher;
From the tallest mount of knowledge
Still we rise and still aspire…

Education, she proclaims here, opens up opportunities beyond what previously could be imagined. Further, it sparked something noble as well as lifelong learning beyond one's school years.

Not shown in this excerpt is Agatha's command and knowledge of the poetry of her time. Agatha's poem consists of 4 stanzas, each with 8 lines. The words at the end of lines 2 and 4 in the stanzas rhymed as well as the words at the end of lines 6 and 8. Like other educated Deaf people, it was important to show one had studied poetic form and could rhyme as well as Hearing writers.

Agatha went on to become a teacher at the Minnesota School for the Deaf an editor, and a poet of some note but her valedictorian address remains a classic piece of oratory to be embraced by future generations of Deaf Women.[8]

2.3 *The Dark Ages, NAD Motion Picture Project and Beginnings of ASL Literature*

When Deaf folks sign MILAN, it conjures up a catastrophic event that has reverberated throughout the DEAF-WORLD for over 100 years. During the 1880 International Congress on Education of the Deaf in Italy, a resolution was passed declaring "the incontestable superiority of articulation over signs for restoring the deaf mute to society." This along with a number of other resolutions led to the banning of sign language from schools for the deaf in Europe, and later, the United States. In Milan, the Congress was made up primarily of voting Italian Hearing instructors. These instructors overwhelmingly had worked to advocate for oral-only instruction, manipulating the entire Congress. The pure oral method swept over Europe traveling across the Atlantic Ocean and seizing every school for the deaf in the United States. Even the American School for the Deaf became an oral-only school.

Earlier in the year of 1880, the National Association of the Deaf (NAD) was founded in the United States. Composed of Deaf school alumni and Deaf community members, one of the first papers at NAD's first convention was Theodore A. Froehlich's *The Importance of Association Among Mutes for Mutual Improvement* (1880) which stated, "We have interests peculiar to ourselves which can be taken care of by ourselves."

During George Veditz's term as president (1904–1910), the NAD achieved two important objectives. First, the NAD challenged the federal government's discriminatory barriers to Deaf people applying for civil service jobs. After several years, the President of the United States announced that Deaf people would be eligible to take civil service examinations, which would qualify them for governmental employment. The second action was to establish a Moving Pictures Committee to counter the increasing encroachment of oralism. Utilizing the recently developed process of filmmaking, the NAD raised money to film second, third and fourth generation ASL signers showcasing a variety of genres (Supalla & Clark, 2015). The second generation of signers, for example, included Edward Miner Gallaudet (a Hearing son of Thomas Hopkins Gallaudet and President of Gallaudet University) and John B. Hotchkiss (a Deaf professor at Gallaudet who had been an ASD student and had met Laurent Clerc).

Since the establishment of ASD, sign language had been the language of most Deaf schools in the United States and in these schools the face to face literary tradition of ASL folklore began. Veditz, a third generation signer, was not aware of any formally recognized literary traditions in ASL as noted in his quote above ("a language with no fixed form or literature in the past"). Because of the possibilities of film for recording and preserving sign language, he could foresee the development of a literary canon. Yet, in truth, as the recording of these Gallaudet Lecture Series films document, the literary development of ASL was well underway. The master signers of the second and third generations were filmed demonstrating literary genres such as oratorical presentations, personal narratives, and humorous storytelling whereas fourth generation signers were filmed performing various literary arts (a short play, translated poem, and translated song) (Supalla & Clark, 2015).[9]

Out of the 15 signers filmed,[10] there were only two Deaf Women—both fourth generation signers who appeared as performers. In the film of a scene from a short play, *A Chapter from the life of Thomas Hopkins Gallaudet*, Ruth Knox appeared as a docile Sophia Fowler Gallaudet, T.H. Gallaudet's wife. Mary Williamson Erd appeared in a sign/gestured interpretation *The Death of Minnehaha*—the only selection that featured a Deaf Women alone. While her performance had mixed reviews, she did use some rudimentary features of ASL poetic signing. Furthermore, this film selection illustrated the tendency of educated Deaf people to translate English poetry into sign and include elements of performance.

Such signed performances by Deaf females seem to have been common in schools, literary societies, and churches of the Deaf. In fact, Schuchman (1988) lists a 1902 film entitled *Deaf Mute Girl Reciting "Star Spangled Banner"* as the earliest known film of a Deaf person signing.

In her analysis of female dynamics in the context of Deaf schools in the nineteenth and early twentieth centuries, Lee (2006) mentioned gender differences related to how sign language was used in residential schools for the deaf:

> Girls [...] had restricted venues in which to express themselves in sign language. Often their use of sign was tied to dramatic performance [...] graceful and highly stylized signed performance by deaf girls had become a staple of deaf schools. Commencement ceremonies traditionally included groups of girls reciting poetry and hymns such as *Nearer My God to Thee*. Girls earned praise for their dramatic and artistic expressions, efforts that emphasized physical beauty and form with signing ability. Boys, in contrast, frequently honed their sign skills through public speeches and competition, displaying their command of sign language in debate teams or valedictorian addresses [...]. In terms of sign language presentation, girls performed and boys communicated. (p. 13)

Yet when oralism took over the Deaf schools, there were no on-stage uses of sign language in Deaf schools. Sign language became a language used only in bathrooms and dorms. Demonstration of speech skills became the only 'performances' that Deaf children gave. Baynton (1996) noted that in 1860 there were hardly any Deaf students taught by oral-only methods. Yet, by the end of the First World War (around 1918), oralism was the communication methodology that dominated eighty percent of the schools, and maintained its hold until well into the 1970s. In addition, the number of Deaf teachers fell from almost half of all teachers to barely one tenth, many of whom were tracked into teaching 'multiply handicapped' Deaf students or vocational trades (Lane, 1992). Thus was the effect of the Milan Conference as well as the influence of oralism's leading proponent in the United States, Alexander Graham Bell. Bell was also involved with the eugenics movement and believed that in order to stop the formation of a "Deaf variety of the human race," Deaf schools should be closed, Deaf marriages disallowed, and sign language forbidden (Bell, 1884; Winefield, 1981). Due to Bell's power as a recognizable public figure and one with vast economic resources, his influence on the field of Deaf education and societal perception of Deaf people was extremely detrimental and is still at work today (viz., the AG Bell Association of the Deaf which has as a goal "advancing listening and spoken language for individuals who are Deaf and hard of hearing," has a powerful lobbying group, and has received money/sponsorship from cochlear implant companies).[11]

While oralism had a hold on educational institutions across the United States, racism also meant that a huge population of Deaf individuals had no access to education. The book, *The Hidden Treasure of Black ASL: Its History and Structure* (McCaskill, Lucas, Bayley, & Hill, 2011), uncovers the history of Black Deaf education which only began in 1852 with a small number of students being admitted to ASD. Following that, a number of northern Deaf schools over the years also educated small populations of Black Deaf students. As outlined by McCaskill et al. (2011), between 1857 and 1938, eighteen states in the South established segregated departments (associated with specific white schools for the deaf) and/or segregated schools for Black Deaf students. In these programs, schooling did not always go to the full 12 grades and there was often a focus on industrial/vocational training rather than academics. Desegregation of these schools was not complete until 1978. Further, Gallaudet University did not accept Black Deaf students until the 1950s. The first Black Deaf graduate was Andrew J. Foster in 1954, and the first Black Deaf Woman graduate was Ida Gray Hampton in 1957, both who later earned advanced degrees. Foster went on to establish over 30 schools for the deaf in sub-Saharan Africa and Hampton was a well-respected educator in Florida. Yet, the history of racial disparities in Deaf education and systematic racism along with pervasive oralism and audism has continued to impact generations of Deaf people.

2.4 *Dawning of a New Age: ASL as a Language, NTD and the First Generation of ASL Poets*

Deaf scholars describe the 'dark ages of oralism' as coming to a close with the linguistic research on American Sign Language at Gallaudet in the 1960s. Dr. William C. Stokoe, who was a Hearing English Professor at Gallaudet, noticed that the English-like signing he was being trained to use in his classroom and that which was taking place among his students outside the classroom were completely different. This led to an examination of that natural form of signing and his establishment of a Linguistics Research Laboratory. The initial analysis showed that individual signs were made up of smaller parts (a limited number of handshapes, locations and movements), and when recombined they created new signs. This discovery, of a visually-based phonology, was accepted as proof by linguists that American Sign Language was a full-fledged language. In 1960, Stokoe published *Sign Language Structure* followed by *A Dictionary of American Sign Language on Linguistic Principles* (DASL) in 1965—the latter work, co-authored by two Deaf researchers, Dorothy Sueoka Casterline and Carl Croneberg. While educators of the Deaf and Deaf people themselves were initially skeptical of the work of Stokoe, Casterline and Croneberg, it was evidence which ultimately discredited and contested the "uncontestable superiority of articulation"—impacting Deaf education, empowerment and literary expression.

While the field of ASL linguistics began to grow producing analyses of further grammatical features such as morphology and syntax, schools and programs for Deaf students held fast to oralism. It wasn't until at least 10 years after the publication of DASL that Deaf schools began to change their communication policies—and even then, they did not fully accept ASL. What they implemented was one of a number of invented sign systems that could be used simultaneously with speech, ensuring that English would remain the dominant language. And often, sign language was only allowed to be used with those in the upper grades or with Deaf students who had been labeled 'failures' under the oral system.

Despite ASL being shut out of the classrooms, there was a thriving Deaf folklore during these dark ages. Bahan (2006) notes that Deaf Gallaudet professor Gil Eastman confirmed that ASL folklore, such as jokes, sign play and ABC stories, had been in Deaf schools at least since the 1930s—and likely back to Veditz's time. ASL folklore as an area of study has since been described as including the genres of anecdotes, material culture explanations, tall tales and legends, personal narratives, sign play, cheers/chants, rituals and customs, as well as folktales (Rutherford, 1993). Particularly valuable are films from the Festival of American Folklife (1981)[12] and San Francisco Public Library (1985) which showcases a number of older Deaf adults who had learned folklore in ASL in their Deaf families, Deaf community settings or during their oral schooling years.

While ASL folklore continued underground, the National Theatre of the Deaf (NTD) was formed in 1967 and sign language was seen on national and international stages. NTD was made up of both Deaf and Hearing actors with the Hearing actors voicing lines signed by Deaf actors. The theatre group innovatively experimented with adapting plays, creative translations, and artistic sign-mime. NTD was extremely popular with Hearing audiences. The response of Deaf audience members was mixed: the primary criticism being the signing was more artistic than comprehensible.[13]

Yet, NTD was important also due to the cultural ramifications of seeing a formerly "forbidden" language up on stage and experimenting with. One of our Deaf community members tells the story of first seeing NTD on stage as a teen with his Deaf family. He recalled it so clearly, not because of the performance itself, but because of what happened later that evening. His family went out for a late dinner following the performance and it was the first time his Deaf mother, father and himself had ever signed openly in a public restaurant. NTD was also the place where future ASL poets Dorothy Miles and Patrick Graybill performed and began thinking about the poetic possibilities of ASL.

Ella Mae Lentz, an ASL poet of distinction today, describes other ways in which NTD impacted Deaf school-aged students such as herself during this time. Ella was a student at the California School for the Deaf, Berkeley (CSD-Berkeley) under Deaf teacher, Eric Malzkuhn ("Malz"). Malz was a well-known master teacher, skilled in translation and knowledgeable about English literature. In 1968, Malz along with Deaf NTD actor Bernard Bragg taught a summer workshop at CSD-Berkeley. Ella remembers Bragg using many poems and haikus from the recent NTD tour for students to memorize and perform. Bragg demonstrated techniques for translating and performing poetry. Ella stated: "We just gobbled it all up! I got the best from both of them—a perfect balance of skills needed by a future poet: creativity (from Malz) and sign art techniques (from Bragg)" (cited in Christie & Durr, 2012).

Despite these positive experiences, Lentz noticed Deaf schools and members of the Deaf community had not yet become empowered in regard to using ASL:

> Still, English was at the forefront—it was clear that English was important and that one needed to start with English and then translate the English works into ASL. English was of high prestige and that was the attitude at that time [...]. At that time, the thought of taking our natural ASL off the streets and up onto the stage was scary for me. We were all fearful [...]. We were constantly trying to prove our worth via speech or Sign English as measures of our intelligence. Prove it, prove it, prove it. This is a hard way to exist, this constant oppression of what is natural and normal for us. There was no pride in our ASL and Deaf culture. None whatsoever. (E. M. Lentz, personal communication, April 8, 2016)

Later as a college student at Gallaudet, Ella states, "for the first time, I realized that ASL and English were separate languages and equal languages" Under the influence of Gallaudet Professors Canney and Eastman, she began

FIGURE 6.2
This is Dorothy Miles
ARTWORK: NANCY ROURKE

"experimenting with this radical idea" of creating poems in ASL. Several years later, she met Dorothy Miles who had left NTD and was working in California.

2.5 *Dorothy Miles: Experimenting with Poetic Forms in English and* ASL

> Courage
> and faith in my experience
> that's all I need.
> Here are my wings…
> …Dorothy Miles, *The Hang Glider* (1976)

Dorothy Miles (1931–1993) grew up in the United Kingdom, coming to the United States to attend Gallaudet University. As a young person, she wrote poetry and at Gallaudet she majored in English, winning prizes for both her poetry and her acting. Having learned British Sign Language in school, Dorothy described learning ASL at Gallaudet as both "confusing" and "like falling in love again" (Miles, 1976; Brown, 1977). During NTD's first year, Dorothy Miles saw one of their first performances and was awed and determined to join. After seeing NTD for the first time in March 1968, she said,

> I saw what they were doing with sign language, things I had never dreamed of. And I went home and started writing poetry that combined English language and signs. That was my first real honest to goodness poetry—before that I wrote, well, just verse—and it was all so exciting for me. (Miles in Sutton-Spence, 2003)

In 1976, Dorothy Miles published *Gestures*, a collection of 36 poems. Fifteen of these poems were a result of her experiments with combining English and sign. She also made a film of her signed performances of these poems that was made available by her publisher.

Dorothy Miles performed these poems using both spoken English and signs (she had become Deaf in childhood and still retained speech skills). She explained her "blending or interlinking" experiments in this way:

> I have tried to blend words with sign language as closely as lyrics and tunes are blended in song. In such poems, the signs I chose are a vital part of the total effect, and to understand my intention the poem should be seen as well as read. This is the difference between these particular poems, and those that have been written for English and are freely interpreted by individual signers. (Miles, 1976, p. 5)

> a number of those poems were written interlinking the two languages. I thought of a way of signing it and then how to write it almost at the same time. [...] couldn't say which happened first [...]. They just fit together. (Miles cited in Sutton-Spence, 2005, p. 150)

Not only is Miles' poetry interesting and important for the forms she was playing with, but also because many of the poems were clearly rooted in the experience of being a Deaf Woman. In *Gestures,* Miles divided her collection of poems into categories such as 'Nature Poems,' 'Animal Poems,' 'Poems of Love and Womanhood' and 'Poems of Experience.' Many of the poems collected under 'Animal Poems' and 'Poems of Experience' are, in fact, poems of the Deaf experience in terms of resistance, affirmation, and liberation.[14]

Here, we look at two of her poems, *To the Men I Love* and *Defiance*. The first, an English poem that doesn't play with sign language nor is performed, appears in the subsection 'Poems of Love and Womanhood.' The second, *Defiance*, grouped with 'Poems of Experience,' is one of the poems that Miles signed and performed on film.[15] In both poems, Miles expressed feelings Women often were told to repress—empowerment and anger.

"To the Men I Love"

Oh, all you men who opened doors for me
    That I might enter exits to myself,
I thank you for me. Who would ever know
    That the way out was the way in? To see
Mirrored in others' eyes my certain wealth
    Has brought it back to me. Now I may grow
To know you and to love you as I ought—
    Incessantly, demanding no return
Yet hoping always. Love cannot be bought
    Or sold, but only given, turn by turn.
Now may I give you back your selves, and say
    Only that I am richer for your care;
Only that I am more myself, this day,
    Because you loved me once, some why, somewhere.

The first line of the poem shows how men who followed social conventions of being polite were, unknowingly, leading the persona to learning more about herself. The poem follows some rules of sonnets in the number of syllables per line (10), number of lines (14) and a pattern of rhyming words at the end of her lines (me/see; myself/wealth; know/grow, etc.). It's interesting to note that one place where she changes the iambic pattern of stressed and unstressed syllables is in the third line—"I thank you for me"—perhaps the most direct comment she intends to communicate "to the men I love." In the poem, the back and forth, coming and going, giving and taking images ultimately result in a Women's empowerment rather than loss.

"Defiance"

If I were I
I would not say those pleasant things I say;—
I would not smile and nod my head—
When you say—
No!
I would not bear, restrain, repress my disagreement,—
But argue every point to puncturing—
Then smile—
If I were I.—

If I were I, —
I would not stand chained to co-operation;—
Give my hand humbly to your lead—
In your way —
No!
I would unlink the ring that binds my neck and gags me—
And let my great hate vomit in your face
Then laugh!

If I were I.

In *Defiance*, Miles introduces the poem in the film by explaining "most of us wear masks … so that the real I is often hidden behind a false I." She describes the struggle to be true to oneself and honestly express emotions such as anger. In the signed version, Miles creatively signs, "if I were I," first making the sign for HYPOCRITE and then blending it with the next sign for I. At a brief pause here, the viewer can see the sign for I, but can also see part of the form of the sign for HYPOCRITE behind it. This is followed by signing INSTEAD and the sign for I again, but this time I is signed singularly, emphatically—clearly meaning the authentic I. Throughout the poem, she continues to show the viewer the sign for I backed with the sign for HYPOCRITE, meaning "the false 'I' that I show to the world while the real 'I' remains hidden behind it." While a person may choose to accept things as they are, often for an individual from an oppressed group (as a Woman, as a Deaf person), passive acceptance and submission means the repression of one's anger and a denial of self. Thus, the poem ends with an explosion of anger—a clear expression of an authentic emotion.

And yet, in the signed version when she ends with the affirmation of "If I were I," she pauses and then slowly adds again the sign meaning 'the hypocritical false I' with an expression of cunningness. Padden and Humphries (2006) describe this as

> Abandoning the literal translation, Miles has gone beyond the English to create a line in signed poetry that has meaning above and beyond the words. Where her poetry had previously matched the two languages faithfully in translation and structure, here she tips the scale in favor of ASL. (p. 136)

The signed version, therefore, not only is performed poetically with creative use of signs and connections between signs, but also extends the meaning of the English poem.

In the written version, Miles again shows her control of poetic form in English by using patterns of repetition and a number of vowel and consonant rhymes. Yet, Miles *defies* expectations in the patterns of rhythm and structure of the poem—using the poem's form to further emphasize its meaning. For example, the first stanza has nine lines and the second mirrors the first until the very end, when she sets apart the final line "If I were I." This technique is effective for emphasis, but it doesn't quite carry the extra layers of meaning that the signed version so subtly expresses.

Dorothy Miles' blended poems have sometimes been called more of a pidgin sign English (Rose, 1992), primarily due to her simultaneous use of speech. It is fascinating to compare Dorothy Miles' version of her poem, *Total Communication*, with a later version signed by Ella Mae Lentz (San Francisco Public Library, 1984). Because Lentz uses ASL (and doesn't use voicing), the comparison helps us to focus on ASL poetic features that Miles did use. Both Miles and Lentz use a lot of ASL poetic elements such as creative use of space and neologisms. Lentz, however, is able to sign the poem with stronger non-manual signals (most simply described as facial expressions), which impact both affect and grammar. Her use of ASL mouthing (not speech, but mouth positions which function as adjectives and adverbs) produces greater visual descriptive power. Additionally, she uses different body shifts and pausing in more distinct ways. With Lentz's version, we see poetry in sign moving further away from English which would eventually be created in and directly inspired by playing with the linguistic features of ASL. Yet, Miles' contribution to the evolution to ASL poetry was revolutionary. Previously, Deaf poets either wrote English poetry or translated the poetry of others into sign. It was even rare for Deaf poets to translate *their own* English poetry let alone create a poem from ASL signs.

Dorothy Miles later returned to England creating poetry in British Sign Language (BSL). She became a BSL teacher and Deaf community activist. Yet, her years in the United States, experimenting with the forms of English and sign, were significant especially in her outright statement that "Signs have a rhythm meter of their own" (Miles, cited in Brown, 1977, p. 18). In the following decade, the first generation of ASL poets such as Ella Lentz, Clayton Valli, Patrick Graybill, and Debbie Rennie as well as Peter Cook and Kenny Lerner of the Flying Words Project began creating and performing, discovering how to artistically capture such rhythm. Thus, Dorothy Miles' work contributed significantly to the evolution of poetry by Deaf people and Deaf Women in particular.

2.6 *ASL Poetry: Coming into Its Own*

Soon after Dorothy Miles' return to England, the first conference on sign language poetry took place in South Bend, Indiana. The 1978 *Poetry in the Palm of Your Hand* Conference organizers invited Ella Mae Lentz as the primary poet of the conference. Lentz performed an evolutionary set of poetry during the conference. In two different performance sessions, she performed twelve different pieces.[16]

As shown in Table 6.1, she creatively translated three well-known English poems into ASL. For the fourth English poem, Lentz gave a nod to the ASL translation and performance of *Jabberwocky* by Joe Velez that has become an identifiable classic. Velez had worked with Lentz's former CSD-Berkeley teacher, Eric Malzkuhn, in the creation of his translation/performance. Another poem she shared was Dorothy Miles' poem, *California Freeways*, which appeared in *Gestures* and the accompanying film. She performed two sign-mime pieces in a style associated with NTD and Bernard Bragg. The authorship of these pieces, like many works of literature with folkloric face to face traditions, is unclear and likely created and adapted by a number of performers. In an explanation of sign-mime to the audience, she mentions how she performs using film techniques such as long shots and close ups (later coined Visual Vernacular by Bragg).

A number of works were her original creations. *Eye Music*, one of Lentz's better-known works today, was originally written in English and then translated into ASL. The poem, *The Glass Wall* was introduced as "blended poem" created to honor the sign newscasts that occurred in the Bay Area. She shared early versions of her original ASL poems, *The Dogs* and *Silence Oh Painful.* A

TABLE 6.1 Content of Ella Mae Lentz's poetry in the *Palm of Your Hand Performances*

Title of poem	Author/Creator	Type of poem/performance
"Barter"	Sara Teasdale	Translated from English to ASL
"Stopping by the Woods on a Snowy Evening"	Robert Frost	Translated from English to ASL
"There is No Frigate Like a Book"	Emily Dickinson	Translated from English to ASL
"Jabberwocky"	Lewis Carroll	Originally translated from English to ASL by Joe Velez with consultation by Eric Malzkuhn
"California Freeways"	Dorothy Miles	Blended Poem ASL/English
"The Horse Race"	The Deaf community folkloric tradition with an "Ella Mae Lentz" signature	Sign Mime
"The Road Runner: The Chase"	The Deaf community folkloric tradition with an "Ella Mae Lentz" signature	Sign Mime
"Eye Music"	Ella Mae Lentz	Created in English and Translated to ASL
"The Glass Wall"	Ella Mae Lentz	Blended poem ASL/English
"The Dogs"	Ella Mae Lentz	ASL poem
"Silence, Oh Painful"	Ella Mae Lentz	ASL poem
"Life and Death"	Ella Mae Lentz	ASL poem

final original ASL poem, *Life and Death*, would today likely be called a classifier poem—that is, a descriptive poem using ASL classifiers that smoothly link to each other creating elegant transformations. All three of these poems did have 'written ASL versions' (i.e., notes with English words), but they were written primarily for interpreters to work from and to help with Lentz remembering the poems. The *Poetry in the Palm of Your Hand* Conference was little known, and film from the conference was not widely shared. Nevertheless, it is likely this was the first national conference in which original ASL poetry had been performed.

At the 1980 National Symposium on Sign Language Research and Teaching conference, Lentz gave a paper/presentation on ASL poetry while Clayton Valli stepped on stage, performing his original ASL poetry. Later, both Valli and Lentz performed during the 1987 National ASL Poetry Conference which also featured poets Debbie Rennie, Peter Cook, and Patrick Graybill.[17] In the 1990s, there were two National ASL Literature Conferences in Rochester, NY and a number of ASL poets began to document their works on videotape (Graybill, 1990; Lentz, 1995; Rennie, 1990; Valli, 1990 & 1995).[18]

During that Second National ASL Literature Conference in 1996, Valli performed a number of ASL poems and also presented on his doctoral dissertation in ASL poetics, the first of its kind.[19] Additionally, there was a focus on educating Deaf students in ASL literature as well as performances by Deaf students from the Lexington School for the Deaf, Rochester School for the Deaf, and the National Technical Institute for the Deaf. Today, ASL poetry has become a vital part Deaf Cultural Studies programs in elementary schools, high schools and colleges. The Internet has become a space where Deaf poets who use sign language share their works beyond what even Veditz had envisioned.[20]

3 Deaf Liberation and Contemporary Deaf Women Poets

As noted previously, Veditz and the NAD worked to secure the right of Deaf people to qualify for government jobs. Deaf people in the United States and Canada also established the National Fraternal Society for the Deaf in the early 1900s that was a response to discriminatory practices for Deaf people striving to obtain insurance.

During the years of the Civil Rights movement, Women's movement and the liberation movements of other disenfranchised groups, Deaf people started to become aware of the concepts of equality and discrimination in our own lives. As we further claimed the linguistic emancipation of ASL, Deaf people turned to advocating for Deaf rights in education and as citizens.

While NAD ensured Deaf people could qualify for governmental jobs, the Rehabilitation Act of 1973 was the first federal legislation to address the civil rights of disabled individuals and prohibit discrimination in federal programs in terms of employment and services. After years of lobbying and protests, the disability movement pressured the government to pass the Americans with Disabilities Act in 1990. In terms of the education of Deaf students, governmental investigations reported on the failure of oral/English-only education of

Deaf children (i.e., the Babbidge report of 1965 and later the Commission on the Education of the Deaf report of 1988). These reports were addressed (in the government's view), in part, by the Education for all Handicapped Children Act (P. L. 94–142) enacted to establish "a free appropriate public education" in the "least restrictive environment" whereby disabled students interact with non-disabled students.

While legislation promoted greater equal protection for disabled individuals including Deaf people and significantly improved our lives in some areas, it did not recognize Deaf people as a linguistic and cultural minority. That is, we do not have protections related to our rights to an education in American Sign Language, to guaranteed provisions of access to information in ASL, and education in which Deaf peers and role models can promote healthy Deaf identities for academic, economic and personal achievement in order to be full citizens.

The NAD worked to advocate for some changes during these years, however, it neglected to advocate for all Deaf citizens. Kristi B. Merriweather explains the purpose for the founding of the National Black Deaf Advocates (NBDA) organization:

> The founding of NBDA wasn't based on one clear-cut cause but on several factors that converged into a determined passion to forge this organization into existence. Some of the factors were historically long-standing, such as persistent systematic racism and audism in the deaf and hearing communities, which manifested itself in inequitable resources and racial disparities in education, employment, housing, legal protection, and health care. The dominant society's devaluation and marginalization of non-conforming language (whether it be ASL, Ebonics, or black deaf dialect) along with the unique black deaf cultural features also planted the seeds for NBDA's inception. Various types of resistance against oppression, exploitation, and degradation have always been an impetus and mainstay of the Black American experience and its deaf members were no exception. W.E.B. DuBois stated that the greatest problem of the 20th century was the color line (racism). For Black Deaf Americans, their challenge was the color line plus the hearing line (audism). Black-oriented organizations like NAACP were strictly combating the color line, and Deaf-oriented organizations like NAD were strictly contending the hearing line. But – who was going to address both? Where would they gather where their shared reality as a people was not going to be treated as a minority footnote? The answer would be revealed in 1981, in the form of a vision of an organization by, for, and about Black Deaf people.[21]

Over the years, Deaf people have established additional organizations to serve vital roles in ensuring advocacy and empowerment of ALL members of the Deaf community such as Deaf Women United, Deaf Women of Color, the Rainbow Alliance of the Deaf, Deaf Queer Resource Center, Turtle Island Hand Talk, and Council de Manos to name just a few.

Perhaps the most notable event of the Deaf liberation movement occurred as a result of a perfect storm of various movements toward civil rights as well as the recognition and valorization of ASL within the Deaf community. In 1988, Deaf students, alumni, community members, and allies protested the appointment at Gallaudet University of a Hearing president from a pool of one Hearing and two Deaf candidates. The Deaf President Now (DPN) movement lasted a week, "seven days which shook the world," during which popular media turned a spotlight on promoting the rights of Deaf people to self-representation and self-agency particularly at a Deaf educational institution of higher learning.

In 2006 during the appointment of the next president of Gallaudet, the Unity for Gallaudet protest demonstrated the power of social media for harnessing GLOBAL Deaf power and discussions related to not simply having a Deaf person at the helm of the University, but having one who was chosen fairly among all qualified applicants and who values ASL as an academic language. Currently, the president of Gallaudet is recognized as one who needs to promote Gallaudet as a bilingual college and one willing to take on the issues related to racial inequality in the college.[22]

One interesting phenomenon resulting from the 1988 and 2006 protests was the creation by Deaf people of a number of literary and artistic expressions. Poems in ASL and English as well as films and performances demonstrated how a liberation movement of a people leads to artistic empowerment and artivism (see Durr on artivism, Chapter 8, and Christie & Durr, 2012 for short videos showing how these protests stimulated arts across various genres). Deaf Women's literary contributions included Kristine Hall's *Gally Protest Story A-Z*, Kristi B. Merriweather's *The Gallaudet Protest From My Eyes*, Mary Beth Miller's improvisational performance on DPN, and Colleen Ryan's *ABC's Gallaudet University Protest: A Poem*.

More recently, the work of Deaf scholar Paddy Ladd (2003) has led to a movement in the United States working to decolonize and empower Deaf individuals and communities. Ladd, who asserted that colonization was the best model that fits the historical 'treatment' of Deaf peoples, coined the term 'Deafhood.' Replacing terminology which has reduced us to a medical condition (i.e., deafness), Deafhood describes both an individual and collective journey. For individuals, it is the lifelong process toward self-actualization as an authentic and whole Deaf person. As a collective process, it describes how Deaf people themselves come to define their 'existential state of Deaf being-in-the-world.' This type of liberation movement focuses within our community, reframing our thinking and leading toward activism. Furthermore, a post-colonial literary theory/Deafhood framework has been used to analyze a significant number of ASL poems (see Christie & Wilkins, 2006; Christie & Wilkins, 2007).

While there have been a number of successful pieces of legislation and protests, the rights of Deaf people in education, employment, economic power and self-governance remain at risk today. Historical sites of linguistic and cultural transmission such as Deaf schools have become endangered. Empowerment as individuals and global citizens has led to greater awareness of strategies in which to advocate for these rights including the creation of literary works, particularly those in ASL.

3.1 *Contemporary Deaf Women Poets*

The Deaf community in the United States today is at least a bilingual community with ASL and English as the primary languages. Contemporary Deaf Women poets in the United States can be found both writing English poetry and creating ASL poetry. Deaf Women who write in English include Alison L. Aubrecht, Abiola Haroun, Kristi B Merriweather and Pamela Wright. Deaf Women ASL poets of note include Shira Grabelsky, Ruthie Jordan, Ella Mae Lentz, Nathie Marbury, and Rosa Lee Timm. Additionally, we are more aware of international Deaf sign language poets who are Women such as Canadian poet Jolanta Lapiak (ASL), British Sign Language poet Donna Williams, South African Sign Language poet Modiegi Moime, Brazilian sign language poet, Fernanda Machado and Swedish Sign Language poet Debbie Rennie (formerly from the United States). While these lists are not exhaustive, they do give a sense of the proliferation

FIGURE 6.3
Kristi B. Merriweather

of poetry in ASL in recent years in addition to the global magnitude of Deaf Women creating in sign language. In this section, we take a closer look at three American Deaf Women poets: English poet Kristi B. Merriweather, ASL poet/performer Nathie Marbury, and ASL poet Ella Mae Lentz.[23]

3.1.1 An In-Depth Look at an English Poet: Kristi B. Merriweather[24]

> "only I be
> tellin' me
> what a blakdeafemale is."

Kristi B. Merriweather self identifies as a Black Deaf Woman who prefers to use the term Ebonics to describe some features of African American Vernacular English that she uses in her poems. She currently lives in Atlanta, Georgia and is the first Deaf teacher in the mainstream program for Deaf students at Clarkson High School. Her passion today focuses on improving the lives of Deaf youth.

Kristi grew up in a Hearing family with strong Black Women role models both at home and at school. One early experience with advocacy was when she and her classmates in her integrated high school worked to demand a Black history class.

Her undergraduate degree was from Spelman College, a historically Black liberal arts college for Women. She describes her experience at Spelman as being empowering both inside and outside of the classroom: There was formal study of Black culture and Black Women's Culture as well as a variety of co-curricular activities where Women modeled leadership and advocacy skills. Kristi was the first Deaf student at Spelman under ADA who used interpreters in her classes. Breaking new ground at Spelman, she also established ASL classes.

Kristi felt that Spelman helped to nurture her identity as a Black Woman and later attended Gallaudet University to develop her Deaf identity: "in this way, I had planned to become a well-rounded person." During her graduate studies at Gallaudet University, Kristi utilized her leadership and advocacy skills to address the concerns of Black Deaf students. She led Gallaudet's Black Deaf Student Union in petitioning the college to include a Black Deaf Studies course in the curriculum. She advised the newly established Delta Sigma Theta (DST) sorority at Gallaudet bringing with her lived experiences as a DST member from Spelman. She became involved with the National Black Deaf Advocates organization, eventually serving in a number of capacities and founding its first youth program, the Youth Empowerment Summit (YES). During this time, Kristi began to turn to poetry writing primarily as a 'mental escape' from the pressures of her studies.

A number of Merriweather's poems are rooted in her experiences as a Black Deaf Woman. Her poem *Hollywood Queens Rap* is a celebration of notable Black Deaf Women in the entertainment field such as the filmmaker Jade, the actress/theatre founder Michelle Banks, and the performer Evon Black. Her poem, *It Was His Movin' Hands* describes the 'magick' of her attraction to particular Black signing Deaf men. Below she discusses two other poems related to Black Deaf Women.

"Remember"

Out of Motherland Africa,
ripped from my people
into the iron-heavy chains,
stifling my motions,
I look at the sea, the dark threatening waters
awaiting
to carry us on an endless, wicked journey,
  I heard my weeping mother yell to me,
    "Remember."

Out of slavery,
Lord knows the scars and horrors of my hands,
body, mind, & soul been through
I've forgotten my language, my home,
my hopes, my culture or even where
my family are.
Yet, as I watch my people heading for the
cities of the North or the farms of the South, no
money, no food, no clear guidance.
    Somewhere I heard my mother
    whisper to me,
      "Remember."

Out of Jim Crow,
with all its burning crosses and
burnt promises,
facing the stony faces of those that wear the
badge of law and order,
holding the nightsticks that have
senselessly beat

thousands of my people while we sang
"We shall overcome" and
trying to keep believing that.
Raise your Black Power fist
Say Right on, Black is beautiful.
Don't know why my head is hurting, some
kind of image is trying
to fight its way into it,
        It's screaming my mother's voice
        and eyes saying,
                "Remember."

Out of the burning riots of LA,
Through the red smoke of anger finally
unleashed,
I stand motionless to see the images finally
flashing before my eyes,
The drug dealers gaining control, the bullets
flying toward our people by
our own brothers,
the punch of the rap lyrics attacking the
dignity of sisters,
poverty, unwanted pregnancies, AIDS,
clarence and anita
        Suddenly, I saw the image of my mother
        Signing to me,
                "Remember."

Out of the cosmos,
Out of Africa,
Stationed here in America,
The Black Deaf Woman,
challenging and transforming systems
shattering restricting definitions
until she becomes in-defin-able,
timeless, progressive, creative,
and unstoppable.

Don't you remember?

In terms of structure, Merriweather creates a free verse poem with strong emphasis on repetition. The words "Out of" begin all stanzas (except the last one-lined stanza). This repetition situates the history of Black Americans—coming from a particular place of origin/homeland, relating oppressive life events whereby they have suffered and successfully moved. The word "remember" is repeated at the end of all the stanzas. Because the title of the poem is "Remember," it is clear that there is an emphasis on knowing the history of one's people in the role of liberation. Variations on the repetition of "remember" at the end of each stanza suggest this strengthening empowerment: from weeping to whispering to screaming to signing.

The poem, *Remember* was meant to explore that experience of looking back to the beginning to where Black people had power in their African homeland. The poem then moves on to the time when Africans were captured, and the impact of the violent disruption slavery inflicted on family ties and the loss of tribal/kinship connections. Merriweather mentions Jim Crow, the LA riots, and Anita Hill's testimony. During our interview, Kristi said,

> Today, I can imagine adding another stanza to this poem related to more current issues in the Black community such as #Blacklivesmatter. I use the word, 'remember,' repeatedly to remind people that it is important not to forget where you have come from.

In addition, repeated images of 'mother' in the poem were used

> because mothers tend to be the most powerful relationship that people have. It is the first relationship with another person in the world you have and it shapes who you are. People who have been abandoned at birth often feel a sense of abandonment in adulthood. It is a very primal connection. It also refers to the very real experience of how we tend to carry our mother's voice, her words with us throughout life. Further, repeating the use of 'mother' denotes the carrying of a cultural legacy and the recognition of Africa as the land of origin, our motherland.

Near the end of the poem, Merriweather refers specifically to Black Deaf Women.

> Because the Deaf movement for civil rights and the recognition of ASL as a language happened after the Black civil rights movement, I also incorporate the image of signing at the end of the poem. By incorporating the signing image, the poem communicates the appreciation of the history of

> both Black culture and Deaf culture. With both traditions valued, Black Deaf Women are empowered—moving on and moving up in the world.

Kristi B. Merriweather's poem *Remember* describes the historical journeys of African Americans, and specifically the role of African American Women. Africa is described as the MOTHERland and the role of mothers is emphasized in cultural remembrance—keeping alive one's family roots and history. Remembering (in the sense of the Akan word, Sankofa) resists forgetting and affirms survival. The poem concludes celebrating the future of Black Deaf American Women today—those who have found their place in the world—who have been born of this history (and the history of the liberation movements of Women and Deaf people that followed) and are now empowered to make history on their own terms.

"Be Tellin' Me"

People tell me
what they think
a black deaf female is
People tell me
what they think
they know
what a black deaf female is
People tell me
they know the deal
behind all the deals
just a simple solution
mix in the deaf culture,
add equal amount of
black culture,
stir well and smoothly,
pronto, the black deaf culture,
I say
excuse my standard English, but
/cursing/
I don't take no
second-handed,
mulatto, prescribed,
whittled-down,
semi-that,
half-here,

part-this
culture,
uh-huh
I be cookin' up my own recipe,
spicy, like my mama taught me,
no, don't need your bowl,
thank you very much,
only I be
tellin' me
what a blakdeafemale is.

Kristi explained the poem, *Be Tellin' Me* in the following way:

> During graduate school, I was caught up in writing my thesis which was about Black Deaf identity. I went to the Gallaudet University library to research the topic and found it was incredibly frustrating to try to find much research on Black Deaf people. This was puzzling to me because it was around 1996–1997, and I thought, of course, there should be a great deal of research by that time. Through my discussions with others, I came to the realization that the scarcity of research in this area was due to the fact that researchers traditionally assumed that Black Deaf people were no different from white Deaf people. It seems that the thinking was that Deaf culture erases any vestiges of Black culture. Therefore, much of the research had not taken into account the impact of Black cultural experiences on Black Deaf people. In addition, while I felt I was exposed to research about Black Women at Spelman, there was hardly any information about Black Deaf Women. In this poem I used "seasonings/spices" as a metaphor for this assumption that all Deaf people are exactly the same regardless of their race and their own unique experiences. In the poem, it says that people associate you with only Black culture, or only Deaf culture. This ignores the fact that Black Deaf culture is unique. It ignores the fact that Black Deaf Women are unique. The poem also includes playing with words—a strong part of Black cultureof creating newly coined words which really express more directly what we want to say.

The poem is created with short lines and infrequent rhymes. The two part adjective phrases in the poem (whittled-down/semi-that/half-here, etc.) give the poem a strong rap beat. The repetition of phrases such as "people tell me," "what they think," and "they know" build up a feeling of irritation.

In the beginning of the poem, *Be Tellin' Me*, Kristi B. Merriweather describes a resistance to other people's ideas, labels, and assumptions about the identity

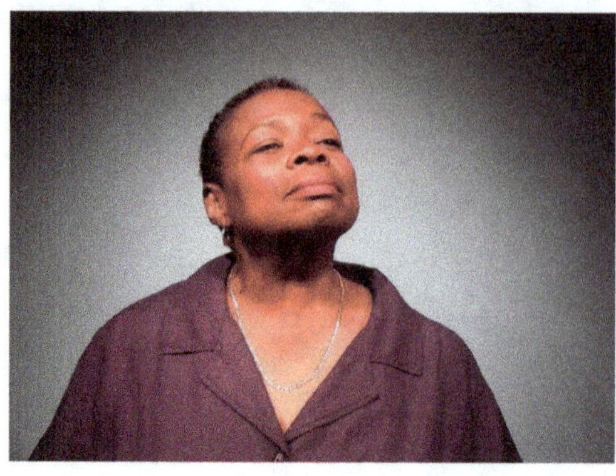

FIGURE 6.4
Nathie Marbury (©Raymond Luczak)

of Black Deaf Women. She challenged negative ideas such as 'mixed race' and 'the melting pot' by writing a poem about self-determination with symbols related to cooking—creating our own recipe of who we are. The poem becomes a self-affirmation. She has created for herself a unique name-word, "blakdeafemale" which celebrates her oneness/completeness.

3.1.2 A Closer Look at ASL Performance/Poetry: Nathie Marbury[25]

> "I thought to myself: WHO was I?"

Nathie Marbury (1944–2013) was a Black Deaf Woman who was a gifted performer and educator. Born into a large Hearing family in Mississippi, Nathie later attended and graduated from the Western Pennsylvania School for the Deaf (WPSD). She received her Bachelor's degree from Gallaudet University, two Master's from California State University at Northridge, and her Doctorate degree from Lamar University. She was the first Black Woman to teach at the Kendall School for the Deaf. An educator par excellence, she promoted ASL-English bilingual education for Deaf children, trained interpreters, and made a number of videotapes as an ASL talent and Deaf Culture expert. In addition, she was a tireless champion of Deaf people and the Deaf community.

In a filmed collection of stories and poetry, *No Hand-Me-Downs* (Clark & Luczak, 2005), Marbury shares anecdotes about her upbringing and background related to her ASL literary works. One of her ASL stories includes a powerful description of the racism she experienced as one of the few Black students at WPSD. The *Ajax Story* tells of girls who cornered her in a bathroom and tried to "rub off her dirt" by using Ajax bleach. The experience remained a powerful memory and Marbury didn't focus only on the individuals but on the systematic racism behind this act. Her story, *Hearing Aids and Headphones* described how she longed for hearing aids like those of the rest of her classmates, as if they were the latest fad. Her comic description of the sense of 'hearing'—the itchy static from hearing aids and vise-like pressure of the headphones used in class are humorously recognizable to most Deaf people. She laughs as she switches from her childish self back to being an adult narrating the story communicating she didn't know any better. In the end, the story affirms pride in being Deaf and the futility of hearing amplification. In another story, she told of her first year at Gallaudet and the registrars' mistaken belief she was a male student. As a freshman, she was summoned by letter to report for football practice. Marbury decided to show up at the first football practice, delighting the discomfort of the coaching staff and team. As these summaries illustrate, Marbury's entertaining stories often served the additional purpose of unmasking the social prejudice of audism, racism, and sexism. As a storyteller, Marbury's signature was her enhanced facial expressions that communicated a wide range of emotions and comic descriptions appreciated by Deaf audiences.

A small sample of her original ASL poetry was included in the *No Hand-Me-Downs* (Clark & Luczak, 2005) with voice over and English captioning. Below we look at two, one sharing her love for her granddaughter and the second related to identity.

"Crystal Marie"

In my arms is a baby named Crystal Marie
She was born in the mountains of Virginia on August 15th.
Her eyes are blue.
Her thick curly hair is dark brown.
Her skin glows.
Her toothless smile is so cute!
Her face is so full of expression.
Her lips frown and pucker.

This baby belongs to my daughter, who's now a mother.
This baby is just like my daughter growing up years ago:
I sign to her. She lights up with excitement and fascination.
I wonder if she'll grow up the same way as my daughter did.
Will she sign too?
Use signs to teach?
Or a pianist?
Or a painter?
Or a surgeon?
What will your future be like?
I'm so curious.

The performance of this ASL poem is unique in that throughout the poem Marbury signs with only her right hand as her left hand/arm holds a baby. At the end of almost each line, she rocks the baby creating a soft rhythm. At the beginning of the poem, Marbury introduces the baby to the audience and then her eye gaze shifts to the baby in her arms. For most of the poem, except when she introduces the baby and in the lines mentioning her daughter, Marbury's eyes remain lovingly on the baby. It's clear from her description that the baby is biracial, hearing and that her ASL heritage may be something she will claim as part of her future. Yet, the poem is truly a poem to a granddaughter, communicating strong unconditional love and the dreams a grandmother has of her granddaughter's future.

"Ones"

Him … a hearing black person.
Me … a deaf black person.
We met.
We talked.
He started learning signs.
We started discussing,
Which got more heated.
We argued.
Disagreeing, we turned away from each other.
He insulted me!
He said I wasn't black or deaf.
I was shocked.
Really … I cried.
Such an insult!
I have deaf friends all over,
Some of whom I'm very close to.
I understand deaf culture
And all of us deaf friends.
But what happened was I'd always thought of myself as Deaf first.
A new thought popped into my head.
And then something else happened.
I was puzzled at the difference.
But I decided not to care.
Then something else happened.
I'd suddenly thought of the hearing black person who's insulted me so.
I realized he was right!

He'd shown me different examples of what he meant.
I'd witnessed them too
He was really right!
I kept thinking about him.
I thought to myself: WHO was I?
I was really black first,
Deaf second.
I changed inside how I'd understood myself
Pah! You understand too?

The performance of this poem is amazingly controlled by handshape alliteration. As Dr. Clayton Valli explains, "Alliteration may be the repetition of the first sound of several words in a line, compared to the handshape rhyme, that is, the repetition of the handshape of several signs in a line" (1993, p. 113). Yet, Marbury basically uses the "one" handshape (index finger) throughout the *entire* poem. To maintain the integrity of the poem in terms of meaning using such constraints, much more control is needed by a performer. Marbury is exceedingly gifted at doing this through her facial expressions, eye gaze, and shifts between signing as the persona and narrator of the poem.

In other sections of *No Hand-Me-Downs*, titled *Learning Black Culture* and *Black First*, Nathie describes experiences that likely were behind this poem. She explains meeting a Black Hearing man when she was a student at UCLA teaching ASL. He was "very strong on Black culture" and ended up teaching her about Black history, culture and heritage. Nathie explained this was "the first time I grasped the concept of Black community and culture" which she had never been exposed to at her (primarily white) Deaf school. In addition, she shared an experience in which she realized for the first time in Deaf community

FIGURE 6.5
Ella Mae Lentz (©Carl Chapman)

settings, such as a Deaf school where she worked, that she was viewed by Deaf people not as 'DEAF-SAME,' but as Black. From that day on she said,

> All along I'd thought of myself as Deaf just like everyone else. I was proud of being Deaf … I realized that people saw my Blackness. From that day, I changed the focus of my identity from 'Deaf' only to 'Black Deaf.'

Nathie Marbury's journey is different and expressed differently than that of Kristi B. Merriweather, yet both create poetically eloquent works of Black Deaf Women.

3.1.3 A Closer Look at ASL Poetry: Ella Mae Lenz[26]

> "we must seize the power of every poem to speak the truth"

Ella Mae Lentz self identifies as a Deaf Woman who is a lesbian and graduate of the California School for the Deaf at Berkeley (CSD-Berkeley) as well as Gallaudet. She is a cherisher and defender of ASL who is also passionate about working toward the liberation of the Deaf community and promoting cultural growth. She has been an ASL researcher, teacher and curriculum developer. One of her primary callings is in using her native fluency in ASL and Deaf cultural knowledge to disseminate current research and critical theories to members of the Deaf community. She was one of the founders of the Deafhood Foundation, "an organization dedicated to achieving economic and social justice for all Deaf people."[27]

Growing up in Berkeley in the 1960s, she had exposure to the Women's movement and the Civil Rights movement which impacted her ideas about advocacy and social justice. Although she had limited information related to these movements as a Deaf person, she had personal experiences with sexism in the Deaf community. At CSD-Berkeley, Ella admits to being treated 'special' because of her English literacy skills and because she was from a well-thought of Deaf family. Most of the students she competed with academically were boys and she could feel the teachers' and administrators' preferential attitudes and greater expectations for the boys to succeed. While she was at college in the 1970s, she met other Deaf people who shared an interest in political movements and she became aware of and had greater access to information about the Women's movement.

As a lesbian, Ella explains "Homosexuality was a powerful taboo in the Deaf community during the years I was growing up and couldn't be discussed. Homophobia was acceptable and I had to suppress that part of my identity." Yet, she felt less impacted by sexism and homophobia than by linguicism—that is, discrimination against those who use ASL and the attitudes that ASL is inferior to spoken/written languages. Unfortunately, members of the Deaf community have grown up internalizing oppression and linguicism toward their own language:

> How exactly the Women's movement fit with our own Deaf community was not yet clear. When I was working in the field of ASL linguistics, I became aware that ASL had been analyzed and shown to be a bona fide language. As a result, I became involved with confronting linguicism as a form of political advocacy, borrowing strategies from the Women's movement. While Deaf Women clearly benefited from the work of Hearing feminists, it was still up to Deaf Women to apply this information and knowledge inside our own community. While being a Woman or being gay is not less important to me, I need to invest in and advocate for a healthy Deaf community. If we Deaf people don't do this, who will? (E. M. Lentz, personal communication, April 8, 2016)

As a Deaf person whose life is deeply rooted in the DEAF-WORLD, a significant number of her poems address audism, linguicism, and preservation of Deaf Culture such as *The Treasure*, *The Rosebush*, *The Door*, and *The Children's Garden* (in Lentz, 1995). Here, we take a closer look at two poems, *To A Hearing Mother* and *The Baseball Game*.

"To a Hearing Mother"[28]

You and I, we are so different ...
Worlds apart,
Language disparate,
Experiences unequal ...
You grew up knowing nothing about Deaf people and our lives
While I grew up knowing too well
The injustices by hearing people ...
And now you give birth to a boy!
And he is Deaf!
You are shocked and desperate ...
While I am surprised and delighted ...
Determinedly, you raise him to be like you ...
Impressive.
However, inside him, he shall be like me.
His hair, eyes and body are so much like yours ...
However, his soul, mind and heart shall be like mine.

He is your son …
But, he is of our people.
To whom then does the boy belong?
Well, he is like a tree …
Who he will be, we don't know.
Without us, he shall be alone and empty.
However, without you, the ground shall forever be barren …
And our wonderful people, our wonderful language shall dwindle.
We struggle about him, like a two-man saw, sawing, sawing
Until he falls.
No! We do not want that to happen!
Will you take my hands, and come join me
And become the doubly fertile ground
For him to grow strong, smart and beautiful!
Yes?

We focus here on one element of ASL poetry, space rhyming. In terms of form, the original ASL performance of this poem is creatively plotted out somewhat akin to a concrete poem on a page. While the narrator/persona (ME) is centralized, the Hearing mother (YOU) is pointed to and addressed to the camera, gaze straight on. Concepts such as WORLD and LANGUAGE are signed in two different spaces: near the narrator (MY-WORLD) and near the camera (YOUR-WORLD). The Deaf child in the poem is placed between the narrator/persona and the mother. Signs such as SAME-AS-ME/SAME-AS-YOU move back and forth between the boy and the narrator/persona as well as the boy and the Hearing mother. The sign STRUGGLE moves back and forth in space between the narrator/persona and the Hearing mother and is echoed in the sign for SAWING. Toward the end of the poem, the two spaces meld in signs that join together such as the signs BECOME SOIL. In this way, Lentz demonstrates via the structure of the poem the closing of separated spaces with the goal of collaboration.

This poem, we felt, was one of Ella Mae Lentz's poems that necessitated a female performer/persona. Lentz agreed that a man signing this would drastically alter the power dynamics in the poem and 'the intention of maternal partnership' would not be communicated. While she mentioned that she created the poem with a particular Hearing Women with a Deaf son in mind, it is truly a poem, which promotes a collaborative relationship between Hearing parents and the Deaf community for the sake of raising a healthy Deaf child. Traditionally, specialists in the field of Deafness/Deaf Education have warned Hearing parents away from such a collaboration saying it would be adversarial.

In this poem, there is an offer to co-nurture a child who is 'different' from the biological family. From a Deaf cultural view, Deaf children born into Hearing families have a birthright to be members of the Deaf community as well as the community of their families. The extended metaphor of the boy as a tree communicates a Deaf person as a part of the natural world, a world rich in biodiversity. It also speaks to one of Ella Lentz's passions—building a stronger Deaf community by investing in the next generation.

Below appears a translated English version of another of Ella Mae Lentz's original poems created in ASL.

"The Baseball Game"[29]

Back when I was a young girl,
we Deaf folks would gather for picnics
in a park near the woods
with a large grass field

We knew what we would find there:
Folks hungering for
good home cooking
and even better conversation.

I noticed then,
all the men would huddle together by the BBQ fire
while the women busied themselves at cloth-covered tables

The men
dissected cars, careers, and sports:
"My new car has a ton of horsepower, you can really feel it."
"My boss is an asshole. Just because I'm Deaf doesn't mean that he can
give me that crap."
"My golf game sucks. Can you believe I shot a 175?"

The women
chatted about food, clothes, and children:
"You know, honey is better for your health than sugar."
"There is a huge clothing sale is going on. You can't miss it!"
"Guess what? My fifteen-year-old daughter finally got her period!"

Meanwhile out on the field,
the call-up
"Who wants to play baseball?"
"Who wants to play baseball?"

My hand reaching high,
I ran over to join them.

The boys eyed me.
Should we let this GIRL play,
their expressions seemed to ask each other.
Grudgingly, they waved me over.

Standing all in a line,
the two opposing captains
surveyed the group.

The first captain carefully chose
the short, stocky kid.

The second captain prudently picked
the beanstalk boy with the burro ears.

One by one,
they were selected
until
I stood alone
opposite them all.

I stood ... looking across at the captains.
They stood ... looking at me
then each other.

"Oh, I think you should take her on your team," said one
"No, no," said the other, "you go ahead."

Finally, one of them called me over.
I thought about women in history,
who had been
belittled, undermined,

demoralized, and minimized.

I squeezed shut
the rage behind my eyes
in my fists.

The game began with my team batting.
After two outs, I was up.

The outfielders moved in.
The pitcher snickered and tossed
an underhanded slow ball.

And my rage connected.

The ball shot over the heads
of the open-mouthed outfielders
who raced to the far back of the outfield.

Passing first base,
I bowed my head to all those brave women
Who struggled to free slaves,
who battled for the right to vote.

At second,
I saluted the women who served in the wars
sneaking behind enemy lines
to save brother soldiers.

Rounding third,
I paid tribute to successful women
who shattered glass ceilings
in the corporate world, in government.

Touching home plate,
another victory.

My teammates, jumped off the bench,
cheering.
Behind them,

the men and women had joined,
applauding

"Wow, way to go!"
"She did it!"

Facing them,
I raised my hand
In a fist.

Twisting my wrist,
I flicked up my finger.

Now,
"Doyoufuckingetit?

Lentz describes her poem, *The Baseball Game*, as "an exploration where story and poetry intersected. I experimented with a free form technique, which pushed the boundaries between storytelling and poetry, using both prosaic and poetic features." Some of the poetic features include rhymes that appear in the beginning of the poem. The signs used to communicate the first two stanzas in the translation above, all rhyme, that is, all are made with a 5 handshape.

At the beginning of this poem, men and Women separate at a picnic. This type of division by gender for social purposes was very common in the Deaf club where Lentz grew up. The men tended to be upstairs in the poker room—smoking cigars and playing cards. Women and children were not really permitted upstairs. Women stayed downstairs in the club with kids. Men tended to run the bar/snack bar. The experience of both Lentz and that of the authors is that when Deaf couples socialize at a party for example, Deaf men and Women couples will separate, interacting more frequently with their own gender. In contrast, Hearing couples more often will stay, sitting and socializing together in party situations.

In this section of the poem, describing the different topics that men and Women chatted about, Lentz uses signing that is recognizably different. The men's signing appears lower, larger and more casual. The Women's signing, in contrast, uses a higher and smaller signing space. When asked about gender sign variation in ASL, Lentz stated, "I do notice different sign styles between men and women, but really there hasn't been enough research to document this." Nevertheless, the signing styles she used in the poem fit the scant research findings.

Later in the poem, attention shifts to the playground where boys gather to play baseball and hesitatingly include the girl narrator/persona. The girl is clearly aware of the reactions and yet takes her place among teammates. Lentz goes on to describe the game, the patronizing attitudes of the players, and the girl's eventual homerun. During the homerun, she thinks back to the accomplishments of Women in various areas and as she crosses home plate, the men and Women gather together to cheer her. The final sign of the poem is a neologism of the sign for UNDERSTAND, typically made with the index finger, is replaced with the middle finger which she signs to the crowd—here translated as "do you all fuckinget it?" While she has brought the men and Women together to the baseball game to cheer her on, her anger is truly at the sexism of the community as a whole.

The poem is instructive in that it shows how the social world of Deaf people was organized and how gender discrimination has existed there. This poem shows how poetry can be used to highlight sexism in the community and lead a charge toward Deaf Women's liberation.

4 Conclusion

Following Paddy Ladd (2003), we could describe the history of Deaf Women poets as a long Deafhood literary journey. As a community, Deaf people have made huge strides combating the audism and linguicism of the majority Hearing American culture and the internalization of those attitudes within our own community. Like other Americans, we have contended with sexism, racism and homophobia and their manifestations in our Deaf community. However, the greatest risk common to ALL Deaf people has been forces working for the elimination of Deaf people via genetic technology and research. In addition, medical technology, legislation and governmental mandates have led to Deaf children increasingly being denied the right to an education in ASL and with Deaf peers threatening our people, our community, our language, and our creative expression. Scholars H-Dirksen L. Bauman and Joseph Murray (2009) argue that Deaf people strengthen the biodiversity of humankind and identify sign language poetry as one aspect of DEAF-GAIN, that is, the unique and variety of ways that Deaf people contribute to humanity.

We are aware that our struggles have only just begun. Our ability to harness the literary power of Deaf Women to fight for liberation has yet to be fully realized. The literary works that DO exist, as shown here, carry the promise. Ella Mae Lentz (cited in Christie & Durr, 2012) has stated,

> poems become an opportunity to confront people, and they are needed to bear witness to the cause ... I want to have a poem right here in my hands that exposes our oppression, right here, right in front of you, right in your face.

Acknowledgements

The authors would like to express appreciation to Dr. Betsy Hicks McDonald and Prof. Patti Durr for their assistance. This chapter is the revised version of Christie, K., & Durr, P. (2012). *The HeART of Deaf Culture: Literary and Artistic Expressions of Deafhood*, an online website. In addition, we thank Nancy Rourke and Ellen Mansfield for honoring our Deaf foremothers and for permission to use images of their artwork. For sharing their poetry and their thoughts, gracious thanks to Kristi B. Merriweather and Ella Mae Lentz.

To the title. Please note that translations, summaries and discussion about ASL literary works continue to be challenging endeavors. To truly appreciate ASL literature, one needs to have access to its original signed performance, fluency in the language and knowledge of the culture from which it arose. While this is true of literary works in most languages, it is particularly true when the language is visually based and does not have a written form.

To the authors. The authors are self-identified as sighted Deaf White Cis Women. We both grew up in Hearing families and we consider ASL our native language. Dorothy attended the Rochester School for the Deaf. KC, public school-educated, taught at the Washington State School for the Deaf for a number of years. We are academics who are still examining our experiences of privilege and our experiences having grown up in a patriarchal, audist, racist, and homophobic (i.e., Kyriarchist) culture.

Notes

1 "The Rosebush" by Ella Mae Lentz is a poem in American Sign Language. It was translated into English by Karen Christie. See http://www.thevoicesproject.org/poetry-library/the-rosebush-by-ella-mae-lentz for the full ASL and English versions.

2 Audism is defined as attitudes and practices based on the assumption that behaving in the ways of those who speak and hear is desired and best. It produces a system of privilege, thus resulting in stigma, bias, discrimination, and prejudice—in overt or covert ways—against Deaf culture, American Sign Language, and Deaf people of all walks of life (Audism Free America, 2009).

3 For example, search the websites of the following organizations: National Institutes of Health, Center for Disease Control, National Human Genome Research Institute, National Institute on Deafness and Other Communication Disorders and Deafness Research Foundation, to name a few.

4 See Article 30 of the UN Convention on the Rights of Persons with Disabilities, https://www.un.org/development/desa/disabilities/convention-on-the-rights-of-persons-with-disabilities.html

5 http://wfdeaf.org/databank/policies/education-rights-for-deaf-children

6 See practices and legislation related to EHDI and NCHAM at http://www.infanthearing.org

7 Other sign languages, such as British Sign Language and New Zealand sign languages use a two-handed alphabet.

8 See https://www.youtube.com/watch?v=Gvv_aIoDP_I for a modern ASL version of this presentation. Since this article has been written, Jankowski (2020) has published a full-length biography of Agatha Tiegel.

9 For a selection of these works, see Christie and Durr (2012).

10 A number of the selections filmed were lost (see Supalla & Clark, 2015, for a discussion).

11 See agbell.org, opensecrets.org, and further reporting in https://handeyes.wordpress.com/2011/09/07/propaganda-and-legislation-a-la-ag-bell/

12 See Festival of American Folklife, Deaf Videos via http://videocatalog.gallaudet.edu/?category=206

13 Undoubtedly, NTD's most popular early production with Deaf audiences was the ensemble-created *My Third Eye* which was directed by Dorothy Miles. *Parade* was also a Deaf audience favorite, but is less well known. See Baldwin (1993) for information about NTD and audience reactions.

14 See Christie and Wilkins (2007) for a discussion of these themes and also symbols in ASL poetry.

15 The filmed version (with annotated text) of *Defiance* can be seen in Christie and Durr (2012).

16 Thanks to Ruth Hoffman for donating the *Poetry in the Palm of Your Hand* conference film of Ella Mae Lentz's performance to the RIT Deaf Studies Archives and for the NTID President's Office and Department of Cultural and Creative Studies for funds to digitalize the films.

17 See Lerner and Feigel's film, *The Heart of the Hydrogen Jukebox* (2009), for further information on this conference.

18 See Heidi Rose's (1992) work on the pre- and post-videotaping periods as they impact ASL literature.

19 See Christie and Durr (2012) for edited versions of his presentation and performance. For more information on his dissertation, see Valli (1993).

20 See ASL SLAM, VV Underground, and The Dandelions: ASL Literature Facebook pages; ASLIzed.org/jasl/ and sections from https://www.deafstudiesdigitaljournal.org/

21 From http://www.nbda.org/history_NBDA.html

22 In July 2016, Roberta J. Cordano became the 11th president and first Deaf Women president of Gallaudet University. At this writing (2016), she has begun to work toward addressing bilingualism, racism, sexism and homophobia at Gallaudet.

23 The poems discussed here were all created prior to the year 2000.

24 Information in this section is based on two filmed interviews with Kristi B. Merriweather. One is available via *The HeART of Deaf Culture: Literary and Cultural Expressions of Deafhood* (Christie and Durr, 2012). The other occurred between the authors and Kristi B Merriweather on January 25, 2016. A written draft of this section was shared with Kristi B. Merriweather for feedback.

25 Biographical information from *No Hand Me Downs* (2005) and http://www.nbda.org/news/nbda-mourns-the-loss-of-longtime-member-dr.-nathie-marbury

26 Information in this section is based on two filmed interviews with Ella Mae Lentz. One is available via *The HeART of Deaf Culture: Literary and Cultural Expressions of Deafhood* (Christie & Durr, 2012) and based on an interview with Miriam Lerner conducted on August 4, 2007. The other occurred between the authors and Ella Mae Lentz on January 20, 2016. A written draft of this section was shared with Ella Mae Lentz for feedback.

27 See http://www.deafhoodfoundation.org/Deafhood/About_Us.html

28 See an ASL version with English captions at: https://www.youtube.com/watch?v=PzpbYDCpyWg. The English translation is by Ella Mae Lentz

29 *The Baseball Game* an original poem in ASL by Ella Mae Lentz appears in her collection of ASL Poetry, *The Treasure* (1995). This English translation is by Karen Christie. Thanks to Ella Mae Lentz and John Lee Clark for feedback on this translation.

References

Allen, E. (1832). *The silent harp; or fugitive poems*. Burlington, VT: Edward Smith Publisher.

Audism Free America. (2009, November). http://audismfreeamerica.blogspot.com

Bahan, B. (2006). Face-to-face tradition in the American Deaf community: Dynamics of the teller, the tale and the audience. In H-D. L. Bauman, J. L. Nelson, & H. M. Rose (Eds.), *Signing the body poetic: Essays on American Sign Language literature* (pp. 21–50). Berkeley, CA: University of California Press.

Baldwin, S. C. (1994). *Pictures in the air: The story of the National Theatre of the Deaf*. Washington, D.C.: Gallaudet University Press.

Bauman, H-D. L., & Murray, J. M. (2009, Fall). Reframing: From hearing loss to Deaf Gain. *Deaf Studies Digital Journal, 1*(1–10). dsdj.galludet.edu

Baynton, D. C. (1996). *Forbidden signs: American culture and the campaign against sign language*. Chicago, IL: University of Chicago Press.

Bell, A. G. (1884). Upon the formation of a deaf variety of the human race. Washington, D.C.: Government Printing Office.

Brown, R. (1977, July-August). Dorothy Squire Miles: Bard of the Deaf theater. *The Deaf American*, 17–18, 44.

Christie, K., & Durr, P. (2012). *The HeART of Deaf culture: Literary and artistic expressions of Deafhood*. https://heartdeaf.com/

Christie, K., & Wilkins, D. M. (2006). Roots and wings: ASL poems of coming home. In B. K. Eldredge, D. Stringham, & M. M. Wilding-Diaz (Eds.), *Deaf Studies Today! 2006 Conference Proceedings* (Vol. 2, pp. 227–235). Orem, UT: Utah Valley State College.

Christie, K., & Wilkins, D. M. (2007). Themes and symbols in ASL poetry: Resistance, affirmation, and liberation. *Deaf Worlds*, 22(3), 1–49.

Clark, J. L. (2005, May). *Melodies unheard. Poetry*. http://www.poetryfoundation.org/poetrymagazine/article/171072

Clark, J. L., & Luczak, R. (2005). *No hand-me-downs* [DVD]. Minneapolis, MN: The Tactile Mind Press.

Festival of American Folklife. (1981). *Deaf Videos*. http://videocatalog.gallaudet.edu/?category=206.

Froehlich, T. A. (1880, August 25–27). *The importance of association among mutes for mutual improvement* [Conference session]. *Proceedings of the First National Conference of Deaf-Mutes. Cincinnati, Ohio*. https://archive.org/details/gu_proceedings1880nati

Graybill, P. (1990). *Poetry in Motion* [DVD]. Sign Media Inc.

Groce, N. E. (1985). *Everyone here spoke sign language: Hereditary deafness on Martha's Vineyard*. Cambridge, MA: Harvard University Press.

Hanson, A. T. (1937). The Victorian era at Gallaudet. *Buff and Blue, 46*, 5–8.

Humphries, T., Kushalnagar, P., Mathur, G., Napoli, D. J., Padden, C., Rathmann, C., & Smith, S. R. (2012). Language acquisition for deaf children: Reducing the harms of zero tolerance to the use of alternative approaches. *Harm Reduction Journal, 9*, 16. http://harmreductionjournal.biomedcentral.com/articles/10.1186/1477-7517-9-16

Jankowski, K. (2001). 'Til all barriers crumble and fall: Agatha Tiegel's presentation day speech in April 1893. In L. Bragg (Ed.), *Deaf worlds* (pp. 284–295). New York, NY: New York University Press.

Jankowski, K. (2019). *Agatha Tiegel Hanson: Our places in the sun*. Karen L. Goss Publisher.

Jewel, A. M. (2000). A brief narrative of the life of Mrs. Adele M. Jewel, (being Deaf and dumb). In C. Krentz (Ed.), *A mighty change: An anthology of Deaf American writing, 1816–1864* (pp. 118–128). Washington, D.C.: Gallaudet University Press.

Jones, J. Y., & Vallier, J. E. (Eds.). (2003). *Sweet bells jangled: Laura Redden Searing-A Deaf poet restored*. Washington, D.C.: Gallaudet University Press.

Ladd, P. (2003). *Understanding Deaf culture: In search of Deafhood*. Clevedon, UK: Multilingual Matters.

Lane, H. (1992). *The mask of benevolence*. New York, NY: Alfred A. Knopf.

Lane, H., & Philip, F. (2006). *The Deaf experience: Classics in language and education*. Washington, D.C.: Gallaudet University Press.

Lee, J. (2006). Family matters: Female dynamics within Deaf schools. In B. J. Brueggemann & S. Burch (Eds.), *Women and deafness* (pp. 5–20). Washington, D.C.: Gallaudet University Press.

Lentz, E. M. (1995). *The treasure*. San Diego, CA: In Motion Press.

Lerner, M. N., & Fiegel, D. (2009). *The heart of the hydrogen jukebox* [DVD]. Rochester, NY: National Technical Institute for the Deaf.

McCaskill, C., Lucas, C., Bayley, R., & Hill, J. (2011). *The hidden treasure of black ASL: Its history and structure*. Washington, D.C.: Gallaudet University Press.

Miles, D. (1976). *Gestures*. Northridge, CA: Joyce Motion Picture Company.

Padden, C., & Humpries, T. (2006). *Inside Deaf culture.* Cambridge, MA: Harvard University Press.

Rée, J. (1999). *I see a voice.* New York, NY: Metropolitan Books.

Rennie, D. (1990). *Poetry in Motion* [DVD]. Burtonsville, MD: Sign Media Inc.

Rose, H. (1992). *A critical methodology for analysing American Sign Language literature* [Unpublished doctoral dissertation]. Arizona State University, Tempe, AZ.

Rutherford, S. (1993). *A study of American Deaf folklore.* Silver Spring, MD: Linstok Press.

San Francisco Public Library (1985). *American culture: The Deaf perspective* [DVD]. San Francisco, CA: San Francisco Public Library/D.E.A.F. Media.

Schuchman, J. S. (1988) *Hollywood speaks: Deafness and the film entertainment industry.* Urbana and Chicago, IL: University of Illinois Press.

Stokoe, W. C. (1960). Sign language structure: An outline of the visual communication system of the American *Deaf. Studies in Linguistics Occasional Papers, No. 8.* University of Buffalo.

Stokoe, W. C., Casterline, D. C., & Croneberg, C. G. (1965). *A dictionary of American Sign Language on lingustic principles.* Washington, D.C.: Gallaudet College Press.

Supalla, T. & Clark, P. (2015). *Sign language archaeology: Understanding the historical roots of American Sign Language.* Washington, D.C.: Gallaudet University Press.

Sutton-Spence, R. (2003, December). *Dorothy Miles.* European Cultural Heritage Online. https://web.archive.org/web/20111002151727/http://www.let.ru.nl/sign-lang/echo/docs/Dorothy%20Miles.pdf

Sutton-Spence, R. (2005), *Analyzing sign language poetry.* New York, NY: Palgrave MacMillan.

Valli, C. (1990). *Poetry in Motion* [DVD]. Burtonsville, MD: Sign Media Inc.

Valli, C. (1993). *Poetics of American Sign Language poetry* [Unpublished doctoral dissertation]. Union Institute Graduate School, Cincinnati, OH.

Valli, C. (1995). *ASL poetry: Selected works of Clayton Valli* [DVD]. San Diego, CA: DawnSign Press.

Veditz, G. W. (1910). The President's Message [Conference session]. *Proceedings of the Ninth Convention of the National Association of the Deaf and the Third World's Congress of the Deaf, 1910* (p. 30). Los Angeles, CA: Philocophus Press.

Winefield, R. M. (1981). *Bell, Gallaudet and the sign language debate: An historical analysis of the communication controversy in education of the Deaf* [Unpublished doctoral dissertation]. Cambridge, MA: Harvard University.

CHAPTER 7

The Transformative Power of Deaf Theatre

Aaron W. Kelstone

Abstract

During 19th century Deaf Theatre emerged as a visual medium to support the Deaf community's development of a shared language (ASL), cultural identity, and creation of a cultural model based on the dichotomy between Deaf, those who are culturally Deaf, as opposed to deaf which refers to a hearing loss. During the 20th century Deaf Theatre's visual qualities attracted hearing artists who were exploring how performances could rely less on the spoken word. These hearing artists became active in Deaf Theatre diverting Deaf Theatre, from an exclusive focus on the Deaf community, to serve mixed audiences of deaf and hearing people. As sign language and voice began to appear simultaneously on stage it challenged the earlier cultural model. Within this intersectionality Deaf Theatre lacked the ability to explain how a physical (sensory) reality for Deaf people is different from hearing people. In the 1980's Women's Studies provided a new perspective on physical differences that enabled representation of multiple voices and communities. This now allows Deaf Theatre, to provide a new transformative experience for a better understanding of human diversity and the rediscovery of our common stories fully shared by all people, in all times, and in all places.

Keywords

American Sign Language (ASL) – cultural – Deaf – Deaf community – Deaf Theatre – performance – sign language – transformation

•••

> Artistic forms are used chiefly for the expression of values, feelings, and ideas whether or not the addressee understands immediately.
>
> PETERS (2000, p. 187)

∴

 | DOI:10.1163/9789004692299_008

1 Introduction

This chapter can only hope to touch on some of the transformative influences of Deaf Theatre.[1] It can neither be exhaustive nor conclusive due to the ongoing nature of social, cultural, and political changes within American society. Deaf Theatre, as it developed in America, utilized a visually defined space to satisfy the Deaf community's need to express its thoughts, beliefs, and experiences. For deaf people sign language in a performance mode using specific elements of American Sign Language (ASL) helped disseminate the cultural experiences of deaf people who today identify themselves as 'people of the eye' (Veditz, 1912). Their deaf experiences are based on a Deaf-World point of view as a linguistic minority with American Sign Language (ASL) providing the defining aspect of their cultural experiences (Bahan & Poole-Nash, 1995; Padden & Humphries, 1988; Lane, Hoffmeister, & Bahan, 1996; Lane, Pillard, & Hedberg, 2011).

Within this context Deaf Theatre offers an opportunity to mediate historical, social, and political misrepresentations of deaf people. Deaf Theatre actively occupies spaces, both real and imagined, to serve as a catalyst for actively reframing the Deaf experience and give shape to an authentic representation of the Deaf community. The active use of visual language on the traditional stage calls attention to what has previously been left unseen. Deaf artists performing on stage potentially challenge the plausibility of the social, cultural, and political perceptions that society has concerning deaf people leading to transformational changes.

When transformation occurs, in whatever form, it is not always a welcoming event for groups who are affected by the resulting changes. This is true of Deaf Theatre where some transformational benefits have unintentionally accrued to hearing people as Deaf Theatre productions increased its public presence within American society after the 1930s. These types of transformational changes have not always been understood or welcomed by the Deaf community. As hearing people moved from the wings to center stage issues of cultural ownership and language privileges generated a heightened realization within the Deaf communities of how ongoing interactions with hearing people continued to impact their daily lives in unexpected ways.

One example of transformational change relates to the unique capability that ASL and English have to perform simultaneously on stage. For many conventional theatrical performances it is difficult to concurrently use multiple languages during performances in close proximity to each another. The audience's ability to retain a sense of coherence becomes awkward as noted during the recent Broadway production of *Chinglish*. Henry David Hwang, a noted

American playwright, wrote the play in 2012 that successfully ran on Broadway for 128 performances. Dialogue, in the play, was presented in English and Mandarin and a New York Times article observed how rare it is for non-English dialogue to occur in Broadway plays. The same article emphasized that "some English-speaking theatregoers will be put off by parts of *Chinglish,* given that about a quarter of the dialogue is in Mandarin" (Healy, 2011).

Another example of multiple language use during performances is the National Yiddish Theatre Folksbiene (NYTF) presentation of plays, concerts, literary events and workshops in both English and Yiddish. Yiddish, in this situation, claims priority during performances due to the clear purposes and cultural priorities of the NYTF. Performances involving other languages, such as English and Russian, are presented as supertitles that effectively 'silences' the two languages and satisfies the expectations of its primary audience. Thus, only ASL and English have appeared to perform successfully together. However, the capacity for both languages to perform simultaneously can mask inherent vulnerabilities which will be explored in more detail later.

2 Historical Overview

Some Deaf people, since the 19th century, used traditional literature and visual arts as powerful tools of self-expression (Panara, 1970; Sonnenstrahl, 2002). However, for many Deaf people access to and use of literature and visual arts were of limited benefit because it depended on individual innate writing, painting, and visual arts talents. When sign language performances and, later on, Deaf Theatre became alternative choices for artistic expression, it expanded significantly the number of Deaf people who could successfully express their innermost thoughts and experiences. As a result, the life experiences of Deaf people could be more broadly revealed to others within American society.

Some Deaf artists have an innate ability to observe language and are naturally curious about how language works. They tend to engage effectively with an audience and can incorporate cultural or social values into their artistic work. Using the body's natural capacity for gesture, body language, and physical expression with the performance elements of sign language enabled them to bypass communication and writing limitations that Deaf people often face in their daily lives. Sign language in this context moved beyond everyday conversational use to become a powerful new medium of expression for the thoughts, experiences, and feelings of the Deaf community while also satisfying the universal need for effective human interaction all individuals desire in their daily life experiences.

As ASL performances evolved during the 19th century the performance elements of sign language were developed to support a creative means of expression and delivery. As the early Deaf artists mastered specific performance techniques added emphasis was given to the non-manual features of ASL. Non-manual features involve use of facial expressions, head tilting, shoulder raising, mouthing features, raised & lowered eyebrows, eye gaze, nose wrinkling, and periodic head movements such as nod and head shakes (Neidle et al., 2014). Other visual, kinetic, and movement features of ASL were refined primarily through post-performance social interaction and feedback from audiences and other Deaf artists.

Ben Bahan identifies these Deaf artists as being equivalent to smooth signers who "as a language artist can weave a story so smoothly that even complex utterances appear simple, yet beautiful" (Bahan, 2006, p. 24). What does a smooth signer look like to someone who does not know sign language? An interview with Marcel Marceau in 1978 by Vicky Herman at the University of Wisconsin Union Theater provides some insight. Marcel Marceau, one of the premiere mime performers of the 20th century, talked about his experiences with Bernard Bragg. As a mime, Marceau offered a unique perspective due to his masterful understanding of physical performance. When asked about his first audition meeting with Bernard in 1956 Marceau provides his first impression:

> it struck me immediately he had very elegant gestures and no vulgarity at all. Pantomime, when you have no technique, is very difficult to handle because if you have not the poetry of the body, if you don't have a technique […] it's difficult to watch, even to follow. (Marceau, 1978)

Marceau emphasized during the interview the importance of conveying emotions by maintaining a sense of timing. Marceau would later teach his mime techniques to Bragg in Paris and afterwards they maintained a friendship until Marceau's death in 2007. He indicated that what he observed of Bragg's' performances was that his sense of timing appeared instinctive. He saw this instinctive quality for rhythm and timing in other Deaf mimes and Marceau felt this was tied to some kind of internalized rhythm. Marceau described the essence of a mime performance as being a similar kind of internalized and intimate silence where the "mime needs, in silence, a musicality. First of all, we use music, second, the way we move in space with time has a resonance, it has a vibration, you hear the silence, people hear it" (Marceau, 1978).

In addition to innate ability that some Deaf artist may have had there was also the need to:

> inherit or learn various specialized techniques: controlling the pauses and tempos in stories, using parallelisms, repetitions, and digressions effectively [...] they also learn from master storytellers a core of narratives that employ basic themes that are meaningful and central to the culture and the audience. (Bahan, 2006, p. 25)

Over time, as these various Deaf artists became comfortable with their performance skills, they began to create indigenous stories grounded in these performance techniques. Eventually through community workshops and academic research these performance techniques became formally identified elements. As film and video became a common experience Bernard Bragg was able to identify certain cinematic features of film that were present within performances using sign language. These various performance techniques were grouped together and named a rarefied form of ASL "emphasizing the flexibility of using the body, face, and surrounding space for better communication" (Bragg & Olson, 1994, p. 27).

Bragg built on this rarefied ASL concept by identifying specific cinematic features found naturally in ASL, focusing primarily on non-manual features of ASL, which he later named Visual Vernacular (VV). Bragg explained VV as a performance process that:

> does not involve the use of words or signs. Close-up views, the long shot, the panoramic view, zooming, slow motion, fast motion—all are movements of the human body. The performer remains all the time within the film frame, so to speak, presenting a montage of cross-cuts and cutaway views. Visual Vernacular liberates latent resources of visual self-expression in creative signing that leads to a new fluency and dramatic impact. (Bragg & Olson, 1994, p. 27)

As skilled Deaf performers improved their ability to move in time and space, using sign language, they visually presented performances richer in potential meaning beyond a representational perspective. These kinds of performances, conducted for the most part in silence, became a transformative experience for modern Deaf audiences. As they watched ASL performances and later Deaf Theatre they began to appreciate the performance capacity of ASL to provide new insights. For example, after viewing an ASL poetry performance one scholar noted that "ASL can be beautiful to watch as music is to hear, but the former is a natural language replete with meaning. Music is sound without meaning; ASL is meaning without sound" (Polansky, 2013, p. 2).

As ASL performances became more common and shared with Deaf peers, it became a critical social and language breakthrough for Deaf people. Through performance and Deaf Theatre, the Deaf community moved closer to the center of public life and this attracted the involvement of hearing artists. These artists, as actors, directors, and writers, already frustrated with the artistic limitations of voice and text, found opportunities to actively participate with Deaf artists to support an alternative means of creative expression. As Deaf or hearing artists strived to break free of the written and spoken word they discovered within the framework of sign language performances an expanded dimensional use of the body for artistic expression. This fascination with the visual capacity of theatrical performance continues to the present day with various organizations, such as QuestFest, located near Baltimore, Maryland, promoting visual theatre available to both Deaf or hearing performers.[2]

From a rhetorical viewpoint, Deaf performance is transformative because it powerfully renders meaning by emphasizing a visual delivery of the message that can at times exceed anything that traditional oratory or literary approaches can hope to offer. While descriptive language, written or spoken, can be effective means of rhetorical delivery, sign language offers access to visual imagery beyond representational meaning to provide a dynamic delivery. Formal rhetorical studies have noted the effects of an oratory presentation depend on how voice, gestures, and facial expressions are incorporated into the speech (Bizzell & Herzberg, 2001). By utilizing kinetic and cinematic elements of sign language, the oratory tradition of delivery can be dramatically enhanced. Scholars of rhetorical studies strongly argue for a deeper understanding and revision of the traditional rhetorical triangle (speaker, audience, subject) to acknowledge the potential power of nonverbal signs, including sign language, to achieve a contemporary understanding and use of rhetorical delivery (Brueggemann, 2005).

3 Historical Background

Before ASL performances could fully develop and offer a viable path to Deaf Theatre productions, creative spaces were needed. Deaf individuals needed to develop skills as performers and benefit from various forms of feedback from other professional artists, teachers, and the Deaf community. At the same time the Deaf community needed opportunities to see these performances in a consistent way to allow them to become valid social, cultural, and artistic sources of feedback. Early sources of creative space were performances in the Literary Societies, broadly popular within early American culture that served as an important resource for the development of Deaf performers. The Literary Society format offered social and intellectual discussion based on orations, debates, and dramatic productions (Blaisell, 2008; Potter, 1944; Synder, 1904). Due to the broad popularity of Literary Societies it was likely to have crossed over into the Deaf community and the residential schools for the deaf. The ability to document this early influence has been difficult, but an article published in the Silent Worker (1912), written by Agatha Tiegel Hanson, describes the founding of the first Women's Literary Society (1881–1892) at Gallaudet College. In this article she commented that the men already had a Literary Society called the "LIT" (Hanson, 1912, p. 56).

When the Women's Literary Society was being founded Hanson explains that the founding members wanted a more varied program different from the men and "not patterned after the state deaf schools" (p. 56). This statement helps confirm the possibility that Literary Societies were active within the deaf schools prior to Gallaudet College. Establishment of the Ballard Literary Society in 1875 at Gallaudet College, along with earlier community efforts such as the establishment of the Clerc Literary Association of Philadelphia in 1865, likely influenced the subsequent development of Deaf Theatre (Mow, 1987). The Literary Society men's program, according to Hanson, involved debates, essay presentations, dialogues, and declamation programs. Hanson (1912) says that the women wanted to add tableaus, charades, storytelling, and characters from books in addition to debates and studying literature.

Deaf culture, traditionally an oral story-telling society based on an indigenous use of oratory, folklore, and performance art, responded well to this approach to exploring literature (Bahan, 2006; Frishberg, 1988; Rutherford, 1987). Students begin to experience different ways of performing ASL based on the use of various recital formats. The gradual development of an informal translation processes between written English and ASL allowed opportunities for the adaptation of songs and stories. With the use of skit formats involving various natural mime and gesture features available in sign language coupled with an iterative process, without an immediate need to create original works, made it possible to focus on their performance skills. This resulted in the modifying and adapting of different types of poems and stories from English literature. These performance and translation processes were gradually improved through teacher, student, and local Deaf community feedback.

When various ASL performances—first for Literary Society events, then in the Deaf clubs, and much later at larger organized events such as conferences and school reunions—became well received by the Deaf community, these artistic works were frequently requested. In time this led to the development of a traditional collection of community-based performances. As a core group of Deaf artists gained confidence in their artistic work they moved away from the exclusive use of these literary adaptations and began to create original content. Through the years the structure of ASL performances would become better understood and, especially after video technology became available, more broadly disseminated. These recorded performances would gain national audiences and with the effects of film editing, use of special effects, and the influence of technical advisors, these performances became more structurally complex (Krentz, 2006).

When Deaf Theatre arrived on the scene, these skilled Deaf artists provided the creative leadership along with other theatre skills necessary to support Deaf Theatre productions. Both sign language performances and conversational ASL, up to this point, had been a private affair within the Deaf-World. To conceptualize this sense of privacy within the Deaf-World we can borrow an example from popular literary fiction. In *The Lord of the Rings*, by J. R. R. Tolkien, the Hobbits represent an overlooked community within Middle-earth. Hobbits were quite content to be overlooked, satisfied by the comforting nature of their customs and way of life. The Deaf-World, during its early formation, was in a similar situation. The experiences of Deaf people were not well understood nor did the general public have any indication that there was a deaf community. Few outside of the Deaf-World understood sign language or its social, cultural, and artistic potential. The difficulties of effective interaction between deaf and hearing people caused deaf people to maintain a communal privacy and allowed them to limit their social interaction to inside the Deaf-World.

As early Deaf Theatre became an active part of the Deaf community, it served a functional role in continuing the 'oral' traditions created by earlier signing communities. Theatre provided a space to preserve, validate, and affirm the experiences of Deaf people. It provided positive social interchanges between Deaf people to develop their own social and cultural understanding of their lived experiences that lead to "strengthening communal ties, inscribing cultural history, affirming and exploring the expressive and communicative potential of ASL, and asserting the right to use ASL and define Deafness on its own terms" (Berson, 2009, p. 43). As the social and political perspectives of deaf people evolved Deaf Theatre provided an avenue to expressing these perspectives and promoting the Deaf community, its cultural norms, values, and status as a linguistic minority based on ASL. Deaf Theatre provided an inclusive style that "in its more indigenous form, the Deaf American play is cultural performance, uniting the community (including its marginal members) and facilitating a bonding and defining of the culture's identity and viability" (Peters, 2006, p. 78).

The ability of Deaf Theatre to provide a supporting role in the development of Deaf culture is likely its first major transformational influence on the Deaf-World. The ability to work through this transformational moment owes a debt to the Literary Societies. Deaf people needed a structural process, which the Literary Societies provided, for supporting the development of specific performance skills uniquely tailored to the creative and expressive purposes of the Deaf community. The development of these performance skills provided a critical bridge for supporting the emergence of Deaf Theatre because traditional theatre is a very formal construct, historically emerging from rich ritualized resources and derived from specific social groups within Western societies (Brockett, Ball, Fleming, & Carlson, 2015). It would have been difficult for the Deaf community to adapt and conform to these traditional expectations for formal theatre without the communal development of an indigenous style of Deaf performances in sign language. This is important because the social and cultural expectations of a social group are often reflected in theatrical productions by either affirming the cultural experience or serving as symbolical acts of resistance that identify the external forces affecting their lived experiences.

Depending on the needs and desires of both the artists and respective audiences, theatre can serve a broad range of social and cultural needs. Deaf people would need to explore and understand the trappings of a traditional theatre before they could adopt or modify certain theatrical practices acceptable to the cultural and social expectations of the Deaf-World. Fortunately, Gallaudet College provided early opportunities to achieve this when the men organized their own drama club in 1891 named the Saturday Night Club. Later, the women, due to social constraints of the time, established a separate women's drama club in 1895 named the Jollity Club. The drama clubs provided the next stage of development towards Deaf theatre and offered informal dramatic events organized and operated by the students without any direct funding by the college. Typical events included solo and group performances, personal narratives, essays, fiction, and other adaptations of literature from canonical sources (Peters, 2006; Ferris, 2005).

As students graduated, they returned home bringing with them their drama club experiences. The Gallaudet College drama clubs complimented the Literary Society activities by providing additional resources to nurture the development of Deaf Theatre. Eventually the drama club activities would lead to a unique style of professional Deaf Theatre later in the 20th century (Baldwin, 1994; Miles, 1974). The productions mounted by these two drama clubs between 1884 and 1949 were at first accessible only to those who knew sign language or were personally associated with the campus community. Deaf Theatre belonged exclusively to the Deaf community and most productions in

American Deaf Theatre significantly involved Deaf people in performances. These performances often were based on the adaptations of plays written by hearing playwrights and translated into ASL. Deaf Theatre borrowed specific styles and performance techniques from traditional theatre using for example shadow theatre during early productions. Later physical slapstick from vaudeville shows and melodramatic action from silent films were incorporated in the sign language performances along with gestures, mime, and sign play (Tadie, 1979; Schuchman, 1999). Spoken English and sound effects were likely absent and a modern example of this style is the ASL Films productions that are presented entirely in ASL without using a traditional soundtrack.[3]

4 Introduction of Voice

The use of voice emerged in Deaf Theatre performances more as a convenience to the hearing audiences rather than a functional need. Gallaudet College theatre productions began to occasionally include oral narrators during their productions through the early part of the 20th century and as Tadie (1979) points out:

> the use of an interpreter who provided oral narration to accompany the Sign Language dialogue enacted on stage was not new. It had occurred before. But after John Gough provided narration for *The Curse of the Idol* in 1932, a narrator was regularly included as part of most drama productions presented at the College. Perhaps this was because more hearing people began to attend plays at Gallaudet. Or perhaps the students found more hearing graduate students and faculty members who were willing to assume the task. (p. 169)

As the use of oral narrators continued another transforming influence at Gallaudet College was the introduction of faculty involvement with theatre productions. *The Curse of the Idol* not only marks the early appearance of readers, but it also involves the first involvement of faculty. Dr. Ted Hughes was an early influence on the drama club. He encouraged the actors to shift the style of theatre performances from improvisational use of skit, narratives, short stories, and non-verbal physical action to traditional theatre performances formally based on the division of scenes and acts. The process for selection of plays focused more on full-length plays that were dialogue driven requiring the Deaf actors to devote more time to the translation process. Adapting these plays from English to ASL was beyond the informal translation skills of the Deaf actors requiring increased involvement of the faculty. With a greater focus on translation the sign language process began to follow more closely an English word-for-word translation process. Continued faculty and student interaction gradually led to the establishment of a formal theatre program with curriculum expectations and greater control of theatre activities by the college.

The Drama Club productions had traditionally relied on an ensemble approach, naturally adopted due to the communal nature of Deaf culture, for the rehearsal process to support planned performances. The development process for plays would gradually shift, as the theatre program at Gallaudet College took shape, and become director driven, usually involving faculty to direct and select the plays. A greater focus on character development and formal processes for adapting the scripts from English to ASL lead to requirements for students to take credit-bearing courses in theatre and participation in college-sponsored activities. As a result the drama clubs lost their ability to influence the seasonal choices of plays and the scheduling of productions by the drama clubs began to decline (Armstrong, 2014).

As faculty involvement generated the establishment of a formal theatre program the seasonal productions became open to the general public. This transition to public access made vocal narration of the performances more of a required accommodation to meet the communication needs of a mixed audience. Deaf Theatre began at this point to move away from its exclusively Deaf-World audience. As hearing people began to gain awareness of ASL performances this shift would become more pronounced. An early example of this was during the 1940's when Eric "Malz" Malzkuhn, a Gallaudet College student, contacted the Broadway producers of *Arsenic and Old Lace* for permission to produce the show. The producers, Howard Lindsay and Russell Crouse, declined permission because the play was currently performing on Broadway. Malz responded back to Lindsay and Crouse explaining that the Gallaudet College production would be uniquely different because of its use of sign language. Much to everyone's surprise, especially the faculty and administration at Gallaudet College, the producers changed their mind and granted permission for the Gallaudet College actors to produce the play (E. Malzkuhn, personal communication, 2005, January 6). The Broadway producers also invited them to Broadway to perform during a night off for the original cast that occurred on May 10, 1942, at the Fulton Theatre. Malz realized that voice readers would be critical to the success of the May 10th performance. Voicing for the Deaf actors was no longer a courtesy because the audience, composed primarily of hearing individuals, would be unfamiliar with sign language. Communication access became necessary and several faculty members were recruited to read vocally (E. Malzkuhn, personal communication, 2005, January 6).

This performance by the Gallaudet College actors represents the earliest known performance, by an all-deaf cast, on Broadway (Baldwin, 1994). The Gallaudet College students' performance represents a significant moment for American Deaf Theatre. The presence of readers was for the benefit of a public audience and not simply a courtesy. It serves as an early indicator of a future transformational change where Deaf Theatre would shift its focus to accommodate the communication needs of the hearing members of the audience. As voice dictated the delivery of sign language perceptions, the value and importance of Deaf Theatre would be redefined by the Deaf community. The presence of voice became a necessity for the ongoing public success of Deaf Theatre productions because the financial success of productions became a greater need than communal, social, and cultural interaction. This became problematic for the Deaf community because the use of voice or speech was already an issue within the Deaf-World. This was due to the educational philosophies existing within deaf education concerning the politics of speech and language modality choices for educating deaf people (Johnson, Liddell & Erting, 1989; Turnbull, Turnbull, Stowe, & Huerta, 2006; Winefield, 1987). The debate regarding use of manual (sign language) and oral methods for teaching the deaf had been ongoing since the establishment of public education for the deaf in France in 1760 (Lane, 1989; Mirzoeff, 1995). As the language debate grew increasingly tense between Deaf and hearing people, the appearance of hearing actors alongside the Deaf actors in Deaf theatre disrupted the historical support by the Deaf community. However, for the moment Deaf Theatre on the Gallaudet College campus continued to perform to their traditional Deaf audience. Over the next thirty years, this specific style of Deaf Theatre at Gallaudet College would begin to fade away.

5 National Exposure to ASL Performances

The addition of voice readers during Deaf Theatre productions was not the sole cause for the eventual changes within Deaf Theatre. Literary Societies were also affected by social changes in American society with the emergence of radio and film. The expansion of extracurricular activities such as sports also offered attractive alternatives (Blaisedell, 2008). Not only was the presence of voice, coupled with changes in social interaction within society, impacting Deaf Theatre, so was also the increasing awareness of the public concerning sign language and deaf people. Similar to the earlier example regarding Tolkien's Hobbit characters, once their private world became apparent to others, the Deaf-World could not avoid the ensuing changes it experienced.

Broadway theatre would continue to be a source for public awareness of deaf people beginning with two successful Broadway productions. *Johnny Belinda*, produced in 1940, for 321 performances, and *The Miracle Worker*, produced in 1959, for 719 performances indirectly increased the public awareness of sign language and the existence of deaf people in American society. *The Miracle Worker* required Anne Bancroft, the actress performing the role of Helen Keller's teacher, to learn sign language. She took private lessons from Martin Sternberg, a noted deaf person active in the field of Deaf education, for six months and gained a further understanding of deaf people through her association with Edna Levine, a prominent administrator associated with the Department of Education. Both Levine and Bancroft formed a deep friendship and supported each other in promoting the idea of establishing a Deaf professional theatre (Baldwin, 1994).

Levine, Bancroft, and Arthur Penn, director of *The Miracle Worker,* encouraged the development of public funding for the establishment of a Deaf professional theatre without much initial success due to their active professional careers. Eventually, David Hays, a set and light designer, who worked with Arthur Penn and Anne Bancroft on other productions, became involved. He went with Levine and Bancroft to a Gallaudet College production of *Our Town* in 1961. As David Hays viewed the production, it sparked an interest in the concept of a professional Deaf Theatre company. David Hays was already looking for a new creative focus and immediately saw the potential for a Deaf professional theatre. After several grant proposal submissions were made by Levine and Hays their persistent efforts eventually led to Federal funding to support the establishment of the National Theatre of the Deaf (NTD).

While Broadway was a significant contributor, another event also directed attention to Deaf Theatre and helped to increase the academic and public awareness of sign language. Linguistic research conducted at Gallaudet College by William Stokoe, the chair of the English Department, resulted in the publication of significant research that officially established sign language as a language (Maher, 1996). Additional national and international linguistic research on sign languages further validated Stokoe's findings. The extensive sign language research led by Ursula Bellugi and Edward Klima at the Salk Institute in California would be influential as well. The validation of sign language at the academic level generated critical support towards the rationale for establishing a professional Deaf Theatre and using it to promote further awareness of Deaf people. Hays from the beginning, however, resisted the rehabilitative approach and emphasized instead the importance of an artistic focus for NTD as he believed it would prove to be the better approach and more beneficial to the deaf (Zachary, 1995).

Finally, a major influence, in addition to Federal funding, was the active involvement of the Federal government for initiating social changes. The Federal enactment of laws to resolve school segregation significantly impacted the Deaf-World as deaf students were integrated into the public school systems (Turnbull et al., 2006). This led to the disintegration of the traditional geographic boundaries that the Deaf community had long associated with the local residential deaf schools. The Deaf school no longer remained the center of social and cultural interaction nor the default site for the enrollment of deaf students. Despite efforts to resist these changes in school placement for deaf children the Deaf community was left with decisions on what would serve as a replacement for the deaf schools to preserve the values, norms, and cultural experiences of Deaf people.

Public school 'mainstreaming' programs contributed to a sense of geographical fluidity and an experience of diaspora. As the Deaf-World searched for alternative solutions Deaf scholars proposed new ways of thinking about the Deaf community grounded in current social understandings of cultural and linguistic models. One of the outcomes of these academic discussions led to the eventual adoption of the cultural model as a viable alternative. Within this model ASL became the cultural keystone for the Deaf community and served as the primary means of promoting the Deaf-World as a linguistic minority (Padden, 1999). The cultural model has served as an abstract 'geographic' boundary for the Deaf experience and helped define the Deaf identity throughout the latter part of the 20th century (Padden & Humphries, 1988).

With the increased academic focus on ASL coupled with the success of Broadway plays, notably *The Miracle Worker,* a growing public awareness of the Deaf community began to change prevailing attitudes towards sign language and deaf people. As significant interest was generated for sign language, it led to the evolution in the traditional composition of Deaf Theatre audiences. Audiences became more mixed with the percentage of hearing members increasing to nearly ninety percent. Essentially, mixed audiences became problematic for Deaf Theatre because it became necessary for productions to satisfy audiences embracing more than one cultural experience. In these circumstances decisions needed to be made as to which culture takes precedence over the other. Since the hearing audience was the majority of ticket buyers, by default it became an economic necessity to focus on the hearing segment of the audience.

Mixed audiences changed how Deaf performers conducted and delivered their sign language performances. It became necessary to adjust their signing style to match the voice actors for the benefit of the hearing audience. Deaf audience members began to experience difficulties following this new style of signing as it was less 'ASL' and followed the linear grammar style of the English language while placing a higher value on the aesthetic qualities of sign language. Sign language was perceived as being beautiful to watch by the hearing audiences and incomprehensible by the Deaf audiences. Consequently, the Deaf audiences felt left out and as these performances placed more attention on the needs of the hearing audience Deaf Theatre became less relevant to Deaf people (Bahan, 2006).

6 Redefining Deaf Theatre

Deaf Theatre would go through a period of transition as the Deaf community claimed their cultural identity. Developing new ways to define what the Deaf experience meant also meant developing new understandings of how Deaf Theatre should represent the Deaf community. As mixed audiences became more of the norm for Deaf Theatre, the politics of language and power took hold and generated renewed efforts to reassess and redefine the purpose of Deaf Theatre. One of the earliest seminal efforts was a thesis co-written by Lou Fant and Dorothy Miles (1976). The two authors proposed that Deaf Theatre consisted of two theatre models, one known as Deaf Theatre and the alternative form named Sign Language Theatre. Fant and Miles described Sign Language Theatre as performances involving both hearing and deaf actors based on plays written by hearing playwrights presented simultaneously in sign language and spoken English.

Deaf Theatre, on the other hand, was defined as the controlled presence or absence of hearing actors and voice during performances. Deaf Theatre, according to their definition, emphasized the sole presence of Deaf actors performing in ASL. Performance style used either the traditional skit format or a traditional play structure for plays written by Deaf playwrights or with topics relevant to the Deaf audience. The two styles of theatre, by definition, appeared in polar opposition to each other, however, Fant and Miles emphasized that these two theatre models did not need to be mutually exclusive. In other words, they proposed that there was room, within Deaf culture, to contain both performance models (Fant & Miles, 1976).

Another Deaf scholar, Don Bangs, took a different approach to defining Deaf Theatre. Bangs (1992) suggested that the two models of Deaf Theatre proposed by Fant and Miles, could coexist on two ends of a continuum. Instead of accepting the models as polarizing conditions, Bangs suggested that the Deaf Theatre experience was influenced by the composition of the mixed audiences. Thus, the production goals for each Deaf Theatre production would be assigned somewhere along this continuum space depending on the focus of each theatrical production (Bangs, 1992). The presence of mixed audiences at Deaf Theatre productions was not necessarily a new experience for the Deaf members of the audience. What was influencing the need to redefine Deaf Theatre was how the presence of hearing people was impacting the traditional performance style of Deaf performers.

What these various redefinitions of Deaf Theatre were attempting to address was the sense of unease within the Deaf community due to the explicit presence of hearing actors in close proximity to the Deaf actors. In the past hearing participation had been off stage or placed in areas not immediately obvious to the audience. Early Deaf Theatre performances involving voice readers, whether off stage or visually nearby, did not tend to dictate the flow of the Deaf artists' sign language delivery during performances. However, as the general public became more interested in Deaf Theatre, especially with the popularity of the National Theatre of the Deaf, the static role of hearing actors came to an end. The hearing actors would no longer be

> disembodied and hidden behind a screen or in the orchestra area, but visibly moving across the stage as they voiced the lines of the Deaf actors [...] but would themselves be actors and deliver as powerful a performance in voice as in sign. (Padden, 2009, p. 108)

As these hearing artists, and particularly artistic and stage directors, took a more active role in Deaf Theatre, just as years before Ted Hughes and other Gallaudet College faculty took control of the drama club productions, it began to change production expectations. These hearing artistic directors insisted that the Deaf performers work closely with the speaking actors to synchronize their ASL delivery to match the linear, non-spatial qualities of spoken English. The spatial qualities of ASL now had to be constrained in order to fit within the boundaries of the hearing actors' spoken lines. This required the Deaf actors to use sign language phrasing significantly different from the grammatical structure of ASL contributing to awkward timing issues. As the Deaf actors tried to synchronize their signing with the hearing actors they were asked to make further adjustments to their signing by utilizing more of the perceived iconic forms of gesture signs and also elongating other signs (Baldwin, 1994). By forcing Deaf actors to synchronize their signing with the hearing actors' voicing styles, the hearing audiences were able to follow the sign language performances because the signing style now followed the more linear phrasing of English. As a result "it altered Deaf actors' style of acting. It changed the direction of translation because the signing now not only needed to match the original English text, but it also had to match the choreography of voiced performance." (Padden, 2009, p. 113)

What was problematic for the Deaf actors using this kind of sign language approach ties back to the traditional use of sign language performances that are typically similar to oral presentations. Signed performances are not oral literature per se, yet still consisting more of an oral composition (Lord, 2000; Frishberg, 1988). Oral (sign) compositions are composed in a manner that allows the performance to proceed more rapidly, adhering to a certain structural flow and not relying on pure memorization. Thus, ASL performances are delivered, as are oral epics, not based on "broad improvisation, but rather are improvised within the restrictions of a particular style" (Frishberg, 1988, p. 152). Thus, the Deaf performers, as they synchronized their signing with the hearing actors, lost their compositional style along with the pacing and timing that is naturally embedded in traditional ASL performances. As their timing was thrown off, it disrupted other features of ASL performances related to physical movement and the use of nonmanual markers (NMM) supporting essential facial expression features necessary to remain grammatically correct as required in ASL.

Performances presented in this way were pleasing to a mixed audience because the inclusion of voice made hearing members of the audiences more comfortable following ASL performances. Voice, in this context, provided the hearing members of the audience with sufficient clues for successfully identifying the iconic aspects of the signs and comprehension of the visual imagery that passed their eyes. Sign Language Theatre, presented in this way, provides accessibility to an expanded national and international audience, but not necessarily to the Deaf community. While Deaf people recognized some of the creative and aesthetic qualities of sign language performed by the professional Deaf actors, they also found this type of sign language performances to be incomprehensible. Deaf Theatre had transformed from a creative means of expression for Deaf artist and a retainer of Deaf culture folklore to a paragon of accessibility that primarily benefitted the hearing members of its mixed audiences.

This pattern of accommodation by Deaf Theatre to the hearing portion of the audience would continue due to the growth of interest in sign language. As ASL became the third most popular foreign language choice across American college campuses it contributed to a heightened level of interest in ASL (Goldberg, Looney, & Lusin, 2015). Career opportunities also encourage the interest in ASL for hearing people working in the professional fields of sign language interpreting, teaching, counseling, and other social services to the deaf. As these hearing individuals gained some fluency in sign language, it created an expanded audience base of sign language users who enjoyed attending Sign Language Theatre performances. For hearing audience members, Sign

Language Theatre provided a safe social event where watching sign language performances produced an accessible way to practice their receptive sign language skills while enjoying the performances.

As a result, Deaf audience members began dwindling in numbers and sought out alternative social and entertainment opportunities where appreciation for their language and cultural experiences remained relevant to them. Deaf Theatre, no longer able to retain a large following within the Deaf community, increasingly focused on developing their audience within mainstream theatre. It would appear to casual observers that Deaf Theatre had lost its original purpose and was no longer a relevant vehicle of expression for the experiences of Deaf people. However, the appearance of hearing actors, voice, and the simultaneous use of two languages triggered other issues that could not be easily named or readily discussed at the time.

7 The Convergence of Diversity, Disability, and Intersectionality

When Deaf Theatre brought deaf and hearing bodies together on stage, these two sets of bodies differed in more ways than language. The Deaf community found these two sets of competing bodies on stage a confusing experience because dual use of spoken English and Sign Language affected the rhythm of sign language. It also disrupted the traditional audience experiences they had come to know. Deaf and hearing actors performing side by side, following the English language pacing, influenced how sign language was performed. The presence of additional actors created a contested space forcing audience members to choose which set of bodies to watch.

The experiences of dealing with two sets of bodies may have been overlooked during the earlier period of Deaf Theatre's performances. These earlier interactions involving simultaneous use of two languages, which many initially assumed was harmonious because one set of bodies (hearing) were kept off stage, may have masked deeper issues that were present on the stage with the appearance of different representational 'bodies.' The arrival of these competing bodies may have been an early signifier for what we now academically identify as intersectionality (McCall, 2005). Often in this context the viewpoint leans towards recognizing how the minority or disabled (abnormal) community appears on a traditional stage. In this case we need to recognize how the minority views the appearance of the majority (normal) into their community. In these moments issues of control long experienced by those identified as disabled come into focus. In these kinds of experiences, the intersectionality concept is reversed with the hearing actors representing the main sector of society. These competing bodies, performing on stage simultaneously, began to behave in ways that became disruptive to the expected norms of both the 'normal' and the 'disabled/linguistic minority' members of the audience. As the Deaf segment of the audience began to become conscious of how the two sets of bodies interacted with one another on stage it raised questions related to power, language, and cultural appropriation that go far deeper than a simple recognition of language differences (Thomson, 2005).

Not only did these bodies 'speak' differently, they also were contrasting representations: one of normalcy and the other body being identified as not normal by the hearing segment of the audience and normal by the Deaf segment of the audience. The categorization of the disabled body, as historically used by greater society, had generally served its social purpose to either remove or divert society's gaze from different bodies that were considered inappropriate to view (Lane, 2002). The Deaf-World lacked this historical reference as to how to address the appearance of hearing people inside of their cultural experiences. As the Deaf audience members became conscious of this presence they faced a quandary. Namely, do they address this presence, or do they remove themselves from this presence?

The obvious presence of different bodies could not be as easily resolved because social experiences of the 'normal' body performing in a 'disabled' space was relatively new. The presence of difference, and how it was traditionally controlled by both groups, conflicted with efforts to accommodate performances based on a perceived communication necessity. This constitutes a potentially new transformational change because once disability, difference, normalcy, and language appropriation between two cultural groups became apparent to all segments of the audience then Deaf Theatre could no longer be viewed simply as a theatre consisting of language differences.

For the Deaf community, their strong use of the 'D/d' dichotomy to establish membership in the Deaf-World served to reinforce an already historical resistance to the disability label. It served as an effective mechanism for keeping the 'other' outside their cultural and social boundaries. Their need to exclude was directly tied to the historical association by society, intended or not, to connect the experience of being deaf as representing incapacity, deprivation, and suffering due to an inability to hear. This prevalent view of the Deaf experience has represented a large part of the Deaf community's heritage (Gannon, Butler & Gilbert, 1981). Thus, for nearly thirty-five years the cultural and linguistic minority models served the Deaf community, both politically and socially, in their fight for improved educational, employment, and accessibility rights. The use of categorization and dichotomy, while useful in some circumstances to illuminate ideas or clarify relationships, will at some point begin to falter because it can overlook issues of complexity contained within lived experiences.

During the 1980s, Women's Studies began to challenge the overuse of categorizations. The lively discussion and dissemination of academic studies by Women's Studies programs helped improve our understanding of the complexity involving human interaction through newly introduced theoretical models. These models have since been used to analyze the inherent complexity existing within categorical assignments in regards to identity, gender, race, and disability (McCall, 2005). Recently, within the field of Deaf Studies some scholars began to question the Deaf community's exclusive reliance on the cultural model. Instead, it has been proposed that there is a need to recognize, just as the Women's Studies programs have done in the past, that the identity of Deaf people is complex, and the cultural model may be inadequate to fully explain the Deaf experience.

To fully understand the lived experiences of Deaf people demands answers that the cultural model may lack because the Deaf experience contains a physical (sensory) reality that is different from hearing people. The Deaf-World has consistently resisted an identity based on physical differences because of how society has focused on the disabled body. Differences based on defects and deficiencies are often viewed from a medical or pathological viewpoint and therefore only require a remedial approach (Baynton, 2008, chapter 1). For the Deaf-World, when bodies are 'different,' whether it is language modality (ASL) or other kinds of difference, these bodies still matter. Regardless of what a normative society identifies as disabling their lived experiences is their new reality and

> physical difference result[s] in a new configuration of abilities. Merely equating disability with impairment reduces a way of life, a complex relation to the environment, and a web of social relationships and cultural meanings to simple and concrete absence. (Baynton, 2008, pp. 296–297, chapter 1)

When one can consider the full complexity of a lived experience, then disability expands beyond the historical perception of an absence. Expanding beyond a cultural model makes room for the possibility that these 'bodies' can be both culturally Deaf and deaf. Thus, as McCall has pointed out, "politics based on identification and opposition" have been rejected by feminists and poststructuralists (McCall, 2005, p. 1779). These D/deaf bodies represent what is usually not seen within the 'hyphens' of society, nor even within the Deaf-World. For Deaf people their marginality lies between dichotomies of 'hearing-deaf' and 'able-disabled.' What happens when society begins to move beyond dichotomy? In this case the recognition of these types of hyphenated bodies on stage can become controversial and later disruptive to the social norms for both hearing and Deaf members of the audience based on how each choose to define normalcy and control privileged appearances within a social group (Linton, 1998; Sun, 2000). To simplify the identity of deaf people along opposing categories of audiology and culture may help demonstrate social and political fault lines, yet it fails to take into account the modern fragmentation of identity. This fragmentation includes multicultural and multilingual lived experiences of deaf people (Call, 2010).

Thus, the theatre stage is unique in that it can provide to an audience, almost simultaneously, a sense of safety based on their distance from the stage and its actors and yet a sense of unease as they observe the presence of each 'type' of body present on the stage. A theatrical play allows for the audience's gaze to be two-fold and within these moments there are opportunities for representation of multiple voices and communities. As a consequence, a "careful manipulation of aesthetic distance can quell, make apparent, or challenge existential and functional anxieties" (Ferris, 2005, p. 58). This causes audiences to engage in a newly perceived reality that potentially provokes new levels of thought. The audience is compelled to reconsider how seemingly disparate groups can find common ground and hopefully meaningful dialogue about what it means to be functional, creative, and human.

Difference becomes not a means of separating ourselves within society; instead, difference defines what is unique about all lived experiences within society. Deaf Theatre, at this juncture, may not be aware of this dynamic new role. This is because the Deaf community is still working toward creating, both socially and culturally, a new understanding of the lived experiences of Deaf people that can be acculturated across the boundaries of difference. Until then Deaf Theatre will need to wait in the wings, so to speak, before it can begin again to provide new transformational changes. The living stage, through Deaf Theatre, offers a way towards a better understanding of human diversity and within that diversity the eventual rediscovery of our common stories that can be fully shared by all people, in all times, and in all places.

Notes

1 It is common in Deaf Studies and Disability Studies to provide a distinction between Deaf (uppercase) and deaf (lowercase). The uppercase was developed by James Woodward (1982) to distinguish those who identify themselves as culturally Deaf as opposed to deaf, which refers to an audiological condition involving hearing loss. This chapter covers a historical time span where deaf people were struggling to discover their cultural identity. For the purpose of this chapter the lowercase and uppercase forms will be used when it relates appropriately to historical or contemporary usage.

2 http://questfest.org/about/visual-theatre

3 www.aslfilms.com

References

Armstrong, D. F. (2014). *History of Gallaudet University.* Washington, D.C.: Gallaudet University Press.

Baldwin, S. C. (1994). *Pictures in the air: The story of the National Theatre of the Deaf.* Washington, D.C.: Gallaudet University Press.

Bahan, B., & Poole-Nash, J. (1995, April). *Formation of signing communities: Perspectives from Martha's Vineyard* [Paper presentation]. Deaf Studies IV Conference, Woburn, MA.

Bahan, B. (2006). Face-to-face tradition in the American deaf community: Dynamics of the teller, the tale, and the audience. In H-D. L. Bauman, J. L. Nelson, & H. M. Rose (Eds.), *Signing the body poetic: Essays on American sign language literature.* Berkeley, CA: University of California Press.

Bangs, D. (1992). Sound of one hand clapping: Performing arts and Deaf people. In J. Cebe (Compiler), *Deaf Studies for educators. March 7–10, 1991, Dallas, TX* (pp. 126–131). Washington, D.C.: Gallaudet University (College for Continuing Education).

Baynton, D. C. (2008). Beyond culture: Deaf studies and the deaf body. In H-D. L. Bauman (Ed.), *Open your eyes: Deaf studies talking* (pp. 293–313). Minneapolis, MN: University of Minnesota Press.

Berson, J. (2009). Performing deaf identity: Toward a continuum of deaf performance. In C. Sandahl & P. Auslander (Eds.), *Bodies in commotion: Disability and performance* (pp. 42–55). Ann Arbor, MI: University of Michigan Press.

Blaisdell, J. E. (2008). *The influence of literary societies in Virginia's colleges and universities from 1904 to 1907* [Master's thesis, California State University].

Bizzell, P., & Herzberg, B. (2001). *The rhetorical tradition.* Boston, MA: Bedford/St. Martin's.

Bragg, B., & Olson, J. R. (1994). *Meeting halfway in American Sign Language: A common ground for effective communication among Deaf and hearing people.* Rochester, NY: Deaf Life Press.

Brockett, O. G., Ball, R.J., Fleming, J., & Carlson, A. (2015). *The essential theatre.* Boston, MA: Cengage Learning.

Brueggemann, B. J. (2005). Delivering disability, willing speech. In C. Sandahl & P. Auslander (Eds.), *Bodies in commotion: Disability and performance* (pp. 17–29). Ann Arbor, MI: University of Michigan Press.

Call, M. (2010). See me through the triplicity of my world: Ethical considerations in language choices. In K. M. Christensen (Ed.), *Ethical considerations in educating children who are deaf or hard of hearing* (pp. 14–37). Washington, D.C.: Gallaudet University Press.

Fant, L. J., Jr., & Miles, D. S. (1976). Sign Language theatre and Deaf theatre: New definitions and directions. In H. J. Murphy (Ed.), *Special Issue of Center on Deafness 2* (pp. 1–54). Northridge, CA: California State University Northridge.

Ferris, J. (2005). Aesthetic distance and the fiction of disability. In C. Sandahl & P. Auslander (Eds.), *Bodies in commotion: Disability and performance* (pp. 56–68). Ann Arbor, MI: University of Michigan Press.

Frishberg, N. (1988). Signers of tales: The case for literary status of an unwritten language. *Sign Language Studies, 59*(1), 149–170.

Gannon, J. R., Butler, J., & Gilbert, L. J. (1981). *Deaf heritage: A narrative history of deaf America.* Silver Spring, MD: National Association of the Deaf.

Goldberg, D., Looney, D., & Lusin, N. (2015). Enrollments in languages other than English in United States institutions of higher education, Fall 2013. https://apps.mla.org/pdf/2013_enrollment_survey.pdf

Hanson, A. T. (1912). The origins of O.W.L.S., *Silent Worker 25*(3), 56. https://archive.org/details/silentworkerv25n3

Healy, P. (2011, October 20). Do you know what I mean? Probably not. *New York Times.* http://www.nytimes.com/2011/10/23/theater/david-henry-hwangs-chinglish.html

Johnson, R. E., Liddell, S. K., & Erting, C. J. (1989). *Unlocking the curriculum: Principles for achieving access in deaf education* (Gallaudet Research Institute Working Paper 89–3, pp. 1–29). Washington, D.C.: Gallaudet University Press.

Krentz, C. B. (2006). The camera as printing press. In H-D. L. Bauman, J. Rose, & H. M. Rose (Eds.), *Signing the body poetic: Essays on American Sign Language Literature* (pp. 51–70). Berkeley, CA: California University Press.

Lane, H. (1989). *When the mind hears: A history of the deaf.* New York, NY: Vintage Books.

Lane, H. (2002). Do deaf people have a disability? *Sign Language Studies, 2*(4), 356–379.

Lane, H., Hoffmeister, R., & Bahan, B. (1996). *A journey into the deaf-world.* San Diego, CA: DawnSign Press.

Lane, H., Pillard, R. C., & Hedberg, U. (2011). *The people of the eye: Deaf ethnicity and ancestry.* Oxford, UK: Oxford University Press.

Linton, S. (1998). *Claiming disability: Knowledge and identity.* New York, NY: New York University Press.

Lord, A. B., Mitchell, S. A., & Nagy, G. (2000). *The singer of tales* (Vol. 24). Cambridge, MA: Harvard University Press.

Maher, J. (1996). *Seeing language in sign: The work of William C. Stokoe.* Washington, D.C.: Gallaudet University Press.

Marceau, M. (1978, February 14). Interview by V. Harvey. Union Theatre, University of Wisconsin. http://bernardbragg.com/homages/homage-7/

McCall, L. (2005). The complexity of intersectionality. *Signs: Journal of Women in Culture and Society, 30*(3), 1771–1800.

Miles, D. (1974). *A history of theatre activities in the deaf community of the United States* [Unpublished master's thesis]. New London, CT: Connecticut College.

Mirzoeff, N. (1995). *Silent poetry: Deafness, sign, and visual culture in modern France.* Princeton, NJ: Princeton University Press.

Mow, S. (1987). Theater, community. In J. V. Van Cleve (Ed.), *Gallaudet Encyclopedia of Deaf People and Deafness* (Vol. 3, pp. 288–289). New York, NY: McGraw-Hill.

Neidle, C., Liu, J., Liu, B., Peng, X., Vogler, C., & Metaxas, D. (2014). *Computer-based tracking, analysis, and visualization of linguistically significant nonmanual events in American Sign Language* (*ASL*) [Conference session]. Ninth International Conference on Language Resources and Evaluation, Reykjavik, 2014, Iceland http://citeseerx.ist.psu.edu/viewdoc/download?doi=10.1.1.475.7590&rep=rep1&type=pdf

Padden, C. A. (1999). The future of deaf people. In Gallaudet University, College of Continuing Education (Ed.), *Deaf Studies VI: making the connection: conference proceedings* (pp. 1–15). Washington, D.C.: Gallaudet University Press.

Padden, C., & Humphries, T. (1988). *Deaf in America.* Cambridge, MA: Harvard University Press.

Padden, C., & Humphries, T. (2009). *Inside deaf culture.* Cambridge, MA: Harvard University Press.

Panara, R. F. (1970). The Deaf writer in America from colonial times to 1970 (part 1). *American Annals of the Deaf, 115*(5), 569–513.

Peters, C. (2000). *Deaf American literature: From carnival to the canon.* Washington, D.C.: Gallaudet University Press.

Peters, C. (2006). American Deaf Theatre. In H.-D. L. Bauman, H. M. Rose, & J. L. Nelson (Eds.), *Signing the body poetic* (pp. 71–92). Berkeley, CA: University of California Press.

Polansky, L. (2015). *The best American poetry you'll never read.* http://aum.dartmouth.edu/~larry/asl_material/writings_2013/The%20Best%20American%20Poetry%20You%27ll%20Never%20Read.pdf

Potter, D. (1944). *Debating in the colonial chartered colleges: An historical survey, 1642 to 1900.* New York, NY: Teachers College, Columbia University.

Rutherford, S. D. (1987). *A study of American deaf folklore* [Unpublished manuscript]. University of California, Berkeley, CA.

Schuchman, J. S. (1999). *Hollywood speaks: Deafness and the film entertainment industry.* Champaign, IL: University of Illinois Press.

Sun, W. H. (2000). Power and problems of performance across ethnic lines, an alternative approach to nontraditional casting. *TDR/The Drama Review, 44*(4), 86–95.

Sonnenstrahl, D. M. (2002). *Deaf artists in America: Colonial to contemporary.* San Diego, CA: DawnSignPress.

Snyder, H. N. (1904). The college literary society. *The Sewanee Review, 12*(1), 78–91.

Tadie, N. B. (1979). *A history of drama at Gallaudet College: 1864 to 1969* [Unpublished doctoral dissertation]. Gallaudet University, Washington, D.C.

Thomson, R. G. (2005). Dares to stares: Disabled women performance artists & the dynamics of staring. In C. Sandahl & P. Auslander (Eds.), *Bodies in commotion:*

Disability and performance (pp. 304–319). Ann Arbor, MI: University of Michigan Press.

Turnbull, H. R., Turnbull, A. P., Stowe, M., & Huerta, N. (2006). *Free appropriate public education: The law and children with disabilities*. Denver, CO: Love Publishing Co.

Veditz, G. W. (1912). The President's Message. *Proceedings of ninth convention of National Association of the Deaf and Third World's Congress of the Deaf, 1910* (p. 30). Los Angeles, CA: Philcophus Press

Winefield, R. (1987). *Never the twain shall meet: Bell, Gallaudet, and the communications debate*. Washington, D.C.: Gallaudet University Press.

Woodward, J. (1982). *How you gonna get to heaven if you can't talk with Jesus: On depathologizing deafness*. Dallas, TX: TJ Publishers

Zachary, S. J. (1995). The National theatre of the Deaf and the teatr mimikj I zhesta: Two views on theatre of the deaf. *Theatre Topics, 5*(1), 53–67.

CHAPTER 8

De'VIA as an Art Form and a Form of Activism

Patti Durr
Interviewer *Ana L. Cruz*

Abstract

In an interview with Ana L. Cruz, Patti Durr discusses in this chapter the nature and significance of the De'VIA movement which stands for Deaf View/Image Art. Founded in 1989 with the De'VIA Manifesto, De'VIA is Deaf-themed visual art with the intent to show the Deaf experience. It incorporates both works of affirmation (celebrating Deaf culture) and works of resistance (focusing on injustice and oppression experienced by Deaf people), and provides visual testimony to Deaf lived experiences. This art movement was important in the revitalization of a distinct Deaf culture and identity. Following along the path forged by De'VIA, the more recent art movement of Surdism is defined more broadly by also incorporating other Deaf-themed art forms in contrast to De'VIA's focus on the visual arts. De'VIA plays an important role in consciousness raising for Deaf people, but also hearing people; it can be considered a form of activism to bring about social justice for Deaf people.

Keywords

De'VIA – Deaf Art – Surdism – ARTivism – Deaf culture – De'VIA Manifesto – Surdism Manifesto – Betty G. Miller – Nancy Rourke – liberation

1 Introduction

Patti Durr is a faculty member (retired) in the Department of Cultural and Creative Studies at the National Technical Institute for the Deaf (Rochester Institute of Technology). As part of her scholarship she published on De'VIA in *Visual Anthropology Review* ('Deconstructing the Forced Assimilation of Deaf People via De'VIA Resistance and Affirmation Art') and *Deaf Studies Today!* ('De'VIA: Investigating Deaf Visual Art'). Patti Durr recently co-curated the exhibit *De'VIA: The Manifesto Comes of Age*; was the director of *People of the Third Eye*—a kaleidoscopic show of ASL performance art, poetry, narratives, monologues, film clips and live painting; and co-organized the *ARTiculating Deaf Experiences Conference*

 | DOI:10.1163/9789004692299_009

that examined literary and artistic works about Deaf experiences. In addition, she is an artist herself and an activist for Deaf rights. Patti Durr is an important figure in the De'VIA movement and she shares her expertise about De'VIA, De'VIA's place within Deaf culture, and ARTivism in the following interview.

2 Interview

Ana L. Cruz [ALC]: *It is my understanding that De'VIA is an art form, am I correct? Could you please tell us about the origin of De'VIA and why it was created?*

Patti Durr [PD]: De'VIA stands for Deaf View/Image Art. The name originated in ASL and is signed "Deaf 'look-at-hand' art." The 'look-at' is to signify Deaf perspectives and points of view. The hand (open palm) is to signify the artwork—it could be a sheet of paper, a canvas, a photograph, a fabric work, etc. De'VIA is often said to be a genre or an art movement. Deaf people had created works about their Deaf experiences long before the term was coined in 1989. Prior to the birth of the De'VIA name and manifesto, a small group of Deaf students at Gallaudet University created the Deaf Art Movement DAM and a Deaf artists colony was formed in Austin, Texas in the late 1970s. Some Deaf artists and scholars still wanted to 'name' works that were specifically about Deaf experiences rather than simply having them housed under the broad and general term of 'Deaf art.' They convened in the Washburn Arts Center at Gallaudet University in 1989 for four days to look over a wide variety of works finding common motifs and styles and thus coined the term and penned the manifesto.[1]

[ALC]: *What would be some of the fundamental characteristics of De'VIA?*

[PD]: According to the De'VIA Manifesto the fundamental characteristics of De'VIA are:

- artists creating visual art with the intention to show Deaf experiences
- using intense & contrasting colors & textures
- having a central focus
- displaying exaggerated features
- incorporating motifs such as eyes, hands, mouths, and ears.

An example is Betty G. Miller's *Ameslan Prohibited* (1972). It is a black & white illustration with strong contrast that focuses on broken exaggerated fingers and shackles and chain. Deaf people readily understand this work to be about oralism—the banning of American Sign Language—which enslaves Deaf people (Figure 8.1). Another example is Harry Williams' *Musign* (1978) with the use of bold color in three paint cans and a super-sized eye iris, contrasting with the black and white illustration of the other items. The central focus is on the eye and paintbrush that is by an exaggerated hand-body figure with musical score and notes nearby. The message is that ASL is music to our eyes (Figure 8.2).

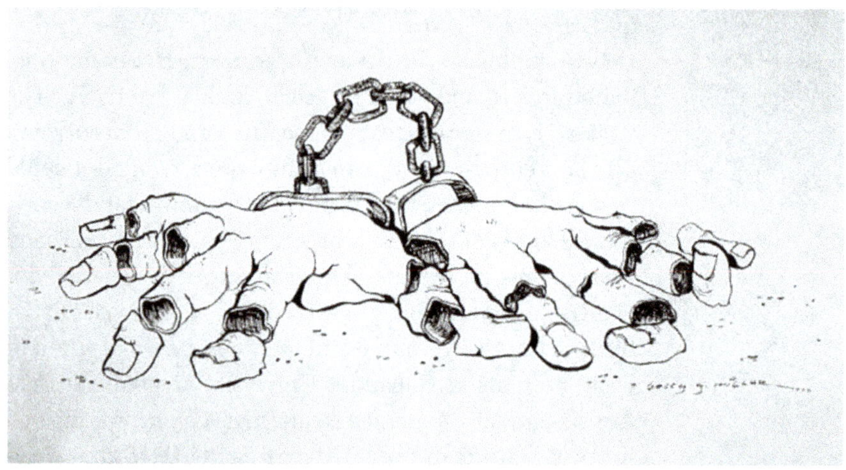

FIGURE 8.1 *Ameslan prohibited* (1972)
ARTWORK: BETTY G. MILLER

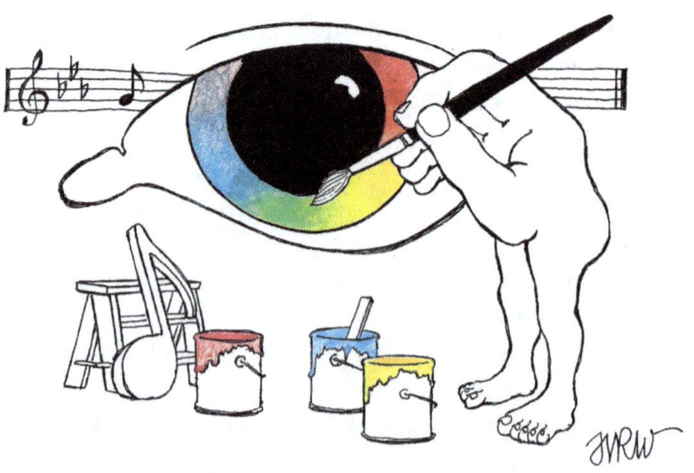

FIGURE 8.2 *Musign* (1978)
ARTWORK: HARRY WILLIAMS

To quote from the De'VIA Manifesto:

> De'VIA represents Deaf artists and perceptions based on their Deaf experiences. It uses formal art elements with the intention of expressing innate cultural or physical Deaf experience. These experiences may include Deaf metaphors, Deaf perspectives, and Deaf insight in relationship with the environment (both the natural world and Deaf cultural environment), spiritual and everyday life.

[ALC]: *Who are some of the artists currently involved in De'VIA? Is De'VIA a national or an international art movement?*

[PD]: De'VIA was originally a U.S. based art movement but other countries have embraced it as well.

Nancy Rourke is the most prolific and active De'VIA artist presently and has been instrumental in fostering other De'VIA artists and helping to develop the De'VIA curriculum with Deaf art teachers across the U.S. Other current Deaf-themed artists who have a large body of work or are currently active are: *Arnaud Balard* (French DeafBlind artist), *Fred Beam* (Black Deaf U.S. artist, actor, director, storyteller, painter), *Levent Beskardes* (Turkish Deaf artist, actor, and poet based in France), *Cizzy Boga* (Black Deaf U.S. ceramic and mixed media artist), *Uzi Buzgalo* (Israeli Deaf artist who creates unique frames to accompany his Deaf-themed paintings), *David Call* (Deaf U.S. artist who specializes in De'VIA linocuts), *Matt Daigle* (DeafBlind U.S. comic artist who creates comic strips about life with his Hearing wife and son), *Susan Dupor* (Deaf U.S. realism painter), *Raymond Fuyana* (African surrealist specializing in linocut and other printmaking), *Randy Garber* (Hard of Hearing Jewish U.S. mixed media, installations, and painting and printmaking artist), *Ixchel Jaxmin Solis Garcia* (Mexican Deaf painter, printmaker, and photographer), *Ashley Hannan* (Deaf U.S. painter who examines her identity as a Deaf person who uses a Cochlear implant), *Takiyah Harris* (Black Deaf U.S. collage artist with a large body of Black Deaf-themed works), *Christine Sun Kim* (Asian American Deaf sound artist based in Germany), *Tomas Kold* (Danish Deaf artist who has many photography pieces that are Deaf-themed and political), *Ellen Mansfield* (Jewish Deaf U.S. artist who works in ceramics and painting), *Alexander Martianov* (Russian Deaf artist and actor), *Theresa Matteson* (Deaf U.S. textile artist with many quilts incorporating ASL and Deaf themes), *Tony McGregor* (Deaf U.S. Native American artist creates Southwestern De'VIA by doing wood burnings on gourds that incorporate ASL signs), *Laurie Monahan* (Deaf U.S. Lesbian artist who creates many Queer De'VIA paintings), *Ann Silver* (Deaf U.S. Lesbian artist, who was one of the founders of DAM in the late 1960s, is most recognized for her use of Deaf-themed pop art works), *Jennifer Tandoc* (Filipino Deaf artist who was raised in the U.S. and does large striking Black and White illustrations that incorporate ASL), *Rosalyn Watson* (Black Deaf artist whose watercolor works honor Black Deaf children and adults). Many of these artists are featured in the Deaf-art.org website. There are many more but these are folks who have a significant body of Deaf-themed work—although not all of them may self-identify as being a De'VIA artist.

Four of the founders of De'VIA are no longer with us—*Betty G. Miller, Chuck Baird, Lai-Yok Ho* and *Guy Wonder*. Five of the founders remain—*Nancy Creighton, Paul Johnston, Deborah Sonnenstrahl, Sandi Inches Vasnick*, and *Alex Wilhite*. In 2016 Ann Silver and Tony McGregor were recognized as elders and added with the living founders to the De'VIA Statement of Philosophy.

[ALC]: *What was the significance of the De'VIA Manifesto and how does it fit into the emergence of a distinct Deaf culture/identity?*

[PD]: The famous Chinese artist and activist, Ai Weiwei, said "Art should live in the heart of the people."

As Deaf people started to assert themselves, their language and their culture (after witnessing the social movements of the 60s and 70s— Civil Rights, Feminism, Gay rights, etc.), they began to advocate for their own rights more and to reclaim a great deal of their past creativity that had been stifled or diminished during the reign of oralism. Oralism is a systematic way of teaching Deaf children speech which forbids the use of signing and often includes punishment to suppress a Deaf child's natural inclination to use their hands and eyes for language. American Sign Language, which is a unique and much beloved language for U.S. Deaf folks, was finally recognized as a bonafide language within academia in the mid-1960s thanks to the work of Dr. Stokoe and his two Deaf research assistants, Carl Croneberg and Dorothy Casterline. Black ASL was an outcome of segregated schools for the deaf in the South and wasn't fully acknowledged until the ground-breaking work of scholars—Drs. Carolyn McCaskill, Ceil Lucas, Robert Bayley, and Joseph Hill.

In the 1980s Deaf communities began to revitalize Deaf theatre and there was an emergence of Deaf poetry and visual art. Even though the National Theatre of the Deaf (NTD) had been founded in 1967, it opted to produce Hearing plays in sign language and only twice in its long and illustrious run ventured to create original Deaf-themed plays. There was a collective approach to sharing and processing Deaf-themed community-based works and many of the most important Deaf theatrical works had political messages about language rights and Deaf pride. The Deaf President Now movement in 1988, where Gallaudet students and community members demanded that the only Deaf college in the world, finally appoint a Deaf president, and the Americans with Disability Act of 1990 helped to raise Deaf folks' critical and collective consciousness. Visual art has been utilized by Deaf communities throughout time as Deaf folks are, as George W. Veditz called us, 'People of the Eye.'

The Deaf View/Image Art thinktank took place at Gallaudet University in 1989 and the manifesto was unveiled a month later at Deaf Way I, an international festival recognizing Deaf culture, pride, sign languages, art, theatre, and more. Drs. Betty G. Miller and Paul Johnston convened the 4-day workshop at the end of May 1989 as a continuation of some of the themes and thoughts that had been percolating since DAM and the Spectrum Deaf Artists' Colony in Austin, Texas and to finally give an unique name to art about Deaf experiences instead of the generic 'Deaf Art' term. It was natural for this meeting of the minds to have taken place after the Deaf President Now movement and before Deaf Way I and the passage of the ADA. Self-assertion, cultural pride, creative expressions, the expansion of the field of ASL linguistics, interpreting and Deaf Studies in academia, all played a key role in the emergence of De'VIA.

De'VIA contributed a great deal to revitalizing a distinct Deaf culture and identity. All cultures produce artifacts and possessions. Things that show and say who they are whether it be music, clothing, food, literature or art. For Deaf folks there is no distinct music, clothing or food associated with us as a marker of Deaf culture. This makes the role of art, language and literature even more important as transmitters of culture. For Deaf people (of whom 95% come from Hearing parents), these cultural markers play an even more important role as vertical transmission is rare within the Deaf world.

Couple that with the classic notion that a picture speaks a thousand words and the fact that many Deaf people have suffered from language deprivation due to oralism, De'VIA plays a special, important and powerful role in giving visual testimony to Deaf lived experiences.

[ALC]: *As one starts to explore the journey of Deaf people, one will encounter the word 'oppression' alluded to or expressed by many Deaf individuals; in what ways could De'VIA be associated with liberation from oppression?*

[PD]: De'VIA has works that are part of *affirmation*—celebrating Deaf culture and ASL—and it also has works that are *resistance*—examining the oppression and injustice Deaf people experience. Creating these works is often an act of liberation even if the pieces seem heavy or dark. When other Deaf folks see Betty G. Miller's classic piece *Ameslan Prohibited* or Susan Dupor's *Family Dog* or David Call's *Your Joy, My Pain,* they readily understand and feel validated that the dark secrets are out. When they see works by Chuck Baird, where he cleverly incorporated the iconicity of ASL—especially with the use of animals and a model showing the ASL sign—Deaf people immediately experience recognition and pride. So, too, with Guy Wonder's mixed media pieces celebrating his ASL heritage given to him by his Deaf grandparents and parents.

Some works include resistance themes evolving to affirmation, which Karen Christie and Dorothy Wilkins termed *liberation* works. For a well-known resistance piece, Mary Thornley echoes Goya's *The Third of May 1808* composition in her piece *Milan, Italy 1880*, where she gives visual representation to the destruction brought on by the ICED conference in 1880 where oralism was declared to be the best way to teach Deaf children. Many people are not aware of the fact that Goya lost his hearing in his mid-40s due to illness. Some have attributed his break from traditional art to become the Father of Modern Art to be due to his struggles with becoming Deaf and wanting to share everyday life struggles and experiences. Nancy Rourke's classic *We Came, We Saw, We Conquered* epitomizes a liberation piece by brilliantly referencing Goya's *Third of May 1808* and Thornley's *Milan, Italy 1880*. Nancy Rourke cleverly twists the theme of destruction by having all the soldiers toppled over while Deaf folks stand strongly doing handwaves in victory and in celebration of the New Era agreement where the International Congress on the Education of the Deaf (ICED) in 2010 recognized the harms caused by the ICED's 1880 declaration of oralism as being the superior method of educating Deaf children.

[ALC]: *How would you position De'VIA in relation to Deaf Art, ARTivism and Surdism?*

[PD]: While many people will use the term Deaf Art to mean specifically Deaf-themed works, Deaf Art is a broader term used to encompass

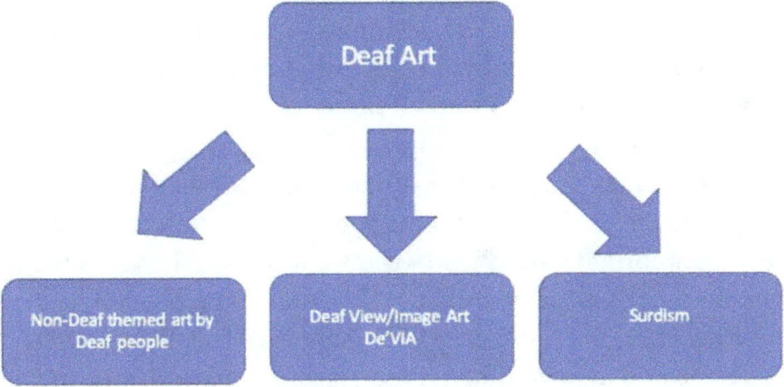

FIGURE 8.3 The Deaf art pyramid

any works by Deaf artists that are not Deaf-themed and works that are (Figure 8.3). De'VIA falls under the umbrella of Deaf Art that is Deaf-themed.

ARTivism, which was introduced in the late 1990s by Chicanos and Zapatistas, is a general term for the use of art as activism. It is not specific to Deaf-themed arts per se. Surdism, which is an art movement that was established in 2009 by Arnaud Balard, a French DeafBlind artist, is Deaf-themed visual art, film, theatre, movement, and literature—written or signed—to bring about social change. Thus, Surdism is a Deaf centered form of ARTivism.

[ALC]: *The theoretical framework of this book is centered on the Critical Pedagogy of Paulo Freire which includes his concept of Conscientização (critical consciousness leading to agency and transformation); in what ways do you see De'VIA raising critical consciousness and as a way of decolonizing the minds of not only Deaf people but hearing people as well?*

[PD]: De'VIA has been instrumental in our consciousness & conscience raising. Many Deaf people will describe an 'awakening' of sort when they see a De'VIA piece. Things will resonate within their core because the works speak to them personally—this making of the invisible visible is very important. Many of my college students would express dismay upon learning about De'VIA for the first time as young adults. Their first question was often, "why didn't my teachers or parents ever teach me about this before?" It is in fact their birth-right and one that they have often been robbed of. De'VIA does have a very powerful impact on Deaf communities and Hearing as well.

Many years ago we were having a Deaf and ASL pride parade from Gallaudet University to the White House to raise awareness about oralism, cochlear implant failures, ASL rights, Deaf pride etc. We handed out small Sign Union flags designed by Arnaud Balard in 2013.[2] Deaf people were thrilled to see a symbol of 'us' as 'a people' (Figure 8.4). The turquois center hand clearly represents sign languages around the world and the outer yellow outlined hand signifies tactile signing as DeafBlind people are an important part of our community and being tactile is an important part of who we are and can be. The yellow color also signifies enlightenment and hope. The outer dark blue on the flag signifies Deafhood and humanity. This flag never fails to attract Deaf people's hope and imagination. I often take a large Sign Union flag to protests for climate, science, women's rights, Black Lives Matter, etc. and Hearing people will ask me what the flag represents. When I point out the hand and gesture signing they readily get it and show their support.

During the 2013 parade we gave out bumper stickers that featured Maureen Klusza's *The Greatest Irony* work which has a Hearing baby signing 'I Love You' and a Deaf baby in shackles—being denied the

FIGURE 8.4 *Everywhere We Stand.* The hands represent 'Stand' for unity and justice—we support each other. It symbolizes the demonstrations for Deaf rights and also displays the 'Sign Union' flag
PAINTING: NANCY ROURKE

right to sign.[3] Baby signs became all the rage several years ago ... FOR HEARING parents and their babies while MANY Deaf babies are still forbidden from signing. As we marched through DC Hearing folks would come up to us and ask what the parade was about. I would give them a bumper sticker and wait until the light bulb would flash for them and it always did. Art is powerful.

The Memorial Art Gallery, a huge museum in Rochester, New York, had a De'VIA exhibit in honor of the 30th anniversary of De'VIA in 2019. I went several times to watch how the Hearing public interacted with the didactics and the works themselves. It was fascinating to see which works touched them and which moved them. I in turn was affected when I watched a woman move in closer to get a better look at a very small painting by Nancy Rourke entitled *Sterilized Without Consent* and return to look at it again after reading the chat label. All the time shaking her head from side to side with her hand over her heart. Many people did not know that Deaf people have been forcibly sterilized. While the work is about the eugenics program in Nazi Germany—it has happened in many countries long after World War II.

It is my hope that more Surdism (not just visual art but film, literature, theatre, etc.) will make its way into the public sphere because those media often have an even greater impact on larger audiences and the arts are often one of the most effective ways to bring about social justice for Deaf people.

[ALC]: *Has De'VIA as an art form called attention to social justice issues affecting the Deaf community and has De'VIA communicated those issues beyond the Deaf community? If so, what were/are the reactions from a Deaf and hearing audience?*

[PD]: De'VIA's Manifesto does not have a social activism component but the works themselves can be considered activism. The Surdism Manifesto specifies creating and using the works to bring about political change and several Deaf ARTivists (surdists) have been committed to that. We could always use more.

Dr. Betty G. Miller explained that at her first solo show entitled *The Silent World* at Gallaudet University in 1972 where Deaf-themed art kinda came out of the closet in force, there were two types of responses by Hearing attendees. Hearing 'outsiders'—folks who did not work in Deaf education understood the work and were moved by it, whereas Hearing folks who worked within the field of 'deafness' often felt threatened and insulted. Betty did share that having just started her recovery journey from alcoholism, she continued to create Deaf-themed works but did not exhibit them regularly after having received a harsh response to her show from some colleagues and peers. Betty was instrumental in the Spectrum Deaf Artists' Colony and the De'VIA think-tank. She presented, published, and created about De'VIA. While Betty was neither the first nor the only person to create and exhibit Deaf-themed works, she was dedicated to doing so and exhibited a fearlessness in presenting our truths to the world. For this reason and many more, Chuck Baird bestowed the title of 'The Mother of De'VIA' to Betty.

Betty's artistic statement said:

> Much of my work depicts the Deaf experience expressed in the most appropriate form of communication: visual art. I present the suppression, and the beauty, of Deaf culture and American Sign Language as I see it, both in the past, and in the present. Oppression of Deaf people by hearing is actually cultural, educational, and political. Another aspect of my work shows the beauty of Deaf culture. I hope this work, and the understanding that may arise from this visual expression, will help bridge the gap between the Deaf world, and the hearing world.

Never one to shy away from resistance works—Betty's classic piece *Ameslan Prohibited* shows how oralism enslaves Deaf people and her *Crucifixion* has a cracked open body aid nailed to a red board with a surgeon general-like warning inserted to state how if a Deaf person does not use the device their life is meaningless. Betty's *Bell School, 1944* shows how repressive Oral education is and her neon mixed media *Hearing Test* depicts how abusive it is to make a Deaf child work for their words. Betty also has many affirmation works such as *Birth of a Deaf Woman*.

Deaf and hearing people are very receptive to Deaf-themed works. There are some folks who say to artists 'you should only make happy art' (affirmation De'VIA) 'because we want to make a good impression' or 'we don't want to scare people off' or 'we need to make money.' Or some will say 'we want the art to look sexy and cool so Deaf folks can have a breakthrough and be accepted and valued,' etc.

But falsehoods don't work and superficial only goes so far and many Hearing folks are really receptive to understanding diversity these days. As Black Hearing author and activist James Baldwin wisely stated—"the artist is here to disturb the peace."

While school children all over the U.S. grow up being taught that Alexander Graham Bell was an amazing inventor who gave us the telephone, Deaf people learn how he advocated against Deaf marriages, Deaf teachers, and ASL in schools. This is why many individuals gathered to have peaceful protests at the AG Bell Volta Bureau as his organization still promotes oral/aural-only approach to Deaf children. During the day, Deaf people would give testimony of workplace discrimination or when their Hearing child had to interpret for their Deaf parents while the child was in agony with an appendicitis or sharing tales of overprotective Hearing parents by adult DeafBlind people. In the evening, vigils would be held and survivors of oralism would share their stories. Some youngsters would create original ABC stories to honor the survivors and to perpetuate the beauty and artistry of ASL literary expressions.

Issues facing Deaf people today include access to information, job opportunities, equal education, cultural appropriation, Hearing actors taking Deaf roles, audism, oralism, genetic engineering, CRISPR, police brutality & murder, solitary confinement in prison, mental health access, human and linguistic rights, intersectionality, racism within the Deaf world, and more. Many of these are addressed via ARTivism.

[ALC]: *The arts in general, in my view, are a powerful way for humankind to re-invent itself and to transcend into a spiritual dimension of existence. Do you believe there is a spiritual dimension associated with De'VIA? If so, have Deaf people—through De'VIA—been able to connect their humanity and Deafhood with their spiritual power?*

[PD]: This is an excellent question. I would say yes. The De'VIA Manifesto mentions spiritual life (see earlier quote in question 2) and the Surdism Manifesto addresses humanity. The first known art on the planet is rock art. Many theorize that the origins of handprints, which are found all over the globe, is to record the signed stories. Early people most likely could not speak and signing would have been their first language. This desire to create, to share, to preserve, to leap at the sun is a fundamental characteristic of human beings and humanity.

Furthermore, Deafhood is an individual and collective praxis to understand what it means to be Deaf and to see the good in having Deaf people as part of the biodiversity of the human family. It was the introduction of the concept of Deafhood by Dr. Paddy Ladd that awoke many of today's current Surdists.

Many creatives will talk about the spiritual experience they have when creating. The meditative, zen-like, 'in the zone' aspect of creating, couple this with creating works that are deeply intimate and often born out of a shared trauma or jubilation—you would be hard pressed not to see the spiritual power in this.

To quote from the Surdism Manfiesto:

Audism denigrates, Deafhood welcomes, Surdism reveals.

[ALC]: *There has been approximately 30 years since the origin of De'VIA; what have been the most significant changes during these years for Deaf people and for De'VIA?*

[PD]: Deaf people have undergone a tremendous amount of changes in the past 30 years—largely because the digital age is changing so much so fast. Mainstreaming and cochlear implantation have impacted Deaf children's entry into the Deaf world. They are still finding it but many more are coming very late to the table due to the fact that such a high percentage of parents do not sign and do not let their Deaf children go to Deaf schools. Fortunately, social media, the internet, and Deaf folks on TV/films and the stage, have increased the visibility and acceptance of sign languages. So it's a good time to be Deaf—there is more captioning, more Deaf interpreters shown on TV, more representation and awareness, etc.

At the same time, CRISPR and genetic engineering are threatening to radically reduce the number of Deaf folks from the planet. BIPOC Deaf folks are also being killed by police—especially those with mental health challenges. The stress and adverse impact of COVID-19 (masks, social isolating, online learning) is still to be seen—especially on Deaf children. We have come a long way baby but still have far to go.

Nancy Rourke, a survivor of COVID-19 herself, organizes a February De'VIA challenge every year and this year the prompt words she created all relate to the year 2020. Many of the works created show how impactful the Corona virus, mask wearing, social distancing, remote learning, etc. have been on Deaf folks.

For De'VIA, I think the most significant change is that more and more people have become aware of what De'VIA is. It is taught to children and adults of all ages. There are more exhibits with Deaf-themed works. When I first began researching about De'VIA, many Deaf folks marveled at and responded to resistance works but they were wary about buying them—often saying they were worried about their Hearing family members seeing the art. In the past 10 years with folks' heightened sense of Deafhood, folks began buying and seeking out resistance pieces. To me that is a good sign of progress and self-actualization for our Deaf communities. Furthermore, as with many art movements, De'VIA did not always seek out and make space for BIPOC, DeafBlind, Disabled and other Deaf folks' expressions. Within the Deaf world—there used to be a heavy push for 'Deaf first' over any other identities and little to no understanding or appreciation of intersectionality. The Dyer Arts Center at the National Technical Institute for the Deaf at RIT has had several exhibits of Black, Latinx, POC, Queer, and DeafBlind Deaf artists. The Deaf Art Central facebook page has featured works by Indigenous, Black, and Latinx Deaf artists on their cover. There is much more to do. No matter if you call it Deaf Art, De'VIA, Surdism or something entirely different—most important to me is that you create.

I am hopeful for the day when cross-pollination between the arts—Deaf literature, film, theatre, visual art, and movement—yields stronger political statements and bring about social change.

Notes

1 An illustrated time line of the development of De'VIA is available at the *The HeART of Deaf Culture* website: https://heartdeaf.com/deaf-visual-art/#tab-321a41b944fd93e8de8

2 A brief video by Arnaud Balard where he explains all the characteristics and components of the Sign Union flag: https://dai.ly/x2wfoh2

3 Maureen Klusza's *The Great Irony* can be seen at the following website: https://deaf-art.org/profiles/maureen-klusza/

PART 3

'Deaf Music:' Visions, Possibilities, and Social Justice

∵

There is no tomorrow without a project, without a dream, without utopia, without hope, without creative work, and work toward the development of possibilities, which can make the concretization of that tomorrow viable.

PAULO FREIRE (2007, *Daring to Dream: Toward A Pedagogy of the Unfinished*, p. 26)

CHAPTER 9

Signed Music and the Deaf Community

Jody H. Cripps, Anita Small, Ely Lyonblum, Samuel J. Supalla, Aimee K. Whyte and Joanne S. Cripps

Abstract

This chapter elaborates on how Deaf people have used hands, movements and facial expressions to create their own music. The term *signed music* is new and emerging in academic circles. It is designed to account for the music performances that are composed by Deaf people. These musical productions are performed in the community, appreciated and accepted by Deaf audiences. Usually, music is seen as simply organized audible sound, a definition that precludes Deaf people from any meaningful involvement in its creative practice. Some attempts to translate the audible music into signed language has been displayed in social media (i.e., YouTube, etc.). This translated work is not characteristic of signed music. Instead, to pursue the possibilities of what the authors refer to as signed music is to draw from Deaf culture and the Deaf community. This shift in cultural perspective requires a detachment from the longstanding traditional perception of music as an auditory phenomenon.

Keywords

Signed music – signed language – deaf people – identity – community – culture – performance

1 Introduction

In academic research, the relationship between music, culture, and authenticity is tenuous. How music is created and how it is presented often obscure the cultural origins of a creative practice. These relationships are further complicated when a set of artistic practices from multiple disciplines are mixed together. The subject of Deaf[1] performance in the context of music offers a unique perspective to the question of what constitutes music in the first place. For many, music is simply organized sound, a definition that precludes Deaf people from any meaningful involvement in its creative practice. To explore the possibilities of what the authors refer to as signed music is to draw from

 | DOI:10.1163/9789004692299_010

Deaf culture.[2] This shift in cultural perspective requires a detachment from the longstanding traditional perception of music as an auditory phenomenon.

Subject to elaboration in this chapter is how Deaf people have used hands, movements and facial expressions to create music. This phenomenon is tied to the fact that Deaf people know and use a signed language. The term *signed music* is new, and designed to account for the music performances that are composed by Deaf people (J. H. Cripps & Lyonblum, 2017; J. H. Cripps, Rosenblum, & Small, 2019; J. H. Cripps, Rosenblum, Small, & S. Supalla, 2017). What is important for music scholars to understand is the language that Deaf people know and use is called American Sign Language (ASL), which constitutes a visual-gestural language in its own right. Like music, language was thought to be exclusively auditory, but that has been changed through linguistic research and scholarship (Meier, 2002). ASL is a fully-fledged human language possessing linguistic properties (i.e., phonology, morphology, syntax, semantics, and pragmatics; Sandler & Lillo-Martin, 2006; Valli, Lucas, Mulrooney & Villanueva, 2011).

By all accounts, Deaf people have struggled with music as an auditory phenomenon. While some enjoy its rhythmic vibration, others do not relate to it at all. The common notion that music equates to a person's capacity to hear cannot be accepted at face value. Only recently has the definition of music expanded through experimentation led by Deaf performers. The experimentation with signed music is now full-blown and numerous. There are also more basic forms of signed music that have been part of Deaf culture over the years.

In the literature, music is known for its deep-seated role within cultures. Hamm, Nettl, and Byrnside (1975) pointed out that every culture has its own music by saying that "there is no culture known to man, no single civilization of the past, that does not have its own body of music" (p. 71). This is evident with how a bone flute was discovered in 1995 as the oldest musical instrument in the world. It was claimed to be approximately 44,000 years old (Kunej & Turk, 2000). Brown, Merker, and Wallin (2000) made an additional argument that "music making is the quintessential human cultural activity, and music is an ubiquitous element in all cultures large and small" (p. 3). These comments reflect that all cultures have music and bring to question, *what characterizes the musical work of Deaf culture that does not include audible sound?* To have a meaningful experience related to a musical performance, Deaf people do not require access to audible sound in order to appreciate music as is expected in auditory culture. Deaf culture and Deaf artists have developed their own points of access for musical expression, which allows them to both appreciate and create music derived from within their own culture. That is, Deaf people have been appreciating and creating music performances in the signed modality. Signed music is as aesthetically pleasing to the eyes as auditory music is pleasing to the ears.

2 Historical Overview of Signed Music

Of special interest for Deaf people and signed music is what ancient Greeks wrote about music. One early form of music theory came from the Greek philosopher and mathematician, Pythagoras (ca. 570 BCE – ca. 495 BCE). He developed a music theory using a mathematical concept called *Music of the Spheres*. This theory describes the movement of the planets reflecting mathematical proportions, shapes, or patterns. These mathematical patterns are present everywhere and direct all temporal cycles that include the seasons and rhythms of nature (Boethius, 1867/1989; Pliny the Elder, 77AD/1938). This mathematical concept does not include or identify any auditory-based music properties. Based on the notion of music being part of the movement of the sun, moon, and planets, Pythagoras stated that humans are 'unable to hear' the Music of the Spheres (Boethius, 1867/1989; Canadian Cultural Society of the Deaf, 2015; Pliny the Elder, 77AD1938). In other words, one can derive meaning from and appreciation of music that is not dependent on hearing it.

The Deaf community has provided its members with some protection from the biases of auditory culture. This is especially true concerning the development of signed music, and it has been around for a long time. Bahan (2006) identified signed percussion songs and English-to-ASL translated songs as two types of music common in the Deaf community. Deaf performers are known for doing signed versions of spoken language songs, and the quality can be high. Two good examples are *A Revival Squirrel* and *Backing to Birmingham* performed by William Ennis that was released in video format (Ennis, 1993). The earliest recorded film of a Deaf person sign singing was 1902. This person was an unknown female who performed the American national anthem, the *Star-Spangled Banner* (United States Library of Congress, 1902/1955). As ironic as it may seem, this black and white film was done during the silent film era when there was no audible sound accompanying film. Deaf people experienced film as including 'talking' that they could clearly understand (since both film and ASL are visual) when the rest of auditory culture experienced it as lacking audible 'talking.'

At the same time, some scholars noticed that Deaf people are uneasy when talking about music in general (Darrow, 2006; Leigh, Andrews, Harris, & González Ávila, 2020; Maler, 2013). This is especially true about what is authentic and not authentic, or even culturally inappropriate. Some hearing individuals who have only started studying ASL perform translated songs in front of a Deaf audience. Inadequate skills in signed language frequently undermine the work and some hearing performers think they are doing a 'favor' for Deaf people (i.e., Deaf people deprived of music deserve 'help' accessing it). The sound of the music would be turned on and a hearing performer signs the song. Some hearing people in the audience may be entertained by the performance for its novelty (i.e., watching the signed performance and hearing it at the same time). Deaf people in the audience are left with the signed portion of the performance that is tied to and limited by the structure of the auditory component of the music. The musicality of the translation tends to not be embedded within ASL grammatical structure, movement and rhythm of the signs as it would be when derived from within Deaf culture.

In contrast, signed music provides Deaf performers with a platform to engage in performance without the support of auditory music. Rhythmic components of signing make the piece far more enjoyable for the Deaf audience. The fact that translation in general is not ideal for music is a critical consideration. Scholars who studied translation works in music have explained that the performances based on different cultural knowledge can result in creating difficulties for audiences to understand the original message from the performer (e.g., Chairo, 2009; Gorlée, 1994; Low, 1994). For example, a song describing a babbling brook or birds chirping would likely not be particularly meaningful or inspiring to Deaf people. In contrast, the visual depiction of a babbling brook and birds soaring could inspire a Deaf audience. This suggests that many musical works created outside the Deaf community would not be appropriate for translation for Deaf people's enjoyment.

Percussion singing, on the other hand, is a type of original song created by Deaf people. This is where signed music reflects authentic Deaf culture. Specifically, the original ASL songs incorporate one-two, one-two-three, one-two, one-two-three rhythm beats using body movements from left to right and vice versa for each word (Bahan, 2006; Padden & Humphries, 1988):

BOAT (left) BOAT (right),
BOAT (left) BOAT (right), BOAT (left),
BOAT (right) BOAT (left),
DRINK (left) DRINK (right),
DRINK (left) DRINK (right), DRINK (left),
DRINK (right) DRINK (left)...

The example above was performed by a Deaf man named George Kannapell, who led a group singing the ASL song, *Boat, Drink, Fun, Enjoy* ... The other example is a group of Deaf men signing *Oh Darn, I Hear Nothing!* ..., in a chorus using ASL with the lyrics intended to be in jest. (These pieces performed in the 1930s and 1940s can be seen in the video documentary, *Charles Krauel: A Profile of a Deaf Filmmaker*, T. Supalla & Dannis, 1994.)

One signed song piece performed in the 1970s deserves mention. Deaf performers of the renowned National Theatre of the Deaf created this piece as part of the *My Third Eye* production for both stage and television during 1971–1972 (Baldwin, 1993). A group of performers performed an ensemble song called *Rescue at the Sea*. This visually powerful performance relied on rhythmic beats. The performers did not include any audible musical instruments. To express the musical quality to the act, one of the performers would create 'up and down' hand motions reflecting the rhythm of ocean waves throughout the majority of the performance.

During the 1990s, the Deaf community had the opportunity to appreciate more original ASL songs either live or through a videotape or DVD. Mary Beth Miller (one of the performers in *My Third Eye*) produced a percussion song in ASL called *Mexican Cowboy* (Miller, 1991). David Supalla produced an American patriotic song in ASL called *A Ballad of the USA Flag* (C. Supalla & D. Supalla, 1991). Like Miller's work, his performance demonstrated rhythmic beats through signed lyrics that incorporated soldiers marching in time from the beginning to the end.

Since 2000, signed music performances have undergone dramatic changes with many performances released through social media. Among the participating Deaf performers are Janis Cripps with *Eyes* (2003), Ian Sanborn with *Caterpillar* (2014), Rosa Lee Timm with *River Song* (2008), and Pamela Witcher with *An Experimental Clip* (2008). They conceived an entirely new level of signed musicianship. Their works are best described as using different rhythmic layers of handshapes and movements—signed musical notes—as well as the use of visual media for their creative expression (J. H. Cripps et al., 2017).

In November 2015, at the *Signed Music: A Symphonious Odyssey* evening performance in Towson, Maryland, a number of Deaf performers presented their signed music pieces live on stage (J. H. Cripps, 2016). The Canadian and American performers were all Deaf: 1) The Fenicle Brothers (Ron, John, and Jonas) performed an ensemble song called *The Food Chain*, 2) Ian Sanborn performed an ASL story-style music called *Rooster Seeks Music*, and 3) Pamela Witcher performed *Nice and Slow* using ASL lyrics and signed musical notes. Each of these live performances was comprised of music properties in the signed modality. At the conclusion of their performances, the audience, predominantly Deaf gave a standing ovation.

3 Signed Music as an Art Form

At this point, it is necessary to quickly review what constitutes music in general to help validate what Deaf people appreciate. Thaut (2005) stated that music is a highly abstract and non-representational art that demonstrates human thought, feelings, and sense of movement. Kramer (2003) made a similar argument by saying that music is frequently perceived as lacking representational-semantic richness. Besides the lack in representational art, individuals must understand the music's "cultural meaning [even] with the lack of referential destiny found in [musical] words or images" (Kramer, 2003, p. 127) in order to appreciate the music performance. Supporting this, Cook (2000) noted that music is embedded within social contexts.

In the late 19th and early 20th centuries, music was categorized as Western Art Music and non-Western forms. Traditional musicologists focused on Western music (e.g., classical) rather than other types of music (e.g., jazz, rap, pop rock, etc.). This binary formed artificial boundaries between the importance of culture in the creative practice of composition and performance. As cultural researchers and music scholars continued to discover new forms of music making, the division between genres began to weaken. Since the 1980s, musicologists, music theorists, and ethnomusicologists have been investigating new types of music and reconsidering old ones with perspectives from across the arts, humanities and social sciences. This paradigm shift, *New Musicology,* studies music through scholarship and performance in addition to any available written notation or musical scores (Cook, 2014). Given that ASL is not written (nor does it have a written literature), such a paradigm shift studying performance and recorded performance is essential to examine signed music. Deaf people are known for maintaining an oral tradition with many stories being transmitted through memory over time (e.g., Byrne, 2017; Christie & Wilkins, 1997; Frishberg, 1988; Padden & Humphries, 1988; Rutherford, 1993).

Music scholars have also begun analyzing music for its meaning beyond a strictly theoretical perspective. For example, scholars are investigating how cultural meaning is captured through performance, revealing details related to the cultural identities of audiences and performers (Cook, 2012). This is made possible through mutual cultural experience from both parties. The earlier mention that musical works outside the Deaf community may not be suitable for Deaf people would be part of this discussion. Middleton (2012) argued that culture has a role in music and so music scholars must think differently. He proposed starting a new approach or paradigm—*Music Studies*. Cook (2008) extended this by stating that Music Studies should include music scholarship from a range of different disciplines including ethnomusicology, historical musicology, and music psychology.

Music has its own basic elements and varies within Western and non-Western cultures. This kind of understanding has ramifications for where signed music fits in. In the former music type, rhythm, timbre, texture, melody, and harmony are the five basic elements identified for music as promoted by people who hear. On the other hand, the popular and folk musics do not require all of these five music elements. Melody and harmony are two elements that are difficult to identify in non-Western music performances (Schmidt-Jones, 2007). J. H. Cripps et al. (2017) synthesized Schmidt-Jones' key definitions for each of the five musical elements as listed:

- Rhythm: the repetitive pulse of the music, or a rhythmic pattern that is repeated throughout the music,
- Timbre: all of the aspects of musical sound that are not based upon the sound's pitch, loudness, or length (e.g., a flute and oboe play the same note, but they have distinctive sonic qualities),
- Melody: a series of notes (of particular pitch and duration) together, one after the other,
- Texture: the overall qualities in the music at any given moment … often described as thick or thin, containing many or few layers,
- Harmony: multiple pitches sounding at a time, which interact with the melody (Schmidt-Jones, 2007, pp. 71–83 as cited in J. H. Cripps et al., 2017, p. 5).

In addition to the five basic elements, the broadest property of music is the motif and Drabkin (2004) defined it as

> a short musical idea —melodic, harmonic, rhythmic, or any combination of these three. [It] may be of any size, and is most commonly regarded as the shortest subdivision of a theme or phrase that still maintains its identity as an idea. (n.p.)

It is the musical theme that contains a combination of rhythmic, melodic, and harmonic elements.

J. H. Cripps et al. (2017) did a preliminary case study on signed music performances specifically *Eyes* and *An Experimental Clip*. They used an ethnomusicological framework using thick description (Geertz, 1973) and comparative analysis as their research methods. In both of these clips, rhythm, timbre, texture, and motif (or series of rhythmic variation) were identified in the signed modality. These three basic elements are known for the non-Western music canon.[3] Equally important is the finding that both signed music performances subject to study incorporated Deaf experience in either an explicit or implicit way. For example, the value of hands (for signing) was expressed in one piece, whereas the issue of alienation that Deaf people experience (in society) was addressed in the other piece. Given evidence that Deaf people have actively pursued music performance derived from within their culture, they are not "trapped in silence and void of music" as is often depicted in the media and Hollywood films (see Schuchman, 1999; Avon, 2006; and McCullough, 2018 for further details regarding Hollywood's perspective on Deaf people).

4 Community, Identity, and Music

Attention now shifts to understanding the relationship between the Deaf community, identity, and signed music. For a better understanding of Deaf people, McMillan and Chavis (1986) defined community using four elements: 1) membership, 2) influence, 3) integration, and fulfillment of needs, and 4) shared emotional connection. All four elements combined, make an effective community where everyone in the community has similar interests. The American Deaf community is known for being closely-knit, well-organized, and vibrant with a broad estimate of 100,000 to 500,000 members (Padden, 1987; Schein & Delk, 1974) (see Mitchell, Young, Bachleda, & Karchmer, 2006 for further details on the demographic of this particular population). The fact that an estimated one in a thousand Canadians uses signed language as a first language is impressive (Canadian Hearing Society, 1998). ASL is understood to play a key role in drawing the community together. With society driven by the use of a spoken language (which is predominantly English), Deaf people have a strong interest in being part of their own community. The space for Deaf people becomes cultural. Deaf people communicate with ease and comfort knowing that in that cultural context they will not encounter communication barriers that they experience in society.

Erting and Kuntze (2008) explained that the Deaf community has a unique trait with so many of its members acculturated rather than being born into it. Demographically, a vast majority of people with hearing loss (between 90 and 95%) are born to hearing parents who typically use a spoken language (Mitchell & Karchmer, 2005). It is true that some hearing parents have learned ASL and used it with their children, but society remains non-signing. True societal integration is easier to achieve in the Deaf community where ASL is used as the common language. Deaf people who are signers, naturally find it easier to be emotionally attached with deep relationships when their communication needs are fulfilled. They share similar experiences as part of a linguistic minority.[4]

Among Deaf people, there are differences in childhood experience. While growing up with hearing parents, there may be some pressure associated with the auditory culture and language. Those parents who lack a good understanding about Deaf culture tend to put emphasis on making the child as 'hearing-like' as possible rather than building on the child's innate strengths. There is research evidence to suggest that positive identity is formed when a child's self-efficacy is fostered. Self-efficacy is formed when children know what they are good at and are encouraged to proactively develop those strengths.

This applies to fostering natural signed language acquisition as well as exposure to and opportunity to develop signed language artistic performance (Small, J. S. Cripps, & Côté, 2012; see Sutton-Spence, 2010 and Sutton-Spence & Müller de Quadros, 2006 for Deaf people's identity associated with performing arts such as storytelling and poetry).

Deaf children with Deaf parents constitute a minority (10% or less) in the Deaf community. They are usually exposed to ASL in a rich manner and in diverse ways (with Deaf parents most likely having a network with many other primary signers for interaction opportunities, etc.). Deaf individuals with Deaf parents tend to have a strong identity along with native signing skills (Lane, Hoffmeister & Bahan, 1996). The impact on signed music is evident. Deaf musicians are almost entirely made up of individuals from Deaf families, which represent the Deaf community disproportionally. They are clearly successful in making emotional connections with the Deaf audience.[5] Individuals who come from Deaf families often are 'core members' of the Deaf community and serve as cultural models, exerting a powerful influence in the Deaf community.[6] Signed music incorporating Deaf experience may serve as a natural enculturation and mentorship experience as well as supporting the solidarity of the Deaf community. This impact is in addition to Deaf people's opportunity to enjoy the universality of music.

Unlike what was discussed related to hearing novice signers, fluent hearing signers have a strong tendency to be cautious in performing signed music with respect to Deaf people and their culture. Children of Deaf adults (CODAS; see Singleton & Tittle, 2000 for more information about this population) who were raised in a signing household with Deaf parents are likely to be native signers. *Earth Move* performed by Sherry Hicks and Michael Velez[7] serves as an example of some native hearing signers who have created signed music performances with great appeal to the Deaf audience. These performers are CODAS. The signed musical piece comprises cultural sensitivity towards Deaf people for two important reasons. One is the independence from auditory music and the other originality. The importance of native or native-like ASL proficiency cannot be ignored for it underlines the power of signed music. The idea that Deaf and hearing individuals need to be fluent signers for creating and performing signed music is a reasonable proposition.

Points for consideration related to signed music follow. J. H. Cripps and Supalla (2012) explained that signing and signed language are directly associated with Deaf people (as there is no known culture that hearing people would rely on for the use of signed language exclusively, for example). Granted, hearing people have gestured as part of making music (e.g., Berry, 2009; Cox,

2006; Davidson, 2012; Hatten, 2004; Gritten & King, 2006, 2011), but nothing amounts to what has been discussed for signed music. Not only does signed music deserve recognition, but also realization that it belongs to the culture of Deaf people. While some fluent hearing signers appreciate signed music as an art form, they see it as exactly that—an artistic form that is defined by its emergence from within Deaf culture. Their appreciation of it is derived from its Deaf cultural source. Music interpreting or reliance on auditory music is not part of signed music. Deaf people are entitled to authentic signed music that has the potential for maximum pleasure. It is important to understand that signed music is not limited to expressing Deaf experience. The Deaf audience is capable of relating to themes from everyday life as much as they do life being Deaf. Two signed music pieces *The Food Chain* and *Rooster Seeks Music* mentioned earlier are good illustrations of general themes expressed by Deaf performers. Although more research is needed, hearing performers who do signed music successfully may emphasize the Deaf-free experiences as they are not Deaf. This can be seen as a way of respecting Deaf culture.

Deaf children will need to be exposed to signed music in their curriculum. Exposure to signed music in the school system is expected to greatly encourage the self-efficacy and identity of the children in question (see Hargreaves, Miell, & MacDonald, 2002 for the importance of music for the development of self-identities for children in general). Signed music performed by accomplished Deaf performers must be part of curricula teaching ASL as a foreign/second language in schools, colleges, and universities. Hearing students studying signed language will benefit from understanding the characteristics and significance of signed music over the years. Signed music serves as one critical basis of knowledge for Deaf culture and the Deaf community after all.

With the implementation of state-of-art resources pertaining to signed music, larger numbers of signers will become more educated and conscious of what constitutes signed music. Signed music resources are available that will impact performers and students in their understanding of the characteristics or properties of signed music. The implementation of signed music in the curriculum using signed music documentaries listed below and *Signed Music: Rhythm of the Heart—Deaf Arts Handbook Series Volume II* will assist performers, teachers, therapists and others to understand signed music. This signed music handbook is available online.[8] Two documentaries are available online: 1) *Signed Music: Rhythm of the Heart*[9] and 2) *Signed Music: A Symphonious Odyssey*.[10] These resources are just the beginning of archiving and analyzing signed music in the future. Finally, the proliferation of awareness of signed music and its exploration are likely to expand signers' sense of community and identity in the sphere of music.

Acknowledgement

The authors would like to acknowledge Dr. Lynn Jacobowitz for her input on the works of Sherry Hicks and Michael Velez.

Notes

1 The capitalized D for 'Deaf' represents a cultural view of the population under review in this chapter. Deaf people have been seen from a medical view with an emphasis on "disability" rather than the fact that they have formed their own signing community that resembles a linguistic and cultural minority group in society (e.g., Charrow & Wilbur, 1989; Johnston & Erting, 1989; Lane, 1999; Lane, Pillard, & Hedberg, 2011; Padden 1980; Reagan, 1995; Rutherford, 1988).

2 For further discussion, see Padden, 1980, Rutherford, 1988, and J. S. Cripps, 2008.

3 Between the time this manuscript was conceived and then submitted for publication, additional work has been undertaken to study other signed music pieces in the Deaf community to identify the two remaining basic musical elements—melody and harmony.

4 Attending a school for the deaf is known as an important factor in the healthy socio-emotional development of Deaf individuals. These schools are inclined to provide signing teachers and a rich signing environment in the classroom as well as opportunities for effective communicative interaction with peers (Erting & Kuntze, 2008; see Patterson, 2009 for further discussion of the impact of schools for the deaf on the Deaf community over the years).

5 Christiansen & Barnartt 1995 made a similar observation in regard to the leadership positions for the historic 1988 student protest at Gallaudet University, a higher education institution for Deaf students.

6 Deaf individuals from Deaf families enjoying high esteem in the Deaf community can also be described as common knowledge and part of Deaf people's daily lives.

7 https://www.youtube.com/watch?v=G9n1L08BWWE

8 https://deafculturecentre.ca/deaf-arts-series/deaf-arts-handbook-vol-two.pdf

9 https://www.youtube.com/watch?v=FLazgI_phNQ

10 https://www.youtube.com/watch?v=2JjFCM8UZHM

References

Avon, A. (2006). Watching films, learning language, experiencing culture: An account of deaf culture through history and popular films. *Journal of Popular Culture, 39*(2), 185–204.

Bahan, B. (2006). Face-to-face tradition in the American deaf community: Dynamics of the teller, the tale, and the audience. In H-D. L. Bauman, J. L. Nelson, & H. M. Rose (Eds.), *Signing the body poetic: Essays on American Sign Language literature* (pp. 21–50). Berkeley, CA: University of California Press.

Baldwin, S. C. (1993). *Pictures in the air: The story of the National Theatre of the Deaf.* Washington, D.C.: Gallaudet University Press.

Berry, M. (2009). The importance of bodily gesture in Sofia Gubaidulina's music for low strings. *Music Theory Online, 15*(5), 1–12.

Boethius, A. M. S. (1989). De institutione musica. In C. V. Palisca (Ed.), *Fundamentals of music* (C. Bower, Trans.). New Haven, CT: Yale University Press. (Original work published 1867)

Brown, S., Merker, B., & Wallin, N. L. (2000). An introduction to evolution musicology. In N. L. Wallin, B. Merker & S. Brown (Eds.), *The origins of music* (pp. 3–24). Cambridge, MA: MIT Press.

Byrne, A. P. J. (2017). American Sign Language Literature: Some considerations for legitimacy and quality issues. *Society for American Sign Language Journal, 1*(1), 56–77.

Canadian Cultural Society of the Deaf. (2015). *Deaf arts handbook series, vol. 2 – Signed music: Rhythm of the heart.* Toronto, ON: Canadian Cultural Society of the Deaf.

Canadian Hearing Society. (April, 1998). *Vibes.*

Chairo, D. (2009). Issues in audiovisual translation. In J. Munday (Ed.), *The Routledge companion to translation studies* (Rev. ed., pp. 141–165). New York, NY: Routledge.

Charrow, V. R., & Wilbur, R. B. (1989). The deaf child as a linguistic minority. In S. Wilcox (Ed.), *American deaf culture: An anthology* (pp. 103–155). Silver Spring, MD: Linstok Press.

Christiansen, J. B., & Barnartt, S. N. (1995). *Deaf President Now!: The 1988 revolution at Gallaudet University.* Washington, D.C.: Gallaudet University Press.

Christie, K., & Wilkins, D. (1997). A feast for the eyes: ASL literacy and ASL literature. *Journal of Deaf Studies and Deaf Education, 2*(1), 57–59.

Cook, N. (2014). Between art and science: Music as performance. *Journal of the British Academy, 2*, 1–25.

Cook, N. (2012). Music as performance. In M. Clayton, T. Herbert, & R. Middleton (Eds.), *The cultural study of music: A critical introduction* (2nd ed., pp. 184–194). New York, NY: Routledge.

Cook, N. (2008). We are all (ethno)musicologists now. In H. Stobart (Ed.), *The new (ethno)musicologies* (pp. 48–70). Lanham, MD: Scarecrow Press.

Cook, N. (2000). *Music: A very short introduction.* Oxford, UK: Oxford University Press.

Cox, A. (2006). Hearing, feeling, grasping gestures. In A. Gritten & E. King (Eds.), *Music and gesture* (pp. 45–60). Aldershot, UK: Ashgate.

Cripps, J. H. (2016). *Signed music: A symphonious odyssey* [Online]. Towson, MD: A Cripps Production.

Cripps, J. H., & Lyonblum, E. (2017). Understanding signed music. *Society for American Sign Language Journal, 1*(1), 78–96.

Cripps, J. H., Rosenblum, E., & Small, A. (2019). Signed music: An emerging interperformative art. In B. K. Eldredge, D. Stringham, & B. Jarashow (Eds.), *Waypoints:*

Deaf Studies Today! 2014 conference proceedings (pp. 179–186). Orem, UT: Utah Valley University Press.

Cripps, J. H., Rosenblum, E., Small, A., & Supalla, S. (2017). A case study on signed music: The emergence of an inter-performance art. *Liminalities: A Journal of Performance Studies, 13*(2), 1–25.

Cripps, J. H., & Supalla, S. J. (2012). The power of spoken languages in schools and deaf students who sign. *International Journal of Humanities and Social Science, 2*(16), 86–102.

Cripps, J. S. (2008). *What is Deaf Culture?* https://deafculturecentre.ca/what-is-deaf-culture/

Cripps, J. S., Small, A., Rosenblum, E., & Cripps, J. H. (2015). *Signed music: Rhythm of the heart.* Toronto, ON: Canadian Cultural Society of the Deaf. https://deafculturecentre.ca/deaf-arts-series/deaf-arts-handbook-vol-two.pdf

Darrow, A. (2006). The role of music in deaf culture: Implications for music educators. *Journal of Research in Music Education, 41*(2), 93–110.

Davidson, J. W. (2012). Bodily movement and facial actions in expressive musical performance by solo and duo instrumentalists: Two distinctive case studies. *Psychology of Music, 40*(5), 595–633.

Drabkin, W. (2004). Motif. In S. Sadie & J. Tyrrell (Eds.), *The new grove dictionary of music and musicians* (2nd ed.). London, UK: Macmillan.

Ennis, B. (1993). *Live at SMI! Bill Ennis* [DVD]. Burtonsville, MD: Sign Media Inc.

Erting, C. J., & Kuntze M. (2008) Language socialization in deaf communities. In P. A. Duff & N. H. Hornberger (Eds.), *Encyclopedia of language and education* (2nd ed., pp. 2845–2858). New York, NY: Springer.

Frishberg, N. (1988). Signers of tales: The case for literary status of an unwritten language. *Sign Language Studies, 59*, 149–170.

Geertz, C. (1973). *The interpretation of cultures.* New York, NY: Basic Books.

Gorlée, D. L. (1994). Prelude and acknowledgements. In D. L. Gorlée (Ed.), *Song and significance: Virtues and vices of vocal translation* (pp. 7–15). New York, NY: Rodopi.

Gritten, A., & King, E. (2011). *New perspectives on music and gesture.* Aldershot, UK: Ashgate.

Gritten, A., & King, E. (2006). *Music and gesture.* Aldershot, UK: Ashgate.

Hamm, C., Nettl, B., & Byrnside, R. (1975). *Contemporary music and music culture.* Englewood Cliffs, NJ: Prentice-Hall.

Hargreaves, D. J., Miell, D., & MacDonald, R. R. (2002). What are musical identities, and why are they important? In R. R. MacDonald, D. Hargreaves & D. Miell (Eds.), *Musical identities, new edition* (pp. 1–20). Oxford, UK: Oxford University Press.

Hatten, R. S. (2004). *Interpreting musical gestures, topics, and tropes: Mozart, Beethoven, Schubert.* Bloomington, IN: Indiana University Press.

Johnston, R. E., & Erting, C. (1989). Ethnicity and socialization in a classroom for deaf children. In C. Lucas & C. Valli (Eds.), *Sociolinguistics of the deaf community* (pp. 41–83). San Diego, CA: Academic Press.

Kramer, L. (2003). Subjectivity rampant! Music, hermeneutics, and history. In M. Clayton, T. Herbert, & R. Middleton (Eds.), *The cultural study of music: A critical introduction* (pp. 124–135). New York, NY: Routledge.

Kunej, D., & Turk, I. (2000). New perspectives on the beginning s of music: Archaeological and music analysis of a middle Paleolithic bone "flute." In N. L. Wallin, B. Merker, & S. Brown (Eds.), *The origins of music* (pp. 235–268). Cambridge, MA: MIT Press.

Lane, H. (1999). *Mask of benevolence: Disabling the deaf community.* San Diego, CA: DawnSignPress.

Lane, H., Hoffmeister, R., & Bahan, B. (1996). *A journey into the Deaf-World.* San Diego, CA: DawnSignPress.

Lane, H., Pillard, R. C., & Hedberg, U. (2011). *The people of the eye: Deaf ethnicity and ancestry.* Oxford, UK: Oxford University Press.

Leigh, I. W., Andrews, J. F., Harris, R. L., & Gonzalez Avila, T. (2020). *Deaf culture: Exploring deaf communities in the United States* (2nd ed.). San Diego, CA: Plural Publishing.

Low, P. (1994). The Pentathlon approach to translating songs. In D. L. Gorlée (Ed.), *Song and significance: Virtues and vices of vocal translation* (pp. 185–212). New York, NY: Rodopi.

Maler, A. (2013). Songs for hands: Analyzing interactions of sign language and music. *Society for Music Theory, 19*(1), 1–15.

McCullough, C. (2018). Six not-so-great messages found in a quiet place: A film critique. *Society for American Sign Language Journal, 2*(1), 64–67.

McMillian, D. W., & Chavis, D. M. (1986). Sense of community: A definition and theory. *Journal of Community Psychology, 14*, 6–23.

Meier, R. P. (2002). Why different, why the same? Explaining effects and non-effects of modality upon linguistic structure in sign and speech. In R. P. Meier, K. Cormier, & D. Quinto-Pozos (Eds.), *Modality and structure in signed and spoken languages* (pp. 1–25). Cambridge, UK: Cambridge University Press.

Middleton, R. (2012). Music studies and the idea of culture. In M. Clayton, T. Herbert & R. Middleton (Eds.), *The cultural study of music: A critical introduction* (2nd ed., pp. 1–14). New York, NY: Routledge.

Miller, M. B. (1991). *Live at SMI! Mary Beth Miller* [DVD]. Burtonsville, MD: Sign Media Inc.

Mitchell, R. E., & Karchmer, M. A. (2005). Parental hearing status and signing among deaf and hard of hearing students. *Sign Language Studies, 5*(2), 231–244.

Mitchell, R. E., Young, T. A., Bachleda, B., & Karchmer, M. A. (2006). How many people use ASL in the United States? Why estimates need updating. *Sign Language Studies, 6*(3), 306–335.

Padden, C. A. (1980). The Deaf community and the culture of deaf people. In C. Baker & R. Battison (Eds.), *Sign language and the deaf community* (pp. 89–103). Silver Spring, MD: National Association of the Deaf.

Padden, C. A. (1987). Sign languages: American. In J.V. Van Cleve (Ed.), *Gallaudet encyclopedia of deaf people and deafness,* (Vol. 3, pp. 43–53). New York, NY: McGraw-Hill.

Padden, C., & Humphries, T. (1988). *Deaf in America: Voices from a culture.* Cambridge, MA: Harvard University Press.

Patterson, L. (2009). Residential schools. In S. Burch (Ed.), *Encyclopedia of American disability history* (pp. 778–780). New York, NY: Facts on File, Inc.

Pliny the Elder. (1938). *Natural history, books I–II* (H. Rackham, Trans.). Cambridge, MA: Harvard University Press. (Original work published 77AD)

Reagan, T. (1995). A sociocultural understanding of deafness: American Sign Language and the culture of deaf people. *International Journal of Intercultural Relations, 19*(2), 239–251.

Rutherford, S. (1988). The culture of American deaf people. *Sign Language Studies, 59*, 129–147.

Rutherford, S. (1993). *A study of American deaf folklore.* Burtonsville, MD: Linstok Press.

Sandler, W., & Lillo-Martin, D. (2006). *Sign language and linguistic universals.* Cambridge, UK: Cambridge University Press.

Schein, J. D., & Delk, M. T., Jr. (1974). *The deaf population of the United States.* Silver Spring, MD: National Association of the Deaf.

Schmidt-Jones, C. (2007). *Understanding basic music theory.* Houston, TX: Connexions & Rice University.

Schuchman, J. S. (1999). *Hollywood speaks: Deafness and the film entertainment industry.* Champaign, IL: University of Illinois Press.

Singleton, J. L., & Tittle, M. D. (2000). Deaf parents and their hearing children. *Journal of Deaf Studies and Deaf Education, 5*(3), 221–236.

Small, A., Cripps, J. S., & Côté, R. (2012). *Culture space and self/identity development among deaf youth.* Toronto, ON: Ministry of Education and Knowledge Network for Applied Education Research.

Supalla, T., & Dannis, J. (1994). *Charles Krauel: A profile of a deaf filmmaker* [VHS]. San Diego, CA: DawnSignPictures.

Supalla, C., & Supalla, D. (1991). *Short stories in American Sign Language* [VHS]. Colton, CA: ASL Vista Project.

Sutton-Spence, R. (2010). The role of sign language narratives in developing identity for deaf children. *Journal of Folklore Research, 47*(3), 265–305.

Sutton-Spence, R., & Müller de Quadros, R. (2006). Sign language poetry and deaf identity. *Sign Language & Linguistics, 8*(1–2), 177–212.

Thaut, M. H. (2005). *Rhythm, music, and the brain: Scientific foundations and clinical applications.* New York, NY: Routledge.

United States Library of Congress. (1955). *Deaf mute girl reciting the "Star spangled banner"* [Motion picture]. Los Angeles, CA: Primrose Productions. (Original work published 1902)

Valli, C., Lucas, C, Mulrooney, K., & Villanueva, M. (2011). *Linguistics of American Sign Language: An introduction* (5th ed.). Washington, D.C.: Gallaudet University Press.

CHAPTER 10

Make the Sign, Make the Mark, Play the Music

Teach the World

Marko Vuoriheimo
Interviewer *Ana L. Cruz*

Abstract

Marko Vuoriheimo (artist name Signmark), in an interview with Ana L. Cruz, describes his journey of becoming a Deaf hip-hop recording artist who performs live to audiences worldwide. Marko recounts his early exposure to music in Finland; his experimentation with musical instruments; the resistance he faced in fulfilling his dream to become a musician and his perseverance in overcoming obstacles; his musical influences; and especially the meaning and significance of music for him personally. He realized early on the power of music to bring people together and to convey messages. He uses his music to advocate for the rights of the global Deaf community (including his work with the United Nations) and to inform a wider audience about the needs of Deaf people.

Keywords

Deaf Finnish musician – hip-hop – music performance – deaf rights advocate – social justice

1 Introduction

Marko Vuoriheimo (artist name *Signmark*) is a congenitally deaf rapper/hip-hop artist from Finland. He performs worldwide with his band and is a recording artist for Warner Music Group. Signmark uses his music to advocate for the rights of Deaf people and supports the view of Deaf people as a linguistic minority with their own culture, history, and community. As a Deaf musician, Signmark competed to represent Finland at the 2009 Eurovision Song Contest and placed a close second in the Finnish qualification. During the interview Signmark revealed his path to music, the significance and meaning of music to him, music and his Deaf identity, the challenges of being a Deaf professional

 DOI:10.1163/9789004692299_011

musician, and the importance of music for raising consciousness and effecting transformation.

2 Interview

The interview was conducted via Zoom in March 2021. The interviewer (Ana L. Cruz) and the interviewee (Marko Vuoriheimo) had communicated before through email, but never had the opportunity to meet. Therefore, before the interview, both had a chance to dialogue, to explore, and to learn a bit about each other's background. Ana L. Cruz talked about her work as a college professor in the U.S. During this part of the conversation Marko Vuoriheimo disclosed that he previously also was a teacher ("I graduated with a Master's Degree in Education in the early 2000s and then I went to a Polytechnic School of Interpretation to work. So I worked as a teacher" [educating sign-language interpreters]). After Marko Vuoriheimo learned that Ana L. Cruz is from Brazil and about her journey that started in the late 80s teaching music to a congenitally deaf student and that her work brought her to the U.S. for graduate studies, he stated that he visited Brazil several times and that he "really loves the culture and people." This time before the start of the interview was also an opportunity to thank the sign-language interpreter Catherine.

Ana L. Cruz [ALC]: *I would like to know, why did you choose Signmark as your artistic name?*

Marko Vuoriheimo [MV]: The name Signmark came about when I decided that I really would go forward with my dream. I wanted to be an artist and I wanted to be a Deaf artist who would be on stage and perform to audiences. I had this big vision that I would be a performing artist and travel around the world, that I would not just stay put in Finland; I wanted to do things and see the world. At that point I started to think about an international name that would work also for the English-speaking world. I wanted to keep my own name in some way in that artistic name and to combine that with sign language and Deaf culture. I was thinking about using 'sign language' and then my own name 'Marko.' Then it was quite obvious to just use 'sign' from sign language, drop 'language,' and then my own name 'Marko' without the 'o,' so that is how it came together. It is a nice name and it is easy to say wherever I am in the world. At first, it was kind of hard here in Finland, but internationally I thought it was a good name.

And then the sign Signmark, which is like this: you have the two fists coming together [*makes the sign for Signmark*]. I think you know that every Deaf person has a sign-name and also the hearing people, who are part of Deaf culture, have a sign-name. It actually was a coincidence when I was at the university studying to become a teacher. At the university where I was studying, there was this visiting professor who was researching different ethnic groups. She came to Finland to give a lecture about this and I was really excited and wanted to go to listen to the lecture. At some point in the lecture, there was a list of different ethnic groups, for instance, Maoris, Muslims, Aborigines, Indians, Sami people, Eskimos; so all these different groups were on the list. I was watching that list and there were no Deaf people on it. I raised my hand and asked the professor: 'why aren't Deaf people on this list?' And the professor said: 'Yes, I was sure that, because we have a Deaf audience here, you would expect to have Deaf people on the list as well. But we have been researching this and we have decided that Deaf people are not an ethnic group.' Then I just wanted her to tell me more about this, how did they come up with this conclusion. She said that in ethnic groups there are five important things that need to come together to call a group an ethnic group: first, you have the language; second, you have the culture; third, you have a history; fourth, you have a community; fifth, you have the genetic inheritance. At this point I asked the professor: 'what is the problem? Why are there no Deaf people on the list?' She said that Deaf people are not that sort of a group that has the inheritance like that. And I stated: 'well, I have Deaf parents and they have the gene, they have the chromosome 26; because I have the same chromosome that my parents have, that's why I'm Deaf; so, obviously, you have this genetic inheritance.' After a while of arguing with her, I just decided to let it go. That same evening I was talking with my friends about the lecture. I really got frustrated in that lecture, because the professor didn't get my point. And how can she say that I don't have that sort of genetic or the inherited history. And I just thought that I needed to wake people up, I needed to kind of smack some sense into people's heads. Many people are just approving everything that is said to them and not thinking for themselves. So that was when I made this sign [the 'Signmark' sign]. My friend was looking at me and he went: 'I like that, that is looking good; that's a powerful sign right there; and that would be kind of suitable when you want to wake people up, and you want to slap some sense into them and make them see things.' That's how the sign for Signmark came to be; [*MV makes the sign for Signmark: left hand closed into a fist pointing forward and then the right hand, also closed into a fist, comes toward the left fist and bumps front ahead into the side of the left fist*] you have the one fist kind of bumping into the other fist [*interviewer tries to make the sign for Signmark*]. You can think about this sign in many ways: as something like 'waking up' to things; also as a bass, like you have the bass feel: bum-bum [*MV points to his heart as imitating the rhythm of the heart*]; you know how Deaf people can feel the rhythm. I think there are multiple explanations of how this sign can be seen.

[ALC]: *What was the professor teaching? What was the discipline?*

[MV]: I will send it to you on chat, because the interpreter might not know the exact term for it.

[ALC]: *Okay, so it was Ethnic Studies.*

[MV]: There you find her information [*info sent through chat*]. She came to our school and tried to tell me things [that MV did not agree with]. But on the other hand, of course, she also gave me more ammunition and more energy, she woke me up to see that I want to have more perspectives from the world about Deaf people, and that I want to have discussions about these things. It is not as clear as many people may think. She also gave me more reasons and more topics that I really want to write songs about. I have to thank her as well.

[ALC]: *When I was in Tennessee, during my graduate studies, I was closer to Deaf people. They also gave me a sign-name. This is my sign-name [ALC makes her sign-name: right hand in the shape of the letter 'A' in American Sign Language to mean Ana, the hand touching the right side of the lips and pulling upward along the right cheek; sign = Ana Smile*]. *They told me I smile a lot.*

[MV]: That I think is a strong American tradition, that they give sign-names with fingerspelled letters. And then you have 'A,' so that's the first letter. In Finland, we don't use these fingerspelling-based names. We are trying to get rid of the fingerspelling. So it wouldn't be Ana with 'A' from fingerspelling; this is not a typical handshape in signed names in Finnish Deaf culture. In Finnish it would be … [*MV makes sign-name: the index finger of the right hand touching the right side of the lips and moving upward along the right cheek; sign = Smile*]. But in American Deaf culture, I think fingerspelling is so much more emphasized. So it makes sense that you have a sign-name that has the letter 'A' handshape in it as well, that is nice.

[ALC]: *How and when did you discover music? Under what circumstances? And what specifically sparked your interest in music?*

[MV]: Everything began in this house where I am actually living now with my family, because this used to be my grandparents' house. After they died we moved here. At Christmas time, we had this tradition that all of my relatives came to this house. Most of my relatives are Deaf; only my grandparents were hearing and they didn't know how to sign. On Christmas Eve we had our dinner and then we had Santa Claus, and presents, and everything. Everybody was mingling and having fun and my grandparents were with us for a while. Then my grandparents went downstairs, because there is another area downstairs and there was also my grandparents' piano. They disappeared downstairs and I always wondered what were they doing downstairs? Why would they go there and nobody else? I was just curious and wanted to see what was happening downstairs. So I went downstairs and saw my grandfather playing the piano and my grandmother singing Christmas carols. I asked them 'what exactly were you singing grandma?' My grandparents said that 'because everybody upstairs was signing to each other and we don't understand what they were signing, we just like to come here, just the two of us and sing and play Christmas music.' I got interested and I said to them 'I want to be with you, I want to see what's happening.' My grandma started singing and I started lip reading what my grandma was singing and started signing that to sign language. And I noticed that this was actually really fun. I could understand what my grandma was singing and then I could kind of make my own music. But it felt quite boring to be signing on my own. So I went back upstairs and said to all my cousins and my parents and all the other relatives to come down with me, and also my godparents who were present as well. So I just asked everybody to come down with me and then showed them how I was signing. I think I was about eight years old at the time. I was quite proud to be doing this in front of everybody and performing for them. Everybody came down and then everybody started signing with me the songs. And that was the moment when I knew at some unconscious level, I think I didn't quite fully understand it yet, that music brings people together, that it is a way to really unite different people. There was something special about that experience; it was like a little spark inside of me that would become a flame. I really got interested in music, because I understood that you can tell people things with music, and that you can go between cultures and languages with music. At the same time you can enjoy music, but you can also give information and so on. I just thought this was so cool to do that. And that's how it all started.

[ALC]: *I mentioned a little bit about my story with the deaf girl in Brazil. She really struggled to find a school where she could be taught how to play the piano. She was the only deaf child in the family and she wanted to participate in the music activities of the family. So her father was looking for teachers to teach his daughter how to play the piano; that was when I came in. I adapted some methodology I used to teach hearing people and I started teaching that deaf girl. After one year of music/piano instruction, she could read classical music notation and play the piano; nobody in the audience could tell that she was deaf. She played the piano with much engagement, enthusiasm and love for music. I taught her (what I was taught when I learned to play the piano) that a music instrument is an extension of her body. And she took the piano as an extension of her body to express herself. So since then, I became really interested in and a big advocate for more opportunities for Deaf people to have entrance to music instruction in schools. So my question is in regard to your music learning. Did you have schools and teachers that would be willing to accept you as a student, and teach you music or a music instrument? Did you have anybody who could teach you? And how was your learning of music?*

[MV]: In our school system we had no music education for Deaf students. Or, if you had some music education, it was always done in a way that the teacher was playing the piano or something and then he or she would ask the students to lip-read and then sign, or make the rhythms with our bodies, or dance, or something like this. It was always taught in the same way. Many times I said to the teachers that I really wanted to learn how to play these instruments. And the teachers answered: 'no, no, this would be too hard on the hearing ears.' So they just didn't understand at all what could have been accomplished. In Spring, we have the end of the school year party and later in the year we have a Christmas party; then people would come to see the students. It was always done in a way that the teacher was teaching us to sign as if we were in a [singing] choir; but I never got to be a part of that in a way that it [the type of performance] would keep my interest.

I've had three ways to learn music. The one I loved the most was at home at night. In the 80s and 90s, when I was growing up, we had these music videos that came on at nighttime on MTV/Music Television. I used to record them on VHS cassettes. When I woke up I would just take my cassettes and go to school. Then, when all the other students went outside on recess, I would just stay in the classroom and watch these music videos and study them. I was so interested in these live performances, to see real-life performances. I could see what the drummer was doing and how the bass player was handling the instrument. For instance, one of the concerts I was watching constantly was AC/DC performing *Thunderstruck*, this big concert by AC/DC. That was something I loved to watch, because it had been recorded at a live event; again, I could see what the drummer was actually doing there on stage and how his hands were moving. I tried to do that at the same time, doing these rhythms on my thighs and just trying to get the feel of it. Or I would read the lyrics and just look at the lips of the singer and sign it simultaneously, kind of translate the songs into sign. I also used to watch Michael Jackson a lot and liked to learn all the dance moves and get some ideas about how you can combine the signs with the dance moves so that the whole signing performance becomes more musical. For instance, *Thriller* was a video that I used to do the moves of the dancers, but at the same time sign the lyrics with my hands. It was really hardcore when you think about it, growing up doing that. So, one way that I used to practice was with videos. But it was quite hard because the teachers punished me many times for not going outside on recess. They would say 'you have to go outside with the other students' and we had these constant arguments about it. That was the attitude at my school. There was another way for me to learn about music, I think I did it maybe 30 or 40 times: after school I would go out and just walk around, because I knew that the school building would be closed before five o'clock. I would then sneak back into the school building before five o'clock and say that I needed to go to the toilet or I needed to get my gym gear. I would hide in the school building and just wait for all the teachers and staff to leave and the school would be closed. I would go back to the music classroom and start exploring music instruments by myself. I would play the drums and study the different books, play the piano and the different instruments I could find, just explore what would be the nicest music instruments I could find and how to feel them. But of course, I got caught at some point. So after that, I got written up, a warning for doing this. My parents were of course very upset with me for doing such a thing. I just had to quit it after that, because they were very furious with me. The third way for me to learn about music was in my neighborhood. There was this neighbor who had a band and his hearing son was my friend. He had these different music instruments at home. I always would go to my neighbor's house and then my friend would say 'of course you can try those out; I can teach you and I can show you how to play the drums and how to play different instruments.' That was really important for me when I was growing up that I had this place where I could go and play. I think these three ways were the most important ones for getting me into music.

[ALC]: *When you talk about schools, those were regular schools, correct?*

[MV]: Yeah, they were regular schools, the classes from the first grade to the ninth grade. Here in Finland we have the regular school from first grade, we start around six or seven years old. And then we finish when we are 14 or 15 years old. So that is the first level [grades 1 to 9, comprehensive school] of school here in Finland. That would be the school I'm talking about now.

[ALC]: *How about music schools, any specific music schools?*

[MV]: No specific music schools in my lifetime. At the university, when I started there, there were music classes as well, but they only had piano. For example, when you are studying to be a teacher, then you study to play the piano so you can teach music to the kids; but I wasn't interested in that. Because at the same time I started studying rap music, hip hop, and hip hop culture and I was more into that. Hip hop culture really caught my eye at that time. I just was not really interested in teaching little kids how to play the piano. So I'm kind of self-taught. In addition, I have many friends that were great sources of information for me; I just would ask around and kind of made my own way. When I started making music myself—it was around 2004—I started making my own music with my friends. I would write the lyrics. At the same time I would ask because I wanted to understand the production of music as well: what does it mean to have a live sample? What is a sample? How do you use samples in your music? I would just educate myself and little by little learn more. That has been my way.

[ALC]: *You mentioned that you explored several instruments. Which one did you feel closer to? You said that your grandmother played the piano, but you also talk a lot about drums. Which one did you feel like: I wish I would be a performer, proficient musician on that instrument. Anything specific or not?*

[MV]: I have had two favorite instruments; first were the drums and then the bass guitar. Those would be the two instruments that I felt the closest to. But I never had any formal music instruction or got any education on how to play C major or C minor or anything like that. I just explored bass guitar without getting any formal music education. Anything that has to do with musical theory, I know nothing about it because I've never studied it, and I never wanted to study the theory of music, either. The most important thing for me has always been the lyrics, the translation of the lyrics, and the beat of the music. I also see as important that you have a good tempo, that you have a good flow, and whether you have a good melody. Those are the things that matter to me. I don't know how to make the background music, I just want to concentrate on the things that are most important to me. I am happy that I have done much research about music instruments; I basically know what kinds of sounds the instruments make, and how they affect the overall sound of the music and the feel, and the visuals. For example, if you have a text about love, I want the signing and the singing to create this little moment when you have these shivers going down your spine, because you find the other person so attractive. I would then explain that I think that maybe a cello or violin would go well with this, but I actually don't know if it is C or E minor that I would be after. That is something I leave to the hands of more capable people. I just know that in this first verse I want to have the feeling that you get these 'cold shivers' and I think that the violin would go well, but I'm not able to write the music key myself. Then I ask other people to do it for me.

[ALC]: *Tell me then about the importance and the meaning of music for you personally; and how does it connect to your Deaf identity?*

[MV]: There are many things to say on this topic. I have to say that music has always been a way of living for me, if I want to unwind or if I just want to relax. If I want to go to do some exercise, I use these headphones and put the volume up so I can feel the beats or I can feel the bass. Or if I'm feeling sad or melancholic, then I would have some music to deal with that. I feel that music supports me and helps me to go forward.

So that is one viewpoint on music. Then other music artists, music videos, and lyrics have always given me much inspiration. I was always very interested in other music artists' work. I have gained much information from their lyrics and I know more about the world because I have been studying other music artists and their lyrics. For instance, Sami people or Maori and their own songs; when I am 'listening' to the music and reading those texts I get a feeling of a shared identity, that I have similar experiences with them, I kind of 'feel' them. At the same time, I am thinking about how I would write my own next song because I was inspired by their song, or how will this affect my songwriting because I am always writing for Deaf audiences. I start to think how could I make this for a Deaf audience, but at the same time, of course, I want the hearing people to be able to enjoy my music as well. I have these two audiences that I'm constantly thinking about. That is important for me in music. Nowadays I do a lot of lectures as well, and I am always trying to support and inspire the teachers and/or the parents of Deaf people about teaching young people how a song is made, what does it mean to have a verse, or a chorus, or what does it mean to have a bridge in a song. They need to teach this to Deaf people, because I have noticed that in my age group, when I think about my Deaf friends who are approximately the same age I am, they are quite lacking in the ability of how to write a logical text that has a beginning and an end. Again, when Deaf people write applications to get a grant or write an article, when I read the words of other Deaf people who are approximately my age, I notice that there are things a bit scattered around and also there are unnecessary repetitions—it's like the whole written structure is incorrect. I feel that it would be really good for young Deaf children to start playing with the structure of a song. That would be a way to show them that you have this intro, and then you have this verse and chorus, and so on. That would maybe help them to understand how to write a logical text when they are older. This [the importance of the connection between learning music and writing for Deaf people], of course, has not been studied but just came to my mind. I think it has something to do with the fact that I understand how a song is made and that I'm able to write a logical text.

[ALC]: *Did you find resistance from Deaf people because you liked music?*

[MV]: Yes, there have been those attitudes as well. There have been always the people who were rooting for me and saying things like 'this is the best thing ever, a Deaf rapper' and 'oh my gosh.' I think the majority of us, especially the younger people who are under 40 years old, they are rooting for me. But then there is the other side as well, the older generation, especially over 50 years old, that is quite resistant. But in a way I understand it because it is the history that affects them. For them, they have always been told that Deaf people and music don't go together and that you are not allowed to enjoy music, and you heard that for 50 or 60 years every day of your life. And then there came this rapper, who is trying to make a difference. Of course it is causing some people not to understand it and to be resistant to that.

[ALC]: *How and when did you decide that being a music performer was the career choice for you?*

[MV]: It was at a night club on a late Friday night in June 2004. That would be the time and the place. I was there that night with my friends just hanging out. There was this song, I realized that I knew it, it was Mr. President's *Coco Jamboo* and I went to the dance floor, just dancing and signing on my own on the dance floor. And then all of a sudden, three hearing guys came to me and they had a glass of beer and they just threw it on me, just poured the beer down my neck and smacked me in the face. There was this full-blown fight going on; they were hitting me and I was trying to defend myself. All of a sudden all the lights went on, the music stopped, and the bouncers came and just wrapped us up and made me stop. The hearing guys said that they just got annoyed with me, this deaf person here just acting like a monkey on the dance floor. I tried to explain my side of the story: that I was just signing. The bouncers were kind of fed up and they said 'okay, you deaf guy just go out, it's better that you just leave; never come back again. You are banned from this place.' And I said 'me, are you kidding me? I was just using my mother tongue on the dance floor; that cannot be restricted.' Well, I left and I thought 'okay, I had enough, this is it; now I will start to write my own songs. I quit translating other people's lyrics, Mr. President's *Coco Jamboo* is the last song I'm ever going to translate. I will start to write my own lyrics and make my own music.' So that was the time.

[ALC]: *So thanks to the three guys and a fight, we have Signmark!*

[MV]: I lost the fight, I have to admit. I wasn't punching back; I am still kind of holding a grudge.

[ALC]: *You gained so much more and so did we.*

[MV]: Yes, I have. It would be great to meet those people again and say to them 'thank you so much; see what I am today.'

[ALC]: *You mentioned Michael Jackson already. But were there other artists or individuals that were instrumental or very inspirational for you to develop into the musician and performer that you are today? Are there any particular names besides Michael Jackson?*

[MV]: When I started looking at different music genres there were different music artists. But then when I started getting into hip hop and rap music, when I saw Coolio's *Gangsta's Paradise*, that was a song for me that made the decision that I wanted to be in hip hop as well. I was so taken by it, it was something extraordinarily cool. I wanted to be a rapper. And at the time when Coolio's *Gangsta's Paradise* came out there also was Run-DMC and it affected me greatly. Also, MC Hammer with his kind of pop, pop/rap music was a great influence at the beginning of my rap career, and the Fugees was also big for me. That is the kind of style I liked in the beginning. I was also really interested in Public Enemy. That was one of the bands, but it was really hard because that kind of rap was too fast for me to follow. So I like the style of Coolio and the Fugees where the flow was more mellow and not as rapid as Public Enemy. Those were the big influences for me.

[ALC]: *For the majority of people being Deaf and engaged in music is a contradiction. What is your response to this very common attitude and belief?*

[MV]: That is hard to say because there are so many things it depends on, such as the environment in which Deaf individuals are growing up, what is the attitude there, and what are the kind of opportunities or stimulation they get towards music. I think the best way would be if we have Deaf professionals teaching Deaf people how to engage in music. There is, of course, nothing wrong with hearing people teaching music to Deaf kids, of course not; for instance, children of Deaf parents, there are many great CODAs in the world. But at the same time—it's such a small thing—you can be a really skilled signer, you may have grown up in a Deaf family, but when you are trying to teach people who don't hear and you yourself are hearing, it is not the same. I myself appreciate CODAs trying to do this. But at the same time you do hear, so you can't identify in the same way as a Deaf person can. Of course you know the language, but you don't have the experience of not hearing. When you have another Deaf person who comes and starts teaching about music, then you have the same experience. Like, if I can learn this you can learn this, because we are the same. So I think that is the most important thing.

[ALC]: *Do you see yourself inspiring other Deaf kids to learn music when you have your shows?*

[MV]: Yes, I do think so; I have gotten a lot of feedback. I have visited schools and I have had these videos and everything else that kids are sending to me all the time. They are trying to do the same I do, like sign my lyrics. I think I have made some sort of a difference. And it has been so great to see that, that my music has had this effect. My music has also been used as teaching material in schools, I know this as well. It has been so nice, because when I think about my time in school and when I was trying to find something to do with music and have sign language in it, there was nothing available. There were mimes or poetry done in sign language, but nothing that would combine music and sign language. So I'm happy to do it myself. I can imagine that when I was 12 or 13 years old, and if there would have been someone like Signmark, I am sure I would have been super excited about that. I would have said: how does he do that, I want to do it as well, and I want to be better than him. I am sure that some kids at least are inspired.

[ALC]: *You obviously travel with your music all over the world. Some people erroneously believe that sign language is the same in every country worldwide. How many sign languages do you speak? How do you handle sign language communication with Deaf communities from different parts of the world? Is International Sign an option?*

[MV]: I have this music career now for 12 years and still in Finnish media they have the same question: is sign language universal? Do you all sign the same? I think I have been asked the same question thousands of times. Still, they haven't learned so this is something I think we will struggle with for eternity.

But to your other question. I myself know six different sign languages. When I travel, it depends on the country and on the audience. If I go to India, Australia, or England I use the British Sign Language. When I travel in Nordic countries, I use the Swedish Sign Language. Then here in Finland, of course, I use Finnish Sign Language. It also depends on what kind of audience we have. In some parts of the world, people know American Sign Language. So if the audience knows that, I use American Sign Language. I think in many countries the most used sign language is American Sign Language, even if it is not the mother tongue. But then if a person doesn't know American Sign Language, then I use the International Sign. I know a little bit Chinese Sign Language, because I've made four songs in Chinese Sign Language as well.

[ALC]: *So I have British Sign Language, Swedish Sign Language, Finnish Sign Language, American Sign Language, Chinese Sign Language, and International Sign, very nice!*

[MV]: But then, three weeks ago, there was this interview for a Russian magazine and they asked if I am hearing; I was confused and said 'No, I am

Deaf.' And the interviewer was just dumbstruck because he had been following my musical career for seven or eight years. He had all the time thought that I am hearing, that I am a child of Deaf adults, that I would be hearing just growing up in a sign language family. When I said 'no, no, I my Deaf' he was shocked; he had been talking with his friends as well and everybody was thinking that I was a child of Deaf adults, a CODA. It was just a puzzling moment for me as well. It seems that in some way, I do belong to both communities, the Deaf community and the hearing community as well, because it's easy for me to get along with both communities.

[ALC]: *Well, you speak the international language of music, that is why. One more question ...*

[MV]: But just to add to this. I meet a lot of people who come from different countries. For instance, a few years ago I was at this festival in France and there were seven thousand Deaf people from all over the world; it was a huge audience. And most of them thought that I was a CODA or that I was an interpreter, because beforehand they didn't know me, most of them were quite young. They had not been around when I started my career. They had been accustomed in their home countries to the way that interpreters are translating songs and signing them. When they came to France and saw me perform, and saw what I was doing on stage, they just couldn't understand that I am actually a Deaf artist performing. They thought I was hearing and they were quite astonished when they learned the truth. Sometimes I get this [misreading of MV's background].

[ALC]: *One of the main foci of the book we are working on is the issue of equity and social justice. How do you see your work in music closing the equity gap for Deaf communities around the world?*

[MV]: The situation varies a lot from country to country I go to. There is a lot of inequality, for instance in the interpreting services. In many countries they just don't have it; the situation is terrible, they don't have these services. Then there is the issue of opportunities, such as the right to go to school and to have an education. There are some countries where a Deaf person is not permitted to get a driver's license. The situation may be different in various parts of the world. It will take two hours for me to tell you about my experiences in different parts of the world and how different each situation for Deaf people is. So there is a lot of work to be done.

[ALC]: *When you come to those countries with your music, do you bring Deaf people together and they realize that they can, perhaps, fight for more of their rights? Do they become more conscious?*

[MV]: Yes, this is the kind of feedback I do get after my performances; they have understood their rights. And, of course, I'm also performing at the UN [United Nations] or the African Union. So there have been a lot of these performances for people in high places, such as ministers [politicians in government] and people who are making the decisions. They come after my gig to thank me that I opened their eyes and made them realize that they do need to work for Deaf people as well. And they might be ashamed that the situation in their countries might be so bad when, for example, in Finland it is much better. It has been really great for me to make this sort of impact on people. And what you just said that through music one can really raise awareness [consciousness] and make a difference. When I started in 2004 making my own music, I never could have imagined that I would be at the headquarters of the UN having a performance or something like this because I was just thinking about beer and alcohol and partying, that was my thing in 2004. I never would have imagined that all of this would happen, but my whole career has been such a huge impact on people's lives.

[ALC]: *That is actually my last question. Could you please tell us about your involvement with the UN?*

[MV]: When I started doing gigs abroad, little by little, I noticed that there were really influential people coming to me and saying that they really think my performance was great and that I do great work. And then I started realizing that with what I do, I'm also a representative of Finland when I go abroad. I tell about the Finnish situation and how we have things here in Finland. And I also promote equality and human rights, and the acceptance of different kinds of people. I realized that I am a role model when I go abroad and perform, and then it occurred to me that I need to emphasize this even more, make it even bigger. I started thinking who would be a Finnish person who is also internationally known. And it came to mind that we have our own Minister [Secretary] of Foreign Affairs, Alexander Stubb was it at that time—and now, of course, it's a different person already. I emailed him a couple of times and just requested an appointment, and at last, I got an appointment. I told him about what I do and who I am, and what are my vision and my dream. And the Secretary himself was immediately taken by my message and wanted to work with me. He was really interested in what I had to say. I asked him 'what's the next place you're going to as Secretary' and he said 'I am actually going with the President of Finland to the UN headquarters for a meeting there.' And I said 'okay, I'm coming with you.' Then he thought about it for a while and said 'okay, let's try it out, you can come,' and that is how it all started. So

I did that for 10 years. I was a special guest of the Secretary of Foreign Affairs of Finland. I have been, for instance, in Geneva, Switzerland, at an annual meeting about human rights. I have been to Brussels for EU [European Union] events, and also to Rome; there was this UN-arranged event on food and water. So I went there to give a lecture. Many, many places, many lectures, many things have happened over those 10 years.

[ALC]: *I don't have any further questions. I just wanted to ask you whether there is anything that you feel is important for people to know about you and your work that I did not ask you?*

[MV]: Well, please stay healthy and take care of yourselves. Don't get sick [the world was still facing the COVID-19 pandemic]. Just follow your dreams and don't let them go. Because following my dream, it's been a nice life. So maybe it's just that.

[ALC]: *Thank you so much. It was a pleasure meeting you. A very enjoyable interview. Again, thank you and big hugs to you.*

[MV]: Good luck with your book. I'm hoping all the best and I think this is just a great idea and an important book in the making.

3 Post-Script

Signmark realized early on the power of music to bring people together and to convey a message. He uses his music to passionately advocate for the rights of the global Deaf community and to make aware a wider audience [hearing and Deaf] about the needs of Deaf people. Although heterogeneous with multiple intersecting identities, Deaf people around the world share characteristics and experiences that forge a distinct community. Signmark started as a teacher and now as an artist and performer he teaches through his music about the tapestry of a global Deaf community and he engages the world with the needs and the rights of Deaf people. His music with signed lyrics makes a mark and teaches the world!

CHAPTER 11

Silence as a Powerful Cultural Mark

Critical Pedagogy, Music, and Radical Deaf Studies

Ana L. Cruz

Abstract

The multitude of oppressive forces faced by a deaf individual to engage in musical activities became apparent to the author when teaching a deaf-born girl to play the piano. This experience of teaching the deaf girl to play the piano also showed, however, the possibilities of exploring music & deafness, where Deaf individuals can 'see' music externally and internally and view musical instruments as extension of their body. The author proposes the tansdisciplinary fusion of Deaf Studies and Freirean critical pedagogy, especially its notions of conscientização and emancipatory literature, for a Radical Deaf Studies. It is argued that Radical Deaf Studies can provide a language and theoretical lens to further analyze and develop a deeper understanding of the oppressive socio-cultural-political forces that affect the lives of Deaf people which in turn can result in true transformation and liberation. The chapter concludes with the author outlining some practical applications of Radical Deaf Studies and the Freirean notion of praxis for the field of Deaf education, including music education.

Keywords

critical pedagogy – Paulo Freire – Radical Deaf Studies – music & deafness – music education – music – audism – oralism – oppression – Deaf education – plural pathways

1 Introduction

The roots for this chapter were planted in Brazil. I was an assistant professor of music education while at the Universidade Federal do Amazonas (Brazil) when I started working with music & deafness in the late 1980s as part of my community service responsibilities at the university. I accepted the challenge to take on a deaf-born (profoundly deaf) girl as a student and worked in teaching her

 | DOI:10.1163/9789004692299_012

how to play the piano. The members of her family were musicians and the deaf girl yearned to learn how to play the piano to be able to participate in family musical activities. I then became aware about the oppression and denial of opportunities faced by Deaf people which were anchored in ableism and audism which consequently led to attitudes such as 'you are deaf, you can't do this, you can't do that.' To engage with music was apparently one of the things that Deaf people 'can't do.' Therefore, engaging with music has become a matter of social justice and equity, it must be a choice for people (including Deaf people) to explore and find fulfillment in music without having these opportunities denied through pre-ordained obstacles (including internalized oppression of what a person can or can't do based on being deaf or hearing). During the *Deaf President Now* protests in 1988 at Gallaudet University, Willard J. Madsen (2007, p. 82)[1] expressed the following about oppression and denial of opportunity and access because of being deaf:

> [...] Let not the stillness hide our cause—it shall abide
> Until we've turned the tide, and the whole world knows
> Our pride! The pride of right, the pride of might,
> The pride of all that's just and fair! There's victory in the air.
> Stand fast and never let go this magnificent torch
> We call "Deaf Pride." It is our hope and it shall be passed
> To every generation from this day. There can be no turning back!
> [...] Oppressed for years and years, It's always been the same:
> "You're deaf! You can't do this; You can't do that!"
> [A]nd so, the "Can't Syndrome" imposed on us
> By a hearing world majority who did not want to see
> Deaf people achieving full equality! [...]

Later on, while pursuing my graduate studies in the United States at the University of Tennessee-Knoxville and continuing the work in music & deafness, I started to investigate how a deaf individual constructs meaning in music and to interrogate oppressive forces and hegemonic relationships based on auditory skills (Cruz, 1997a; additional work on music & deafness by Cruz, 1997b; 1997c). By reimagining and incorporating the tenets of critical pedagogy, as espoused through the work of Paulo Freire (e.g., 1970; 1985; 1992; 1994a, b; 2010; 2011), it provided a template for analysis and praxis. The merging of critical pedagogy with Deaf Studies for a critical/radical Deaf Studies to offer a framework for analysis of oppressive forces on Deaf people was developed (Cruz, 2007; 2010; 2012; 2015; 2017; 2019) and is explored further in this book chapter.

Experiencing and practicing music are commonly perceived as requiring the hearing sense (direct pathway). However, Deaf persons engage in musical activities without (necessarily) the hearing sense (e.g., Straus, 2011; Loeffler, 2014) as they experience and even practice music using *plural* pathways (Cruz, 1997a: a combination of visualization, feeling vibrations, developing an image of sounds in the mind, and the 'internalization' of sounds) and not just relying on the *indirect* pathways (i.e., moving, feeling). Deaf persons can derive meaning from and enjoy experiencing music (Cruz, 1997a; see also Edwards, 1975; Kapla, 1975; Robbins & Robbins, 1980; Darrow, 1985). At present, there are prominent Deaf/hard-of-hearing musicians who engage professionally with music, including live concerts and release of recorded music, mostly based in the genre of hip-hop (e.g., Jones, 2015; Best, 2015/2016; Vuoriheimo, Chapter 10, this volume). Deafness & music are not mutually exclusive but certainly there is a lack of equal opportunity for Deaf persons to experience and engage with music. It seems, therefore, that what we know about experiencing and practicing music is still in its infancy since we yet need to understand music itself. With respect to music, Lucien Price (n.d.) enunciates:

> No one knows what music is. It is performed, listened to, composed, and talked about; but its essential reality is as little understood as that of its first cousin, electricity. We know that it detaches the understanding, enabling thoughts to turn inward upon themselves and clarify; we know that it releases the human spirit into some solitude of meditation where the creative process can freely act; we know that it can soothe pain, relieve anxiety, comfort distress, exhilarate health, confirm courage, inspire clear and bold thinking, ennoble the will, refine taste, uplift the heart, stimulate intellect, and will do many other interesting and beautiful things. And yet, when all is said and done, no one knows what music is. Perhaps the explanation is that music is the very stuff of creation itself.[2]

A physicist will equate music with sound waves that travel by pressure variations (vibrations) through a medium, such as air.[3] An equally important element of music, however, is silence, currently understood as the complete absence of sound,[4] a definition challenged by John Cage (2011). Within the world of music, John Cage's piece *4'33"* is a provocative 'silent composition:' the pianist sits at the piano in the concert hall, lifts the keyboard cover, but does not engage in playing the piano.[5] The sounds of Cage's *4'33"* music piece are generated by the audience present and the physical environment of the concert hall. Even with a musical score that does not involve intentional sounds, there never is complete silence because there is always an existing ambient sound of one form or another. Cage (2011, p. 8) states "There is no such thing as an empty space or an empty time. There is always something to see, something to hear. In fact, try as we may to make a silence, we cannot."

Silence, as an absence of sound, is often correlated with deafness. However, considering that a deaf person might still possess a level of residual hearing, has the experience with sounds produced by the human body (e.g., heartbeat, abdominal sounds, etc.), or perceives sound through the use of senses other that the hearing sense, there truly is never a 'total silence'—just as with Cage's music piece *4′33″*. There is always a constant dynamic involving silence, as if a constant dialogue occurs through which messages are conveyed and shared. The Brazilian poet Carlos Drummond de Andrade in his poem *O Constante Dialogo/The Constant Dialogue*[6] also explicates the notion that people can communicate in silence and with silence, that the spoken word (perceived through the hearing sense) is not a necessity:

> O CONSTANTE DIÁLOGO (Portuguese excerpt)
> [...]
> Escolhe teu diálogo
> E
> tua melhor palavra
> ou
> teu melhor silêncio
> Mesmo no silêncio e com o silêncio
> dialogamos.

> THE CONSTANT DIALOGUE (excerpt)
> [...]
> Choose your dialogue
> And
> your best word
> or
> your best silence
> Even in silence and with silence
> we dialogue.

Moreover, the use of silence in the title of this book chapter refers to the cultural and political importance of silence for the Deaf community: for instance the silence that attests to the resistance of Deaf people to the oppression from oralism and contributes to the formation of identity. And yet, this silence is a distinguishing mark of d/Deaf people who approach it as a different way to organize, interact with, and attach meaning to sound. This distinguishing mark is not a deficit or disability but can be seen as a special ability: studies indicate, for example, the augmentation of other senses (e.g., vision, touch; Karns et al., 2012) in lieu of the hearing sense in deaf persons and not to the same degree in hearing persons. The concept of Deaf Gain emphasizes the unique contributions the Deaf community and d/Deaf individuals can make to society and humankind in a wide variety of fields (Baumann & Murray, 2014): therefore, silence is also a means of empowerment showing the importance of d/Deaf persons within the global human community.

2 A Brief Exploration of Deaf Studies

Deaf Studies, as an academic discipline, can be broadly defined as "the study of anything linked to deaf people" (Kusters et al., 2017a); more specifically it focuses, according to Kuster et al. (2017a), on "deaf people's ontologies (deaf ways of being) and epistemologies (deaf ways of knowing), communities, networks, ideologies, literature, histories, religion, language practices, political practices, and aspirations." Bauman (2008a, p. 9; italics in the original) posits that Deaf Studies (also including here African American Studies, Women Studies, etc.):

> critique existing social arrangements that have served to marginalize their kind; they explore the complexities of identity construction within a political context, and they celebrate what is most unique in their ways of being. As such, Deaf Studies has explored a wide spectrum of topics, many of which fall under the more general notions of *identity*, *power*, and *language*.

The scope, emphasis, and evolution of Deaf Studies as an academic discipline was presented in two important edited books: *Open Your Eyes: Deaf Studies Talking* (Bauman, 2008b) and *Innovations in Deaf Studies: The Role of Deaf Scholars* (Kusters et al., 2017b); the overview section outlined below is based on the works of Kusters et al. (2017a), Murray (2017), and Bauman (2008a).

2.1 *Overview*

Deaf Studies was established in the 1970s principally steered by scholars in the United States and the United Kingdom. Its roots lay in the work of linguists studying sign language. The breakthrough came with the work of Stokoe (e.g.,

Stokoe et al., 1965) establishing American Sign Language as a bona-fide language on par with other (spoken) languages (Murray, 2017). During this phase, Deaf Studies scholars concentrated on describing and justifying a distinct Deaf culture, Deaf community, Deaf identity, and Deaf ethnicity researching and documenting the rich history of Deaf experiences in society. Grounded in the verve of the U.S. civil rights movement and activism, and countering the medical-pathological view of deafness and of deaf people (and the hegemonic shadow of oralism), the view of Deaf people belonging to a distinct cultural and linguistic minority emerged. With this work came the realization of a Deaf world with unique characteristics separate from the hearing world; however, it also led to stratification within the Deaf world based on the concept of Deaf culture and who belonged to it and to what degree. Seminal contributions to this phase of Deaf Studies were made by Padden (1980), Padden and Humphries (1988), Erting et al. (1994), Lane et al. (1996), Wilcox (1989), Ladd (1992), and Van Cleve and Crouch (1992).

A second phase of Deaf Studies (in the 1990s and 2000s) broadened the geographic reach beyond the United States and the United Kingdom and centered on detailed studies of Deaf ways of being (Deaf ontologies) and Deaf ways of knowing (Deaf epistemologies). A continued and intensified focus was on countering oppression experienced by Deaf persons in society and on Deaf liberation. The concepts of Deafhood (Ladd, 2003) and Deaf Gain (Bauman & Murray, 2009; 2014a) played a crucial role during this phase of Deaf Studies (please see sections below). In addition to the survey on the status of Deaf Studies by Bauman (2008b), other important contributions to Deaf Studies include Lane (1992), Ladd (2003; 2008), Bauman (2008a), Dunn (2008), and Gertz (2008). It is also crucial to highlight here the criticisms of Deaf Studies by authors such as Turner (1994), Fernandes and Myers (Fernandes & Myers, 2010; Myers & Fernandes, 2010), Baynton (2008; Chapter 1, this volume), and Davis (2006). These authors criticized: (1) essentialist aspects embedded in Deaf Studies' core concepts of Deaf culture, community, identity, and Deafhood; (2) the emphasis on perceiving Deaf people as a 'monolithic' block even beyond national borders (contrasting with the broad diversity within the Deaf community where individuals can be recognized by different intersectional identities); and (3) the perceived static nature and uncritical application of Deaf Studies' core concepts. Furthermore, (4) it was proposed to (re)evaluate the emphasis on Deaf culture and ethnicity in Deaf Studies.

According to Kusters et al. (2017a), the current research on Deaf ontologies and epistemologies (a third phase) is further broadened by expanding the geographical reach, by putting a focus on the political context within which Deaf persons are positioned in society, and by emphasizing the need to influence policy making. An important recent development is also the more prominent role of Deaf scholars as lead researchers and as holders of academic positions in researching Deaf ontologies and epistemologies and the expansion of the methodological approaches involved in such research (Kusters et al., 2017a). Related to that is the realization of the importance to reach beyond the confines of Deaf Studies, contribute to, and interact with other academic fields; while Deaf Studies scholars are predominantly associated with different and diverse academic disciplines, this current phase of Deaf Studies is opening the field to interdisciplinarity and transdisciplinarity (Kusters et al., 2017a).

The concepts of Deafhood and Deaf Gain, introduced as part of the second phase of Deaf Studies, are further elaborated in the following sections.

2.2 *Deafhood*

The concept of Deafhood was conceived by Paddy Ladd in the 1990s and formally introduced through his book *Understanding Deaf Culture: In Search of Deafhood* (Ladd, 2003). It emphasizes the "positive, collective, worldwide deaf experience" (Ladd, 2005, p. 14). Ladd (2003, p. XVIII) also stresses that:

> Deafhood is not seen as a finite state but as a process by which Deaf individuals come to actualize their Deaf identity, positing that those individuals construct that identity around several differently ordered sets of priorities and principles, which are affected by various factors such as nation, era, and class.

And further (Ladd, 2005, p. 15):

> it is a *process* through which each deaf man, woman, and child implicitly explains his/her existence as a deaf being in the world to him/herself and to each other [...] the precise epistemological and ontological "content" of those explanations.

Kusters and De Meulder (2013) emphasize that the Deafhood concept encompasses two components. The first one is the ontological dimension, focusing on the visual-gestural-tactile skills of Deaf persons; the second one is the emancipatory-liberatory dimension, meaning Deaf persons experiencing and overcoming barriers and oppression connected to being deaf.

Deafhood, therefore, was and still is a useful concept to empowering the Deaf community. It was conceived to highlight Deaf persons' experiences and ways of being, emphasizing a positive view of Deaf persons (Ladd, 2005; Kusters & De Meulder, 2013). It is also a vehicle to allow Deaf persons to address oppression brought about by the long history of oralism and the effects of colonialism. The Deafhood concept was designed with 'strategic essentialism,' focusing on Deaf commonalities, as a first step in Deaf cultural studies (Ladd, 2015). The Deafhood concept emphasizes sameness, shared experiences among the Deaf, and Deaf universalism—defined by Kusters and Friedner (2015, p. x) as "a (belief in a) deep connection that is felt between deaf people around the globe, grounded in experiential ways of being in the world as deaf people." More recently, differences within the Deaf community, the broad diversity within the Deaf community, and the importance of the concept of intersectionality (e.g., a Deaf person can have multiple intersecting identities, such as deaf-female-Latina-Christian) is emphasized. The dichotomy between sameness (DEAF-SAME) and difference within the Deaf community is examined by Kusters and Friedner (2015) and contributing authors in the book *It's a Small World* (Friedner & Kusters, 2015; see also Bauman, 2008a; Dunn & Cooke, Chapter 3, this volume). Nevertheless, while recognizing and respecting diversity in the (global) Deaf community, Ladd (2015) emphasizes the shared profound global commonalities among Deaf people.

2.3 *Deaf Gain*

The concept of Deaf Gain was formally introduced by Bauman and Murray (2009; 2010; 2014b) and defined as "a reframing of 'deaf' as a form of sensory and cognitive diversity that has the potential to contribute to the greater good of humanity" (Bauman & Murray, 2009, p. 3). The concept of Deaf Gain underscores the distinctive contributions the Deaf community and Deaf individuals can make to society in a wide variety of fields, based on the Deaf ways of knowing: the unique lived experiences, sensitivities, understandings, and life stories of Deaf people;[7] Bauman and Murray (2014a) provide examples of philosophical gains, language gains, sensory gains, social gains, and creative gains. Therefore, emphasizing Deaf Gain highlights the importance of the Deaf community for human diversity and with it, potentially, for human survival. bell hooks (2013, p. 26) addresses the fundamental importance of human diversity:

> Diversity is the reality of all our lives. It is the very essence of our planetary survival. Organically, human survival as a species relies on the interdependence of life. Fundamentalist thinking, supporting dominator culture, denies this truth, socializing citizens to believe that safety resides in upholding the tyranny of the same, in protecting homogeneity.

3 Deaf People and Oppression

Deaf people have faced a long history of oppression. The medical-pathological model views deafness as a deficit, something that is deviating from the normal and that needs to be fixed. Normalcy is a mid-19th century social construct (Davis, 2006) based on a statistical analysis of measured human traits. Plotting the frequency distribution of measured traits will show a bell-shaped curve: individuals that fall around the mode are considered 'normal,' individuals that fall within the lower frequencies away from the mode are considered 'abnormal' (Davis, 2006), and this deviation from the constructed notion of normalcy led to the label of being disabled. Branson and Miller (2002) in their book *Damned for their Difference: The Social Construction of Deaf People as Disabled* examine society's orientation and behavior toward Deaf people within a wider historical and cultural context (Branson & Miller, 2002); they show that being disabled is not a natural but a cultural construct and that Deaf people classified as disabled (individuals in need of being 'fixed') experienced marginalization and oppression because of it. Interestingly, Branson and Miller (2002, p. 67) point out that long before the constructed notion of disabled, Deaf people were viewed "as part of God's complex world" and, therefore, it was not considered "as right or proper … [to] change [to 'fix'] deaf people."

The 'push' for 'fixing' deafness subjected Deaf people to *oralism*. Ladd (2005, p. 13) defines oralism as "policies actively intending to eradicate or marginalize sign languages and deaf cultures." Starting in the 1880s, oralism aimed at teaching deaf persons to communicate exclusively through speech and lip-reading instead of using sign language with the purported goal to assimilate deaf people into mainstream society. The consequences of oralism were severe, including low educational attainment by deaf children (resulting in a lack of employment or further education), and internalized oppressions (lack of self-esteem, identity crises, self-hatred) (Ladd, 2005). Related to the label disability attached to Deaf persons, they are also confronted by *ableism*, that is discrimination in favor of able-bodied people. Deaf people also suffer under *audism*, a concept conceived by Tom Humphries and defined as "[t]he notion that one is superior based on one's ability to hear or to behave in the manner of one who hears" (Humphries, 1975, as cited in Bauman, 2008a). Furthermore, Lane (1992, p. 43) expanded on the notion of (systemic) audism by stating that it represents:

> the corporate institution for dealing with deaf people, dealing with them by making statements about them, authorizing views of them, describing them, teaching about them, governing where they go to school and, in

> some cases, where they live; in short, audism is the hearing way of dominating, restructuring, and exercising authority over the deaf community.

In the search for 'curing' deafness in the 20th and 21st centuries and (for the most part) ignoring Deaf people's culture and lived experiences, modern medicine and modern technology have become a threat to the existence of Deaf communities. Marginalization, discrimination and oppression toward Deaf people, Deaf culture and the Deaf community can be present through modern medicine, for example, with the imposition of cochlear implants for, once again, curing deafness. In addition, genetic engineering (such as CRISPR [Clustered Regularly Interspaced Short Palindromic Repeats] genome editing technology), especially, may not only be a threat to Deaf culture/Deaf world—where silence is not a sign of deficiency (negative) but a sign of strength (positive), an embodied cultural difference—but could eventually lead to eradication of the Deaf community (Bauman, 2008a). Moreover, Deaf people not only face oppression based on the fact that they are deaf, but also based on additional intersecting identities (e.g., deaf-female-black) and the concept of intersectionality becomes important when analyzing oppression and inequality (Dunn, 2008; Dunn & Cooke, Chapter 3, this volume; Kusters & Friedner, 2015).

In addition, there is also oppression exerted within the Deaf community, something Ladd (2005) referred to as 'horizontal violence.' The strong dichotomy between the Deaf world and the hearing world leads to 'prescribing' acceptable norms of behavior and attitudes as means to being perceived as 'really' Deaf and committed to being Deaf. Engaging in behaviors not 'approved' as part of the Deaf world is frowned upon and such Deaf individuals then are not fully embraced by the Deaf world based on the premise that such Deaf individuals have a 'hearing mind.' This can be illustrated by the experiences of a Deaf individual who enjoys, plays, and composes music. Although these activities are portrayed as very meaningful by the Deaf individual (e.g., as a 'cleansing vehicle;' help in dealing with frustrations and emotions; as a tool for self-expression; being of spiritual value; Cruz, 1997a), he experienced significant resistance, ridicule, snide remarks, and even hostility from fellow members of the Deaf community (Cruz, 1997a) because music is perceived by a segment of the Deaf community as part of the hearing world (only).

Overall, it is apparent that discrimination and oppression of Deaf people (including internalized oppression) are still prevalent in society. And, therefore, it is important that the work on social justice, equity, and critical literacy continues.

4 Critical Pedagogy

Critical pedagogy (see for example McLaren, 2015; Darder, Baltodano, & Torres, 2003; Kincheloe, 2008) has its origin in the work of the Brazilian educational philosopher Paulo Freire (1992; 1994a; 2011) most fundamentally in his *Pedagogy of the Oppressed*, but further elaborated in his numerous subsequent publications (e.g., Freire, 1985; 1998a; Shor & Freire, 1987). Critical pedagogy is rooted in the field of education, but notions and approaches developed from critical pedagogy, such as the oppressor-oppressed relationship and how to address and overcome it, has found application in other academic disciplines as well.

Macedo (2007, p. 394) expresses that critical pedagogy:

> is a state of becoming, a way of being in the world and with the world—a never ending process that involves struggle and pain but also hope and joy shaped and maintained by a humanizing pedagogy.

Furthermore, Leistyna and Woodrum (1999, p. 2) state that critical pedagogy:

> challenges us to recognize, engage, and critique (so as to transform) any existing undemocratic social practices and institutional structures that produce and sustain inequalities and oppressive social identities and relations.

Freirean critical pedagogy encompasses several concepts. The concepts of conscientização and critical literacy/emancipatory literacy, for example, are especially important in our context.

Conscientização, commonly translated into English from the original Brazilian Portuguese as conscientization, is considered as one of the key concepts of Freirean critical pedagogy (for an overview of the concept, including its origin and history, see Cruz, 2013). Freire (1970a, p. 452) defines conscientização as:

> the process in which men [and women], not as recipients, but as knowing subjects, achieve a deepening awareness both of the sociocultural reality that shape their lives and of their capacity to transform that reality.

Freire (1972, p. 5) continues:

> Conscientization [conscientização] implies, then, that when I realize that I am oppressed, I also know I can liberate myself if I transform

> the concrete situation where I find myself oppressed. Obviously, I can't transform it in my head: that would be to fall into the philosophical error of thinking that awareness "creates" reality, I would be decreeing that I am free, by my mind. And yet, the structures would continue to be the same as ever—so that I wouldn't be free. No, conscientization [conscientização] implies a critical insertion into a process, it implies a historical commitment to make changes.

Cruz (2013, p. 173) emphasizes that Freire's concept of conscientização:

> is the active process through which a critical understanding of the social-political-economical circumstances is gained that enables one to actively change oppressive circumstances. To consider the concept of conscientização as a process merely to increase awareness is inaccurate; conscientização always will include the next step, to actively transform the circumstances that cause oppression.

Freire's concept of conscientização, thus, is a powerful vehicle for liberation; it implies developing a thorough understanding of the oppressive circumstances coupled with action to overcome them once these are recognized. Once again, it is not a process to merely increase awareness.

Moreover, as we continue to embrace critical pedagogy, the concept of *critical literacy/emancipatory literacy* is of paramount importance. Based on the work of Freire and Macedo (1987) and Giroux (1987), emancipatory literacy is not just a technical skill, the ability to read and write, but it is "a necessary foundation for cultural action for freedom, a central aspect of what it means to be a self and socially constituted agent" (Giroux, 1987, p. 7). Freire and Macedo (1987, p. 157) emphasize that emancipatory literacy:

> becomes a vehicle by which the oppressed are equipped with the necessary tools to reappropriate their history, culture, and language practices. It is, thus, a way to enable the oppressed to reclaim "those historical and existential experiences that are devalued in everyday life by the dominant culture in order to be both validated and critically understood." (see Giroux, 1983, p. 226)

Kincheloe (2008, p. 85) succinctly states that emancipatory literacy "involves revealing the ways dominant power operates in a manner that allows an individual and groups to act in resistance to its efforts to oppress them." Emancipatory literacy, therefore, includes practices that ultimately can enable individuals/groups of people to critically analyze and change their current circumstances.

5 Radical Deaf Studies

Radical Deaf Studies, crossing established disciplinary boundaries, encompasses the transdisciplinary fusion of Freirean critical pedagogy (emphasizing concepts of critical pedagogy such as conscientização and emancipatory literacy) and Deaf Studies (Cruz, 2019) (Figure 11.1).

Notions of critical pedagogy and publications by Paulo Freire (particularly his most cited book Pedagogy of the Oppressed) have been mentioned (see Fleischer, 2008; Ladd, 2003) within Deaf Studies but have not yet been applied systematically. In addition, Gertz (2016), based on tenets of critical race theory (CRT), introduced the concept of Deaf Crit. It is important, however, to mention here that critical race theory, initially conceptualized to highlight how racism within the legal field subordinates some racial and ethnic groups, was then applied as a theoretical lens outside the field of legal studies (e.g., Ladson-Billings & Tate, 1995—the application of CRT in the field of education). Furthermore, Deaf Crit is the adaptation of critical race theory themes to the Deaf world (Gertz, 2016) with audism as the central oppressive force. Gertz (2016, p. 160) posits that Deaf Crit can provide a framework to analyze the "audistic subordination and marginalization of Deaf people." Moreover, Ladd's (2003) emphasis on the hegemonic relationship between the Deaf world and the hearing world, the framing of Deaf people as being colonized, and calling for a decolonization of Deaf people correlates with critical pedagogy as espoused

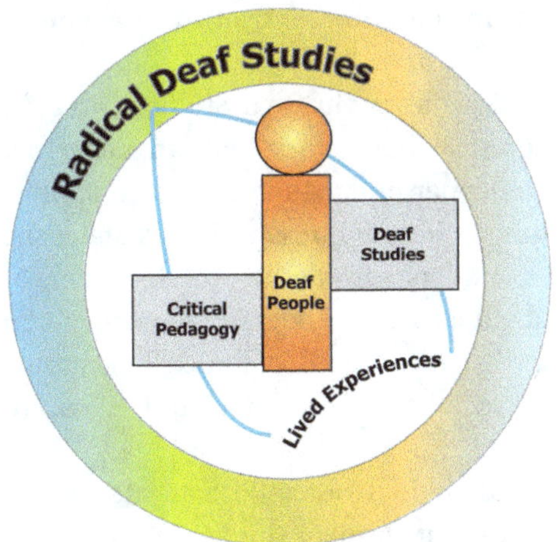

FIGURE 11.1
Radical Deaf Studies: Lived experiences of Deaf people examined through the fusion of critical pedagogy and Deaf Studies

by Paulo Freire; Freire, in turn, in his efforts to elucidate and disrupt any form of oppressor-oppressed relationship (Freire, 1994a), clearly was influenced by the work on de/colonization by Frantz Fanon (2004) and Albert Memmi (1991) and embraced the term 'decolonization of minds' coined by Aristides Pereira (Freire, 1977; see also 1985; Cruz & Dorsch, 2022).

Thus, the notion of working with critical pedagogy as a theoretical foundation of Deaf Studies—Radical Deaf Studies—can constitute a fruitful approach for analyzing and devising means for overcoming oppressive forces affecting the lives of Deaf people.

The use of the adjective 'radical' stems from the work of Paulo Freire. Paulo Freire, in the Preface to *Pedagogy of the Oppressed* (1994a, p. 21), addresses what it means to be a radical:

> The radical, committed to human liberation, does not become the prisoner of a "circle of certainty" within which reality is also imprisoned. On the contrary, the more radical the person is, the more fully he or she enters into reality so that, knowing it better, he or she can better transform it. This individual is not afraid to confront, to listen, to see the world unveiled. This person is not afraid to meet the people or to enter into dialogue with them. This person does not consider himself or herself the proprietor of history or of all people, or the liberator of the oppressed; but he or she does commit himself or herself, within history, to fight on their side.

For Freire, then, being radical means to understand reality and working to change this reality on the side of those affected by this reality. Radical entails a deep commitment to transformation as expressed by Freire (1994a, p. 19) "[r]adicalization involves increased commitment to the position one has chosen, and thus ever greater engagement in the effort to transform concrete, objective reality."

Once again, the application of critical pedagogy in Deaf Studies can offer an analytical and transformative theoretical framework and language that can guide the examination and lead to deeper understanding of the oppressive socio-cultural-political forces and how these oppressive forces affect the lives of Deaf people. It can also support understanding the evolving forms of intersectionality that impact Deaf individuals. This understanding then can develop agency to disrupt these oppressive forces, decolonize hegemonic meanings, and consequently result in social transformation and transcendence of all types of oppression.

The argument for a Radical Deaf Studies does not reflect an attempt to impose critical pedagogy on Deaf Studies, but through the fusion of critical pedagogy and Deaf Studies to develop together a better understanding of the complex, varied, and unique lived experiences of Deaf people as an oppressed group; consequently, this will expand our comprehension that our differences should not be the basis for oppression. Furthermore, it can inspire all of us to become cognizant that human diversity constitutes the strength, the resilience, and the richness of the fabric of humankind.

With respect to the significance and application of Radical Deaf Studies, conceived through the transdisciplinary fusion of Deaf Studies with critical pedagogy, Cruz (2019, p. 48) posits that (also linking to Paulo Freire's *Pedagogy of Freedom*, 1998a):

> Radical Deaf Studies can be a pathway for [...] Deaf [people] to find their 'voice' through their 'silence' in order to actively (re)construct their own history and to claim their own future. It can become the means of liberation not only for the oppressed but for the oppressor as well, which can result in a more inclusive and democratic society emphasizing human rights and social justice for all of society.

6 Radical Deaf Studies and Praxis

Praxis is another concept in critical pedagogy. It emphasizes action and reflection, and the important articulation of theory and practice. Radical Deaf Studies can provide a theoretical foundation to investigate socio-political and economical circumstances that lead to oppression, but there is also, in addition, a 'practical' aspect to Radical Deaf Studies. With respect to critical pedagogy and praxis, Freire and Macedo (1995, p. 382) posit:

> I am not suggesting an over-celebration of theory. We must not negate practice for the sake of theory. To do so would reduce theory to pure verbalism or intellectualism. By the same token, to negate theory for the sake of practice [...] is to run the risk of losing oneself in the disconnectedness of practice. It is for this reason that I never advocate either a theoretic elitism or a practice ungrounded in theory, but the unity between theory and practice.

Radical Deaf Studies and the concept of praxis can find an important role in the education of Deaf students. Teachers (be they hearing or deaf) of Deaf students need to be acquainted with Deaf culture and the background and lived experiences of the students: an understanding of students' lived experience and cultural identity is of paramount importance (Freire, 1998b) and will result in better teaching and learning. The suggestions of critical pedagogue Christopher Emdin (2017, 2022) with regard to the education of black and brown students (i.e., teachers need to understand and value the students' experience, the students' way of being in the world; teachers, in addition, need to understand that the struggles and obstacles faced by the students makes them unique) can also be applied within the context of education of Deaf students. Moreover, international students living in diaspora with diasporic identity (e.g., Wright, 2003, with respect to diasporic identity) is another important aspect to be considered in the education of Deaf students since international Deaf students can be also present in the classroom. Deaf students need to be valued for who they are and that also involves dialogue[8] between teachers and students (Freire, 1994a) and, if necessary, a constant re-inventing of the (prescribed and scripted) curriculum to make it culturally relevant. Such a dialogue and the resulting changes can support Deaf students to be more successful. It is important to curtail an educational system that often replicates oppression, a hegemonic system that tries to mold individuals to become who they are not, individuals who are often perceived as being inferior. Thus, Radical Deaf Studies is a call for action and transformation also within the practice of educating Deaf students.

As for music education for Deaf people: this is where this journey began—starting in Brazil, moving to the U.S., learning about Deaf culture and Deaf Studies, leading then to Radical Deaf Studies. The pedagogy anchoring music education for Deaf people must be developed from the principles of 'seeing music' externally and internally and utilizing musical instruments as the extension of the human body for means of expression. Therefore, sounds of musical instruments must be visualized as Deaf people learn the mechanics of musical instruments,[9] feel the sounds produced by such musical instruments, internalize those sounds, and create a mental image of these sounds (similar to mental images developed by a conductor of all the sounds of the musical instruments in an orchestra), and realize that by engaging with a musical instrument that this particular instrument becomes an extension of the human body. Such pedagogy (almost still inexistent) not only makes the experience with music by a Deaf person more real but also more meaningful and fun. Engaging with music is a challenging endeavor because the musician not only engages in the production of music but also in the (re)discovery what music is all about and its effects on the body and soul. In other words, music is a process of constant exploration of the self and the opportunity to always push the boundaries of ideas and creativity in the search for new ontologies, new epistemologies, and new concepts of axiology. Deaf people can lead the way in showing all of us (hearing and deaf) a new way to think of, experiment with, and understand the dynamics between sound and silence or redefining music by following John Cage's view of music as the "organization of sound" (2011), sounds that we all can then 'see' (as we adjust our sights to what is possible) and 'feel' in space and time in a more holistic way. Consequently, this could be one example of how conscientização can open eyes to the *possibility of the impossible*—Radical Deaf Studies for true transformation and liberation.

Notes

1 The poem was originally published in 1988 in *The Buff and the Blue*—the Gallaudet University student newspaper.
2 This quote is accessible online from various sources, e. g., https://www.compofactur.com/blog/zitate-zur-musik/lucien-price-1883-1964/
3 https://method-behind-the-music.com/mechanics/physics/
4 Definition from The New Oxford American Dictionary (2001).
5 An example of a performance of Cage's *4'33"* can be accessed at https://www.youtube.com/watch?v=JTEFKFiXSx4
6 Poem in Portuguese is accessible over the internet (e.g., http://www.algumapoesia.com.br/drummond/drummond19.htm).
7 Ladd (2005; p. 15) stated "One might ask therefore just what other powerful gains for humanity might be achieved through utilizing the skills of deaf communities."
8 Dialogue is another important concept of critical pedagogy (see Freire, 1994a).
9 This also includes percussion instruments which are many times preferred by Deaf people.

References

Bauman, H.-D. L. (2008a). Introduction: Listening to deaf studies. In H.-D. L. Bauman (Ed.), *Open your eyes: Deaf studies talking* (pp. 1–32). Minneapolis, MN: University of Minnesota Press.

Bauman, H.-D. L. (Ed.). (2008b). *Open your eyes: Deaf studies talking*. Minneapolis, MN: University of Minnesota Press.

Bauman, H-D. L., & Murray, J. J. (2009). Reframing: From hearing loss to Deaf Gain. *Deaf Studies Digital Journal, 1*(1–10).

Bauman, H-D. L., & Murray, J. J. (2010). Deaf Studies in the 21st century: "Deaf-gain" and the future of human diversity. In M. Marschark & P. E. Spencer (Eds.), *The Oxford handbook of Deaf Studies, language, and education,* (Vol. 2, pp. 210–225). New York, NY: Oxford University Press.

Bauman, H.-D. L., & Murray, J. J. (Eds.). (2014a). *Deaf Gain: Raising the stakes for human diversity*. Minneapolis, MN: University of Minnesota Press.

Bauman, H.-D. L., & Murray, J. J. (2014b). Deaf Gain: An introduction. In H.-D. L. Bauman & J. J. Murray (Eds.), *Deaf Gain: Raising the stakes for human diversity* (pp. XV–XLII). Minneapolis, MN: University of Minnesota Press.

Baynton, D. C. (2008). Beyond culture: Deaf studies and the deaf body. In H-D. L. Bauman (Ed.), *Open your eyes: Deaf studies talking* (pp. 293–313). Minneapolis, MN: University of Minnesota Press.

Best, K. E. (2015/2016). "We still have a dream": The Deaf hip hop movement and the struggle against the socio-cultural marginalization of deaf people. *Lied und populäre Kultur/Song and Popular Culture, 60/61*, 61–86.

Branson, J., & Miller, D. (2002). *Damned for their difference: The cultural construction of deaf people as disabled.* Washington, D.C.: Gallaudet University Press.

Cage, J. (2011). *Silence (50th anniversary edition)*. Middletown, CT: Wesleyan University Press. (Original work published 1961)

Cruz, A. L. (1997a). *An examination of how one deaf person constructs meaning in music: A phenomenological perspective* [Unpublished doctoral dissertation]. University of Tennessee: Knoxville, TN.

Cruz, A. L. (1997b). Music for the deaf: A qualitative approach. In L. D. Labbo & S. L. Field (Eds.), *QUIG 1997 Conference Proceedings.*

Cruz, A. L. (1997c). Critical thinking in music: Insights from teaching music to a deaf teenager. *Canadian Music Educator, 38*(2), 35–38.

Cruz, A. L. (2007). *Music for the* Deaf *and the importance of Freire's concept of conscientização* [Paper presentation]. Annual Meeting of the American Educational Research Association (AERA), Chicago, IL.

Cruz, A. L. (2010). Paulo and me: A personal narrative of encounters. In T. Wilson, P. Park, & A. Colón-Muñiz (Eds.), *Memories of Paulo* (pp. 157–160). Rotterdam: Sense Publishers.

Cruz, A. L. (2012). *Re-imagining the education of the deaf: Music, critical pedagogy and radical literacy* [Conference Abstracts]. 9th International Conference Crossroads in Cultural Studies, Paris, France.

Cruz, A. L. (2013). Paulo Freire's concept of conscientização. In R. Lake & T. Kress (Eds.), *Paulo Freire's intellectual roots: Toward historicity in praxis* (pp. 169–182). New York, NY: Bloomsbury.

Cruz, A. L. (2015). From practice to theory & from theory to praxis: A journey with Paulo Freire. In B. J. Porfilio & D. R. Ford (Eds.), *Leaders in critical pedagogy: Narratives for understanding and solidarity* (pp. 169–183). Rotterdam: Sense Publishers.

Cruz, A. L. (2017). A world in special need(s): Diversity and social justice. *Tijdschrft Voor Orthopedagogiek*, *56*(7/8), 358–365.

Cruz, A. L. (2019). New directions for Freirean critical pedagogy: A transdisciplinary reach for radical Deaf Studies. In J. Dabisch, D. Gipser, & H. Zillmer (Eds.), *Dialogisches Denken und Bildung als Praxis der Freiheit* (pp. 48–50). Oldenburg: Paulo Freire Verlag.

Cruz, A. L., & Dorsch, J. (2022). Freirean critical pedagogy and the decolonization of minds: Importance for community colleges in the U.S. higher education system. *Postcolonial Directions in Education, 11*(2), 248–273.

Darder, A., Baltodano, M., & Torres, R. D. (2003). Critical pedagogy: An introduction. In A. Darder, M. Baltodano & R. D. Torres (Eds.), *The critical pedagogy reader* (pp. 1–21). New York, NY: RoutledgeFalmer.

Darrow, A.-A. (1985). Music for the deaf. *Music Educators Journal, 71*(6), 33–35.

Davis, L. J. (2006). Constructing normalcy: The Bell curve, the novel, and the invention of the disabled body in the nineteenth century. In L. J. Davis (Ed.), *The disability studies reader* (2nd ed., pp. 3–16). New York, NY: Routledge.

Dunn, L. (2008). The burden of racism and audism. In H.-D.L. Bauman (Ed.), *Open your eyes: Deaf studies talking* (pp. 235–250). Minneapolis, MN: University of Minnesota Press.

Dunn, L. M., & Cooke, K. F. (2025). Black and Deaf in America: Exploring intersecting identity. In A. L. Cruz (Ed.), Culture, deafness & music: Critical pedagogy and a path to social justice (pp. 60–71). Leiden: Brill.

Edwards, E. M. (1975). Music and the hearing impaired. In R. M. Graham (Ed.), *Music for the exceptional child* (pp. 48–60). Reston, VA: Music Educators National Conference.

Emdin, C. (2017). *For white folks who teach in the hood... and the rest of y'all too: Reality pedagogy and urban education.* Boston, MA: Beacon Press.

Emdin, C. (2022). *Ratchetdemic: Reimaging academic success.* Boston, MA: Beacon Press.

Erting, C., Johnson, R., Smith, D., & Snider, B. (Eds.). (1994). *The deaf way: Perspectives from the international conference on deaf culture.* Washington, D.C.: Gallaudet University Press.

Fanon, F. (2004). *The wretched of the earth.* New York, NY: Grove Press. (Original work published in French 1961)

Fernandes, J. K., & Myers, S. S. (2009). Inclusive Deaf Studies: Barriers and pathways. *Journal of Deaf Studies and Deaf Education, 15*(1), 17–29.

Fleischer, L. (2008). Critical pedagogy and ASL videobooks. In H.-D. L. Bauman (Ed.), *Open your eyes: Deaf Studies talking* (pp. 158–166). Minneapolis, MN: University of Minnesota Press.

Freire, P. (1970a). Cultural action and conscientization. *Harvard Educational Review, 40*(3), 452–477.

Freire, P. (1972). Conscientizing as a way of liberating. In Anonymous (Ed.), *Paulo Freire* (pp. 3–10). The LADOC "Keyhole" Series, 1. Washington, D.C.: USCC Division for Latin America.

Freire, P. (1977). *Cartas à guiné-bissau: Registros de uma experiência em processo.* São Paulo: Paz e Terra.

Freire, P. (1985). *The politics of education: Culture, power and liberation.* Westport, CT: Bergin & Garvey.

Freire, P. (1992). *Educação como prática da liberdade*. São Paulo: Paz e Terra. (Original work published 1967)

Freire, P. (1994a). *Pedagogy of the oppressed*. New York, NY: Continuum. (Original work published 1970)

Freire, P. (1994b). *Pedagogy of hope: Reliving pedagogy of the oppressed*. New York, NY: Continuum. (Original work published in Portuguese 1992)

Freire, P. (1998a). *Pedagogy of freedom: Ethics, democracy, and civil courage*. Lanham, MD: Rowman & Littlefield. (Original work published in Portuguese 1996)

Freire, P. (1998b). *Teachers as cultural workers: Letters to those who dare teach*. Boulder, CO: Westview Press. (Original work published in Portuguese 1993)

Freire, P. (2010). *Educação e mudança*. São Paulo: Paz e Terra. (Original work published 1979)

Freire, P. (2011). *Education for critical consciousness*. New York, NY: Continuum. (Original work published 1974)

Freire, P., & Macedo, D. (1987). *Literacy: Reading the word and the world*. Westport, CT: Bergin & Garvey.

Freire, P., & Macedo, D. (1995). A dialogue: Culture, language, and race. *Harvard Educational Review, 65*(3), 377–402.

Friedner, M., & Kusters, A. (Eds.). (2015). *It's a small world: International deaf spaces and encounters*. Washington, D.C.: Gallaudet University Press.

Gertz, G. (2008). Dysconscious audism: A theoretical proposition. In H.–D. L. Bauman (Ed.), *Open your eyes: Deaf studies talking* (pp. 219–234). Minneapolis, MN: University of Minnesota Press.

Gertz, G. (2016). Deaf crit. In G. Gertz & P. Boudreault (Eds.), *The SAGE Deaf studies encyclopedia,* (Vol. 1, pp. 158–161). Thousand Oaks, CA: Sage.

Giroux, H. A. (1983). *Theory and resistance in education: A pedagogy for the opposition*. South Hadley, MA: Bergin & Garvey.

Giroux, H. A. (1987). Literacy and the pedagogy of political empowerment. In P. Freire & D. Macedo, *Literacy: Reading the word and the world* (pp. 1–25). Westport, CT: Bergin & Garvey.

hooks, b. (2013). *Writing beyond race: Living theory and practice*. New York, NY: Routledge.

Humphries, T. (1975). Audism: The making of a word. Unpublished paper.

Jones, J. D. (2016). Imagined hearing: Music making in Deaf culture. In B. Howe, S. Jensen-Moulton, N. Lerner & J. N. Straus (Eds.), *Oxford handbook of music and disability studies* (pp. 54–72). New York, NY: Oxford University Press.

Kapla, P. S. (1975). Music and the hearing handicapped child. In R. M. Graham (Ed.), *Music for the exceptional child* (pp. 48–60). Reston, VA: Music Educators National Conference.

Karns, Ch. M., Dow, M. W., & Neville, H. J. (2012). Altered cross-modal processing in the primary auditory cortex of congenitally deaf adults: A visual-somatosensory fMRI study with a double-flash illusion. *The Journal of Neuroscience, 32*(28), 9626–9638.

Kincheloe, J. L. (2008). *Critical pedagogy primer* (2nd ed.). New York, NY: Peter Lang.

Kusters, A., & De Meulder, M. (2013). Understanding Deafhood: In search of its meanings. *American Annals of the Deaf, 157*(5), 428–438.

Kusters, A., De Meulder, M., & O'Brien, D. (2017a). Innovations in Deaf studies: Critically mapping the field. In A. Kusters, M. De Meulder & D. O'Brien (Eds.), *Innovations in Deaf studies: The role of deaf scholars* (pp. 1–53). New York, NY: Oxford University Press.

Kusters, A., De Meulder, M., & O'Brien, D. (Eds.). (2017b). *Innovations in Deaf studies: The role of deaf scholars*. New York, NY: Oxford University Press.

Kusters, A., & Friedner, M. (2015). Introduction: DEAF-SAME and difference in international deaf spaces and encounters. In M. Friedner & A. Kusters (Eds.), *It's a small world: International deaf spaces and encounters* (pp. IX–XXIX). Washington, D.C.: Gallaudet University Press.

Ladd, P. (1992). Deaf cultural studies. In M. Garretson (Ed.), *Viewpoints on deafness* (pp. 83–88). Silver Spring, MD: National Association of the Deaf Press.

Ladd, P. (2003). *Understanding Deaf culture: In search of Deafhood.* Clevedon, UK: Multilingual Matters.

Ladd, P. (2005). Deafhood: A concept stressing possibilities, not deficits. *Scandinavian Journal of Public Health, 33*(Suppl. 66), 12–17.

Ladd, P. (2008). Colonialism and resistance: A brief history of Deafhood. In H-D. L. Bauman (Ed.), *Open your eyes: Deaf studies talking* (pp. 42–59). Minneapolis, MN: University of Minnesota Press.

Ladd, P. (2015). Global Deafhood: Exploring myths and realities. In M. Friedner & A. Kusters (Eds.), *It's a small world: International deaf spaces and encounters* (pp. 274–285). Washington, D.C.: Gallaudet University Press.

Ladson-Billings, G. & Tate, W. F. (1995). Toward a critical race theory of education. *Teachers College Record, 97*(1), 47–68.

Lane, H. (1992). *The mask of benevolence: Disabling the deaf community*. New York, NY: Knopf.

Lane, H., Hoffmeister, R., & Bahan, B. (1996): *A journey into the deaf-world.* San Diego, CA: DawnSign Press.

Leistyna, P., & Woodrum, A. (1999). Context and culture: What is critical pedagogy? In P. Leistyna, A. Woodrum & S. A. Sherblom (Eds.), *Breaking free: The transformative power of critical pedagogy* (pp. 1–7). Cambridge, MA: Harvard Educational Review No. 27.

Loeffler, S. (2014). Deaf music: Embodying language and rhythm. In H-D. L. Bauman & J. J. Murray (Eds.), *Deaf gain: Raising the stakes for human diversity* (pp. 436–456). Minnesota, MN: University of Minnesota Press.

Macedo, D. (2007). Afterword: Reinserting criticity into critical pedagogy. In P. McLaren & J. L. Kincheloe (Eds.), *Critical pedagogy: Where are we now?* (pp. 391–395). New York, NY: Peter Lang.

Madsen, W. J. (2007). The Gallaudet message from the DPN. In W. J. Madsen (Ed.), *Moods of silence: Reflections in prose through a deaf poet's eyes* (p. 82). Bloomington, IN: Xlibris Corporation.

McLaren, P. (2015). *Life in schools: An introduction to critical pedagogy in the foundations of education* (6th ed.). Boulder, CO: Paradigm Publishers. (Original work published 1989)

Memmi, A. (1991). *The colonizer and the colonized.* Boston, MA: Beacon Press. (Original work published in French 1957)

Myers, S. S., & Fernandes, J. K. (2009). Deaf studies: A critique of the predominant U.S. theoretical direction. *Journal of Deaf Studies and Deaf Education, 15*(1), 30–49.

Murray, J. J. (2017). Academic and community interactions in the formation of deaf studies in the United States. In A. Kusters, M. De Meulder, & D. O'Brien (Eds.), *Innovations in Deaf studies: The role of deaf scholars* (pp. 77–100). New York, NY: Oxford University Press.

Padden, C. (1980). The deaf community and the culture of deaf people. In C. Baker & R. Battison (Eds.), *Sign language and the deaf community* (pp. 98–104). Silver Spring, MD: National Association of the Deaf.

Padden, C., & Humphries, T. (1988). *Deaf in America.* Cambridge, MA: Harvard University Press.

Robbins, C., & Robbins, C. (1980). *Music for the hearing impaired: A resource manual and curriculum guide.* St. Louis, MO: Magnamusic-Baton.

Shor, I., & Freire, P. (1987). *A pedagogy for liberation: Dialogues on transforming education.* Westport, CT: Bergin & Garvey.

Stokoe, W. C., Casterline, D. C., & Croneberg, C. (1965). *A dictionary of American Sign Language on linguistic principles.* Washington, D.C.: Gallaudet College Press.

Straus, J. N. (2011). *Extraordinary measures: Disability in music.* Oxford, UK: Oxford University Press.

Turner, G. H. (1994). How is deaf culture? Another perspective on a fundamental concept. *Sign Language Studies, 83*(1), 103–126.

Van Cleve, J. V., & Crouch, R. (1992). *A place of their own: Creating the deaf community in America.* Washington, D.C.: Gallaudet University Press.

Vuoriheimo, M. (2025). Make the sign, make the mark, play the music: Teach the world. In A. L. Cruz (Ed.), *Culture, deafness & music: Critical pedagogy and a path to social justice* (Cruz, A. L. interviewer, pp. 213–228). Leiden: Brill.

Wilcox, S. (Ed.) (1989). *American deaf culture: An anthology.* Silver Spring, MD: Linstock Press.

Wright, H. K. (2003). Editorial: Whose diaspora is this anyway? Continental Africans trying on and troubling diasporic identity. *Critical Arts, 17*(1–2), 1–16.

PART 4

Understanding the Auditory System and Portraying the Diversity of Deaf Voices through Research

∴

To live our lives based on the principles of a love ethic (showing care, respect, knowledge, integrity, and the will to cooperate), we have to be courageous.

BELL HOOKS (2001, *All About Love*, p. 101)

CHAPTER 12

Understanding the Auditory Pathway and Hearing Loss

Wafaa Kaf

Abstract

This chapter begins by providing readers with a general overview of the anatomy and physiology of the ear and auditory pathway. Through the brief overview, it provides basic knowledge and understanding needed to understand the underlying mechanisms of hearing loss. This chapter also provides common pathologic causes of hearing loss and auditory processing disorders, along with an overview of the different types of hearing loss. In addition, this chapter introduces readers to common audiological procedures used to test for and identify hearing loss, along with candidacy and treatment options for people with hearing loss.

Keywords

hearing loss – ear – auditory system – audiology – Cochlear implants – amplification

1 Introduction

To understand the auditory pathway and how hearing loss occurs, it is important to learn about the anatomy and physiology of the entire auditory system. There are different parts of the auditory system that all work together to perform the amazing function of hearing. The anatomy of the ear is divided into three sections including the outer ear, the middle ear, and the inner ear. Beyond the inner ear lie the auditory nerve and the central auditory system which carries information to the auditory cortex in the temporal lobe of the brain.

1.1 *Outer Ear*

The outer ear is the most visible part of the auditory system. It consists of the pinna and the external auditory canal (EAC) (Figure 12.1). This mechanism is used for collecting acoustic sounds and transferring that sound to the middle

 | DOI:10.1163/9789004692299_013

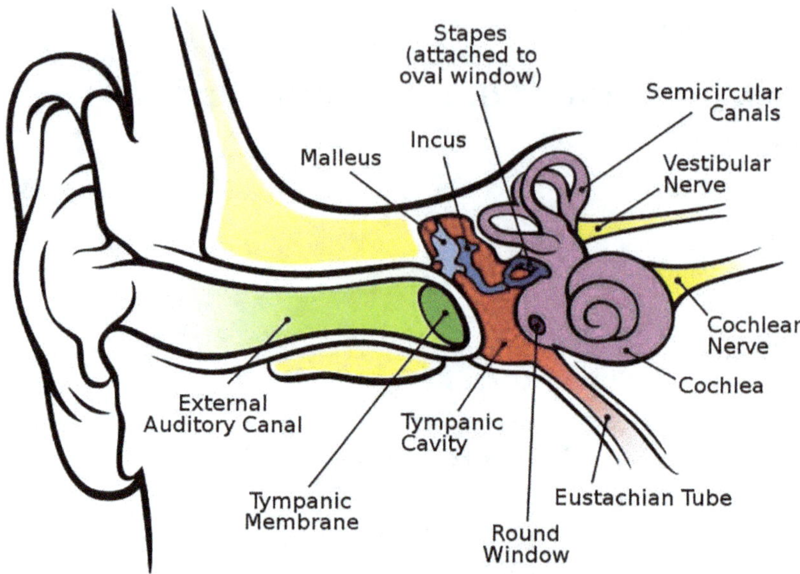

FIGURE 12.1 The auditory system. A sagittal section of the ear showing outer ear, ear canal, middle ear, inner ear, and auditory nerve (from Hain, 2021, reprinted with permission)

ear. The pinna of the outer ear has many curves, ridges, and grooves, which serve the purpose of collecting and resonating sound. This ultimately helps in localization of sounds, or helping the brain decide where sound is coming from. The pinna is made up of skin and cartilaginous tissue, which continues into the outer one-third of the EAC. The cartilaginous portion of the EAC contains hair follicles and sebaceous (oil) and ceruminous (wax) glands, which produce cerumen, more commonly known as ear wax. Cerumen as well as oils within the EAC serves as protective lubricant of the ear to keep the EAC clean. The inner two-third of the EAC is made up of a thin lining of skin which covers the bony wall of the EAC. This bony portion of the canal contains no ceruminous or sebaceous glands. The EAC has an average length of 2.5 cm with a small S-shaped curve about halfway into the canal. The EAC leads to the tympanic membrane, which marks the boundary between the outer and middle ear.

1.2 *Middle Ear*

The middle ear consists of the tympanic cavity, an air-filled space that houses the ossicular chain, middle ear muscles, and ligaments. The middle ear is located between the tympanic membrane and the inner ear. The most lateral portion of the middle ear is the tympanic membrane (TM), more commonly known as the ear drum. The TM is about 9-mm in diameter and 0.1 mm thick.

Its physical appearance is generally described as a pearly gray, cone-shaped, semi-transparent structure. The TM consists of two portions: pars tensa (larger part) and pars flaccida (smaller, superior part), and it is composed of three layers including a lateral epithelial layer, a middle fibrous layer, and a medial mucosal layer. The TM serves as the entryway into the middle ear.

Moving past the tympanic membrane is the tympanic cavity, which houses the ossicular chain that consists of three ossicles. As shown in Figure 12.2 the first ossicle, the malleus, attaches to the medial side of the tympanic membrane by the handle of the malleus. The malleus also attaches to the incus, the second ossicle, within the malleoincudal joint. The lenticular process of the incus connects with the head of the stapes, the third ossicle, within the incudostapedial joint. The footplate of the stapes rests on the oval window, a connective tissue membrane that marks the boundary between the middle and inner ear. Thus, the three ossicles form a chain that connects with the lateral wall of the middle ear at the TM and with the medial wall of the middle ear at the oval window, thus allowing sound transmission to the inner ear. Inferior to the oval window is the round window, which also separates the middle and inner ear. Both oval and round windows vibrate in opposite phase to each other, allowing fluid in the cochlea to circulate to stimulate the hair cells of the cochlea.

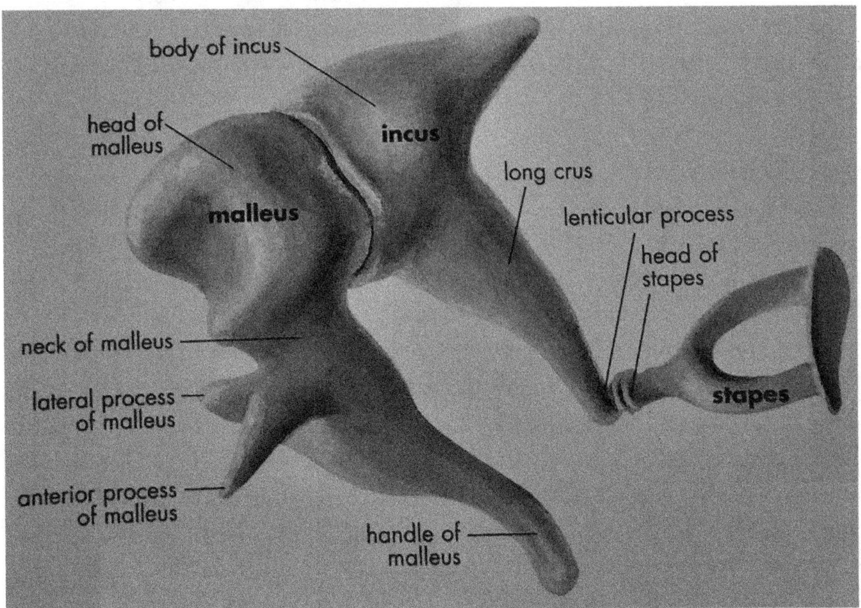

FIGURE 12.2 Middle ear ossicles and muscles. The three ossicles are malleus, incus, and stapes. The two muscles of the middle ear are tensor tympani and stapedius muscles (adapted from Hofymeyr, 2019)

Also within the tympanic cavity are two small muscles, called the tensor tympani and the stapedius muscles. These muscles are attached to two bony structures: a fixed bone (origin) and a movable bone (insertion = site of action). For example, the tensor tympani muscle originates from the bony canal of the Eustachian tube and is inserted into the handle of the malleus, whereas the stapedius muscle originates from the posterior bony wall of the middle ear and is inserted into the neck of the stapes. Both muscles reflexively contract when loud sounds are presented to the ear, resulting in stiffening of middle ear space and reducing ossicular vibration, which ultimately dampen sounds entering the inner ear. These muscles thus help protecting the inner ear from the damaging effect of loud sounds. In addition, the tympanic cavity communicates anteroinferiorly with the nasopharyngeal opening of the Eustachian tube and posteriorly with the mastoid antrum and air cells. The Eustachian tube connects the middle ear to the nasopharynx, allowing the air-filled space of the middle ear to remain ventilated in order for air pressure to be equalized.

Because of its function, the middle ear is often called the energy transducer. As acoustic sound first enters the ear and travels through the pinna and the EAC, it is considered acoustical energy. The middle ear transduces this acoustic energy into mechanical energy. As sound enters the EAC, acoustic energy comes into contact with the TM, causing it to vibrate. This causes a lever action within the ossicular chain. The movement of the ossicles forces the foot plate of the stapes, situated within the oval window, to displace the fluid within the inner ear.

1.3 *The Inner Ear*

The inner ear consists of the cochlea and the vestibular system, which are responsible for hearing and balance, respectively. Within the cochlea lies the sensory organ for hearing, the organ of Corti. The cochlea is a fluid-filled, snail-shaped structure that winds around a bony core in two and a half turns and is approximately 10 mm in diameter at its base (Elliot & Shera, 2012). The cochlea is divided into the bony and membranous labyrinths. The bony portion of the cochlea consists of the petrous portion of the temporal bone, the modiolus, and the osseous spiral lamina. The membranous labyrinth is a fluid-filled sac that follows the shape of the bony labyrinth of the cochlea. Within the membranous labyrinth of the cochlea are two membranes called the basilar membrane and Reissner's membrane. These membranes divide the cochlea into three sections: the scala vestibuli, scala media (cochlear duct), and scala tympani. Both the scala vestibuli and the scala tympani are filled with a calcium rich fluid called perilymph, which has the same chemical composition as cerebrospinal fluid, and are linked by a small opening at the apex of the cochlea called the helicotrema. On the other hand, the medial section, the scala media, is filled with a potassium rich fluid called endolymph, which is produced by the stria vascularis. The scala media houses the organ of Corti (Figure 12.3) that rests on the basilar membrane, and it consists of supporting cells, nerve fibers and thousands of hair cells: 3 rows of 12,000 outer hair cells and 1 row of 3,500 inner hair cells.

Although the outer and inner hair cells are very different in their structures and functions, the outer hair cells communicate the information through cross-links to the inner hair cells, which deliver it to the auditory nerve, VIII cranial nerve. The top part of the outer hair cells, stereocilia, is embedded in the tectorial membrane, whereas the bases of the hair cells rest on the basilar membrane. The stereocillia are more numerous at the basal end of the cochlea and are relatively stiff. The basilar membrane is tonotopically organized, meaning high frequency sounds are represented and stimulate hair cells at the base of the cochlea, whereas low frequency sounds must travel farther to the apex of the cochlea in order to stimulate the hair cells. These hair cells play a key role as they are the sensory cells for hearing. The outer hair cells through

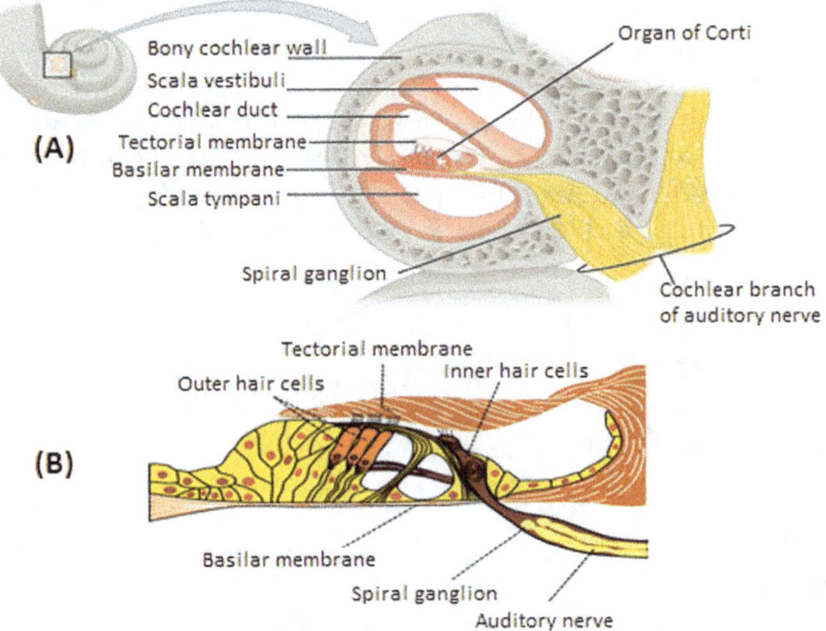

FIGURE 12.3 The cochlea and organ of corti. (A) Cross-section of the cochlea through the organ of corti (Top) showing the three spaces within the cochlea (scala tympani, media that houses organ of corti, and scala vestibuli) (adapted from OpenStax College, Rice University, n.d.). (B) Cross section of the organ of corti (bottom) showing position of the hair cells on the basilar membrane (reprinted from Wikipedia, n.d.)

their electromotility function serve two main purposes. First, they act as a cochlear amplifier that helps us hear soft sounds. Second, they help with the transduction mechanism through their elongation and shortening in length, pulling the tectorial membrane down, resulting in sharpening the traveling wave (frequency resolution) of the basilar membrane, and causing an influx of potassium ions. These mechanical and ionic changes are communicated through the cross-links to the inner hair cells, which send this information via spiral ganglion to the auditory nerve, which generates neural impulses that propagate up the auditory pathway to the auditory cortex.

The vestibular system is also located within the inner ear and is formed by the membranous labyrinth of the inner ear (Figure 12.4). This system is composed of the semi-circular canals and otoliths. The three semicircular canals—posterior, horizontal (lateral), and anterior, which are located at right angle to each other—are filled with perilymph and are the sensory receptors of angular movements involving the head. Within the vestibule lie the two otoliths, the saccule and utricle, which are also located at right angle to each other to help detect vertical and horizontal linear acceleration involving the head. Also, the vestibular system via the vestibulo-ocular reflex

1.4 *The Central Auditory Pathway*

Beyond the inner ear lies an extensive auditory pathway where the neural signal must travel and synapses with other fibers in order to reach the primary auditory cortex in the temporal lobe for sound processing. After the signal leaves the hair cells of the cochlea, it then travels through the auditory nerve fibers to synapse with the cochlear nuclei, located in the medulla of the brainstem.

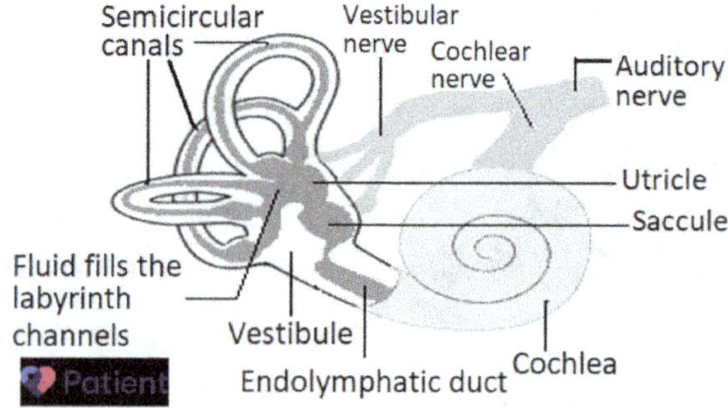

FIGURE 12.4 The inner ear. It houses both the cochlea and the vestibular system. The cochlea is the snail shape structure, whereas the vestibular system includes three semicircular canals, vestibule, saccule, and utricle (reprinted from Knott, 2020) helps control eye movements to stabilize images during head movements from side to side

Next, the afferent auditory pathway splits into two divisions, an ipsilateral pathway which remains on the same side of the brainstem and a contralateral pathway which crosses the midline to travel through the opposite side of the brainstem. Both pathways lead to the superior olivary complex (SOC) that is located in the pons of the brainstem. The SOC is responsible for binaural processing of sounds from both ears (stereo hearing) then transferring the auditory signal to the lateral lemniscus, which is also located in the pons. The next stop for the auditory signal along the pathway is the inferior colliculus within the midbrain. The pathway then extends to the medial geniculate bodies in the thalamus. Finally, the pathway ends at the primary auditory cortex at the superior temporal gyrus of the temporal lobe of the brain. Because certain neurons receive inputs from both ears (ipsilateral and contralateral afferent pathways), binaural processing of sounds is possible at several crossing points starting at the SOC, then at the inferior colliculus, then at the auditory cortex. Because the afferent fibers are complex and distributed bilaterally, unilateral damage at any level of the afferent pathway does not usually result in hearing loss in either ear; instead, auditory processing disorders may result depending on the site and extent of the damage.

1.5 *Physiology of Hearing—How Do We Hear?*

Normal anatomy of the auditory system from the outer ear to the auditory cortex is required for proper physiologic hearing and processing of sounds. The outer ear helps funneling the sound, acoustic energy, to the ear canal. The pinna and the ear canal amplify mid-high frequency (2,500–5,000 Hz) sounds by about 27 dB and help with spatial perception (Shaw & Teranishi, 1968). Also, the middle ear acts as an impedance mismatch transformer that transfers the acoustic energy to mechanical energy by three different mechanisms: the vibration of the tympanic membrane, the area ratio (large tympanic membrane area to the small stapes footplate area), and the lever ratio of the ossicular chain (the long length of the manubrium of the malleus to the short length of the long process of the incus). This impedance mismatch transformer function of the middle ear allows a transfer of energy from a low-impedance air medium in the ear canal to a high-impedance fluid medium in the cochlea of the inner ear (Kurokawa & Goode, 1995). As a result, the middle ear provides an additional amplification of 20–27 dB mainly to low and mid frequencies (250–1000 Hz), which allows 99.9% of the acoustic energy in ear canal to enter the inner ear (Schuknecht, 1993). For example, in the absence of the middle ear, only 0.1% of the acoustic energy in the ear canal would enter the inner ear (Schuknecht, 1993), resulting in a conductive hearing loss. The Eustachian tube is an important structure for the proper function of the middle ear. It adjusts the middle ear pressure to be equal to that of the ear canal pressure.

The resultant mechanical vibrations from the middle ear and the rocking movement of the stapes footplate cause the oval window to move back and forth causing a waving motion in the perilymph of the scala vestibuli and tympani. The perilymph motion is then transferred to the endolymph in the scala media, causing the stereocilia of the outer hair cells to bend resulting in depolarization of the hair cells and releasing of chemical neurotransmitter. As a result, the wave motion is transformed into electrical impulses that are picked up by the inner hair cells and sent to the auditory nerve. Then, neural impulses and sound cues are extracted, processed, and recognized while traveling through the central auditory pathways, to reach their final destination at the Heschyl's gyrus at the primary auditory cortex within the temporal lobe. If any disease affects any of these structures, an individual will suffer from some degree of hearing loss. Damage to the outer, middle and inner ear usually results in some degree of hearing loss. In contrast, changes in the effectiveness of the central auditory pathways often result in processing issues such as inability to understand speech despite normal hearing, inappropriate responses, difficulty hearing in the presence of background noise, and inattention.

2 Hearing Loss and Deafness

Normal hearing is considered a bilateral hearing threshold of 25 dB hearing level (HL) or better (World Health Organization [WHO], 2015). According to the WHO (2015), a hearing loss is constituted as not being able to hear well. The term, 'hearing loss,' is used as a general term. It can be seen as an umbrella that encompasses many types, degrees, and configurations of hearing losses. The term 'deafness' is often used to depict hearing loss. However, the term, 'deaf,' usually refers to those with a significant degree of hearing loss, such as a profound hearing loss, which results in very little hearing ability to no hearing at all (WHO, 2015).

3 Causes of Hearing Loss

Table 12.1 shows a variety of causes of hearing loss that can occur throughout the auditory system. A lesion, malformation, or disruption at any structure of the auditory system, outer, middle, and inner ear as well as central auditory pathway may very well cause a hearing loss and/or a processing disorder.

TABLE 12.1 Causes of hearing loss and their location

Outer ear	Middle ear	Inner ear	Central
Malformation	Malformation	Malformation	Malformation
Atresia	Otosclerosis	Noise exposure	Auditory neuroma
Impacted ear wax	Otitis media	Meniéré's disease	Auditory neuropathy
Obstructed ear canal	Cholesteatoma	Presbycusis	
Anotia	Ossicular disarticulation	Virus/Infection	
	Ear drum perforation	Ototoxic drugs	

3.1 *Outer Ear Pathologies*

The majority of outer ear pathologies result in a structural change which can cause hearing loss. Many of these malformations of structures occur during embryonic development (MacKenzie, 2011). The lateral-most site where we see malformation that causes hearing loss is at the external auditory canal. Atresia and stenosis are both congenital anomalies resulting in narrowing (stenosis) or complete closure (atresia) of the EAC. Stenosis and atresia can, along different portions of the EAC, affect sound differently depending on the site. In cases of atresia, obstructions of the canal make it difficult for sound to travel via air conduction through the EAC through the rest of the auditory system. The total amount of hearing loss in these cases will depend on the severity of the obstruction (Stach & Ramachandran, 2008).

Obstructions of the EAC are not always due to structural malformations. Excessive, impacted cerumen, foreign bodies, ear canal infections, and tumors can also cause blockage and attenuate the sound traveling through the ear. These obstructions are usually seen during an otoscopic examination. The amount of hearing loss, if any, will depend on the amount/size of the blockage present. Over-production of cerumen is a common obstruction of the EAC. In some cases, large amounts of cerumen can be pushed back and become impacted in the osseous portion of the EAC. Once impacted in the osseous portion of the canal, cerumen will harden and can become difficult to remove. A common cause of this impaction is the use of cotton swabs for cleaning the ear or it may be a sign of cholesteatoma, a serious middle ear pathology.

3.2 *Middle Ear Pathologies*

Pathologies of the middle ear can affect the tympanic membrane, the ossicular chain, and any space within the middle ear cavity. The lateral-most portion of the middle ear, the tympanic membrane (TM), is susceptible to perforation, tympanosclerosis, and atrophy. TM perforation (hole in the TM) can be caused by a variety of factors including trauma, excessive pressure or fluid in the middle ear due to otitis media with effusion, or sudden change in pressure (MacKenzie, 2011). Figure 12.5 shows a TM perforation. When the TM is perforated, there is no longer an air tight seal separating the outer ear to the middle ear. This disrupts the efficiency of the TM to transfer acoustic energy into mechanical energy, which may result in conductive hearing loss. This loss will often increase as the perforation increases in size (Mehta, Rosowski, Voss, O'Neil, & Merchant, 2006). While some perforations require surgical repair, many TM perforations are able to heal naturally specifically if the middle ear mucosal lining and the ossicular chain are intact. This spontaneous healing process can cause atrophic or thinning of the TM due to the loss of the fibrous, middle layer of the TM. Atrophic TM does not necessarily result in a hearing loss but can result in high static admittance during tympanometry testing to assess middle ear status. Tympanosclerosis is a condition in which the TM develops scarring and calcium plaques, causing the TM to thicken. This can add mass to the TM which can interfere with its function, but not always cause a hearing loss (Martin & Clark, 2014).

The common middle ear pathology, otitis media, is commonly known as the middle-ear infection, which is known for its widespread effects on children. This infection of the middle ear involves inflammation of the mucous membrane surrounding the middle ear (MacKenzie, 2011), mostly due to Eustachian tube dysfunction from upper respiratory infection (MacKenzie, 2011). Without proper ventilation of the middle ear, negative pressure build up begins in the middle ear, which can then lead to acute otitis media. As the disease progresses, fluid can start to accumulate in the middle ear cavity, the so-called otitis media with effusion. As the fluid accumulates, the middle ear becomes stiff and rigid, disrupting the transfer of sound, and causing a conductive hearing loss. The severity of the loss is related to the amount of remaining air within the middle ear (Ravicz, Rosowski, & Merchant, 2004). If the infection does not subside within 48 to 72 hours after close monitoring of the acute manifestation, antibiotic treatment is required (Lieberthal, Carroll, Chonmaitree, Ganiats, Hoberman, Jackson, et al., 2013). If antibiotic treatment is not enough, surgical treatment such as myringotomy and pressure equalization (PE) tubes is considered. Myringotomy consists of making a surgical incision within the tympanic membrane then placing a tube opened from both ends to allow the fluid to drain from the middle ear and to equalize pressure within the middle ear.

Cholesteatoma is another pathology affecting the middle ear. A cholesteatoma is a benign tumor in the middle ear caused by the abnormal growth of skin cells. This growth will disrupt the transfer of sound depending on the size and location of the tumor (Moller, 2006). These growths have the potential to grow and possibly erode the ossicular chain and other middle ear structures, causing permanent damage to the middle ear, mastoid, inner ear, and even causing intracranial complication. Therefore, surgical removal of cholesteatoma is imperative.

Otosclerosis, often an inherited autosomal dominant disorder mainly in women, is a slowly progressive pathology that affect the otic capsule and/or the stapes of the middle ear. It is due to accumulation of new bone growth, which causes the footplate of the stapes to become fixated in the oval window. This stiffening of the stapes results in attenuation of the transfer of sounds from the middle ear to the inner ear, causing a tinnitus, vertigo, and conductive hearing loss or sensorineural hearing loss if the otic capsule is involved (cochlear otosclerosis).

On the contrary, ossicular disarticulation has the opposite effect on the ossicular chain. This results in the separation or disruption of the ossicular chain, which then causes attenuation of sound resulting in a conductive hearing loss. Both otosclerosis and ossicular dislocation require surgical treatment if indicated to reconstruct the fixed stapes in case of otosclerosis and to repair the disrupted ossicular joint in the case of ossicular dislocation. Figure 12.5 shows several otoscopic tympanic membrane middle ear structures and pathologies.

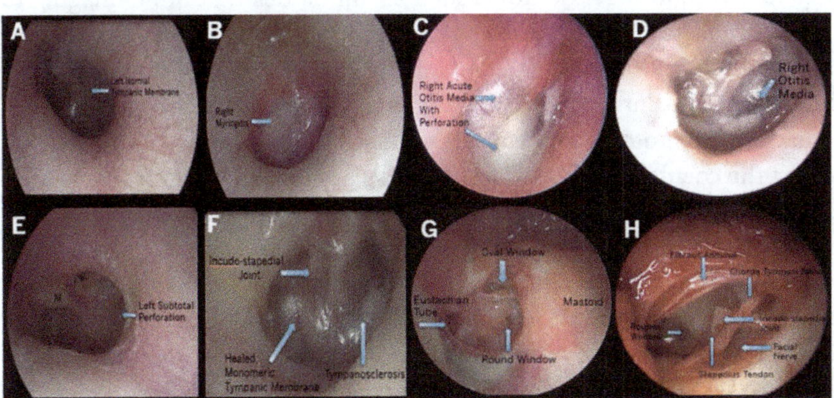

FIGURE 12.5 Otoscopic images of normal and abnormal middle ear. (A) Normal looking left tympanic membrane (TM), (B) Right myringitis (inflammation of TM). (C) Right acute otitis media with a ruptured TM and purulent drainage. (D) Right otitis media with effusion with an intact TM. (E) Left large, subtotal TM perforation revealing two of the middle ear ossicles (malleus "M" and Incus "I"). (F) Healed TM perforation with a very thin scar, hypermobile TM (monomeric TM) and another area with a thick white scar (tympanosclerosis). (G) Left infected radical mastoid cavity exposing the middle ear space and few structures (e.g., Eustachian tube opening in the middle ear cavity, oval and round windows). (H) A surgical view of the left middle ear exposing the middle ear space and few structures (e.g., fibrous annulus, chorda tympani nerve, facial nerves, incudo-stapedial joint, stapedius tendon, and round window) (adapted from Gadre, 2021)

3.3 *Inner Ear Pathologies*

Inner ear pathologies are those affecting structures within the cochlea and causing sensorineural (cochlear) hearing loss. There are a variety of inner ear pathologies including genetic syndromic and non-syndromic causes, and non-genetic causes such as prenatal, natal and postnatal causes, ototoxic medications, noise exposure, Meniéré's disease, and presbycusis. Congenital, genetic syndromic hearing loss are due to disorders such as Alport syndrome, Treacher Collins syndrome, Down syndrome, and Usher syndrome, which cause malformation within the cochlea (American Speech-Language-Hearing Association, 2015). Other non-genetic, congenital disorders can be acquired through illness during pregnancy (prenatal causes). Common viruses contracted during pregnancy that can result in congenital hearing loss include rubella, cytomegalovirus, herpes, syphilis, and the human immunodeficiency virus (HIV). Trauma during pregnancy or during the birthing process can also cause damage to the cochlea resulting in a hearing loss. Oxygen deprivation and premature birth are also high-risk factors to congenital hearing loss. A common postnatal disease that is known for causing sensorineural hearing loss is meningitis, which can lead to destruction of the hair cells within the cochlea causing a permanent, severe to profound hearing loss.

There are certain ototoxic drugs such as antibiotics that are damaging to the cochlea and result in sensorineural hearing loss and balance problems. Aminoglycoside antibiotics include kanamycin, gentamycin, amikacin, and streptomycin. Also, large doses of aspirin and some chemotherapeutic drugs are known to be ototoxic and cause sensorineural hearing loss. These drugs can affect the cochlea differently and can result in differing degrees of hearing loss. It is recommended that those taking ototoxic drugs be monitored closely before, during, and following the administration of these ototoxic drugs for any early or late development of sensorineural hearing loss, tinnitus, and/or vertigo.

Noise exposure is one of the most common causes of sensorineural hearing loss due to damage of the outer hair cells of the cochlea. Listening to high levels of noise for a period of time has the potential to damage these hair cells. Depending on the intensity and length of the sound exposure, noise exposure can result in either a temporary hearing threshold shift or a permanent threshold shift. A temporary threshold shift is a hearing loss from noise exposure that eventually recovers not long after exposure. A permanent threshold shift however, is a hearing loss that does not recover and is permanent. Many environments and objects we are exposed to every day can contribute to dangerous noise exposure without hearing protection. Figure 12.6 shows some of these environments and objects that contribute to noise exposure and their

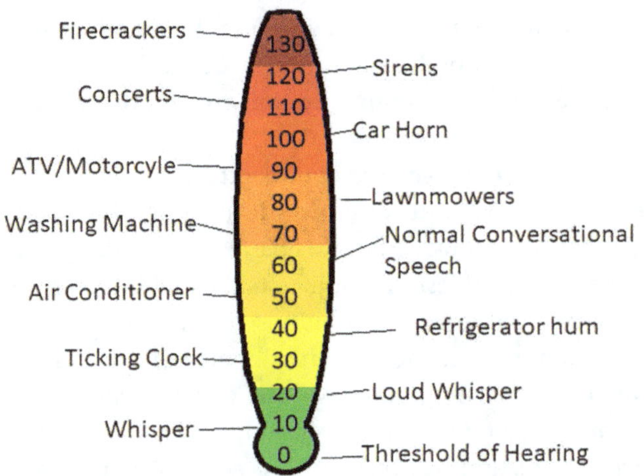

FIGURE 12.6 Noise levels. The above figure depicts a range of hearing levels accompanied with typical examples of everyday noise

approximate intensity. Many professions require people to work in loud environments that are potentially dangerous to a person's hearing. In the Unites States, the Occupational Safety and Health Administration (OSHA) has set legal standards for working conditions and noise exposure. OSHA (1983) states that daily exposure to noise in the workplace is limited to 90 dBA (A-weighted decibels; an expression of the relative loudness of sounds in air as perceived by the ear) for an 8-hour period. However, sudden exposure to loud sounds such as gunshots or explosions can cause instantaneous, permanent sensorineural hearing loss.

Meniéré's disease is another inner ear pathology that not only affects one's hearing, but the vestibular mechanism as well. This disorder is the result of over-production of endolymph within the inner ear. The episodic symptoms of Meniéré's disease include fluctuating sensorineural hearing loss, vertigo, fullness of the ear, and tinnitus (ringing of the ear) (VanDerHeyden & Handelsman, 2015). The oncoming of these symptoms can be abrupt and unexpected, making this disorder very debilitating. These episodes of symptoms fluctuate and can last for hours at a time.

Presbycusis or hearing loss due to aging is one of the most commonly known causes of sensorineural hearing loss that affects the inner ear structure. As we age, the auditory mechanism ages with us. The function of the outer hair cells in the inner ear along with our middle ear structures begin to decline and not perform as well as they once did. Presbycusis generally begins by affecting perception of the higher frequencies at the base of the cochlea, causing a high frequency loss. Because of this loss, individuals with presbycusis will often struggle with speech understanding, particularly in noise. Phonemic regression, or the slowing of auditory comprehension (Martin & Clark, 2014), will often co-occur with presbycusis, making comprehension even more difficult.

3.4 *Retrocochlear and Auditory Processing Pathologies*

Beyond the cochlea lies the central auditory pathway leading up to the auditory temporal area of the brain. Lesions within this pathway have the potential to cause a hearing loss. One such lesion that affects the auditory nerve is an acoustic neuroma, also referred to as a vestibular schwannoma, which is known to grow on the schwann cells of the vestibular branch of the auditory nerve. These tumors are benign, slowly progressive, and occur unilaterally or bilaterally. Audiologic symptoms of a vestibular schwannoma include unilateral or asymmetrical hearing loss, tinnitus, and vertigo (Lee, Choi, Lim, Chung, Yeo & Na, 2015). These tumors are fairly rare but can have a huge impact on the patient's ability to understand speech and may cause facial numbness and weakness when they grow in size. Surgery is usually the recommended form of treatment for vestibular schwannomas, but radiation therapy and close monitoring are also recommended.

Another pathology of the retrocochlear system is auditory neuropathy spectrum disorder (ANSD) that is believed to originate beyond the outer hair cells. ANSD affects the processing of sounds. Given the spectrum nature of the disorder, every case is different and often shows varying symptoms and severity. For example, hearing loss may vary from perfectly normal hearing in some cases to profound sensorineural hearing loss in other cases. Also, there are reported cases of unilateral or bilateral asymmetrical hearing loss. Because it is a neural disorder it includes several characteristic behavioral and electrophysiologic findings that demonstrate abnormality with speech and neural processing. First, the patient will have severe difficulty understanding speech even in cases with only mild degree of hearing loss or even within normal hearing sensitivity. Second, audiological evaluation will show evidence of normal cochlear, outer hair cells function as measured by presence of otoacoustic emissions responses or cochlear microphonics, ruling out inner ear lesion. Third, evidence of abnormal neural brainstem findings as shown by elevated or absent acoustic reflex thresholds and abnormal auditory brainstem response when expected to be present.

Central auditory processing disorder (APD) is another retrocochlear disorder where individuals may exhibit a variety of listening problems. These include difficulty understanding speech in the presence of noise, following directions, discriminating speech sounds, and difficulty with spelling and reading. Although a multidisciplinary team approach is needed to assess and distinguish APD from other pathologies with similar manifestations, the audiologist is responsible to diagnose the condition using auditory processing test battery that are administered when the child is at least 7 or 8 years of age. Treatment of APD generally focuses on three main areas: direct remediation using auditory activities to remediate specific auditory deficits, changing the learning or communication environment to improve delivery and access of auditory information, and using compensatory strategy and active listening and problem-solving techniques to teach children to be active listeners and to recruit higher-order skills to help compensate for the deficit.

4 Types of Hearing Loss

Audiologists classify hearing loss by a certain type, either conductive hearing loss, sensorineural (cochlear) hearing loss, mixed hearing loss, or sensorineural loss of a retrocochlear (neural) origin. As shown in Table 12.2, the type of hearing loss depends on the location of the pathology within the auditory system that is causing the decline in hearing.

4.1 *Conductive Hearing Loss*

A conductive hearing loss (CHL) is due to a pathology within the conductive system of the ear, which is made up of the outer ear and the middle ear. The pathologies mentioned under outer ear pathologies and middle ear pathologies would all be considered causes for CHL if a decline in hearing was present from the pathology. With a CHL, the inner ear is functioning as it should, but since sound intensity is reduced due to the pathology in the outer or middle ear, increased sound intensity is needed to overcome the conductive problem and be transmitted to the cochlea. Most conductive hearing losses are not permanent and can be treated medically or surgically (MacKenzie, 2011). For the conductive losses that do cause hearing loss and for which medical

TABLE 12.2 Types of hearing loss

Types of loss	Site of lesion
Conductive	Outer and middle ear
Sensory/Cochlear	Inner ear
Mixed	middle and inner ear
Neural/Retrocochlear	Beyond the inner ear/cochlea

management is not possible or recommended, amplification is usually the best option for treatment.

4.2 *Sensorineural Hearing Loss*

Sensorineural hearing loss (SNHL) is due to a pathology within the sensory or neural structures of the auditory system. Any pathology within the cochlea of the inner ear or along the auditory pathway of the auditory system that results in a hearing loss is considered sensorineural or cochlear hearing loss in nature. When dealing with a SNHL, it is important to determine where the site of lesion is located, and whether it is sensory (within the cochlea) or neural (beyond the cochlea). Treatment will often differ depending on the pathology and the site of lesion, so it is important to distinguish between sensory and neural losses. The most common cochlear loss in SNHL is due to dysfunction/damage to the hair cells. As mentioned previously, noise exposure, Meniéré's disease, ototoxic medications, aging, genetic conditions and other inner disorders are known to cause dysfunction/damage to the hair cells. Retrocochlear or neural pathologies are also considered SNHL, however they do not impact the hair cells of the cochlea, but are caused by lesions along the central auditory pathway. Unlike conductive losses, SNHL is normally a permanent hearing loss that requires amplification.

4.3 *Mixed Hearing Loss*

Mixed hearing loss is a combination of both conductive and sensorineural hearing loss, meaning there is a pathology within both the conductive (middle ear) and the sensorineural (inner ear) mechanisms. In order for a hearing loss to be considered mixed, both conductive and sensorineural components are shown on the audiogram.

5 Hearing Evaluation

5.1 *Pure Tone Audiometry*

Pure tone audiometry is considered one of the most significant tests of the hearing evaluation that is measured using an audiometer (Figure 12.7). The purpose of pure tone audiometry is to obtain the hearing thresholds for both air conduction and bone conduction testing across a range of frequencies. Pure tones are used as the stimulus presented to the patient, hence the name 'pure tone audiometry.' A pure tone is a signal comprised of one particular frequency. Thus, pure tone audiometry testing is conducted at 250 Hz, 500 Hz, 1000 Hz, 2000 Hz, 3000 Hz, 4000 Hz, 6000 Hz, and 8000 Hz (ASHA, 2005). Threshold is measured in decibels (dB), which represents the intensity or

FIGURE 12.7 Audiometer. This device is used for pure tone audiometry, speech audiometry, and other various hearing evaluation procedures. Pictured here is the GSI Audio-Star Pro Audiometer

amplitude of the pure tone that is presented. The patient's threshold is the lowest level of intensity the patient is able to hear at least 50% of the time at a particular frequency. The frequencies that compose human speech fall within this frequency range, allowing for the evaluation of hearing sensitivity at frequencies essential for auditory communication. Pure tone audiometry results are recorded on a graph called an audiogram. The x-axis of the audiogram represents the frequencies tested, and the y-axis represents the intensity in decibels presented. Measuring pure tone air and bone conduction thresholds provides information about the degree of hearing loss, type of hearing loss, and configuration of the hearing loss, allowing audiologists to recommend the most beneficial treatment for their patients.

5.2 *Air-Conduction Pure Tone Audiometry*

Air conduction testing is performed with the patient wearing headphones or insert ear phones in order to test each ear separately. The patients are instructed to raise their hand or press a button each time they hear a tone. As mentioned before, pure tones are presented to the patient's ear to determine the threshold at octave frequencies of 250 Hz-8000 Hz. Air conduction testing generally begins at 1000 Hz at an intensity level the patient is able to hear (ASHA, 2005). The audiologist steadily decreases the intensity of the tone until the patient is no longer able to hear it. Then, the audiologist will increase the tone until the patient is able to hear it again. This testing is done by decreasing intensity by 10 dB and increasing by 5 dB to track for threshold (ASHA, 2005). This will continue until the audiologist finds the patient's threshold at each tested frequency. The patient's threshold results are then recorded on an audiogram, using circles (o) for the right ear responses and x's (x) for the left ear responses (ASHA, 1990). Air conduction testing gives the audiologist a significant amount of information because it evaluates the entire auditory system, including the conductive (outer and the middle ear), the sensory (the inner ear), and the neural, retrocochlear (the auditory nerve up to the auditory cortex) pathways. We hear every day through air conduction, so this test gives us a good representation at how well we are able to hear.

Air conduction testing allows the audiologist to determine the degree and configuration of the hearing loss. The degree of hearing loss refers to the severity of the hearing loss. Table 12.3 shows ASHA (2015) qualifications for degrees of hearing loss. Configuration of the hearing loss refers to the shape of the audiogram recorded. Different configurations include flat, rising, sloping, saucer, and notched. Using configurations to describe a hearing loss gives one an idea of what frequencies are suffering from a loss. Some configurations are associated with particular causes of hearing loss. Figures 12.8 depicts some examples of puretone air conduction audiograms including their degree and configuration of hearing loss. Audiogram A depicts a *flat* configuration, with patient's right ear responses are all within 10 dB of each other, configuring a fairly flat line. This is also a mild hearing loss because the responses were all poorer than 25 dB HL (between 30 dB and 40 dB HL) across all frequencies. Audiogram B depicts a *sloping/high frequency loss* configuration. As the frequency increases, the patient's responses start to decline, depicting a sloping line across the audiogram. This is a mild to moderately severe hearing loss. The patient has normal hearing within the low frequencies of 250 Hz–1000 Hz. However, at 1500 Hz the patient's responses start to decline into the mild hearing loss range at 30 dB HL, and continue to decline until 70 dB HL at 8000 Hz,

TABLE 12.3 Degrees of hearing loss (Clark, 1981)

Degree of hearing loss	Range in dB
Normal	10–15
Slight	16–25
Mild	26–40
Moderate	41–55
Moderately severe	56–70
Severe	71–90
Profound	91+

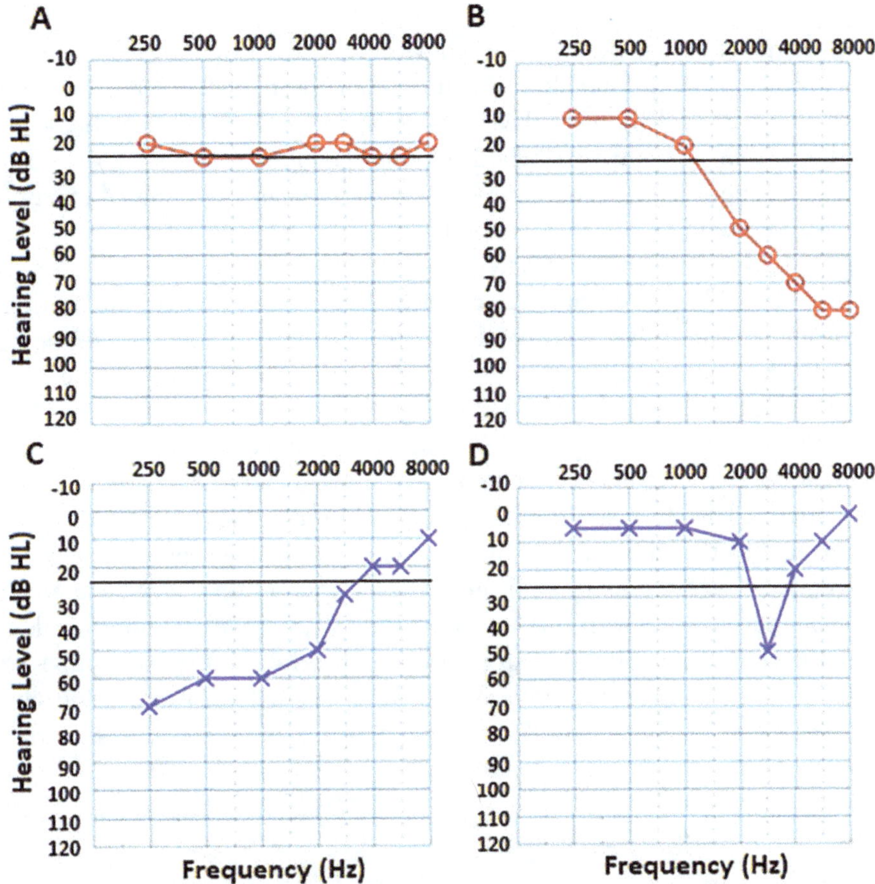

FIGURE 12.8 Audiogram configurations. Audiogram **A** depicts a flat configuration. Audiogram **B** depicts a sloping/high frequency loss configuration. Audiogram **C** depicts a rising configuration. Audiogram **D** depicts a notched, V-shape configuration. Note that the straight line represents the upper limit of normal hearing thresholds (25 dB HL). Audiograms (A and B) with the "o" shapes are responses from the right ear, whereas audiograms (C and D) with the "x" shapes are responses from the left ear

the severe hearing loss range. Audiogram **C** depicts a *rising* configuration. The patient's responses were at a moderate hearing loss at low frequencies (250–500 Hz), mild hearing loss at mid frequencies (1000–1500 Hz), and within normal hearing at high frequencies (2000–8000 Hz). This is a mild to moderate hearing loss since the range of hearing loss was between 30 dB and 50 dB HL. Audiogram **D** depicts a *notched, V-shape* configuration; the patient has within normal hearing thresholds at all frequencies except at 3000 Hz, where it drops to a 35 dB, mild hearing loss. Presence of a notched hearing notch at 4000 Hz or 3000 Hz may be due to noise exposure.

5.3 *Bone Conduction Testing*

Bone conduction testing is performed with the patient wearing a bone oscillator placed on the mastoid bone behind the ear or on the forehead. The bone oscillator is a small vibrating device that when stimulated vibrates the bones of the skull including the cochlea. Thus, bone conduction testing assesses the inner ear bypassing the conductive system of the ear. The bone conduction procedure is similar to that of air conduction testing, but without testing hearing at high 6000 Hz or 8000 Hz frequencies (ASHA, 2005). When a tone is presented via the bone oscillator, the cochlea of the inner ear is set into motion, allowing the hair cells to move and detect sound. Bone conduction responses are also recorded on the audiogram, using these symbols (< or [for the right ear and > or] for the left ear) (ASHA, 2005).

By comparing air conduction thresholds to bone conduction thresholds, the audiologist is able to determine the type of hearing loss of the patient: a conductive hearing loss, a sensorineural hearing loss, or a mixed hearing loss. As shown in Figure 12.9A, when there is a difference of 15 dB or more between air conduction responses and bone conduction responses, this is considered an air-bone gap. In cases with conductive hearing loss, the patient's bone conduction thresholds are within the normal range of hearing (better than 25 dB HL), but the air conduction thresholds fall out of the normal range of hearing with an air-bone gap. If the patient's bone conduction responses and air conduction

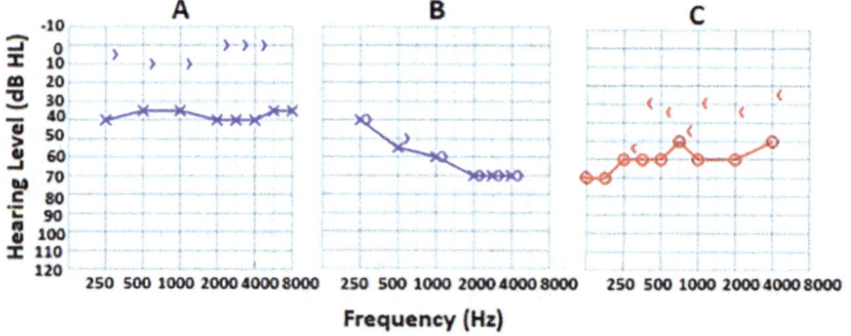

FIGURE 12.9 Types of hearing loss. Audiogram **A** depicts left ear conductive hearing loss of mild degree: bone conduction thresholds fell within the normal range of hearing and air conduction thresholds fell within the mild hearing loss range (26–45 dB HL), leaving an air-bone gap between air and bone conduction thresholds. Audiogram **B** depicts left ear sensorineural hearing loss of mild degree sloping to moderately severe degree at high frequencies: both air and bone conduction responses were in line with one another with no air-bone gap. Audiogram **C** depicts right ear mixed hearing loss of moderate-to-moderately severe degree: both air and bone conduction responses fell outside normal range with an air-bone gap. Hearing loss in both Audiograms **A** and **C** has a relatively flat configuration and Audiogram **B** shows a high frequency sloping hearing loss

responses both fall out of the range of normal hearing without an air-bone gap, it is considered a sensorineural loss (Figure 12.9B). In cases with mixed hearing loss, there is a combination of both conductive hearing loss and sensorineural hearing loss (Figure 12.9C).

5.4 *Speech Audiometry*

Speech audiometry is another important process in the hearing evaluation. While pure tone audiometry provides us with information of the patient's pure tone thresholds/audibility, speech audiometry provides us with information concerning the patient's ability to hear and understand speech. This is significant information considering we use speech every day to communicate, and without understanding speech one can really struggle with everyday life activities. There are several speech audiometry procedures used in the hearing evaluation, which include speech detection threshold, speech recognition threshold, and word recognitions testing as well as other special test battery for auditory processing testing.

Speech detection threshold (SDT) refers to the estimate level at which an individual perceives speech to be present 50% of the time (ASHA, 1988). In other words, this is the threshold at which a person is able to detect and notice speech, not necessarily understand what is being said. This is indicated in babies or in subjects with severe to profound hearing loss. Speech recognition threshold (SRT) is done using spondee words, and it is defined as the level at which a person can hear and repeat back the presented speech 50% of the time. The results of an individual's speech recognition threshold are generally similar (or about 6 dB better speech threshold) to their pure tone average from pure tone air-conduction testing (Wilson, 1973). The pure tone average is an average of pure tone threshold results at 500 Hz, 1000 Hz, and 2000 Hz. If there is a discrepancy between speech and puretone thresholds, retesting should be considered.

Word recognition testing (WRT) is performed using monosyllabic words that are presented at a supra-threshold level (30 or 40 dB above threshold) everyday conversational level. Unlike SDT and SRT, which are used to find the threshold of speech, WRT testing is used to assess an individual's ability to repeat back monosyllabic words that are presented to the patient's ear. This measure is represented as a percentage score rather than a threshold, because it is presented all at one level.

5.4.1 How is Speech Audiometry Conducted?

Both SRT and WRT are presented to each ear individually. Each measure can be presented either via monitored live voice (the audiologists own voice) or through recorded material available on a compact disk or pre-recorded in the audiometer. Each procedure involves presenting speech stimuli from word lists to the patient. For SRT, spondee words are used as the speech stimuli, which consist of two syllables with equal stress (ASHA, 1988). Some examples of common spondee words used for this measure include 'baseball' and 'hotdog.' The SRT procedure consists of presenting the speech stimuli to the patient, who is instructed to repeat back these spondee words. While this is happening, the audiologist is reducing the intensity level of the spondee until a threshold is reached. For WRT, the speech stimuli presented are monosyllabic words. Unlike the SRT procedure, WRT presents speech stimuli at one intensity level for the whole test. This intensity level is generally 30 to 40 dB above the patient's SRT threshold (Martin, Champlin, & Chambers, 1998). The WRT procedure consists of presenting the monosyllabic words to the patient one at a time, who is instructed to repeat back the words. Meanwhile, the audiologist is keeping score of how many words the patient is able to repeat back correctly. This score is then calculated as a percent. If a list of 25-monosyllabic words were presented and the patient missed one word, the score will be 96% (excellent score), but if he missed 15 words the score is 64% (poor score).

6 Amplification

6.1 *Hearing Aids*

The hearing aid is one of the most common sources of amplification for individuals with hearing loss. The basic purpose of the hearing aid is to amplify sound to a level which is audible to the user. Candidates for hearing aids usually fall between a mild to moderately severe hearing loss. The hearing aid is composed of three basic parts: the microphone, the amplifier, and the receiver. Sound enters the hearing aid through the microphone, where it is converted into an electrical signal. This signal is enhanced by the amplifier and then converted back into acoustic sound at the receiver, where it is channeled into the ear canal. Today, most hearing aids are digital and use digital signal processing strategies to amplify the incoming signal. These digital processing strategies allow for alteration of the input signal in order for the output signal to be most appropriate for the listener with hearing loss. For example, some digital hearing aids have noise reduction strategies whereby input signals identified as noise are reduced at the output of the signal. Since speech is the most common signal of interest when using a hearing aid, these processing strategies are designed to facilitate the amplification of incoming speech signals.

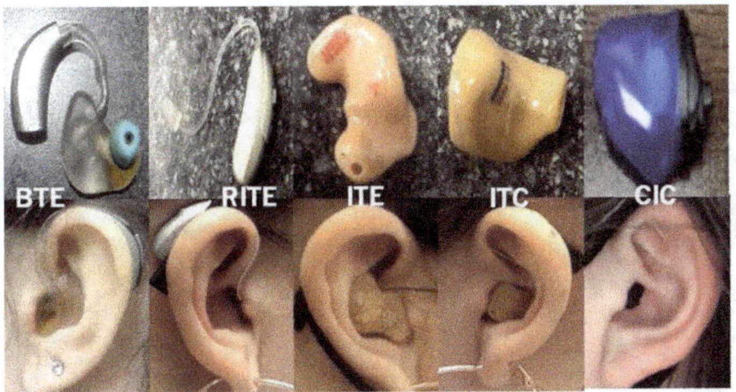

FIGURE 12.10 Hearing aids with different styles. Behind the ear (BTE), receiver in the ear (RITE), in the ear (ITE), in the canal (ITC), and completely in the canal (CIC) hearing aids

There are several styles of hearing aid available, including behind the ear (BTE), receiver in the ear, (RITE), in the ear (ITE), in the canal (ITC), and completely in the canal (CIC) aids (Figure 12.10). The style of the hearing aid is chosen based on type and degree of hearing loss as well as patient preference. The BTE aid is used in cases with severe hearing loss, whereas the ITC and CIC can be used for mild degree of hearing loss. In situations where hearing aids alone are not sufficient to provide the individual with hearing loss the appropriate access to auditory information, other amplification options may be deemed necessary.

6.2 *Cochlear Implants*

Cochlear implant may be considered when there is severe to profound degree of hearing loss and the powerful BTE hearing aids do not provide the needed amplification. The cochlear implant is an electronic prosthetic device that is surgically implanted within the cochlea for direct stimulation of the auditory nerve. Compared to the hearing aid which presents an amplified acoustic signal to the ear canal, a cochlear implant provides direct electrical stimulation of the auditory nerve. There are two components of the cochlear implant: the internal and the external devices (Figure 12.11). The internal device is surgically implanted and consists of a receiver which sits on the temporal bone of the skull and is connected to the electrode array which is implanted within the cochlea. The external device is worn behind the ear, and it consists of a microphone to pick up sound, and a sound processor that will convert sound into a digital signal, which is transmitted through the headpiece connected magnetically to the receiver of the internal device. The first multichannel cochlear

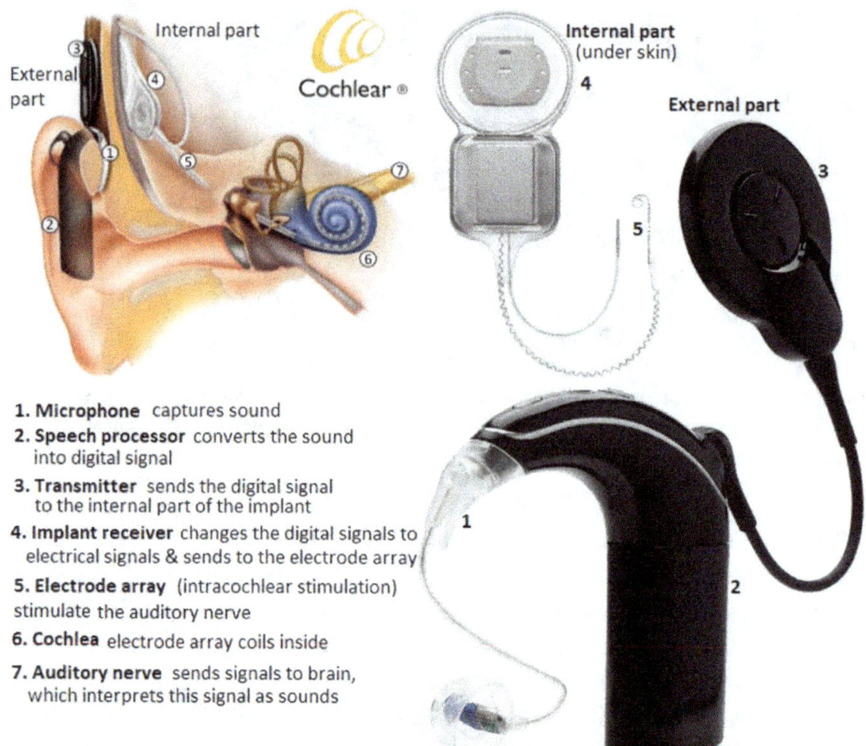

FIGURE 12.11 Cochlear implant. An illustration of its components and how it works (adapted from Cochlear Americas, n.d.)

implant was approved as medically safe for use in adults in 1984 and children in 1990 by the U.S. Food and Drug Administration. Multichannel cochlear implants are used to mimic the place representation of frequencies along the basilar membrane of the cochlea by tonotopic arrangement and stimulation of electrodes.

6.2.1 Candidacy

For those patients with severe to profound sensorineural hearing loss, cochlear implant is an option for amplification depending on several criteria. The candidacy criteria depend on Food and Drug Administration (FDA) regulations, the manufacturer of the cochlear implant, and the age of implantation. General criteria which may inform the decision for implant candidacy include the medical status of the patient, expected communication benefit with cochlear implants compared to other amplification strategies (such as hearing aids), and the support system the patient has in place (ASHA, 2004). Manufacturers of the cochlear implant devices also provide criteria for implantation with their devices. For example, Cochlear® criteria for cochlear implant candidacy in adults includes a moderate to profound sensorineural hearing loss binaurally and little amplification benefit defined by preoperative testing (Cochlear, 2016). However, before a decision be made for cochlear implantation, it is recommended that parents (or guardians) and the child, if age appropriate, be fully informed about alternatives to implantation and Deaf culture.

6.2.2 Pre-operative Testing

Before cochlear implant surgery, several evaluations are performed by the audiologist and physician to ensure the patient meets candidacy requirements for cochlear implants and is ready for the surgery. These tests include physical and physiological examinations of the entire ear (outer, middle, and inner), a hearing evaluation, hearing aid trial, CT and MRI scans, and even a psychological exam (United States Food and Drug Administration [U.S. FDA], 2014). The pre-operative testing allows the physician and audiologist to ensure cochlear implants are the best course of action and will provide the most benefit to the patient.

6.2.3 Implantation Surgery

The cochlear implant surgery is done under general anesthesia and generally takes between 2–5 hours to complete. To begin, the hair around the ear is shaved and the skin is prepped for incision. An incision is made behind the ear, and a hole is drilled into the mastoid, where the receiver portion of the cochlear implant is placed. The electrode array is then inserted into the scala tympani of the cochlea, and the incision is closed.

6.2.4 Post-surgery

In most cases, recovery from cochlear implant surgery is fairly fast. Most patients will be able to leave the hospital within 24 hours of the surgery and often will return to their normal daily routines within a week of the surgery (Zwolan, 2016). The audiologist usually waits 2–3 weeks post-surgery to activate and program the implant in order for the surgery site to heal. When the cochlear implant is activated the initial programming of the device is conducted to best fit the needs of the patient. After initial programming, implant recipients are usually seen several times during the first year of cochlear implant use for follow-up and additional programming adjustments and changes are performed as needed. For some patients, particularly for young children, it is strongly recommended that comprehensive auditory habilitation and training are continued after implantation to maximize the benefit of their cochlear implant in areas such as speech perception, communication, and listening.

6.2.5 Benefits

The benefits of receiving multichannel cochlear implants often vary from patient to patient depending on several factors such as age of onset of hearing loss, age of implantation, amount of cochlear implant experience, and educational training. In general, the shorter the time period of deafness and the earlier the time of implantation, as well as auditory training post implantation, the more likely the patient will benefit from a cochlear implant. Research has shown that children receiving implantation before the age of two demonstrated faster improvement in sound detection and auditory perception skills following implantation (Manrique, Cervera-Paz, Huarte, & Molina, 2009). When young children with a profound hearing impairment are implanted early enough, their language, speech intelligibility, and spoken language can develop in a manner similar to that of their hearing peers because their brain is ready to learn language (Moeller, Hoover, Putman, Arbataitis, Peterson, Wood, et al., 2007a; Moeller, Hoover, Putman, Arbataitis, Bohnenkamp, Peterson, et al., 2007b). However, regardless of age of implantation, most cochlear implant recipients (adults and children) will find some sort of improvement in auditory and speech perception to their everyday life activities. Communication is made easier through more perceptible auditory sensation, and maximum benefit post implantation can be found with further auditory rehabilitation and training. This requires close otological follow up and ongoing audiological programming and monitoring of the performance of cochlear implant management to assess improvement in sound and speech detection and auditory reception of speech.

6.2.6 Future Considerations

As our experience with cochlear implants and technology continues to improve, further developments are being made in order to improve the benefit of these devices. Today, bilateral cochlear implants are becoming more popular. Bilateral cochlear implants have shown to give patients the benefits of binaural hearing such as listening in noise and sound localization (Litovsky, Johnstone, & Godar 2008). Technological advancements have certainly made a difference in these devices (Hardesty, 2014). Another significant area of research in the field is the examination of the benefit of combined acoustic and electrical stimulation. When the patient maintains preserved hearing, typically in the low frequencies, a hybrid implant, a cross between a cochlear implant and a hearing aid, may be suggested. These devices work well on patients with mild or moderate hearing loss in the low frequencies and severe to profound hearing loss in the high frequencies. This allows the low frequencies to be amplified and presented acoustically by the hearing aid, while the high frequencies are electrically stimulated the cochlear implant electrodes. In addition, more research is under way to assess the benefits of cochlear implantation in patients with single sided deafness. As technology continues to improve, we can only expect to see further benefits in cochlear implantation for individuals with significant hearing loss.

References

American Speech-Language-Hearing Association. (1988). Guidelines for determining threshold level for speech. *American Speech-Language – Hearing Association, 30*, 85–89.

American Speech-Language-Hearing Association. (1990). Guidelines for audiometric symbols. *American Speech-Language- Hearing Association, 32*, 25–30.

American Speech-Language-Hearing Association. (2004). *Cochlear implants.* www.asha.org/policy

American Speech-Language-Hearing Association. (2005). Guidelines for manual pure-tone threshold audiometry. Rockville, MD. http://www.asha.org/policy/GL2005–00014/

American Speech-Language-Hearing Association. (2015). *Causes of hearing loss in children.* Audiology Information Series, 10802. http://www.asha.org/public/hearing/Congenital-Hearing-Loss/

Gadre, A. (2021). *Otology & Neurotology Skull Base Surgery.* Geiseinger Commonwealth Medical School.

Chittka, L., & Brockmann, A. (2005). Perception space—The final frontier. *PLoS Biol, 3*(4/e137), 564–568. https://doi.org/10.1371/journal.pbio.0030137

Clark, J. G. (1981). Uses and abuses of hearing loss classification. *American Speech-Language-Hearing Association, 23*, 493–500.

Cochlear. (2016). *Candidacy.* https://www.cochlear.com/us/en/professionals/products-and-candidacy/candidacy/cochlear-implant

Cochlear Americas. (n.d.). Cochlear.com/us. https://www.cochlear.com/us/en/corporate/media-center/media-center

Elliot, S. J., & Shera, C. A. (2012). The cochlea as a smart structure. *Smart Materials and Structures, 21*(6), 1–11.

Hain, T. C. (2021). *Meniere's disease.* https://dizziness-and-balance.com/disorders/menieres/menieres.html

Hardesty, L. (2014, February 9). Cochlear implants – with no exterior hardware. *MIT News.* http://news.mit.edu/2014/cochlear-implants-with-no-exterior-hardware-0209

Hawke, M. (2007). *Tympanic membrane*. https://commons.wikimedia.org/wiki/File:Traumatic_Perforation_of_the_Tympanic_Membrane.jpg#filelinks

Hofymeyr, L. (2021). *3D-printed titanium ossicular chain reconstruction—Hype or reality?* https://lmhofmeyr.co.za/3d-printed-titanium-ossicular-chain-reconstruction-hype-or-reality/

Knott, L. (2020). *Ménière's disease*. Egton Medical Information Systems Limited. https://patient.info/ears-nose-throat-mouth/tinnitus-leaflet/menieres-disease

Kurokawa, H., & Goode, R. L. (1995). Sound pressure gain produced by the human middle ear. *Otolaryngology Head and Neck Surgery, 113*(4), 349–355.

Lee, S. H., Choi, S. K., Lim, Y. J., Chung, H. Y., Yeo, J. H, Na, S. Y, et al. (2015). Otologic manifestations of acoustic neuroma. *Acta Otolaryngology, 135*(2), 140–146.

Lieberthal, A. S., Carroll, A. E., Chonmaitree, T., Ganiats, T. G., Hoberman, A., Jackson, M.A., et al. (2013). Clinical practice guidelines: The diagnosis and management of acute otitis media. *Pediatrics, 131*(3), e964–e999.

Litovsky, R. Y., Johnstone, P., & Godar, S. (2006). Benefits of bilateral cochlear implants and/or hearing aids in children. *International Journal of Audiology, 45*(Suppl), 78–91.

OpenStax College, Rice University. (n.d.) *Lumenlearning. The Ear*. Retrieved April 1, 2021, from https://courses.lumenlearning.com/atd-herkimer-biologyofaging/chapter/audition-and-somatosensation/

MacKenzie, D. J. (2011). Audiology and hearing loss. In R.E. Owens, D. E. Metz, & K. A. Farinella (Eds.), *Introduction to communication disorders: A life-span evidence based perspective* (pp. 404–465). Upper Saddle River, NJ: Pearson Education.

Martin, F., Champlin, C., & Chambers, J. (1998). Seventh survey of audiometric practices in the United States. *Journal of the American Academy of Audiology, 9*, 95–104.

Martin, F. N., & Clark, J. G. (2014). The outer ear. In F. N. Martin & J. G. Clark (Eds.), *Introduction to audiology* (12th ed.). Old Tappan, NJ: Prentice Hall.

Manrique, M., Cervera-Paz, J., Huarte, A., & Molina, M. (2009). Advantages of cochlear implantation in prelingual deaf children before 2 years of age when compared with later implantation. *Laryngoscope, 114*(8), 1462–1469.

Mehta, R., Rosowski, J., Voss, S., O'Neil, E., & Merchant, S. (2006). Determinants of hearing loss in perforations of the tympanic membrane. *Otology & Neurotology*, 27(2), 136–143.

Moeller, M. P., Hoover, B., Putman, C., Arbataitis, K., Peterson, B., Wood, S., et al. (2007a). Vocalizations of infants with hearing loss compared with infants with normal hearing: Part I – phonetic development. *Ear Hear, 28*(5), 605–627.

Moeller, M. P., Hoover, B., Putman, C., Arbataitis, K., Bohnenkamp, G., Peterson, B., et al. (2007b). Vocalizations of infants with hearing loss compared with infants with normal hearing: Part II – transition to words. *Ear Hear, 28*(5), 628–642.

Möller, A. R. (2006). Hearing impairment. In A. R. Möller (Ed.), *Hearing: Anatomy, physiology, and disorders of the auditory system* (pp. 205–251). Burlington, VT: Academic Press.

Occupational Safety and Health Administration (OSHA). (1983). *Occupational noise exposure, hearing conservation amendment. Rule and proposed regulation.* Washington, D.C.: Federal Register, United States Government Printing Office.

Ravicz, M., Rosowski, J., & Merchant, S. (2004). Mechanisms of hearing loss resulting from middle-ear fluid. *Hearing Research, 195*(1–2), 103–130.

Schuknecht, H. F. (1993). *Pathology of the ear* (2nd ed.). Philadelphia, PA: Lea and Febiger.

Shaw, E. A., & Teranishi, R. (1968). Sound pressure generated in an external-ear replica and real human ears by a nearby point source. The *Journal of the Acoustical Society of America, 44*(1), 240–249.

Stach, B. A., & Ramachandran, V. (2008). Hearing disorders in children. In J. R. Flexer (Ed.), *Pediatric audiology: Diagnosis, technology, and management* (pp. 1–11). New York, NY: Thieme Medical Publishers.

United States Food and Drug Administration. (2014). *Before, during and after implant surgery.* http://www.fda.gov/MedicalDevices/ProductsandMedicalProcedures/ImplantsandProsthetics/CochlearImplants/ucm062899.htm

Van Der Heyden, C., & Handelsman, J. A. (2015). *Evaluation and management of Ménière's disease.* http://www.asha.org/aud/articles/menieres-disease-eval-management/

World Health Organization. (2015). *WHO deafness and hearing loss* (*Fact Sheet No. 300*). http://www.who.int/mediacentre/factsheets/fs300/en/

Wikipedia. (n.d.). *Organ of Corti.* Retrieved April 15, 2021, from https://en.wikipedia.org/wiki/Organ_of_Corti (Free licensed Encyclopedia).

Wilson, R. M. (1973). A proposed SRT procedure and its statistical precedent. *Journal of Speech and Hearing Disorders, 38,* 184–191.

Zwolan, T. (2016). Cochlear implant. In J. Katz, L. Medwetsky, R. Burkard & L. Hood (Eds.), *Handbook of clinical audiology* (pp. 912–933). Philadelphia, PA: Wolters Kluwer.

CHAPTER 13

Analyzing the Meaning of Numbers and Words to Portray Deaf Experiences

Stephanie Cawthon

Abstract

This chapter provides a guide to developing research studies that consider the context and characteristics of deaf participants. Ethical inquiry with marginalized populations requires specific attention to decisions made throughout the research development and implementation process. Research must both adhere to the rigorous standards for each domain while at the same time being transparent about what conclusions may or may not be drawn from the resultant data. This chapter offers both emerging and seasoned scholars considerations on how to improve research so that it meets the aims of reducing inequities and injustices that deaf people face. Study conceptualization, including the chosen theoretical frame, the experiences of who is involved in the study, and reflecting on one's own motivation for the research project, lay the groundwork for the formal work of research design and data collection. Measure selection and methodological approaches are then framed within this introductory section, with particular attention to how assumptions about research and methodology need to be critically considered as fair and unbiased for deaf participants. The chapter concludes with discussion about inference-making, tying back to the effect of theoretical frames and researcher positionality, as well as the role of research in work towards equity and justice.

Keywords

research design – measurement – sampling – validity – reliability – literature review – deaf

1 Introduction

We live in a data-driven culture, one that prioritizes making decisions based on evidence. As research designs have become more sophisticated, the rigor of research in social sciences has been under greater scrutiny when evaluating

 | DOI:10.1163/9789004692299_014

the impact of research on recommendations for practice (e.g., What Works Clearinghouse Standards). There has thus been an increasing emphasis on the "how" of research—how our choices about research design, sampling, and research methods affect what inferences we can make from the findings.

Data are not collected in a vacuum and inferences made from them occur within a socio-political context. People and programs with different epistemologies seek information for different purposes. Yet the majority of research is conducted from the point of view of a hearing person, living in a world that is designed to be maximally accessible for hearing individuals. For example, *Deaf Epistemologies: Multiple Perspectives on the Acquisition of Knowledge* (Paul & Moores, 2012), is a collection of contributions that focus on how one's identity as a deaf researcher or within a deaf community has an impact on how one views history, science, and education. I am also co-editor on a volume on research in deaf education, and several chapters focus on issues such as positionality, ethics, and connections within the community (Cawthon & Garberoglio, 2017). Collectively, these works serve as an important reminder of ways in which we as researchers in deaf studies and deaf education interact with the content and context in which we work.

The purpose of this chapter is to discuss the research process with considerations for what it means to do so within deaf studies and deaf education. Beyond simply focusing on research that is about deaf individuals and systems surrounding them, this chapter provides a critical look at factors that affect how decisions are made about how one analyzes the meaning of numbers and words to portray deaf experiences. The chapter first describes different kinds of data collection activities and provides examples of how one might think about how the purpose of the project affects the kind of interpretation of numbers and words one might provide. After a brief overview of ethical considerations, the chapter then describes and provides examples about factors to consider throughout the research process: Deciding what to study, how to approach your study design, and how you describe your findings to your chosen audience.

1.1 *My Positionality*

Before continuing with the heart of this chapter, I want to contextualize what is said here with a statement of my own positionality in relation to research in deaf studies and deaf education. I am an education researcher who has been studying issues related to language development and deaf education for just over 20 years. I work with deaf colleagues and students in a public university that has a heavy emphasis on research publications and external funding. I am hard of hearing and wear hearing aids in most situations, with a heavy emphasis on lip reading. I am an emerging sign language user, functional in a flexible work environment but by no means fluent. Outside of my early intervention experience, I grew up in mainstreamed education settings, mostly in private schools. My context is thus largely in the realm of education, particularly in the development of professionals in the service fields and furthering the evidence base upon which instructional decisions and policy are made.

1.2 *Types of Data Collection*

Research and data collection is not a monolithic process. There are many purposes behind research, and these different motivations for systematic inquiry impact various aspects of the research process. For the sake of this discussion, I will highlight five different types of data collection:

- *Exploration of an idea or phenomenon.* This type of data collection is more about understanding a behavior or an outcome than the impact of an intervention or type of instruction. Much of the groundbreaking research related to deaf individuals falls into this category of descriptive work. This work can vary in the extent to which it uses quantitative (i.e., numbers) or qualitative (e.g., narratives of what people say) information. For example Lissa Stapleton (2015) describes the experiences of d/Deaf Students of Color (her term), highlighting the importance of intersecting identities, particularly within the context of navigating postsecondary education settings. This study took a fundamental qualitative approach to research with the expressed purpose of summarizing the experiences of an often hidden population in the research literature.
- *Evaluation of a program or policy.* A second type of data collection is one that is evaluative, a design that looks at a specific case or program or policy and seeks to understand its implementation and potential impact. Often there is also a question of finances. Is there an adequate Return on Investment (ROI) to continue support for a program, such as an after-school program, or a policy, such as tuition support for a credentialing program in the health sciences? Data collection for evaluation purposes also seeks to uncover any roadblocks to success, such as lack of participant buy-in, unfunded demands, or a misallocation of resources including time and physical space. Evaluations also use descriptive data, including interviews and focus groups as well as counts of the number or proportion of target audience served. Their purpose is different than for the exploratory research because the context and activities are largely already known at the onset of data collection. For example, many grant-funded programs or projects include a required evaluation component, often from an external professional or organization. This distance allows the evaluator to assess what areas are going well in the

program or policy, and what areas could either be improved or may not be at an ROI that is needed for continued implementation.

- *Measure validation.* In quantitative research, we depend highly on the validity of scores from our study measures to be able to make inferences about the meaning of study results. By saying a test score is (more or less) valid we mean that the score (more or less) accurately represents what we think it does—this applies to measures of a person's knowledge of course content as well as to measures of their level of mental health or sign language skills. One particular challenge in measure validation is the development of norms, or expected benchmarks, that allow one to compare a person's score with the overall population. The Stanford Achievement Test – Hearing Impaired (terminology at the time) is one example of an effort by Gallaudet to gather enough data from deaf students to create norms that draw on this specific subpopulation (Qi & Mitchell, 2011). There has been much discussion as to the lack of measures with norms for deaf individuals, and the implications of this for research in the field. We will explore this issue further as we discuss measure selection as part of the research process.
- *Relationships between variables.* Another type of research that is important to consider when thinking about the research process is work that seeks to understand the relationships between constructs and variables. This approach could be taken either quantitatively or qualitatively, depending on the nature of the question and how those relationships are being analyzed. The bulk of research in deaf education follows either this approach or experimental designs, described below. Variable selection becomes critically important in these two types of projects. The advantage of looking at relationships is that it reflects the very complex nature of the lived experience of deaf individuals. One of the challenges, however, is that we must be mindful of the possibilities that factors exist that we are not aware of and have not included in our designs. One of the great needs in the field is for deaf individuals to participate in the design phase of research projects so that factors that they see as having a potential significance can be included.
- *Experimental designs.* Experimental designs that are used to investigate the impact of interventions is the last type of research effort that will be relevant to the discussion in this chapter. There are many different types of experimental designs, ranging from large-scale randomized trials to quasi-experimental models to meta-analytic approaches to synthesis of research literature. The goal in each of these designs is to identify the effect of independent variables on a defined set of outcomes (e.g., whether or not obtaining cochlear implant results in improved expressive language development). Experimental research comes from the tradition of the

"hard" sciences that emphasizes the ability to control for multiple possible explanations for an outcome and tease apart, or identify, the contribution of discrete factors on an outcome. There are many requirements related to sample selection and measurement that are required to be able to use inferential statistics to make causal claims; research within deaf studies and deaf education has only recently started to have access to the types of datasets required to make robust use of experimental designs.

1.3 *Ethical Considerations in Research*

Before we walk through the steps of the research process, a few words about ethical considerations in research, particularly when including deaf participants, their families, and work within their context. In all social science research, under which most deaf studies and deaf education research falls, researchers must always be aware of the ethical guidelines that we must adhere to as part of our responsibility to our participants and to the field. This means maintaining spirit of both confidentiality and transparency throughout the process. While these two ideas, confidentiality and transparency, may seem at odds with one another, they both work to help ensure trustworthy and authentic research is disseminated in a way that benefits our participants. Here are a few questions to think about as you pursue your research project:

- *Have all project materials been reviewed and approved by your Institutional Review Board (IRB) process?* The IRB process is meant to support researchers in thinking clearly about the ways in which they will engage with participants and to pay particular attention making sure that they fully understand what is being asked of them, and are able to give consent freely and without coercion. Transparency is particularly important here in sharing with the IRB what your intended research plan looks like, and confidentiality is important here because IRB wants to make sure you have taken the steps required to keep information you obtain secure.
- *Have your data been represented accurately and honestly?* There are many ways in which it can be tempting to tweak data, leave out information that doesn't confirm your hypotheses, or otherwise misrepresent your data in an effort to make your study seem stronger. In the end, research misconduct only undermines the efforts to raise the quality of research available to support deaf individuals as they seek equity and access in the field. Along those lines, when you discover a mistake in your research, it is imperative that you report it immediately to the publishers. By publishing research you are a public figure in the field, and that comes with responsibilities to uphold the highest standards of integrity in your work.

– *Are you mindful of the degree of social interaction you have with study participants?* Conducting research nearly always requires leveraging relationships you have to recruit participants and gather support for your study. In a small field such as deaf studies and deaf education, it is very likely that you may know your participants, or (if you use them) interpreters, or related persons during the course of your study. For many of us, we have multiple roles in the lives and organizations that are affiliated with our research projects. It can sometimes be challenging to engage with participants to the degree appropriate given the bounds of the study. In every case, it would be important to establish clear guidelines for what is discussed within the research context and thus separate from other communications. It may be helpful to discuss these social role challenges with your research team, individuals you respect, or your IRB review board to ensure that you are able to keep the appropriate level of confidentiality required to maintain proper boundaries around your research.

2 The Research Process

The remainder of this chapter will focus on steps within the research process. Although each type of data collection may approach the research process from a different vantage point, these steps apply broadly to most data collection activities and are relevant when thinking about research within deaf studies and deaf education.

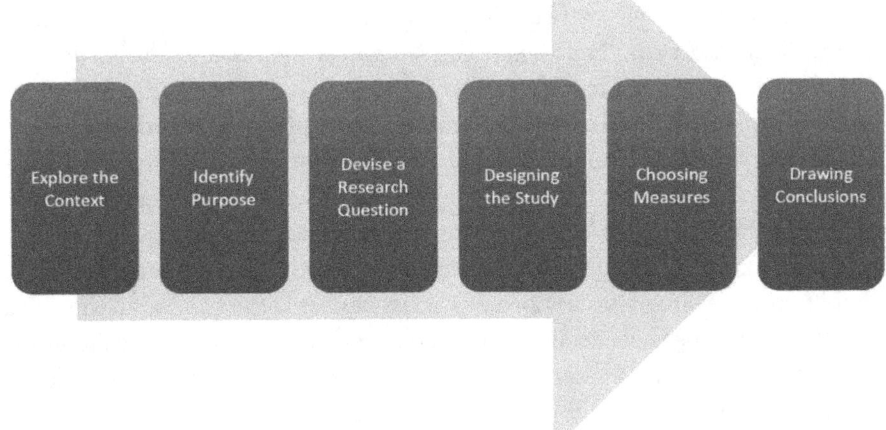

FIGURE 13.1 The research process

2.1 *Exploring the Context*

The first step in the research process is to gather information about the context for your chosen research area. There are both informal (e.g., conversations with colleagues, reading what is happening in the news) and formal approaches to understanding the context to your research topic. Informal approaches might include one's own experiences or those of people you know, providing a 'aha!,' a 'PAH!,' or place of recognition of important factors to consider in your work. For formal approaches, typically this includes reading the research literature, both historical documents and recently published work. In addition to the standard strategies for reviewing research in any area, there are considerations that are important to keeping in mind when exploring the context of a potential research topic within deaf studies and deaf education. Initial search strategies using online databases typically use key words to flag articles that include those terms in either the title or the abstract of the paper. There are a broad range of words used to describe research that addresses issues related to deaf individuals; it can be helpful to use many different ways that authors (now or in the past) have described the population. This may mean conducting searches with terms such as deaf, deafness, hearing impairment, deaf-blind, cochlear implants, hearing aids, hearing loss, sign language, and so forth, even if all of those terms do not directly relate to your area of interest.

Second, it can be helpful to do a manual search through the research literature in addition to the automatized key word searches described above. I recommend going back as far as one's theory motivates a search (more on theory in the next section) to see if there are articles that can help provide needed context for our contemporary understanding of the construct you wish to study. There are some journals that are dedicated to topics in the field, such as *American Annals of the Deaf, Deafness and Education International, Volta Review, Deaf Studies Digital Journal, Sign Language Studies,* and *Journal of Deaf Studies and Deaf Education.* After a set of relevant documents has been identified, it can also be helpful to cull the reference list and see where other research has been published. When identifying articles, be sure to have some balance between articles published in different journals as well as by different authors so as to include multiple perspectives on the topic. Although it is not always possible to know from the articles themselves, including deaf authors within your literature search is an important step in exploring the context of the field.

A third step, one that can arise from a comprehensive review of the literature as well as a broader understanding of the history of theory in social and educational research, is to identify the range of theoretical perspectives or paradigms that are present in the research literature. Theoretical frameworks provide an important contextual feature for interpreting study findings. For example, if a study about identity development is drawing from an ecological systems theory approach, the variables examined should include those that relate to the individual but also to community, schools, families, and other larger system factors. I often make a checklist of characteristics of research articles in my corpus, with one column that identifies what, if any, theoretical frame is named in the research article. If my own proposed project is within the same theoretical frame, this is a useful point to discuss within the rationale and later discussion of results. Without this anchor, it can be challenging to have a robust discussion of alternative explanations of one's findings, or of why the study results contribute to the understanding of the construct of interest. Lack of clear theoretical rationale leads to weaker research base within a field. In a project examining the characteristics of research related to social skill development in deaf individuals, we found that very few studies explicitly articulated a theoretical rationale for their study approach (Cawthon, Schoffstall, Wendel, & Jassal, 2016).

Each discipline, such as social work, economics, and education, has very different specific theoretical frames or rationale that are alive in the field. One of the more basic categories of theories or frameworks is whether or not the study portrays deafness from a medical model or deficit perspective, focusing mainly on the loss of hearing, or if it considers cultural components and other strengths of what it means to function as a deaf person. Although this is a broadly construed continuum, the stated motivation or context for the study is often indicative of underlying assumptions behind the piece. Knowing where the bulk or the spread of research in the field lies on this continuum is an important part of understanding the context for your own work.

Finally, it is important to recognize the effect of cohort both in the lives of deaf individuals and in research. Cohort effects refer to how time in history and the socio-political-economic-cultural-religious context of living in that time period affects how we live. Even just attention to location within modern time acknowledges the influence of cohort. Living as a deaf person in rural China may call one's attention to different factors than living as a deaf person in Los Angeles. Ecological systems theory is a commonly used framework that acknowledges the impact that cohort has on understanding human functioning within a broader system of factors (Bronfenbrenner, 1992). While some studies name cohort effects as part of their analysis, most research occurs at a level more proximal to both the researchers and the studied constructs. When conducting a review of literature in a field, make note of shifts not only in terminology, but also in the types of questions asked and the use of theory to understand the lived experience of deaf individuals.

2.2 *Identifying the Problem or Goal*

The second step in the research process is to identify what needs to be done, and why. Most literature reviews begin with a basic description of a topic, a discussion of why it is important, and what gaps within the field need to be addressed with new research. It is not sufficient to simply say that a project has not been done, but that investing the time and energy into a research project will move the field into deeper understanding. There are places in the field where there is already a research trajectory, but typically not enough to say that we have evidence-based practices. For example, reading interventions has been one of the most highly researched areas in deaf education (Luckner, Sebald, Cooney, Young, & Muir, 2005/2006; Trezek & Wang, 2017). But there are few interventions that meet the current standards for evidence-based practices. Therefore, one important gap to fill in reading research is to design studies that do meet those standards.

A second area for consideration is whether or not the gap in the field is one of understanding a construct, a phenomenon. If this is the case, studies that are needed are largely exploratory or descriptive in nature. Even with the rise in the amount and rigor of research in the field, there is still much that is not known about experiences of deaf individuals. Some of the limitations in the field stem from the fact that, until recently, there were very few deaf individuals who were conducting research or who were participating in the design of research studies. Other gaps are due to the challenges in obtaining a sufficient sample size or a diverse enough sample of deaf individuals to adequately study a specific topic. For example, when looking at experiences of deaf individuals in the workplace, there are very few studies that examine experiences of diverse groups (Johnson & Garberoglio, 2016). Without this nuance, the field is limited in what it can understand about the ways in which deaf individuals engage with what is predominantly a hearing-centric world of work.

Finally, a point of reflection for all authors is to think about why they are pursuing the study. What is the motivation? Research is not an easy task and it takes a significant amount of resources to pursue. For deaf individuals who are working in the field, we often have our own personal experiences that inform the types of research that we do. For myself, I was first inspired to do research on language development when I took a course in college and thought—this is going to look different for deaf individuals, and it was different for me as a hard of hearing individual. It was then that I started building my understanding of how language and communication develops within deaf individuals and their families. Later, I was working in schools, thinking about school policies and doing research in classrooms. I saw that there were differentiated levels of access to education for students depending on the communication skills of the teachers and peer interactions (Cawthon, 2001). Those early experiences have guided, in some way, the rest of my research career (thus far!). Combining my own personal experiences with the last twenty years in the field has been both intellectually and personally enriching.

2.3 *Devising and Revising a Research Question*

A clear research question or guiding study aim is essential to a successful research study. In order to write a clear research question, one must have a deep knowledge of the characteristics of the population you want to study, the constructs you want to measure or explore, and the research approach you wish to take. Research within deaf studies and deaf education requires specialized knowledge and expertise both of the population and constructs being studied. This expertise includes an understanding of the ways in which one's own perspectives reflect the diversity of the deaf population. Although there are many similarities in how deaf individuals experience their lives with other populations, there are differences, sometimes large, sometimes small, in how constructs are manifest across the deaf population. Diversity characteristics are many, and range from language modality to educational setting to family context. Ensuring that one's research questions reflect an appropriate scope can be as straightforward as being clear about both the range of the population in the study and what aspects of the construct are relevant in a study of deaf populations. For example, consider the following research question:

2.4 *What Is the Relationship between Deaf Children and Their Peers?*

This example is intentionally vague in a number of ways, but it is not uncommon to see studies motivated by questions such as these. The construct, 'relationship between children and peers' does not take into account the complexities of communication and peer interaction that may occur. It is also unclear whether the peer group referred to here are also deaf, whether the context is in formal or informal social setting, if there is an interpreter mediating conversations, and so forth. Each of these factors is critically important and has an impact on how the construct of interest presents itself in the studied population. Without care, it would be possible to over generalize from this question with findings that are not precise enough to answer the question. Consider this revised research question:

2.5 *What Is the Role of an Interpreter in Classroom Conflict Resolution between Deaf and Hearing Peers?*

Of course, researchers are typically limited in their access to study participants and need to take those resources into account. When thinking about the final drafting of a research question, it may be an important reality check to see if you have sufficient access to reach their research goals. Particularly with populations that are in specialized settings, such as a school or program that specifically serves deaf students, there are often additional requirements before researchers can conduct their study. One of the most important resources of any participant is time—if your study design is a naturalistic approach, without intrusive measures or time completing study tasks, you may have different opportunities than if the study requires a lot of time or is disruptive of daily life. For example, a brain imaging study would require much more significant amounts of time than a study where the researcher is observing classroom behavior, which in turn may affect the representativeness of one's sample of a larger population. So, fundamentally, the research question needs to reflect what is possible in YOUR context in terms of interaction with potential participants.

2.6 *Designing the Study*

Research designs tend to be classified into one of three categories: quantitative, qualitative, and mixed methods, with the last category a distant third behind the first two. Mixed methods design tends to bring together aspects of quantitative and qualitative design, such as a survey with both multiple choice and open ended responses. Some researchers find this appealing because they wish to elicit some input from participants that is more flexible than typically available in a strictly quantitative design. Yet for the sake of this conversation we will address considerations for the first two categories. When discussing research designs with my students I often get this comment early in the process: "Well, I am going to propose (insert a study design type) because I am a (insert either quantitative or qualitative descriptor) person." On the one hand, it is important to know one's aptitude for different types of data analysis, whether it is working with numbers and statistics or more directly with people and eliciting and documenting their stories, their experiences. There is a great deal of training that goes into developing skills in each area, and each research approach has a wealth of knowledge that is handed down from generation to generation.

On the other hand, and more to the point with regard to the development of a research design that answers a drafted research question, there are some research questions that are better answered using quantitative approaches and others that lend themselves to a qualitative approach. When thinking about the type of study to design, and the type of research question that leads to a particular design, it is important to be aware of how different research questions are better answered by different design types. For example, if the review of the literature and identification of a gap in the research base really shows the need for descriptive data, particularly rich descriptive data, the research design really lends itself to a qualitative approach. Given how little empirical information there is in many areas of deaf studies and deaf education, there may be an opportunity for new researchers to use rigorous qualitative techniques to really build a robust understanding of how deaf individuals experience their lives. From a broader and more nuanced qualitative research base, quantitative designs would be able to potentially capture elements that may be currently missing from the literature.

When conducting research within a minority or marginalized community, there is an inherent political context, one of injustice, injustice that often goes unnoted in the development and discussion of research results. This is particularly true for qualitative work within deaf populations. When thinking about research design, entry into a context and buy in from the community, knowing what challenges or issues the participants face can be useful in a number of ways. First, it shows respect for the community. How can research both serve the development of greater understanding while at the same time serving as a way to advocate for better conditions for the Deaf community to thrive? What is our responsibility as researchers not just to have a successful, valid, and meaningful study, but also to study topics that will add to the greater good for deaf individuals? When we consider that our research may have significant ramifications for how policy decisions are made, as well as the potential dismantling of deficit models of functioning, engaging with the study population as part of design phase is critical.

There are several considerations with regard to sampling that are helpful to keep in mind when conducting research with deaf individuals. For quantitative studies, one early decision is whether or not the research question and study design include a comparison of deaf and hearing individuals, interaction between deaf and hearing individuals, or focuses only on deaf individuals. Although this may seem to be a straightforward decision, it can be helpful to check one's assumption about what is the best fit for the purpose of the study. For example, if the focus of the study is on interaction between deaf and hearing peers, it might also be a useful reference point to analyze interactions between deaf and deaf peers, as a further comparison point to understand how communication modalities, identities and other complexities influence peer-to-peer interaction. If the purpose of the study is to understand communication dynamics between deaf and hearing individuals, assuming there will be differences in this study than what has already been established in the research literature between hearing-hearing dyads, it may be useful to also know what communication dynamics look like in deaf-deaf dyads to show both parallels.

Cohort effects are also very important when thinking about experiences of deaf individuals. In the Western world, there have been many changes in what access deaf individuals have to education and work opportunities, but also an increase in the level of education required to obtain entry-level positions. There are also additional factors related to race, gender, and socio-economic status that interplay with education and deaf identity. These different factors mean that employment experiences and outcomes are not the same for all deaf individuals within the broader workforce (Johnson & Garberoglio, 2016). Overall statistics of workforce participation rates mask what are very real differences between deaf individuals of different ages and demographic backgrounds (pepnet2, 2014). Descriptive statistics that are sensitive to these cohort effects and accompanying demographic factors are essential to drawing appropriate conclusions regarding many socio-economic outcomes for deaf individuals.

2.7 *Choosing Measures*

Once the research question has been defined and the research design chosen, it is time to identify exactly what measures, or tools, are going to be utilized to gather information. The choice of measures is a critical component of the study design process, and often one that early researchers find to be the most challenging. Because measure selection can be very specific to individual constructs, it can be challenging to make general statements about the appropriate fit of a measure to investigate a particular content area. The discussion below is meant to raise considerations that researchers will want to keep in mind when selecting measures for use in studies that include deaf populations.

For quantitative research, there is an emphasis on using standardized measures that have been previously validated and shown to be reliable measures of the intended construct. Some of the research in the field is specifically looking at how validity of test scores may be true (or not) across different populations (Cawthon, Leppo, Carr, & Kopriva, 2013). More sophisticated methods such as a differential item functioning (DIF) analysis can help to pinpoint potential issues that may not be obvious on the surface. Even if a tool was not designed specifically for deaf populations, knowing whether the psychometric properties assumed to be true for the original design of a tool holds true when used with research in deaf populations is a great resource for the field. If you decide to use a standardized measure that has not been previously validated with deaf populations, any information you can provide about the psychometric properties of its use within your current study would be a service to the field.

A variation on the use of standardized measures is when a researcher adapts a previously developed measure to fit for use with deaf participants. For example, in a study of teacher confidence in educating deaf students, a simple adaptation would be to add the specific descriptor of 'deaf' in front of any clause that referred to 'students' more generally. If this descriptor is aligned with the scope of the research question, and does not require further delineation to reflect the diversity of one's deaf student population, that might be a reasonable approach to adapting a measure. If it is not, there are further caveats, perhaps in the directions for answering the question, which might be needed for the participant to be able to apply their experiences to their responses to the test items. A second variation when adapting a measure is to delete or replace items that are not relevant to a deaf population. This means that there are different questions, and perhaps a different structure, to the standardized scale than in its original form. Deleting an item might be necessary when a question is related to an experience that a person in your population is not likely to have, and thus may create tension or a feeling of alienation in your participation. If possible, having a way in which the respondent can simply say 'not applicable' alleviates many of the challenges that may occur in a forced response situation. Take home message: conduct due diligence in making sure that the participants have sufficient experience with the content to be able to respond to the questions asked.

Researcher-designed measures make up the bulk of tools used in studies in the field. For qualitative studies, researcher-designed include interview or focus group questions, as well as structured observations and other naturalistic coding protocol. For quantitative studies, researcher-designed measures might include survey questions or a set of Likert scale items that are developed locally because there are no previously developed measures on that area. In either case, careful wording of items and questions is essential in accurate measurement of your intended construct. Although pilot studies are highly recommended in any development of a new measure, in the case of researcher-designed measures in deaf studies and deaf education, pilot testing is needed for (at least) two reasons. The first is to understand how the text of the question, for participants who are reading those items, is perceived and understood. Having a cognitive lab (where a participant sits with a researcher and describes what they think the items mean) during measure development is key (Desimone & LeFloch, 2004). Cognitive labs are also a place where the delivery of the items can be examined. If participants may be accessing the questions or the prompts in different languages (e.g., spoken vs. signed) or language modalities (e.g., text vs. oral), it is important to have pilot studies to verify the questions are being interpreted as meaning similar things.

For any method of collecting data, written, oral, or signed, or observed, it is critical that researchers are aware of the required language, reading, and auxiliary skills (e.g., interview, statistics, personal relationships) needed to be a successful researcher. Because participants are diverse, research teams must also have diverse skills to accurately measure the constructs of interests. This may mean having multiple assessors or data collectors, those with a range of proficiencies that can meet the range of communication modalities. Having this kind of staffing is time and resource intensive, and often requires many more logistical and technological considerations than when only one language modality is a part of data collection.

2.8 *Drawing Conclusions*

The end of the research process—looking at the data and interpreting findings—comes at the end of a very long series of steps. Across most designs, this is a process of identifying patterns. For qualitative research, the patterns are often relational—how does discussing the importance of a deaf community highlight the relationships between people and within one's own lived experience? Themes that connect across participants, organized in a way that creates a model for understanding behavior, become the pattern recognition task. For quantitative research that involves inferential statistics, the distribution of the underlying data is synthesized to see if the pattern is different than one would expect if there were no impact of an intervention, or change in variability in responses. Group designs examine differences in patterns between groups; single case designs examine differences in patterns across time within individual participants.

In any case, when we are looking at numbers and what they mean, inferences about their significance rely upon both the patterns within our data, as well as how those patterns compare with an expected or hoped for outcome. This is most explicit in a study that utilizes standardized measures with "norms", either of performance of deaf individuals or of the general population. Comparing the results of deaf individuals as either representative or not relative to a reference group, either deaf or hearing, becomes the task of the researcher at the end of the study. Yet this assumption of "what is expected" is present in all studies across methodologies. Why is it important to know that the measured experience of deaf individuals is or is not within the expected behaviors or outcomes? Explaining the significance of data patterns, and its relationship to what is already known in the field in a way that respects that there may be value judgments from within those assumptions is the creative task of researchers as they disseminate findings.

The beginning of the research process was to review the literature and consider different theoretical perspectives. After the end of data collection, there is an opportunity to consider the theoretical rationale or study framework in light of the findings: Does the theoretical rationale provide a way to interpret the meaning of obtained results? Qualitative analytic paradigms tend to encourage researchers to consider both the consistencies and the outliers in their dataset. When a participant describes a unique experience, what is it that led to that outlier? Is it a systemic factor that differentially impacts a subgroup within the studied population? Or, perhaps, does the theoretical framework not capture that kind of experience, and thus there may be a need for a more complex or dynamic approach?

Returning to the specificity required to draft a research question that aligned with the sample and constructs in the study design can create helpful boundaries around description of data and their significance. Be precise. Avoid strident and extreme language. Make the point clearly, without overstating one's claim. It's easy to want to advocate when one sees discrimination and injustice, but without caution in how those findings are portrayed, it is possible to lose the credibility that comes from a conclusion that stays within the bounds of one's findings.

One of the greatest checks on one's conclusions from data analysis is a robust and honest limitations section. There are limitations to any study, and providing a clear explanation of those limitations helps to prevent (some) misinterpretation of the significance of your study findings. Many journals will expect to see discussion of limitations that derive from the generalizability of findings from the studied sample to a larger population. Understanding the variability and diversity in the deaf population is thus critical to writing a purposeful limitations section, as well as the implications that come from the relative representativeness of your study sample. A second key area is that of measurement. The extent to which measures are known to or could possibly contribute to invalid interpretation of test scores should be explained within a limitations section. No measure is perfect, and considerations of how one could improve the measurement in future studies are appreciated by reviewers. A final key area that could be addressed in the limitations section is challenges in implementation. Were there any parts of the study that did not proceed as planned? Was there a high attrition rate or other kind of missing data? Was the time involved in obtaining needed data compromised in anyway? A thoughtful discussion of the study implementation, beyond design implications, is an important part of being transparent about the interpretability of study findings.

The purpose of research is to deepen our understanding of our respective fields. Within deaf studies and deaf education, there are specific audiences that may read our research looking for ways to apply that information to their practice. Research articles tend to have a section on 'Implications' or 'Recommendations for Future Research' or 'Application to Practice.' It can be tempting here to be expansive and show many connections between our study results and its potential use in different arenas. One of the greatest challenges is to refrain from 'causal statements' (Robinson, Levin, Thomas, Pituch, & Vaughn, 2007). A causal statement is one that implies that we have evidence for a directional relationship that is generalizable to a given population. While not as commonly an issue in qualitative studies, where contextual factors are often integrated into the presentation of findings, some quantitative study designs provide information that is useful, but not yet at a level that meets standards for causal relationships. Without controlling for many factors, or engaging in experimental designs (e.g., with randomized control groups), it is nearly impossible to claim causality. This can be frustrating within deaf studies and deaf education because there are so few causal claims that can be made, and it feels like we are often implementing practices that suggest effectiveness, but cannot stand on a rigorous scientific foundation. Policy makers often seek information about 'what works,' and research from our field is often left saying 'research is still emerging.'

In the final phase of the research process, after all the detailed analysis and precise thinking and comprehensive discussion, we are often left with the need to distill what we have done. In other words, what is the message you wish to leave your readers? Does your tone reflect a hopeful approach, or one that is a warning of deeper challenges in the future? It is useful to consider how the presentation of your findings shape that message. For example, do you report your findings in text form only, or is there a way to provide a sign language vlog, or video excerpt from your data that are primarily visual in nature? Are there images or graphics you can design that can convey meaning alongside an abstract or summary data table? Thinking about one's audience, and their diverse ways of accessing information may lead to the development of multiple representations of key points, is a key way to consider how deaf individuals will continue to be a part of how research findings are disseminated, and later utilized, in the field.

References

Bronfenbrenner, U. (1992). Ecological systems theory. In R. Vasta (Ed.), *Six theories of child development: Revised formulations and current issues* (pp. 187–249). London, UK: Jessica Kingsley Publishers.

Cawthon, S. (2001). Teaching strategies in inclusive classrooms with Deaf students. *Journal of Deaf Studies and Deaf Education*, *6*(3), 212–225.

Cawthon, S., & Garberoglio, C. L. (Eds.). (2017). *Research methods in Deaf education: Contexts, challenges, and considerations.* New York, NY: Oxford University Press.

Cawthon, S., Leppo, R., Carr, T., & Kopriva, R. (2013). Towards accessible assessments: The promises and limitations of test item modifications for students with disabilities and English language learners. *Educational Assessment, 18*(2), 73–98.

Cawthon, S., Schoffstall, S., Wendel, E., & Jassal, Y. (2016, February). *Social skills in deaf students: How do we know what we know?* [Poster presentation]. Association of College Educators – Deaf and Hard of Hearing (ACE-DHH) Annual Conference, New York, NY.

Desimone, L., & Le Floch, K. (2004). Are we asking the right questions? Using cognitive interviews to improve surveys in education research. *Education Evaluation and Policy Analysis, 26*(1), 1–22.

Johnson, P., & Garberoglio, C. L. (2016). *Employment and wellbeing for deaf individuals* [Poster presentation]. Association of College Educators – Deaf and Hard of Hearing (ACE-DHH) Annual Conference, New York, NY.

Luckner, J. L., Sebald, A. M., Cooney, J., Young, J., & Muir, S. G. (2006). An examination of the evidence-based literacy research in deaf education. *American Annals of the Deaf, 150*, 443–456. (Original work published 2005)

Paul, P., & Moores, D. (Eds.). (2012). *Deaf epistemologies: Multiple perspectives on the acquisition of knowledge*. Gallaudet University Press.

Pepnet2. (2014). *Employment data for adults who are deaf and hard-of-hearing.* www.pepnet.org

Qi, S., & Mitchell, R. (2011). Large-scale academic achievement testing of deaf and hard-of-hearing students: Past, present, and future. *Journal of Deaf Studies and Deaf Education, 17*(1), 1–18.

Robinson, D., Levin, J., Thomas, G., Pituch, K., & Vaughn, S. (2007). The incidence of "causal" statements in teaching-and-learning research journals. *American Educational Research Journal, 44*(2), 400–413.

Stapleton, L. (2015). When being deaf is centered: d/Deaf women of color's experiences with racial/ethnic and d/Deaf identities in college. *Journal of College Student Development, 56*(6), 570–586.

Trezek, B., & Wang, Y. (2017). Evaluating evidence-based practices in reading interventions for deaf students. In Cawthon, S. & Garberoglio, C.L. (Eds.), *Research methods in deaf education: Contexts, challenges, and considerations* (pp. 277–308). New York, NY: Oxford University Press.

What Works Clearinghouse. http://ies.ed.gov/ncee/wwc/

Afterword

Paddy Ladd

I am very appreciative of being asked to contribute to this important book, with authors who are building on and expanding the movement towards Deaf diversity. I'll take this opportunity to reflect on our collective journey to arrive at this moment in time, relating it to the themes of the papers in the book. I'll interweave this with my own journey, reflecting on my own multiple identities to see if that is helpful in respect of the intersectional discourses we are starting to embark upon.

Awareness of our histories is vital; they help us take a step back to assess progress made, and gain some perspective on our achievements and our current tensions and issues, whilst maintaining our commitment to pushing onwards and opening ourselves up to personal reflection. What follows will focus mainly on the UK and U.S., but I hope it will still stimulate readers from other countries into identifying their own similarities and differences.

Sociological awareness is also crucial, and one problem we have is the virtual absence of analysis of the dynamics and differences within our 'traditional' Deaf communities, so that we can measure how, where and why they have changed over time. 'Hearing' world sociology has invested in analyses of its own societies to gain a better understanding of these characteristics, enabling the possibilities of 'filling in gaps' and advocating changes to address imbalances and oppressions.

Institutional audism has refused to fund the equivalent Deaf research, preferring to favor medical and paternalistic studies.[1] This has made it very difficult for Deaf communities' discourses to move beyond a simple assertion of their communities as monolithic entities, thus hindering the study of Deaf diversities. In *Understanding Deaf Culture: In Search of Deafhood*, I hacked away at that iceberg, but since then there have been very few attempts to examine our other traditional communities. And without an understanding of how our traditional cultures already contain important internal differences, future diversity research risks being one-dimensional, because we will not be able to 'join up the dots,' and relate one to the other.

1 Developmental Stages in the Oralist Era—Stage One

For reasons of space, this is a simplistic analysis in which important local variations cannot be explored. UK Deaf culture has moved through (at least) three

 | DOI:10.1163/9789004692299_015

stages in the Oralist era. In the first, from around 1900 onwards, those who were most 'successful' in surviving Oralism—deafened and hard of hearing persons—possessed English language and/or speech privileges. Often these persons also came from middle class hearing families, so these two factors—class and language privilege—have intersected. Those who wished to were able to use these privileges to acquire *overt* Deaf cultural capital and power in Deaf communities that were compelled to follow the norms of the majority Hearing society.

However, 'underneath' them was a form of *covert* Deaf cultural capital utilized by 'grass roots' Deaf persons, usually those from Deaf families, albeit with limited powers. These two groupings I termed the 'comprador' and 'subaltern' classes respectively. The former used to downplay or hide their Deaf identity and sign language in public; the latter would be more upfront about both, leading to clashes with hearing people that served to teach them how Deaf people should be respected. So these two groupings defined their Deaf identities differently.

The former collaborated with the hearing missioners and paternalists, whose negative views of Deaf people ruled the Deaf clubs and Deaf associations, whilst the latter grumbled to themselves but could do little to change the system. A third group, that I termed the 'pub rebels' were those who had been banned or walked out from Deaf clubs because they disagreed with the system, and met in hearing pubs. They used writing and fingerspelling to glean information from their denizens, thus picking up many useful new ideas about how the hearing world operated, and trying to bring this information back to the communities.

2 Stage Two—The Deaf Resurgence

In the mid to late 1970s, a second stage began to emerge, first in the U.S. and then across Europe, and thence—more slowly—to other parts of the world—a 'Deaf Resurgence.' This developed as a consequence of (1) political/cultural changes in hearing societies in the 1960s, (2) growing awareness of the failures of Oralism, and (3) the confirmation of sign languages as bona fide languages. The latter resulted in a paradigm shift: those with BSL skills—usually from Deaf families—became valued and were recruited by universities and television, eventually forming a 'subaltern elite.' These new cultural tensions between compradors and subaltern often manifested in what we now know as 'D versus d' discourses. The subaltern elite and the new hearing allies aimed—not least through the new bilingualism movement—to create an era that they assumed would 'float all Deaf boats,' whether white, BIPOC or other minorities, but had to focus on the primary struggle—to defeat the medical and paternalistic forces that controlled Deaf lives.

3 Situating Myself

As one of the very first to be mainstreamed, as a (then partially deaf) working-class white male,[2] I had English language and speech privileges, and a degree of knowledge about how the hearing world operated. Whilst at college I entered the atmosphere of the 1960s and became both a hippie (with a concomitant love of music and the arts that challenged the status quo—to the extent that I could participate in it) and a political activist. The hippies were a new sub-culture that challenged Western cultural norms, looked to other societies and minorities for different ways of being and living, and campaigned to support oppressed peoples around the world. This was a life changing experience, but I could never fully 'belong' because group communication was just too difficult, leaving me unable to relax and become myself—whoever that was.

The hippie movement moved on to divide into (at least) two different paths—either drop out of 'straight society' and set up communes, live off the land and so on, or to enter the system and try to change it from within. So I decided to apply to become a teacher of Deaf children. But the very people who had told me when I was growing up that 'I was not really deaf' were the ones who then rejected my application, saying that 'We don't accept deaf people'! That was my first abrupt awakening to the lies of Oralism. So I applied to be a social worker with Deaf people, and was fortunate to be accepted by a far-seeing boss, who saw something in me and felt I would learn to sign 'on the job.'

On entering UK Deaf life in 1974, I was shocked to find that I seemed to be in a minority of one. It felt like the sixties had never happened. The dark hand of Oralism was in absolute control of the lives of children and families. And the atmosphere of Deaf clubs and Deaf associations—grey suited missioners and Deaf stooges ruling Deaf clubs and Deaf associations—felt like travelling back in time to the 1930s. Dissent was almost unthinkable because of the immense power they wielded over Deaf lives, whilst the number of Deaf professionals could be counted on two hands.

Taking the plunge into my lifelong journey towards what we now know as Deafhood required me to first 'decolonize' my own mindset and accept myself as a Deaf person. The work with Deaf teenagers—first to actually find them, then setting up a youth club, a soccer team, vacation projects and so on—was work that today we would call 'rescuing the children'—helping build resilience and Deaf identity.

At this time, the first wave of Deaf BIPOC children of immigrants (from what is known in the UK as the 'Windrush generation') were just entering their teenage years, and undergoing truly awful educational experiences in mainstream education. The spread of mainstreaming meant that, unlike the previous generations of white Deaf children, they were not getting the chance to attend residential schools to build their Deaf identities, and there were as yet no BIPOC Deaf elders to inspire and guide them.

The teenagers came from Deaf schools and 'partially hearing units' (PHUs)—so my own nascent Deaf identity chimed with the latter, and the work itself made it easier to gain acceptance (and my sign name) from them all. In those days there were no sign language classes, so my first steps towards what was later called BSL developed from what they taught me. For all this to happen, my 'main' identity as a hippie activist had to be set aside, minimized, because society was still hostile to hippies and their ideas.

4 Resurgence and Identity

I realized it was not enough to spend my life working in one small locality—that a national rebellion was needed. But rebels were few on the ground. Eventually some of us—from the 'pub groups' around the country—found each other and were able to set up the National Union of the Deaf (NUD) in 1976 to campaign for Deaf issues. We were, amongst other activities, (1) fighting for Deaf control of organizations, (2) making a model Deaf TV program, then campaigning for a regular BBC TV program (*SeeHear*—achieved in 1981 and still running), and (3) fighting Oralism and mainstreaming.[3] At that time, Total Communication (TC) was the goal—sign languages were not acknowledged as bona fide languages, so envisaging bilingualism was not yet possible and even teachers who supported TC refused to countenance the idea of Deaf teachers.

At this point in history, the NUD had no problem with framing ourselves as both Deaf and disabled.[4] We met frequently with the disabled organizations to both learn from them and to argue against their advocacy of mainstreaming. My still-developing Deaf identity was not a problem in the NUD, since (1) the skills I had learned as a hippie activist were very useful to our people, and (2) Deaf people who wanted to work for change welcomed anyone, Deaf or hearing, who was willing to do this. We were a very disparate group that included inspiring models from the oldest generations of fingerspelling-only 'Deaf and Dumb' people, like the legendary A.F. Dimmock.[5] However, the missioners and their supporter still argued that I was not a 'proper Deaf person'—because 'Deaf people do not get involved in politics'!

In the 1980s, BSL research—and thus bilingualism—was a game changer, enabling the crucial paradigm shift described earlier. Another—achieved by the NUD's pressure—was the politicization of the British Deaf Association (BDA) upon its change of leadership. They finally employed Deaf staff—myself among them—and we developed a Manifesto that began to press political parties on Deaf issues, including BSL recognition, bilingualism, and so on. Working for them felt like finally 'coming home' to a Deaf identity, and from then onwards I always signed when communicating with hearing people. However, 'respectability' was important for this work, so my hippie identity still had to be suppressed—cutting off my hair being the most obvious example—so I was still a very divided person.

But 'home' did not last, because the BDA persuaded me that, with the experience I had gained through making the NUD TV program, I had to go and work for *SeeHear,* which was riven with audism, and needed to be turned into the national consciousness-raising tool the NUD had always intended. I accepted this with a heavy heart, which sank further because the program's presenters had to use 'Simcom.'[6] So part of my mission was to utilize my speech privilege in order to fight from the inside to achieve BSL presenters on the program. Being a Simcom presenter gained me some credit with the comprador class, but severely damaged my acceptance as a Deaf person with the subaltern elite. This was a very painful experience—but someone had to do it. After two years of fighting, we finally achieved BSL presenters, and this has remained the norm ever since.

In terms of program content, one priority was to push for the inclusion and thus initial recognition of Deaf arts—Signpoetry, storytelling and Signed Song. Another was to address Deaf minority issues. BIPOC friends were telling me horrifying stories of their rejection by white Deaf clubs, and had very few allies. So in 1983 we ensured that they could make their own edition of *SeeHear* to try and raise awareness of these issues, and then did the same for LGBTQ+ Deaf people, whose own club was refused membership to the BDA. After I left *SeeHear* to create the LDVP (London Deaf Video Project) under the BDA, we focused again on those two communities, training presenters who would go on to work in Deaf TV and arts.

UK Deaf arts and Deaf history slowly began to re-emerge. The British Signpoet Dorothy Miles, plus the influence from the U.S. of the National Theatre of the Deaf (NTD) and the De'VIA movement were key to the former, and were important for many reasons. Deaf arts challenge and expand the limits of what Deaf cultures had formerly thought was possible or significant, as Kelstone, Durr, Christie and Wilkins, and Sutton-Spence have shown us in this book.

Other important U.S. influences included the historico-political writings of Harlan Lane, who also effected a paradigm shift, asserting for the first time in the post-Oralist era that these so-called hearing-impaired individuals actually constituted multi-generational communities with their own cultural histories and noble battles against Oralist oppression.

Since around 1977 I had dreamed of seeing Deaf Studies becoming an academic discipline. The initial inroads were made by sign linguistics and the training of BSL teachers and by the end of the decade, the dream of Deaf Studies itself was starting its own journey in the newly established Centre for Deaf Studies (CDS) in the University of Bristol.

Padden and Humphries in the U.S. had made a start on explaining aspects of U.S. Deaf culture itself, and I identified this as the most important challenge—proving the existence of that concept. There were many reasons for this, including boosting Deaf morale and raising consciousness, but one of the most important was that Oralists were claiming that the Deaf persons challenging them were 'not typical Deaf people,' but isolated individuals with chips on their shoulders! Thus it was necessary to prove that Deaf communities had traditional *collective* values, norms and beliefs that disagreed with those imposed on the community by Oralists, missioners and compradors.

I joined CDS in 1992, and my PhD, covering the approximate period from 1930 to 1970, resulted in *Understanding Deaf Culture: In Search of Deafhood,* which was published by Multilingual Matters in 2003. This was intended to be Volume 1, and the second volume was to be focused on modern diversity, covering BIPOC, youth, Deaf families, Deaf arts, and so on. Because of institutional audism, it was not possible to get research funding for Volume 2, so the only route to developing those subjects was via our MSc in Deaf Studies, plus students' dissertations and PhD topics.

Ironically, people's attention worldwide focused not on the Deaf culture concept, but the concept of Deafhood itself, and so I had to respond to that demand. This required giving workshops that were essentially 'Deaf 101,' since very few people knew anything about their own history, or realized that their low self-esteem was not their own fault, but a consequence of Oralism. As such, Deafhood has been very valuable.

But what was often overlooked (despite being explained in my own workshops) was that Deafhood already stressed intersectionality—before that term had come into use. In 'Volume 1' this focused on (1) unpacking the importance of class diversity in Deaf identities, (2) challenging the Deaf cultural binarism of 'Deaf world' versus 'Hearing world', and (3) flagging up the importance of Deaf minority identities, together with understanding/respecting the cultures from which some had emerged. This had to be undertaken whilst also respecting traditional Deaf cultural perspectives, and how and why they had come to take their existing forms. It is thus heartening to see the work of Hill, Dunn and Cooke in this book, and I hope there will be much more of this in years to come.

5 The Emergence of Stage Three

During the 21st century, stage three—the assertion of Deaf diversity, hand in hand with a growing Deaf internationalism that has benefited from Internet developments and cheaper travel—has been able to emerge. These privileges also emerged from the work of the battling pioneers of the previous decades, both white and BIPOC, who opened doors that previously did not exist, creating new spaces and platforms, and inducing changes in societies' attitudes. And generations who benefited from signing educations now had more confidence and better academic results, enabling the possibilities of gaining professional positions, and experiencing the positive changes in many hearing people's attitudes. A wide range of forms of Deaf creativity are now becoming visible, and sign language recognition campaigns, such as the BSL movement formed by our Federation of Deaf People (FDP) (which was also the first UK organization with BIPOC co-leadership), are spreading around the world.

The creation of a conceptual base of Deaf community and cultural information in Deaf Studies has also enabled the opening of doors for the long overdue emergence of young Deaf academics, who now have their own international organizations and activities such as *Dr. Deaf*. What has been most encouraging is that, instead of taking a solipsistic path focused on their own individual careers, they have immediately embraced the need to focus on diversity, to include the Global South in their praxis, and to start thinking about how to share their findings with grass roots community members. The work of Yang in this book is also heartening—there is so much more we need to learn about all our countries' communities.

Another significant extension of 21st century Deaf identity diversity has been the gradual acceptance of Deaf signed song. Pioneered by Musign in the U.S. in the 1980s, it has always been a contentious development—seen by many as 'not a Deaf thing.' This of course is understandable, not least because of the many instances where it has been used by partially Deaf, deafened and hearing persons in ways that rendered it inaccessible to most Deaf persons. There is also an interesting intersectional feature here. As that wise U.S. Black Deaf elder Carolyn McCaskill pointed out to me back in the 1990s, love of (Black) music was often a marker of Black Deaf cultural difference that problematized the white-centred 'D-d' binary construction.

The work of Cruz, together with Cripps and colleagues in this volume offers significant insights into Deaf musical possibilities, whilst Signmark has shown us that Deaf-political hip-hop—with beats that *all* Deaf people could feel—can be an important contribution in carrying the Deaf message to wider society, and others have since followed. A parallel development, the growth of sign interpreters at hearing concerts has also begun to break down barriers and place Deaf people in the public eye, and has its own significance—although this is a contentious field that I do not have space to explore.

The third stage is also notable for less positive reasons—the spread of mainstreaming and the closure of Deaf schools—and also the closure of Deaf clubs, which were so vital for local community health, and also served as bases from which national activities of all kinds, including political action, could be built. The irony was that the subaltern elite who used to support the clubs had expended their energies entering the newly opened professional doors, and mostly stepped back from Deaf club responsibilities. And, despite the short term efforts of pressure groups like the NUD and the FDP, the lack of consistent campaigning courage by national Deaf associations has allowed Deaf schools to be pushed to the point of closure. So much of the progress of the Deaf Resurgence is now under threat.

So on the one hand we see very positive *'external'* Deaf gains, resulting in a new nascent young middle class, albeit that many do not have (or even know of, or value) traditional Deaf cultural roots in Deaf club life. Some of these have placed individual careerism above traditional Deaf collectivism, whilst large numbers of ex-mainstreamed Deaf people are being left behind in a classless limbo. This is where the loss of Deaf clubs, and thus learning to socialize with, understand and support Deaf subaltern, has hurt us. I am not the person to evaluate the pros and cons of social media in this respect, but it is clear that holding forth from behind a keyboard as an individual is no substitute for real Deaf collective interaction.

The '80s pioneers' are retiring, and we are in a race against time to find enough people to 'rescue' Deaf youth, to save Deaf schools, and to ensure they are well-run and Deaf-led. So we are still in crisis mode, battling to ensure that our communities have a future in an era of neo-eugenics. In this respect, some might argue that this issue—which benefits *all* Deaf people—should be a priority. But of course we are also now in an era of long-needed diversity recognition, that requires us to turn *inwards* and work through all the issues that involves—at the same time.[7]

6 Connecting My Identities

Whilst attending the *Deaf Way* milestone conference in Washington DC in 1989, events occurred that finally enabled me to connect my 'two selves'—Deaf and hippie—for the first time. The hippie band the *Grateful Dead* were in town at the same time, and I chanced upon Deaf folks who were attending the concerts. There were around 30 of us, Deaf and hearing, and that experience changed my life. I had finally found people who shared some of my cherished values and beliefs, whilst also being Deaf. This then became a springboard for more activism—to get the band to agree to establish a DeafZone in which interpreters could operate. My knowledge of their songs (as well as the shortage of hippie interpreters!) meant that I became one of the interpreters until my hearing finally faded out. This, we think, was the world's first DeafZone, and one that continues to this day, drawing together like-minded Deaf and hearing people, and creating some new allies. However, this connecting of my identities could only happen within the Zone—the rest of my life had to be lived outside of this experience, with brief vacation journeys to replenish those energies.

Another important part of my identity is centred in Deaf arts and in my own creativity. I had already started to write political SignSongs in the 1980s, with the aim of giving Deaf teenagers their own artform they could be proud of when surrounded by mocking hearing peers, and one of these was eventually broadcast on BBC television in 1991. My commitment to Deaf community duties meant that this project had to be put on ice until 2020, when I published *Signs Of Freedom* and *Songs Of Deafhood.*[8] I continue to believe that this can be a vital tool in Deaf liberation, since we can 'exploit' hearing people's love of music to build bridges and create spaces for our own signing talents to break through—provided the SignSongs are, where possible, Deaf-created and accessible to *all* Deaf people. I still live in hopes that this part of my identity can find a way to blossom and be sustained.

A similar more explicitly political Deaf theatre is also possible too, and much needed. We have to learn to present our *history* of oppression to hearing people if we are to achieve meaningful change.[9] These and many other forms of 'Deaf-Gain' are also key to making progress in this third stage.

There are other points to make in respect of identity, however. Many people seem to be under the illusion that self-identification as Deaf is all that needs to happen. But identity has two dimensions—the other being Deaf peoples' *acceptance* of oneself as being Deaf. This is a complex and tense issue that generates much informal discourse—but as yet lacks research into these dynamics.

The other point is that being bi/multilingual and multicultural may also mean that *one does not fully belong anywhere*, does not feel 100% at home every minute of their lives. There are always parts of ourselves that make us feel different from others, whether those be class, gender, race, disability, and so on. This is certainly still true for myself. The subject needs more discussion than we have space here to analyze, because different groupings will experience these differences to different degrees at different times. But it is vitally important that we start to recognize the complex psychological dimensions involved—doing so by *sharing and listening to others* is a part of the movement towards stage four.

7 Moving to Stage Four

I envisage stage four as one in which the recognition of diversity is now translated into permanent *action*. This requires Deaf cultures to move on from the 'Deaf-hearing' binary so common in White Deaf Resurgence discourses, to accept that *all* Deaf people are inherently multicultural—that is, that we contain within ourselves our national Deaf culture *and* our hearing cultures. In other words—and I am being mischievous here—even the 'most Deaf' person among us can be said to have a hearing person inside us! All our societies' creations—from laws, social structures and religions, through to sports, entertainments, hobbies, and so on—are *'hearing'* creations. Deaf communities have adopted and adapted many of these—but we still need to acknowledge their origins.

Instead of pretending to have a monolithic Deaf identity that merely pays lip service at best to the existence of the UK, U.S., etc. cultures that permeate us, we have to own these sides of ourselves. Then we can debate and consciously draw from these whatever positive cultural and political features we deem worthy of use for the betterment of *all* our own Sign Language Peoples.

And conversely, we must (1) recognize that our Deaf cultures have absorbed negative features of those hearing cultures, like racism, sexism, classism, ableism, audism, and so on. We must then (2) examine these in (Deafhood) consciousness-raising workshops, guided by those Deaf minorities, in order to identify these negative features, recognize that these do not serve our peoples well, and discard them. In so doing we must address our privileges and strive by our actions to ensure greater Deaf equity. We also need to acknowledge that *almost all of us* have some privileges, whether they be race, class, gender, language skills, speech skills, and so on (although of course some have more than others!) and these need to be calmly unpacked in supportive environments.

All this is a crucial part of Deafhood philosophy; embracing multiplicity and diversity in order to *empower, unify and advance* our own communities—and *enlarging* them by welcoming deaf persons, hearing parents and families and other potential allies in a process of mutual sharing and understanding.[10] This will help move the Deaf Resurgence into the next era of *Deaf Reconstruction.*

Another example of the work that lies before us in this stage is ensuring that Deaf communities—and especially Deaf 'leaders'—understand that Deaf educational oppression is a *political* issue, *worthy* of being seen as equivalent to racism, sexism and so on. Decades of Oralism have diminished the self-respect needed to make this claim and act on it, as well as isolating us from the progressive hearing political arenas.

So we need to develop a *real* understanding of how politics works in the hearing world, both at the parliamentary level and—crucially—in campaigning organizations. Our peoples have been shut out for so long that very few people in the UK, for example, have that knowledge, and often those who do were formerly mainstreamed, and thus not sufficiently involved in the day to day lives of Deaf communities to become leaders there. Although the progress being made is heartening—for example in the sign language recognition movements—Deaf education is often omitted from that battle.

There are two potential 'models' for such unifying work. One is to look to the remarkable 21st century developments in Brazil—the rapid growth of the Deaf movement, and how it has managed to organize national campaigns for multilingualism, with the huge growth in numbers of those holding degrees and doctorates—and consider how these activities might be applied to one's own country.

We should also look to learn from positive examples of Deaf-hearing relationships in and around Deaf minorities, for example the relationships LGBTQ+ Deaf groups have with their hearing peers, and also in certain BIPOC communities. Because those hearing groups and communities have been battling oppression for so many years, they have much life experience and cultural wisdom to teach Deaf people how to find the courage to overcome fear and low self-esteem (still key features of Deaf cultures) and about the importance of working for the benefit of their peoples above individualist careerist aspirations.

Recently, in working on my *Deaf Pedagogies* books, (and this despite my lifelong commitment to anti-racism), thanks to BIPOC colleagues I have become even more aware of the sheer enormity of racism as it plays out in U.S. Deaf communities.[11] They are right to say that the traditional concept of 'Deaf culture' is White—and that the U.S. actually contains distinct Deaf *cultures*. And there is so much more to be learned if we ensure that we are open and listen with our hearts to what people are telling us.

This present historical moment is tense—we are on rocky ground. The emergence from oppression of so many Deaf minorities—and the ongoing resistance to what they are telling us—means we are entering an era of competing claims for priority. Our communities are too small to be able to continue maintaining divisions and resisting the unity of diversity. This is why we need to appreciate the importance of understanding history and its trajectory; accept that these are not only challenging times, but *necessarily* challenging times, that we have to pass through and resolve if we are all to make progress in the fourth stage towards genuine equity and equality. This book and its authors have thus made a significant contribution towards the important task of assisting Deaf Studies and other Deaf domains to understand power relationships throughout history—including Deaf histories—in order to embrace these ongoing challenges and advance towards a more positive future.

Acknowledgements

Deep thanks to Dai O'Brien and Maartje de Meulder for their feedback. All remaining shortcomings are my own.

Notes

1 Following the Deaf Resurgence, sign linguistics practitioners have managed to obtain significant funding—but only a small proportion of that has been expended on sociolinguistics. Similarly, interpreter funding has largely omitted to examine sociological and cultural issues.

2 Unpacking my white male and working class 'selves,' their privileges and oppressions is too complex and lengthy a process for this essay, so I focus on my 'Deaf,' 'hippie' and artistic selves.

3 One especially notable example was creating a book—*'Rights of The Deaf Child'*—in 1982, explaining how mainstreaming fulfilled UN definitions of genocide, and trying to engage with the UN on this.

4 Baynton's paper in this book (Chapter 1) forms an excellent platform for exploration and debating this issue.

5 Dimmock was a Deaf activist and writer, also known for his regular columns in the *British Deaf News*, that ran for over 50 years. These collected Deaf news and information around the world, utilising his many international contacts, and his ability to translate from French, German and other languages, including Latin. His educational travel holidays that he organized and led for decades, were also virtually unique during this era. At the age of 75, on being awarded the MBE (Member of the British Empire) by the Queen, he stated that the most important thing about the award was that it would assist in continuing to campaign for Deaf rights.

6 Signing and speaking at the same time.

7 Cawthon's chapter will be most helpful in designing such appropriate, Deaf-centered, research.

8 See www.deafhoodsignsongs.com

9 Cf. the recent UK play, *The Extraordinary Wall Of Silence,* partly based on Deafhood principles: see https://ad-infinitum.org/extraordinary-wall-of-silence

10 One thing I noticed with both the NUD and the FDP—both took positive attitudes to having hearing allies whilst insisting on Deaf leadership. They preferred political activism to get on with trying to make big changes, rather than being content to sit around simply criticising 'The Hearing,' engaging in d/D arguments, or finding small weaknesses in others in order to 'cancel' them.

11 The UK, and indeed the rest of the world, has plenty of its own racism to face up to, of course, but the U.S. history of racism in respect of its Deaf cultures is much longer and more deeply embedded.

APPENDIX A

De'VIA Manifesto

Deaf View/Image Art
De'VIA represents Deaf artists and perceptions based on their Deaf experiences.[1] It uses formal art elements with the intention of expressing innate cultural or physical Deaf experience. These experiences may include Deaf metaphors, Deaf perspectives, and Deaf insight in relationship with the environment (both the natural world and Deaf cultural environment), spiritual and everyday life.

De'VIA can be identified by formal elements such as Deaf artists' possible tendency to use contrasting colors and values, intense colors, contrasting textures. It may also most often include a centralized focus, with exaggeration or emphasis on facial features, especially eyes, mouths, ears, and hands. Currently, Deaf artists tend to work in human scale with these exaggerations, and not exaggerate the space around these elements.

There is a difference between Deaf artists and De'VIA. Deaf artists are those who use art in any form, media, or subject matter, and who are held to the same artistic standards as other artists. De'VIA is created when the artist intends to express their Deaf experience through visual art. De'VIA may also be created by deafened or hearing artists, if the intention is to create work that is born of their Deaf experience (a possible example would be a hearing child of Deaf parents). It is clearly possible for Deaf artists not to work in the area of De'VIA.

While applied and decorative arts may also use the qualities of De'VIA (high contrast, centralized focus, exaggeration of specific features), this manifesto is specifically written to cover the traditional fields of visual fine arts (painting, sculpture, drawing, photography, printmaking) as well as alternative media when used as fine arts such as fiber arts, ceramics, neon, and collage.

Created in May, 1989, at The Deaf Way.

The signatories were: Dr. Betty G. Miller, painter; Dr. Paul Johnston, sculptor; Dr. Deborah M. Sonnenstrahl, art historian; Chuck Baird, painter; Guy Wonder, sculptor; Alex Wilhite, painter; Sandi Inches Vasnick, fiber artist; Nancy Creighton, fiber artist; and Lai-Yok Ho, video artist.

Note

1 Text of the De'VIA Manifesto (1989) retrieved from http://www.deafart.org/Deaf_Art_/deaf_art_.html

 | DOI:10.1163/9789004692299_016

APPENDIX B

Manifesto of Surdism

Surdism is an artistic, philosophical and cultural movement initiated by Arnaud Balard (2009). This movement offers a renewed and strengthened affirmation of Deaf culture. A manifesto was written and published by Arnaud Balard in 2009, which defines the philosophy targeted by this groundbreaking project of cultural expression.

Reputedly 'invisible,' the Deaf* community paradoxically offers a visual and linguistic culture ready to be seen and shared. And artists have this specific advantage of being able to give life to this identity originality. They support, narrate and reveal this culture of signs, this very particular experience of being Deaf in a world which is not.

Concretely, the movement of Surdism offers a shared name under which each one can individually exist and assert oneself. If an artist creates alone, he can easily be thought of as isolated and be said to represent no one except himself. When several artists opt for the approach which consists in getting united under a single movement, they gain—each one individually—credibility and visibility. And through a snowball effect, they provoke another perception of the Deaf community they claim they belong to. The goal is clearly to gather all the artists (sculpture, painting, photography, literature, signed poetry, cinema, theater, installations, videos …) who are willing to, in order to strengthen the focus on the existence of the Deaf world.

Through exchanges and exhibitions on Deaf cultural, philosophical and artistic topics (experiences, history, politics, language, audism, deafhood …), surdism offers to consolidate the emergence of Deaf artists. It is important to understand that there are very few ways to save records of history, values and traditions of the Deaf culture. Art is one of these ways. By naming Deaf art, we give it life and we define it. A legitimate, strong, unique act which conveys the idea of belonging to the world. Naming oneself means purely and solely to exist.

Surdism therefore aims to be a powerful act of emancipation, and to support an improved mutual recognition of Deaf creation.

(*) = by Deaf we mean any person who is included into the Deaf community. This term encompasses and connects people who master sign language, who share the fundamental values which consolidate the community. Thus, it does not refer to audiograms.

Arnaud Balard artist august 2012

We, Deaf, turn down any discrimination created by the exclusive and oppressive socio-medical vision—called AUDISM—from which springs imprisonment, depreciation and denial of our identity.

 DOI:10.1163/9789004692299_017

Indeed, if audists consider being deaf as an infirmity, a suffering to be looked after and cured, a sensory lack to repair, and think it is necessary to act very precociously on this impairment, we, Deaf, do not perceive it this way, and wish to express it vigorously but proudly.

This manifesto is a vibrating appeal to express once again that we are Deaf, yes, but not disabled people. We don't want to be seen through this single frame of reparation, which mentally and intellectually alienates us by summarizing us with a mere stereotype of hearing impaired individual.

To be able to stand up for ourselves as 'other' but certainly not 'less,' we must oppose this reductive trend of thought. Together, we must mobilize to restore, to its right social, political and public place, being Deaf.

Being Deaf is a relationship, it implies an exchange between two people, and it reveals an unshared communication. It is only that, at the beginning.

No one is deaf alone, one is in relation to the other.

And it is the vision from the other that the most urgently needs to be fixed.

Manifesto of Surdism

Surdism is an artistic, philosophical and cultural movement which aims to carry militant values against the still lingering obscurantism which make us prisoners, we Deaf, of judgements, and above all of a destiny, on which we don't really have the right to sign.

Surdism is thus a revendication and a signing out in public space, and to get its aim, it must be clearly written, read, signed and shared in order to exist.

This is why this manifesto conveys with visibility this act of emancipation which refutes audism and its dominant and censuring point of view.

It is a Deaf intellectual and artistic movement through which we signify:

- We, surdists, offer to express ourselves by literature, theater, cinema, painting, sculpture or any other form of expression, by exploring anything which concerns, in one way or another, being Deaf, Deafhood, Deaf people and their position in social space.
- We claim that our movement carries creativity, inclusion, complementarity and mutual enrichment.
- We will artistically mobilize in order to create a frame of mind of Deafhood—which intends to be an enlightened attitude that anyone can share.

As long as the linguistic specificity is acknowledged and accepted for its true worth, and as long as the values of exchange, respect, communication and equality are shared.

We want therefore surdism to create and sharpen a Deafhood in other people; let it be a bridge between you and us, a walkway that each one can cross freely.

- We support and mobilize ourselves through our artistic means, unambiguously, to carve a space for the Deaf community's linguistic and sociocultural specificity.
- We stand up for artistic expression about, of and through Sign Language as a link of social union, and not as a linguistic and cultural division.
- We pay tribute to those who openly and publicly supported and carried our potential, despite of and against obstacles, through Deaf History.

Well-known or obscure, they carried up the faith of surdism to us, even though they did not name it explicitly. It is incumbent to us to redefine it, to connect to each other, and to work to make our social place visible and real.

Surdism wants to be an international collective movement which carries a positive, constructive, militant and inclusive philosophy. You people who share these values, do join us!

Let's denounce the prejudices, let's stimulate our creativity and call in a new Community force in the spirit of universality, beyond our national borders.

Fellow members, express ourselves through surdism !

Audism denigrates,
Deafhood welcomes,
Surdism reveals.

Reference

Balard, A. (2009). Surdism manifesto. Text of the surdism manifesto. https://surdistsunited.com/devia-history/surdism-manifesto/

APPENDIX C

Music for the Deaf

A Qualitative Approach

Ana L. Cruz

Note: The article discusses a case study that was presented in January 1996 at the Conference on Qualitative Research in Education *at the University of Georgia-Athens. The article, based on the presentation, was published online as:* Cruz, A. L. de C. (1997) Music for the Deaf: A qualitative approach. In L. D. Labbo &S. L. Field (Eds.), QUIG 1997 Conference Proceedings (n. pp.). *The Proceedings website is not active anymore and the article, therefore, is no longer accessible. The article has been cited and reprinting it in this book, with permission from the Proceedings editors, makes it available again for the interested reader. Please note that the article is a reprint and reflects the status of 1997. Based on developments in the field of Deaf Studies, Deaf education, and the author's growth since the late-90s, the author today would refrain from using the phrase 'the Deaf' in the title and instead would choose a title such as 'Music for Deaf Students: A Qualitative Research Study.' Once again, the article was not updated (except for the few added endnotes and correction of some typos), thus, Theoretical Framework, Review of the Literature, and References are not current. Nevertheless, the data, interpretation, and the case study itself provide an interesting example of the application of music in working with d/Deaf children in a school setting and its ramifications. It also illustrates that there are teachers of d/Deaf students, who since the 1990s (and before), have been using music as a teaching tool with their d/Deaf students. The study is a view from the past guiding possibilities for the future.*

1 Introduction

The literature in music and deafness reveals that Deaf individuals' experience with music has not yet received much attention. For many years Deaf people were not allowed to participate in any form of musical activity as a consequence of their hearing impairment. 'Music as something that Deaf people cannot do' is a common belief which many people have repeated throughout the years, without really reflecting upon the veracity of this statement. It became an ideological concept which was either imposed (through hegemonic relationship) upon those with hearing impairment or was learned (by Deaf people) as a means of cultural identity, or both. All of this is

 | DOI:10.1163/9789004692299_018

based upon the 'scientific' or medical fact that without the auditory skills music could not be experienced.

There are cases of Deaf individuals, however, who have overcome the ideological 'barrier,' and have had successful experiences with music[1] (see Edwards, 1974; Kapla, 1975; Robbins, 1980; Darrow, 1985). In order to address issues directly associated with ideological concepts in music and deafness, this study follows the theoretical framework of critical theory, because it is believed that the Deaf community has a disadvantageous position in relation to the hearing society. The hearing society, underestimating the capacity of Deaf people, reduces their opportunity to be exposed to music by claiming that without the sense of hearing music is an invalid experience.

The present case study was conducted at a [U.S.] southeastern school for the Deaf at the middle school level, taking specifically into consideration the instructional techniques employed and the teacher's perspectives. The study was designed to address and better understand the phenomenon of Deaf people successfully engaged in music activities.

2 A Synopsis of the Relevant Literature

According to the literature in music and deafness, teaching the whole body through body movements in order to perceive musical vibrations, rhythms, musical dynamics or any musical elements is a way of helping a Deaf individual to construct his/her own concepts of music and consequently to understand them. Robbins and Robbins (1980) state that all children, including Deaf children, benefit from activities in which *movement* is necessary. Movement and music used together to motivate and help a child to control his/her own body can be a particularly valuable means of expression for a Deaf child (Robbins and Robbins, 1980).

Research has shown that there are no significant differences between normally hearing and Deaf children with respect to music caused solely by limitations in auditory skills (Edwards, 1975). In this context it is important to note that Deaf individuals always have some residual hearing and that only approximately 10% of the Deaf population is considered to be 'completely' deaf (Robbins and Robbins, 1980). Therefore, it is important to provide Deaf individuals with the opportunity to use their residual hearing in the appreciation and understanding of music.

There are some Deaf individuals who, because of the nature of their hearing loss, are able to appreciate the lower sounds better. Therefore, if musical stimuli are accentuated in the frequency range in which the Deaf individual is most sensitive, along with providing the opportunity to experience music in a concrete way, the process of learning and appreciating music might become more meaningful.

In the case of music instruction, Robbins and Robbins (1980) state that music should be used not solely to support body movements, but as a *meaningful* part of the activity. The way music becomes meaningful to some Deaf individuals still has to be explored in depth. Exposure and experience cause the child to build musical concepts and to express them, which might consequently result in understanding and appreciating music. Edwards (1975) emphasizes that *understanding*, as a means of gaining concepts in music, is crucial for Deaf children engaged in musical activities. Thus, without the opportunity to experience music, Deaf children are not able to make music a meaningful experience.

A meaningful and effective experience with music is largely affected by the qualification of the professionals involved. A special qualification for educators attempting to provide music for Deaf students is necessary and requires expertise in aspects of both music and special education (Kapla, 1975; Darrow, 1991).

The teacher, specifically, plays an important role in devising methods which can provide Deaf children with meaningful musical experiences. Methods which involve the principle of 'learning-by-doing' with emphasis on extensive sensory experience (Shehan, 1986) are crucial to the development of Deaf children's neuromuscular feeling for music. As a result of the exposure to concrete experiences with music (learning-by-doing), children can develop feelings and construct images in their minds in which an "understanding" of music concepts might occur (Shehan, 1986).

Normally hearing people tend to view music as a phenomenon which must be experienced primarily auditorially. Therefore, to experience music without the ability to hear is considered a difficult if not impossible task. For these reasons, some people still think negatively about the possibility of having Deaf people experiencing and making music (Edwards, 1975). Ignoring these prejudices, some educators have used music with Deaf children (Darrow, 1985).

A hegemonic relationship appears to be established between normally hearing people and Deaf people based on auditorial skills. This hegemonic relationship appears to limit Deaf people's opportunity to be exposed to music by suggesting that without normal hearing music is an invalid experience. As Gibson (1986) notes in describing the critical theory of Gramsci (1971), hegemony is fabricated through ideology; through ideology the dominant class [hearing community] shapes the beliefs of the subordinate class [Deaf community] to the extent that the subordinate class starts to accept its own oppression. Thus, the Deaf community has learned to accept the belief promulgated by the hearing community of its "inability" to understand or experience music.

3 Methods of Data Collection and Data Analysis

This study is based on three sources of qualitative data reflecting the teacher perspective in applying music for Deaf students: 1) 15 hours of participant-observation were conducted for the purpose of watching the classroom teacher develop music activities in her classroom; 2) informal conversations with the teacher were carried out focusing on the applicability of music for Deaf children (included in this category are Deaf children with multiple handicaps); 3) a ninety minute tape-recorded interview was conducted, particularly scrutinizing how music has been used in the classroom context and what reasons have led a teacher to devote time to music activities for Deaf children. The tape-recorded interview took place in the participant's classroom during the time the students were involved in an outside-the-classroom activity under supervision of the teacher's assistant.

The analysis of the information was based on the following procedures: 1) the notes taken during the participant-observation and the notes obtained from the informal conversations were read; 2) the tape-recorded interview was transcribed, and the transcription was read several times. Rereading the notes and the interview transcription allowed the researcher to organize the collected information into categories. Once the categories were established, the next phase involved the identification of patterns and themes. These patterns were used in developing the study's interpretation. The interpretation was constructed by finding linkages and relationships among the patterns which emerged from the analysis.

4 Description of the Participant

4.1 *Susan Cox: The Teacher*

Susan Cox,[2] a middle school teacher, was selected as the participant for this case study. The selection was based on the participant's involvement with Deaf education, shown through discussions on a computer network. Susan Cox has worked in Deaf education for twenty-nine years. Her academic background includes a master's degree in special education with a concentration in learning disabilities. In the field of music, the participant possesses, what she calls, "a basic elementary music [education]" with knowledge of musical reading and rhythms. Susan learned how to play percussion instruments and started to take accordion lessons as well. Further, as part of her education in music, Susan has sung in choirs and has attended workshops in music. Susan's work experience includes teaching auditory training for seven years. This was how (and when) she started to use music for Deaf students. Since then, Susan applied music as a daily activity in the classroom. Presently, she teaches a class of profoundly Deaf children with multiple handicaps using music.

4.2 *Susan Cox's Students*

Susan has a group of six profoundly Deaf students with multiple handicaps (e.g., physical handicaps, mental retardation, learning disabilities).[3] A few of them possess some behavioral problems, making the whole process of teaching even more difficult. The participant states: "in my room are the students nobody wants. They have so many things wrong with them, that it is very difficult to teach them." The students' mental age varies from two to two-and-half to six or seven years. Their chronological age is between eleven and fifteen years.

The students seem not to have received proper education/attention throughout the years; consequently, they seem to exhibit some odd behaviors that usually are not very well accepted by our society. Susan says:

> some of their behavior are weird or odd,[...] I think that back in the old days, they [people in general] are used to put kids into institutions, because they don't know how to work with them. They don't have patience. It takes a lot of patience, a lot!

5 Data Presentation and Discussion

The analysis revealed that Susan Cox had a set of beliefs or guiding principles about teaching, learning, and students' performance that were related to the process of making music part of the Deaf children's daily activities in school. Several patterns or themes emerged in the analysis of her beliefs or guiding principles. Although they are interwoven with one another, these themes (and subthemes) can be listed separately: 1) independent exposure to music through multi-media;[4] 2) aspects of teaching music for Deaf children; 3) benefits related to exposure to music; 4) problems: outside environment (practical and conceptual), inside environment (the students and the fellow teachers).

5.1 *Independent Exposure to Music through Multi-media*

Music has become more popular among Deaf children in the last five years because of the influence of the media. Television, specifically, has shaped many of the attitudes of Deaf children toward music. Currently, the influence of the multi-media is greater because all media sources have become more accessible to the population, including the Deaf population. Susan Cox states:

> before not everybody had television, and not everybody could go to movies. [...] recently, the media exposes everything. They [Deaf children] see, they want to be the same as everybody else, even the severely [handicapped] kids. They know that there is something else out there.

While Deaf children may not understand the message that the media brings, media sources have made them aware of information that is not a natural part of their environment. Some decades ago, music was considered a 'hearing person's thing.' Therefore, music was not part of Deaf children's lives. However, exposure to a variety of multi-media seems to be changing that.

5.2 *Aspects of Teaching Music to Deaf Children*

To teach music to Deaf children has become easier because of the exposure to the media discussed earlier. Consequently, Deaf individuals show more interest and involvement in music activities in the classroom.

Music activities in the classroom are not restricted to helping Deaf students learn only music concepts. Deaf students participate in singing activities or even in musical instrument performance. Again, the television influences greatly the way they react to these activities. The teacher participant, Susan Cox, says: "If I give him [Deaf student] this playdrum, he pretends like he is on television. He sits in there and he just pounds on that, like he is on television."

In musical activities such as singing, the students use sign language to sign the songs. Sometimes they will also, as Susan notes, "have the intonation and rhythm to go up and down [with their voices]." To conduct the singing activity, Susan uses her hands to indicate high/low sounds, so that the Deaf students' voices (pitch) go up and down.

To keep the students interested and involved in the activities with music, Susan is constantly looking for new ways to approach the (same) musical concepts. She goes from playing the drum, to playing the tambourine, to "listening" to the radio, to moving the body according to the music, etc. The reason for changing the activities is that the majority of the students have short attention spans. Further, to keep their positive attitude toward music, it is necessary either to keep changing the activity constantly or to stop when they are still interested. In this way the students will not become tired or bored. According to the participant, it is also very important to observe their mood. The students are not always inclined to receive musical instructions. Susan states: "If they are accepting [the musical activity], do it; if they are not, change it."

Musical instruments are not only a tool for increasing the children's motivation, they are also a tool for supporting music instruction. Susan introduces the concept of low, medium and high sounds by using instruments such as the drum (low sound), the triangle (medium sound), and some bells (high sound). While Susan plays the instrument, the students are supposed to have their backs to her. When she finishes playing, the students have to turn back to her and identify which instrument was played. The entire activity is approached as a "game" by the teacher and her students. If the students are not able to identify the musical instrument played, Susan helps them by moving the instrument from one place to another. In this way, the students notice that an instrument has been moved and that it probably was the one previously played. To be successful is very important for these children because it improves their self-image, while helping them to better enjoy musical activities. This is one reason why Susan helps them to succeed. She says, "I make them to succeed, so that they will want to do."

In teaching music to the Deaf students, Susan employs many techniques. The use of balloons is one of them. With the balloons, Deaf children can feel the vibrations caused by a musical instrument being played because their fingertips are very sensitive. Some musical activities approached in class are related to Susan's past experience in teaching auditory training. She uses syllables (one, two or three syllables) to introduce some musical concepts such as beat and measurement.

Effective music instruction for Deaf children necessitates good physical conditions such as a wooden floor and good acoustics. A variety of musical instruments is important as well as current information on advances in technology. The amount of computer software in music has significantly increased. Such software provides visual clues for some musical sounds. Therefore, Susan states, "if they can't hear [the musical sound], they can look at [the computer screen] and follow it."

According to the teacher, any special education music teacher has to be constantly attentive to the way his/her students learn music. Each Deaf child learns music in his/her own way. "Some learn better through feeling, some learn better just through vision, and some just have the skill or talent to pick that [music] up and be able to get it." Sometimes in teaching music "things [new techniques] are discovered just by accident, and you [teacher] say: oh! that works," said Susan. Thus, what is really important, Susan continues, is that "there is always a way to show them [Deaf students] what to do, whether it is to teach them a musical beat, or to perform on a musical instrument."

Susan believes that music for Deaf children goes beyond music instruction in the classroom. She believes that Deaf children can become professional in music. She says:

> I met [Deaf] people, [...] I met a girl that plays and plays professionally in a big huge orchestra in Connecticut. She is totally deaf and she plays the flute. [...] I know some few other people that play, but they play other visual [instruments], like drums. I have seen someone [a Deaf person] playing the piano before. [...] I did see a Deaf man playing xylophone, and he played exquisitely perfect.

Thus, for the participant, the process of teaching music to Deaf children may awaken an inherited talent for music which can lead more Deaf individuals to become professionals in music. Susan also believes that music should be available to everybody. She states:

> We all enjoy music. I enjoy music, it is uplifting. Sometimes it makes me cry, sometimes it makes me feel good, sometimes it is just real romantic [...] if it is all that for me, why not for them [Deaf students]?

5.3 *Benefits Related to Exposure to Music*

In order to be more effective and successful in our society, the participant in this study believes that "we need to be social." This socialization, however, is limited for Deaf students because they are still victimized by ignorance about their needs. Susan states:

> The way they handle handicapped children at home is sticking them in front of the television and leaving them alone. Therefore, music for the Deaf is also an opportunity for social training. Music is one way to help them [Deaf children] to perform physical things, related to fine and gross motor activities that are fun [...]. Music makes them to feel good about themselves. They want to be the same as everybody else. It gives them a more positive self-image.

Thus, through music, Deaf students might improve their self-image. By participating in musical performances, they feel themselves more productive and engaged within society. Susan says: "in front of people, they are as everybody else performing on stage." Susan also states that some of the benefits of exposure to music carry over to reading and writing performance. This happens because she relates music activities to language, and she asks the students to talk and to write about their experiences with music.

5.4 *Problems*

In using music with Deaf students Susan faced some problems:

5.4.1 Outside Environment

The problems coming from outside of the participant's environment were divided into problems of a practical and conceptual nature.

a) Practical: Normally hearing teachers, who work close to the participant's classroom, complain about the noise generated by the musical activities. Susan states:

> I am flexible, I go with the flow [...] I wait until the teachers go to PE [physical education], her whole class goes to PE; then I have music. So I just change my schedule. I don't have to have music at 'that' time. I just change my music time.

These teachers also think that the musical activities which Susan conducts are 'just' games, and that instead of teaching she just spends time playing with her students.

b) Conceptual: According to Susan, the major reason why not more teachers use music with Deaf children is their conceptual understanding about the application of music in the class. The teachers don't interrelate music with other class activities. Susan states:

> they [teachers] think [about music] as a separate entity. [...] I think that it is not that they really don't want to do. I think that someone has to show them how it [music] can fit in. How it can be part of the everyday activities, and not as separate entities.

5.4.2 Inside Environment—The Students

In her classroom, Susan also faces some problems concerning the students' involvement in musical activities. She confessed having heard from Deaf students statements such as "I can't hear, do you remember?" "What do you want me to do music for?" However, she also says that these problems have been reduced because of their exposure to multi-media.

5.4.3 Inside Environment—The Teacher

Susan pointed out that, although she has never felt frustrated with the difficulties or with the results obtained in teaching music to Deaf children, frustration might constitute a problem for many teachers. This can cause them to stop looking for alternative pathways to teaching music to Deaf children. Susan also pointed out that the results in this field of instruction are slow and that it requires a lot of patience. However, there is always a way to teach those special kids. She states: "There has to be a way to get through […] it might take me a year or two."

6 Personal Reactions and Conclusions

The study data suggest that Susan has been providing a good level of education to her students by using music as a vehicle of instruction. Although her students have other disabilities in addition to deafness, they don't appear to have affected her commitment to using music. She also does not demonstrate frustration with the results that surface in very slow increments.

Indeed, from the perspective of critical theory there are additional problems to be overcome. These problems involve the power difference between the normal and hearing community (dominant class) and the Deaf community (subordinate and oppressed class) in relation to music. A specific example of hegemonic relationship, in this study, is provided by the reactions and attitudes of some of Susan's colleagues. These colleagues regard music activity for Deaf children simply as a waste of time, because the students are unable to hear musical sounds.

Even though Susan belongs to the normally hearing community, she does not seem to underestimate the capacity and musical skills of Deaf people. Susan works to provide her Deaf students with positive feedback. Her teaching philosophy puts emphasis on the 'ability' and not on the 'inability' of her students. Consequently, this fosters a more positive attitude towards musical experiences in her students.

For this reason, the study has implications for how music may be used as an instructional tool in schools for the Deaf, and how the teachers (in schools for the Deaf) who have used music in their classrooms are viewed by others, including colleagues, students and supervisors.

This study showed that an educator of Deaf students should also be prepared to work with Deaf children with additional disabilities, such as learning disabilities and mental retardation.[5] The results of this study suggest that music can play a very important role for improving Deaf (and multi-handicapped[6]) children's learning ability as well as their social skills. To be effective, music activities for Deaf children must be viewed as serious academic exercises and not just as games. However, to keep the students' interest in these activities, they must also be fun. Thus, musical activities for Deaf children can be fun and effective, if they are presented in a meaningful and motivational context.

Notes

1 The study was conducted in 1996; at present, there are several successful Deaf musicians who perform their music in concerts, especially in the genre of hip-hop (see for example Signmark/Marko Vuoriheimo, Chapter 10, this volume).
2 The name is a pseudonym.
3 The use of these terms is no longer appropriate; nowadays, physical disability, intellectual disability, learning disability are the preferred terms.
4 The study was conducted in 1996; at present, exposure to music and, more importantly, to the work of Deaf musicians is much more widespread and more common for Deaf people—especially Deaf youth — through the Internet/social media, such as YouTube (Vuoriheimo/Signmark, Chapter 10, this volume).
5 The use of this term is no longer appropriate, please see end note 3.
6 The use of this term is no longer appropriate, multiple disabilities is the preferred term nowadays.

References

Darrow, A.-A. (1985). Music for the deaf. *Music Educators Journal, 71*(6), 33–35.

Darrow, A.-A. (1991). A study of public school music programs mainstreaming hearing impaired students. *Journal of Music Therapy, 28*(1), 23–29.

Edwards, E. M. (1974). *Music education for the deaf.* South Waterford, ME: Merriam-Eddy.

Edwards, E. M. (1975). Music for the hearing impaired. In R. M. Graham (Ed.), *Music for the exceptional child* (pp. 48–60). Reston, VA: Music Educators National Conference.

Gibson, R. (1986). *Critical theory and education.* London, UK: Hodder & Stoughton.

Gramsci, A. (1971). Selections from the prison notebooks. In Q. Hoare & G. Nowell-Smith (Eds.), New York, NY: International Publishers.

Kapla, P. S. (1975). Music and the hearing handicapped child. In R. M. Graham (Ed.), *Music for the exceptional child* (pp. 61–71). Reston, VA: Music Educators National Conference.

Robbins, C., & Robbins, C. (1980). *Music for the hearing impaired: A resource manual and curriculum guide.* St. Louis, MO: Magnamusic-Baton.

Shehan, P. K. (1986). Major approaches to music education: An account of method. *Music Educators Journal, 72*(6), 26–31.

Index

www.ingramcontent.com/pod-product-compliance
Lightning Source LLC
LaVergne TN
LVHW020603110826
845149LV00002B/361